CHARLESTON B

CHARLESTON BELLES ABROAD

*The Music Collections of Harriet Lowndes,
Henrietta Aiken, and Louisa Rebecca McCord*

CANDACE BAILEY

THE UNIVERSITY OF SOUTH CAROLINA PRESS

© 2019 University of South Carolina

Published by the University of South Carolina Press
Columbia, South Carolina 29208

www.sc.edu/uscpress

Manufactured in the United States of America

28 27 26 25 24 23 22 21 20 19   10 9 8 7 6 5 4 3 2 1

Library of Congress Cataloging-in-Publication Data can be found at
http://catalog.loc.gov/.

ISBN 978-1-61117-956-9 (cloth)
ISBN 978-1-61117-957-6 (ebook)

To

E M M A *and* G R A H A M

Contents

Preface

On spring break in 2003 I had planned to spend a few days doing research in the South Carolina Historical Society in Charleston as I began studying women and music in the antebellum South. Finishing earlier than I had expected, I contacted Jennifer Sheetz at the Charleston Museum to inquire if the museum held anything that might be useful to my work. She responded that there might possibly be some items of interest to me there, so I headed down Meeting Street to see them. What I found took me completely by surprise: numerous books and individual pieces of sheet music whose owners were well known in southern history. Jennifer graciously spread some of them out on the floor, on cardboard mats, and allowed me to take some photographs for future use. The books with "Louisa McCord" on them particularly struck me as important because they ranged from European scores to Confederate imprints to a bound collection of Clementi and Kuhlau. At that time I was able to make only a few notes and photographs, as I had other research appointments in Savannah on this particular journey.

In the intervening years I traveled back to the Charleston Museum several times. Jennifer McCormick presides over the collection, and her help proved invaluable in collecting the data needed for the current study. I continue to be astounded by the music in the Charleston Museum archives. I am unaware of any other single collection that documents the musical experiences of a specific segment of society better than does the one at the Charleston Museum. This book presents information on music from several prominent families in Charleston, but there is more work to be done. The collection includes music that belonged to Harriet Lowndes, Henrietta Aiken, Louisa Rebecca McCord, Elizabeth Waties Alston Pringle, Mariane Porcher, Sally Kinloch, Frederika "Freddy" Knobloch, Elise Rhett, Mary Rhett, and many other Charlestonian women—and this is only one part of the museum's archives.

Acknowledgments

Any project that requires detailed accounts of numerous primary sources depends heavily on the cooperation and assistance of the custodians of archives, and I have been fortunate to work closely with several of these people. First and foremost, my utmost thanks and appreciation extend to Jennifer McCormick, collections manager at the Charleston Museum. She has made this book possible with her unending help and generosity. Her thorough knowledge of materials relating to the families discussed here greatly aided my understanding of context in Charleston society. Karen Brickman Emmons, archivist with the Historic Charleston Foundation, graciously assisted my work with the Aiken-Rhett House, and I appreciate her willingness to work with me while in Charleston and away. Valerie Perry, the Aiken-Rhett House museum manager, provided me with insight into the Aikens and the Rhetts, and I fondly remember discussing the characters of these women with her. Anna Smith of the Charleston Library Society graciously helped by finding and retrieving the books purchased by the Aikens while abroad. Other archivists have made aspects of this book possible, especially those at the South Caroliniana Library in Columbia and those working with the South Carolina Historical Society, who provided much insight in the early stages of this work. The editor and staff of the University of South Carolina Press and the anonymous readers who offered suggestions have contributed to this book and made it better in many ways.

Several scholars gave generously of their time and ideas as I developed this book. Nicholas Butler, whose knowledge of music in Charleston is unrivaled, helped me think through some of the problems presented by the material and by the absence of material. Rebecca Geoffroy-Swinden assisted with my inquiries on French music of the early nineteenth century, and Kristen Turner was always available to assist by answering my questions or pointing me in the right direction. Katherine Preston has been most supportive in various aspects of the scholarly process, offering advice, writing letters, finding time to meet, and assisting me with access to the Earl Gregg Swem Library at the College of William and Mary in Williamsburg, Virginia. Others to whom I owe thanks include Annegret Fauser, Christine de Bellaigue, and David Kennerley for their knowledge of French and English culture of this period. To these and many others I offer my thanks and appreciation.

As just about anyone who has written a book knows, I could not have completed this project without the love and support of my family. Julian Prosser continues to provide encouragement through the intellectual process, and his willingness to traipse around the South in search of collections never wanes. Without my extended family I could not manage, and I especially thank Lisa Tew for the many times she has made me laugh throughout this process. Finally, my children, Emma and Graham, have grown into young adults who never fail to ask about my projects, listen to me talk about successes and failures, and offer hope in times of frustration. This book is for you.

Editorial Notes

Capitalization in English-language publications of the nineteenth century knew no standard: sheet-music title pages include titles in all capitals, a haphazard use of capitals, or a variety of fonts on a single page, rendering the concept of a "correct" usage impossible. In the main text of *Charleston Belles Abroad,* titles of songs in English appear in standard, or headline, style capitalization, as do English titles of larger collections and operas. Foreign titles follow the capitalization rules of the given languages. In appendix A and the tables, titles are given as they are found on the actual sheet music.

Determining how to refer to the subjects of a book such as this one often means developing a system whereby people with similar names can be easily distinguished. As a general rule, after their initial introduction most of the South Carolinians mentioned in *Charleston Belles Abroad* are referred to by their first names only. The main women whose music forms the basis of this study are mentioned by their maiden names and consequently referred to by their first names. Because there were two women named Louisa McCord in the 1850s, I use "Mother Louisa" and "Louisa Rebecca" to distinguish them. Referring to composers by last names is in line with writings on music. Full names are given to distinguish those with the same last name—such as Clara Schumann in order to distinguish her from Robert Schumann. A list of pertinent composers' full names is provided in appendix C.

Published sheet music sometimes contains more information than is necessary in the tables presented here. If more than one publisher is listed on a given piece of music, only the first is retained in tables of inventories unless there is a compelling reason to include more than one. For example, if a song was published in Boston as well as in New Orleans, the latter, being a southern city, will also appear in the entry. Lists of places where a particular item was sold are also generally not included, except for some Confederate imprints. Much of the music discussed in this book originated with foreign publishers but made its way to Charleston via import dealers in New York and elsewhere. When a piece has the stamp of a seller, it is listed after the publisher information. Dates given in brackets have been found in places other than the sheet music under discussion, such as worldcat.org or libraries from around the world. I have not designated specific libraries as that would be tedious to read for the many titles listed throughout this book. Most have been gleaned from the British Library, the Bibliothèque nationale de France, or American university archives.

A brief definition of each music genre encountered in *Charleston Belles Abroad* is given near the first mention of that genre. Nineteenth-century writers adopted fluid uses of terms, particularly "opera," and some clarification yields a better understanding of stylistic changes that occurred throughout the period encompassed in this book. A list of musicians discussed in this work can be found in appendix C, making information on them available but not disruptive of the narrative. Genres in general are not italicized even if they are foreign words or come from foreign terms originally, because their definitions are well known—for example, aria or nocturne. I use scientific pitch notation to indicate octave placement: "middle C" is C4.

Introduction

As someone who began her academic career researching English seventeenth-century keyboard music, I used to believe that those who did their work on nineteenth-century music had it comparatively easy because so much information existed about composers such as Beethoven, Verdi, and Wagner. Moreover, in the 1980s archival work not only was not a part of the purview of those who worked in the romantic period but also was a source of disdain: subjective exploration ranked higher on the epistemological ladder than objective studies of sources, composers, and similar topics.[1] But for the seventeenth century, we were still uncovering fundamental materials and discovering essential sources for repertories long silenced. How can one write about the "deeper" issues of music history without the basic facts of who, when, and where?

This conundrum came full circle in a postpaper discussion at the 2015 Southern Association of Women Historians in Charleston, South Carolina, when members of the audience asked what had prompted me to look at dealer stamps in nineteenth-century binder's volumes. With almost no secondary sources on antebellum southern women and music, I have frequently found it necessary to apply archival research methods here as well. I realized long ago that our knowledge of nineteenth-century music practices in the southern United States has been largely ignored or subsumed under those of the Northeast and that critical data in understanding musical experiences south of the Mason-Dixon Line lay in women's binder's volumes, of which there are thousands.[2] The romantic period, therefore, required some further elementary source work, complemented by consideration of interdisciplinary methodologies. In looking specifically at women's cultural practices, several attendant subjects, such as gender studies, cultural and intellectual histories, and musicological studies, intertwine to tell the complete story of how music functioned through time among nonprofessionals.

The intellectual historian Michael O'Brien confirmed this when he observed that "each generation of Southern historians must begin afresh at the archives." He asserted that diaries and letters be included as sources of self-commentary and integrated this idea into the generalization that southerners assume a listener—and not a dialectician—when they express themselves. Noting that "the archives are heavy with such conversation," he stressed that "it is evident that they do not speak with one voice."[3] Music collections function similarly because they follow the conventions of polite society, allow agency on the part of the owner, and permit a similarly one-sided dialogue between performer and listener. In this case, as with O'Brien's, the listener enjoins in the convention by not responding, except to acknowledge the performer. Even more, binder's volumes are a practice in gentility, even if no one is listening to the owners perform. The purpose of the present study is to illuminate both the conversations and the disparate voices.

The women considered here should, theoretically, speak with the same voice, articulating similar ideas and opinions, prejudicing similar types of music, and enjoying consistent experiences in private and in public because all were white women who lived at least part of their lives in Charleston and part in Europe, and who belonged to powerful political and wealthy families. Their interconnectedness can be expressed in a number of ways. Harriet Lowndes was Henrietta Aiken's mother. Only nine years separated the births of Henrietta and Louisa Rebecca McCord, and both young women traveled to Europe in the late 1850s. Each owned music purchased at Flaxland's music store in Paris. All were born in South Carolina and descended, in part at least, from Huguenots. Louisa Rebecca's sister married Henrietta's brother-in-law. The sum of these factors suggests that their music practices would resemble each other's closely.

But they did not, and here lies perhaps the most important contribution that this book makes to our understanding of American music history. With all they had in common, their music collections make evident that Harriet, Henrietta, and Louisa Rebecca did not speak with one voice. Their individual practices demonstrate the variation possible among a small group of women with many cultural similarities. Authors write about white women of the middling and upper classes as if they participated in the same musical experiences, at home at the very least. We assume that such women attended performances in public venues, but the evidence for such pales in comparison to that for parlor practices. The fact that an opera played in Savannah does not mean that elite women attended, although they may have done so.[4] Occasionally letters and diaries mention musical performances, but the frequency of such entries depends on the personalities and writing habits of the diarists and cannot provide more than isolated examples of practices.[5]

The most consistent artifact of southern women's musical culture is the binder's volume, many of which have stood the test of time and survive to the present day. Indeed, often a woman's binder's volume is one of only a few items of hers to remain intact.[6] Moreover, the vast number of binder's volumes that exist in archives, libraries, private homes, and antiquarian shops suggests that the practice of collecting sheet music and binding it together ran across many different cultural groups, from free women of color to the daughters of white yeoman farmers to the aristocracy of Charleston.[7] Most of these volumes range in thickness between one and two inches, contain twenty to fifty musical compositions, and have been bound with paper-covered boards and leather spines. Such attributes belong to thousands of mid-century binder's volumes from New Orleans to Louisville to Charleston.

Amid such conformity lies great variation. Geography influenced the options young women had because repertories differed according to trade routes. Binder's volumes from along the Mississippi River contain composers and titles not found in those from the Eastern Seaboard. Music that was available in New Orleans often did not appear in stores in Macon or Richmond. Even among the tightly connected women of Charleston's elite, other factors come into play and influenced the type of music a young woman might sing or play. The three women examined here collected markedly different types of pieces. Some of these variances are easy to explain. Styles changed between the time Harriet first used her music in the 1820s to when her daughter studied music in the 1840s and 1850s. More striking, however, is the distinct difference between the music of Henrietta and that of Louisa Rebecca. A comparison of their collections requires consideration of nonmusical stimuli.

An undercurrent running through this text is a mother's role in shaping her daughter, preparing her to enter society and representing the family among the elites of South Carolina. In this regard, the maternal guidance of Harriet Lowndes Aiken and that of Louisa Susanna Cheves McCord contrasted significantly. Both women saw that their daughters received quality instruction in music. These daughters, Henrietta and Louisa Rebecca respectively, achieved considerable skill as vocalists, surpassing many of their contemporaries—based on the evidence written into their music. Their similarities and differences are made plain by the music now housed in the archives of the Charleston Museum, one of the best resources to investigate the music practices of antebellum women. For this book, I have included information for more than six hundred titles from its archives, and all are directly connected to Harriet, Henrietta, Louisa Rebecca, or their immediate relations.

This museum is one of many in the city. Charleston is rich in historical properties, collections, and societies whose purposes are to preserve its traditions. In the late eighteenth century and the first half of the nineteenth century, at least, it stood as a cultural beacon in the young nation. The Swedish writer and feminist Fredrika Bremer wrote of Charleston during her 1850 visit that it "resembled a city of the European continent more than . . . Boston or New York."[8] Musically too the city differed from others in the nation. Nicholas Butler has meticulously documented musical life in Charleston from 1766 to 1820, noting composers, styles, performers, entrepreneurs, and businessmen invested in some aspect of music. His research on the influential St. Cecilia Society and its constituent parts has illuminated the variety of performances one could have experienced in the city during these early years.[9] There were other performances too, as well as music teachers and performers who passed through on their way north or south.

Many of these aspects of musical experiences can be seen in collections in the Charleston Museum. It houses numerous artifacts from Charleston's history: for example, a piano connected with George Gershwin and *Porgy and Bess;* exhibits devoted to agricultural practices in eastern South Carolina; and even Louisa Rebecca McCord's wedding dress. The music collection remains a hidden gem of exceptional breadth and scope, encapsulating the musical lives of some of South Carolina's most famous antebellum women. How the music came to the Charleston Museum is significant because it clarifies how the collection has remained intact for more than a century.

The Charleston Museum Collection

In 1975 Frances Hinson Dill Rhett, the widow of I'on Lowndes Rhett, transferred ownership of the Aiken-Rhett House, the antebellum residence of William and Harriet Aiken, to the Charleston Museum. At this time a substantial collection of music from the house also came to the museum. It is an extraordinary collection—perhaps the single most impressive gathering of music representing the musical world of elite southern women. Among its riches is the binder's volume of Elizabeth "Bessie" Waties Allston Pringle, the famous author of *A Woman Rice Planter* and *Chronicles of Chicora Wood.* Bessie's volume corroborates a love of the piano that she emphasized when she wrote in *A Woman Rice Planter* that she had owned six Steinways and no other type.[10] Several other books of music that belonged to prominent Charleston women of the mid–nineteenth century, such as Sallie Kinloch, Meta Morris Grimball, M. P. Alston, Anna Smith, Rachel Ross Porcher, and Mary Mickell, figure as well among the treasures in the Charleston Museum.

Naturally the lion's share of the music belonged to members of the extended Lowndes-Aiken-Rhett family, including in-laws, cousins, and nieces. That the music belonging to the family remained intact in the Aiken-Rhett House is a happy coincidence indeed and provides a wealth of material for considering the musical life of antebellum Charleston women in situ. This study examines the music of the two women most directly connected to the house: Harriet Lowndes Aiken, who moved into the house in the 1830s; and her daughter, Henrietta Aiken Rhett, who lived in the house her entire life.

The music collection seems to have been discovered in a storehouse at the Aiken-Rhett House in the early 1970s.[11] Given that family members shut off rooms in the house, a practice beginning at the time of Harriet's death in 1892, continuing with Henrietta's in 1918, and extending into the 1970s, the music collection has survived essentially untouched since the nineteenth century. Thus we can reasonably assume that the collection now housed in the Charleston Museum includes most, if not all, of the music that survives from this family. As such, it encapsulates the degree of musical accomplishment attained by two of Charleston's most respected women and elucidates aspects of their personal tastes.

Inexplicably, Frances Dill Rhett's gift to the Charleston Museum also contains music books that belonged to family members of one of the most famous literary women of South Carolina: Louisa Susannah Cheves McCord. The binder's volumes are not hers but rather those of her daughter and granddaughter. How they came to be part of the Frances Dill Rhett bequest is unknown. Hannah and Louisa Rebecca McCord, daughters of Louisa Susannah, fled Columbia with Mary Chesnut in 1865. When Union soldiers looted the house that year, they destroyed all of the family papers, including the library.[12] Perhaps the young women took their music books with them when they evacuated. Members of the McCord family spent most of their time either at Lang Syne, their plantation in what is now Calhoun County—between Columbia and Charleston—or at their home in Columbia. They did visit Charleston frequently and eventually moved there, however, so it is not too far removed to include them here.

What truly ties these three music collections together is the impact of European music on them. Some of the other binder's volumes from the Aiken-Rhett House that belonged to members of the Lowndes family include music purchased in Europe, but none of them contains so many pieces or indicates such a strong connection with European music as do the books that belonged to Harriet Lowndes, Henrietta Aiken, and Louisa Rebecca McCord.[13] Indeed, I have seen close to a thousand southern binder's volumes from the antebellum period, and the music owned by these women stands alone because it so vividly illustrates the young women's identification with music that was popular and available in London, Brussels, Naples, Basel, Paris, and Liverpool, but not in the United States. Moreover, the sheer volume of their collections as well as the European music within them mark them as worthy of careful study.

All three women spent at least a year in Europe, and the music purchased there forms a significant part of their individual collections. In this respect theirs differ from almost every other binder's volume or set of binder's volumes in southern archives, and it is this feature that makes them worthy of meticulous study. These books provide physical evidence for the impact of the "grand tour" on southern women and provide a gauge by which other narratives may be compared.[14] Moreover, this collection of music contains much evidence, such as marks for breathing in songs or pedaling in piano music, that it was used by the women who owned it. Whether their descendants also performed from these scores is less clear. Styles changed, and most young women preferred to have music appropriate to their generation. Some overlap exists in the Aiken-Rhett Collection, such as Henrietta's French romances that belonged to her mother's youth, not her own.[15]

Harriet's music, collected prior to her marriage, provides a glimpse into music in Charleston during the 1810s and 1820s. It supplements Butler's engaging work on the St. Cecilia Society by providing further evidence of how one wealthy young woman experienced music in the city: it is a microscopic view of elite women's music in 1820s Charleston. Its emphasis on French romances, a genre that dominated the salons of Paris but not the parlors of Charleston, is uncharacteristic and therefore noteworthy. Later, scores of complete operas owned by Harriet reveal her interests while she was traveling abroad between 1831 and 1858. During these sojourns she purchased a number of items in various cities in Europe, including music, paintings, sculptures, furniture, and other items with which to decorate the family's home on 48 Elizabeth Street. She made four trips to Europe with her daughter, Henrietta Aiken, and the latter's music collection reveals the influence of her mother as well as changing styles in the mid-century. Their final voyage, in 1857–58, took place only months before Louisa Rebecca McCord journeyed with her mother overseas in 1858–59. Taken together, the collections of Henrietta and Louisa Rebecca exemplify the types of music wealthy southern Americans sought while abroad in the late antebellum period. In contrast, Louisa Rebecca's fourth binder's volume brilliantly demonstrates the effects of the Civil War on young women of this class. Her daughter's slim volume of music dedicated to only two composers reflects changes in repertory and preservation practices after the war.[16]

Southerners Abroad

Since the earliest years of the republic and even before, Americans continually traveled to Europe. Why they did so, what views they carried there and how those were subsequently shaped by their experiences abroad, and even what they did while in Europe varied considerably. Simple economics tie together a few of the factors that influenced these experiences: those who had the most dispensable incomes tended to spend more freely, while those with less traveled in more constrained circumstances. Businessmen with ties to European manufacturing sailed back and forth to look after their interests, and diplomats of different sorts made numerous journeys across the Atlantic. Before the Civil War, women did not travel without a chaperone, meaning that the women who made the journey came from situations where at least two people could afford to do so. Those with blood relations in the old country, such as Huguenot families in Charleston, often traveled more frequently than those who did not.

The historian Daniel Kilbride has asserted that before 1820 most of the Americans who went to Europe were overwhelmingly male and privileged and that, while homogenous as a group, these men disagreed about how the new nation should relate to those in Europe. These conflicting views, however, seemed to disperse after 1820. One perplexing problem that remained was how people with a certain definition of social ranks interacted with those of a different ilk. Lacking a true aristocracy, by design of the founding fathers, Americans did not divide into nobility, gentry, and so forth as their counterparts in Europe did. However, social interface with Europeans necessitated some sort of distinction. Thus the term "aristocracy" represented a segment of American society, and it was often used to describe certain people in Charleston. Planters, such as Henry Middleton of South Carolina, represented the "self-styled" American aristocrat who sought to mingle with Frenchmen of equal status.[17] Since southerners were preoccupied with an aristocratic past, many maintained ties to distant relatives in the Old World. O'Brien further explained this need for class distinctions that followed those across the Atlantic when he wrote that "southerners imagined themselves as the 'custodians of empire' and drew deeply from European history and culture to provide 'order' for their world and to establish their place in it."[18]

With the advent of regular transatlantic steam travel in the 1840s, the number of Americans traveling from the United States to Europe grew exponentially.[19] Decreasing costs meant that more Americans could experience life abroad, and a market for travel literature, especially books full of travel advice, developed simultaneously.[20] These opportunities extended to a variety of people: European experiences had long been markers of social status, but by the 1830s upper-class Americans disdained the growing number of social inferiors who began to seek their fortunes in Europe. For example, Henry Middleton, a South Carolina planter, complained in an 1836 letter that Paris was "crowded at present with a perfect ravel of Jonathans," noting that the Americans he had met in Paris were vulgar, ignorant, and socially awkward.[21] As more and more Americans traveled overseas, the lines between gentry and the rest of society became even further blurred. Those who considered themselves members of an elite class, as did most South Carolina planters, sought ways to delineate themselves from their middle-class contemporaries. Richard Bushman has seen this as a push toward the refinement of America: "The spread of gentility speaks for the enduring allure of royal palaces and great country estates, for the enticing mystery of nobility and gentry, for the enchantment of these seemingly charmed and exalted lives, for the enthrallment with their grace of movement, speech, and costume."[22] As seen through the music collections evaluated here, the search for refinement in Europe varied: for the Aikens, it formed the primary reason for their journeys; for the McCords, this was not so much the case. While Bushman added that "the hold of the old regime on the imaginations of Americans cannot be overlooked," it did not affect them equally, not even those from roughly the same geographic region and social class.[23]

Southerners who could afford to do so built magnificent homes to rival those of Europe, perfected French accents, and bought their clothes from Parisian couturiers. This was plain in the case of Harriet Lowndes, whose aspirations for herself and her daughter extended to an adoption of French culture as a means of self-expression. Harriet's famous full-length portrait exposes these traits: both her position and her clothes resemble those of European aristocracy. In her study of the Aiken-Rhett House and its art collection, Elizabeth Garrett determined the portrait to be the "*magnum opus* of the collection in the house"; and others have described it as a "grandly conceived full-length portrait" that is "perhaps the last of Charleston's antebellum portraits conceived in the Grand Tour mode."[24] Considering the vast number of artistic items purchased abroad by the Aikens, Harriet's portrait serves as a defining comment on her view of her status and position.

The Aiken women were not alone in their desire to experience the Old World. Southern women traveled from the United States to Europe for a number of reasons. Lucy Petway Holcombe Pickens (1832–99), "the Queen of the Confederacy," accompanied her husband, Francis Wilkinson Pickens, to the imperial court in Russia when he was named ambassador in 1858. Pickens would later be governor of South Carolina. Charleston-born Hortensia Mordecai went to Italy in 1859 to assuage her grief over the loss of her brother. A few, such as Louisa Susannah Cheves McCord (1810–79), sought medical treatment. Most, however, went as tourists and consumers. Some travelers kept diaries of their adventures, but unfortunately most did not describe music in any detail other than to mention attendance at an opera or ball or perhaps to note a famous singer. The degree to which these women were changed by their experiences varied tremendously, with many aspects influencing their receptions to European culture and how they negotiated it as a cultural imperative for their class.

This book considers the extent to which musical experiences overseas affected Harriet, Henrietta, and Louisa Rebecca, and how these experiences contributed—or not—to their lives back in South Carolina.[25]

Travelers' European destinations varied for a number of reasons. Many regions of Europe were involved in armed conflict during this period. Furthermore, southerners did not view each place equally, and this book illuminates distinctly personal preferences on the part of South Carolina women. An Anglo-American connection elicited perhaps the most obvious bond, and many southerners arrived in England (usually Liverpool) as their first destination in Europe. Early in this period, southern men of means traveled to England for an education.[26] In England southern women bought furniture, mingled with aristocracy, shopped, attended the theater, and of course conversed more easily than on the Continent. Such influences showed in Charleston. One Englishman wrote of a visit to the city in the late 1830s that "all around me—the place, the people, the language . . . seemed so thoroughly English, that I could scarcely think I was in a foreign land. . . . There is, indeed, a sincere respect for England and English people, felt by all the more intelligent and opulent classes, and a high veneration for 'the land of their fathers.'"[27] Louisa Rebecca's music collection contains several British publications, affirming this connection.

Nonetheless, the lure of Paris and all things French drew many southern women to French culture. The most tangible evidence of this attraction exists in the numerous fashion plates published in American periodicals that illustrated the latest clothing styles from Paris.[28] French fashions were all the rage. As one young woman wrote in 1844, "We on this side feel as if everything is so much handsomer, and better, and desirable that comes from Paris."[29] As if reiterating this point, the Alabamian Mary Fenwick Lewis commented while at school in Paris, "The French have the best taste in the fashionable world."[30] While on a European grand tour, the South Carolinians Robert Francis Withers Allston and his wife Adèle Petigru Allston purchased ball gowns enhanced with the "most beautiful artificial flowers" in Paris for their daughter Della. A less obvious French influence existed in a popular method of instruction, Emily Thornwell's well-known *Lady's Guide to Complete Gentility: In Manners, Dress and Conversation, in the Family in Company, at the Pianoforte* . . . (first published in Philadelphia in 1856), which contained many untranslated French terms and probably derived from an unidentified French book.[31]

Elite southern women, and some of the middling classes, were frequently exposed to aspects of French culture. As students, either at home or in the academy, southern girls learned French as a second language, and many used it whenever possible. For example, on at least one occasion when P. G. T. Beauregard, the hero of Fort Sumter, wrote to Octavia Walton Le Vert of Mobile, he did so in French.[32] Many teachers and professors were French, such as Madame Acélie Togno (she had married an Italian), who ran a fashionable boarding school in Charleston and later Columbia. The composer Theodor von Hacke realized the importance of a French connection in the South and changed his name to Theodore von La Hache when he moved to New Orleans. Thus French culture, even if affected, permeated elite women's culture in the South.

As the musical center of Europe, Paris held other attractions. It boasted several well-respected opera venues, a conservatory, an informed press, and the premieres of some of the period's most important musical works. Most of the composers whose names are today associated with the period lived in Paris for some time, including many who were not French, such as Rossini, Donizetti, and Wagner. While English music and musicians held strong ties to Americans early in the century, during the 1840s popular preferences moved toward French and Italian music, particularly operas by Meyerbeer, Bellini, and Donizetti.[33]

South Carolinians seem to have been particularly destined to go to France. Once in Paris, southerners tended to flock together. In his diary Gabriel Manigault wrote after meeting Kirkwood King, Robert Pringle, and Thomas Pinckney Alston—all members of Charleston's elite families—that "it was interesting to see so many Americans collected together. I knew quite a number, as there were many Southerners in Europe then." He also noted the "difficulty of becoming intimate with French families" and was amused by the number of rich American heiresses marrying poor French titled men. Others remarked on the number of southerners abroad: in 1854 the Virginian John R. Thompson described the Hôtel Meurice on the rue de Rivoli as "the head-quarters of Americans in Paris" and wrote that he was somewhat surprised at all of the southern food (such as Virginia ham) in French restaurants. David Henry Mordecai (1833–59) mentioned meeting the Middletons, Prestons, Rhetts, and Hamptons while in Europe in 1857–58. In Paris his sister Hortensia mentioned meeting Ransom Calhoun and Mr. Preston, Mr. Ogier, Dr. Horlbeck and family, Senator Charles Sumner (of Boston, with an allusion to his caning by Preston Brooks), as well as "Miss Lewis, the poetess," and the Boston editor Bigelow. She also recorded a visit to a synagogue.[34] While in Paris, the Aikens and the McCords socialized with some of the same people.

Several southerners sent their daughters to school in France, Harriet's aunt Elizabeth Pinckney being one example. Another was Sara Yorke (1847–1921), born in Paris to parents from Louisiana. She attended Cours Remy and later remained in Paris when her parents returned to the United States. Sara studied for one winter in New Orleans, but her family deemed the experience unsatisfactory and sent her to Institution Descauriet, a boarding school in Paris, where she remained from 1858 until 1862. The Alabamian Mary Fenwick Lewis traveled to Paris to study in the 1840s.[35]

Sometimes an entire family would move to Europe so that their children could attend French schools. Charles Izard Manigault of Charleston took his family to Paris for several years so they could be educated there. He wrote to a friend, "*Our* boys & girls of home are too apt to take things Carelessly all the time, just as they happen to come without ever feeling themselves called upon for a great excitement to ambition energy or reflection. They consider themselves young men at 16 or 18, and young women at 14 or 15, but at *these* French Boarding Schools our young ladies are made to perceive that *Such American ideas* are all nonsense." While in Paris, his daughter Henriette took piano lessons with a French instructor.[36] The next year Charles wrote to his brother that "we would not know what to do with her [Henriette] in Charleston now for she is neither *one thing* nor *the other.* Neither woman nor child with no experience. . . . We therefore want to give her some ideas, & something to talk about by shewing her some of the most interesting Parts of Europe."[37] This letter gave the impression that Charles wanted his daughter to have a more substantial immersion in French culture. That he still maintained ties with his French cousins must have made this endeavor easier. The presumption that in Charleston she would be "neither woman or child with no experience" also foretold the expectations that she would enter society, and her father wished her to be prepared for this important part of her life.

With linguistic ties to England and a cultural focus primarily on France, southern women nevertheless visited other noteworthy places in Europe as well. Italy tempted them with sculpture, art and architecture, opera, and a freedom not found in London or Paris. Hortensia Mordecai's 1859 travel diary details her journey through Nice, Monaco, Genoa, Florence, Mantua, Milan, and Venice. In Leghorn (Livorno) she saw a carnival, and in Trieste she watched Emperor Franz Joseph III pass by. As she traveled south to Pompeii, Hortensia visited the American sculptor Harriet Hosmer, as well as other sculptors' studios in Rome. In what must have been an exciting and yet frightening moment, she witnessed Mount Vesuvius erupt at Herculaneum.[38] All three of the women in this study— Harriet Lowndes, Henrietta Aiken, and Louisa Rebecca McCord—traveled a similar course during the 1850s.

Hortensia Mordecai's younger sister, Isabel (1842–1927), attended Madame Achet's school in Paris from 1858 until 1861. This well-known school was located in a specially constructed building that originally served fifty-six students in 1846. It included a chapel, three classrooms, two dormitories, an infirmary, a dining area ("*salle a manger* [*sic*]"), three practice rooms for music, a gymnasium, and a *parloir.*[39] Isabel traveled in between sessions at school, and the final page of her diary illustrates the type of journey a southern woman might have had in France and England in 1861: Paris for school, then Fontainebleau, St. Germain, back to Paris, Versailles, back to Paris, Rouen, Dieppe, Brighton, London, "Christal palace [*sic*]," Richmond, Hampton Court, Windsor, London, Liverpool.[40] Like Henriette Manigault, Isabel experienced the advantages of Parisian schooling and travel.

Some southern women also toured cities in what is now Germany and in Switzerland. Spas, such as those in Interlaken, drew women suffering from poor health. Exotic Vienna appealed to some, but that was about as far east as most traveled. The Aikens and McCords made visits to this area, as did (again) Hortensia Mordecai, who moved through Dresden, Leipzig, and Berlin. German-speaking areas appear to have been places to pass through, though, and most southern women did not spend a lot of time there.[41]

War occasionally interrupted their journeys. The mid–nineteenth century was a particularly turbulent time in Europe, and southerners abroad sometimes found themselves dangerously close to battle lines. In France alone in the first half of the century, periods of the First Republic (1792–1804, under Napoleon), the First French Empire (1804–14/15, Napoleon I), the Bourbon Restoration (1814/15–30, Louis XVIII and Charles X), the July Monarchy (1830–48, Louis Philippe d'Orléans), and the Second Republic (1848–52) occurred. The Second Empire (1852–70), under Napoleon III, was a period when Henrietta and Harriet and Louisa Rebecca were in Paris. Such change had implications, and Americans in the French capital found themselves having to adjust accordingly. Moreover, the Risorgimento, which led to the unification of Italy, inconvenienced southerners traveling on the peninsula. The Italian wars of independence (first, 1848, and second, 1859) affected how the main subjects of this book spent time in Italian-speaking lands.

Music Abroad and in Charleston

Many southerners, men and women, frequented the opera while in Europe. They went to the Opéra, the home of completely sung operas and eventually of grand opera; the Opéra Comique, where the productions included spoken dialogue; or the Théâtre-Italien, featuring opera in Italian. For example, Octavia Le Vert saw Auber's *Haidée* and *L'ambassadrice* at the Opéra Comique in 1853 and Meyerbeer's *L'étoile du Nord* there and his *Le prophète* at the Opéra in 1857. At a performance of Rossini's *Otello* at the Théâtre-Italien in 1844, Mary Fenwick Lewis of Alabama wrote that she heard "the divine 'Grise' [Giulia Grisi] warble, La Blache [Lablache], Mario Salvi, Motellit, Nocello and Belini [*sic*] sing with a band of from fifty to sixty musicians. I was perfectly enchanted. The splendour of the theatre, the magnificence of the 'toilettes' and costumes all tended to complete the brilliant representation of that fairyland which so much charmed my infant imagination in the marvelous Arabian Nights and Childs Own book." To this young southern girl, a night at the opera was nothing short of magical. James Johnson Pettigrew of North Carolina saw a number of operas while in Europe and made a list in his travelogue of 1850–51. His choice of concerts differed from those described by contemporary southern women, though. Notably, he attended performances of Beethoven's symphonies, which are not mentioned in women's diaries of the same period.[42]

From all accounts, European opera productions differed substantially from what audiences in Charleston might have seen and heard. A common summary is that the orchestra was much larger, the set more magnificent, and the quality of the chorus impressive. These differences were natural, given that the spaces in which operas were staged in Europe were theaters designed for such a purpose, while those in Charleston were multipurpose venues for significantly smaller audiences. The St. Cecilia Society, the first musical society in what became the United States, sponsored activities in at least eight different spaces before 1820. Venues known as "long rooms" hosted dances and concerts; in Charleston these included McCrady's Long Room and Fayolle's Long Room. The Carolina Coffee House was another place where music took place, as was the statehouse. Some buildings were named for such purposes, Sollée's Concert Hall among them.[43] None of these, however, compared to the grand theaters of London, Paris, Milan, Venice, or Naples.

Moreover, throughout the federal period Americans usually did not hear operas presented in their entirety, and often selections from other works were interpolated into them.[44] In the United States recitatives were frequently changed to simple dialogue, yielding a different musical experience. Hearing entirely sung operas in foreign languages did not always please touring Americans. They also did not have the opportunity to socialize in the same manner they were accustomed to at home because Europeans sat comparatively quietly through performances—much to the amazement of the Americans present.[45]

The types of entertainments Charlestonians attended abroad differed from what they heard at home. Few women mentioned any type of performance other than opera of some sort while they were abroad. This fare diverged from what they would have attended at home, where benefit performances—such as a sort of mixed recital or concert—were the norm. Such benefits were frequent in London, Paris, and smaller towns as well, but southern women rarely mentioned them in their letters or diaries when abroad. Octavia Le Vert mentioned attending a few such events, but her experiences abroad differed from those of most American women. Perhaps the cachet of going to the opera, with all its trappings such as the gowns, jewels, and escorts, made it a more memorable occasion while in Europe. Benefit concerts were plentiful enough at home.

The Binder's Volume

Most of the music examined in this study exists in what musicologists call "binder's volumes." These are books in which individual pieces of sheet music have been bound together into a single volume, and most extant binder's volumes belonged to women, for whom musical accomplishment was deemed a necessary skill in order to be eligible for marriage.[46] The tradition of the binder's volume began in the late eighteenth century and continued into the twentieth, but its heyday was the middle of the nineteenth century: this was the period when sheet music became widely available in individual selections but before the rise of complete books of music.[47] Pieces of sheet music could be had for as little as $0.25 each, the cost of Siegling's publication of Henry Bishop's popular "Home! Sweet Home!," found in Harriet's SMB 49.[48] During the mid-century the cost of music rose. Some titles cost more, especially if they had illustrations in color—a feature that became more popular in the mid-century.[49] Strawinski's *Guitar Instructor,* a method book for learning how to play the guitar, cost $1.50 in 1846. Inflation steeply drove prices up during the Civil War, and some of the pieces in Louisa Rebecca's collection went for $2.50—an exorbitant price considering the significantly lower price tag of $0.35 that one expected only a few years earlier.

The term "sheet music" as it is used here refers to a single composition, such as a song or piano solo, that was printed and then sold. Occasionally several songs or dances, for example, might be grouped together, and where to draw the line between sheet music or booklet is not standardized. Early nineteenth-century sheet music for strophic songs often had the words to only the first verse written under the music, with words to successive verses printed at the end of the music. The publisher's firm and place as well as the author's name often appeared on the music, and many pieces also included the names of famous performers as a marketing ploy. French, English, and American pieces of sheet music discussed in Harriet Lowndes's binder's volumes exemplify these publications. Publication dates were not common early on, but by the second and third decades of the century American printers included them. This was not the case with music purchased in London, Brussels, Paris, or Mainz.[50]

Until the mid–nineteenth century, most books were sold unbound so that owners could choose how they wished to present them. Parents had their daughters' volumes bound to match other binder's volumes belonging to the same young woman or to blend in with other books in the family library. The sizes of these bound music books vary, depending on the owner's collection, but earlier binder's volumes tend to be smaller, with fewer pieces, than those of the 1840s and later. Frequently binders trimmed music so that all the pages matched in height and width, which means that sometimes information we might deem valuable today—names, places, and dates—has been cut off. The volumes were occasionally bound completely with leather but more frequently with paper coverings and leather spines and corners. Usually there is a plate on the front that bears the name of the owner. Such books were ubiquitous in middle- and upper-class homes of the mid–nineteenth century.

The music in binder's volumes was almost always bound prior to marriage, although a few exceptions can be found scattered throughout archives in the South. Binder's volumes constituted one of the few things that young women truly owned and that went with them, no matter the circumstances. Most women of means had one volume, but the more affluent might own more. Perhaps the largest single extant collection belonged to Ann Beaufort Sims, whose six binder's volumes can be found in the Charleston Museum.[51] She was the daughter of the state librarian in Columbia, and her music reveals much about music education at the South Carolina Female Institute at Barhamville, located just outside Columbia during the antebellum period.

Young women acquired their music through various means. Family members and friends (male or female) gave sheet music pieces to them, and some inherited music from older sisters or their mothers. Sometimes there is an inscription indicating a gift on a piece of music, such as "to Miss so-and-so from her friend Mr. X." In other cases another family member's name or initials might have been written on a piece before it came to the person who owned a particular binder's volume, as was the case with Louisa Rebecca's sister Hannah, whose name appears on one of the pieces in SMB 42.

The size and tight bindings of volumes from the 1850s and 1860s make them unwieldy for practical use on a piano or music stand, or to be held while singing. Frequent use could break the spines. These facts imply that binder's volumes might not have been used after they were bound, although we cannot be certain. Uncharacteristically, Henrietta's were not bound, and in chapter 10 possible reasons are suggested as to why no bound volumes of individual sheet music pieces survive from her collection.

Women in Charleston obtained their music through a number of means. Locally they could have shopped at John Siegling's store. Born in Erfurt, Saxony, in 1789, Johann (later John) Zacharias Siegling studied harp with the most famous professional of the early nineteenth century, Nicolas-Charles Bochsa. Siegling first entered the business world in Paris, where he worked in the musical instrument factory for Sébastien and Jean-Baptiste Érard. He immigrated to the United States in 1819 and opened a business in Charleston on the south side of Broad Street, opposite the courthouse, in November of that year. Soon thereafter he moved to the southeast corner of King and Broad Streets and specifically advertised as a music store. As early as 1820 he began importing from London pianos, called pianofortes, that had been specially manufactured for the climate extremes of the South. He also claimed to have imported the first harp to the United States. In 1828 Siegling moved to the southwest corner of Meeting Street and Horlbecks Alley, but he settled finally on the southwest corner of King and Beaufain Streets, where the Siegling Music House remained until 1970. He opened a Havana, Cuba, branch in 1830. John eventually passed the business to his second son, Henry (1829–1905). John and Henry published a considerable amount of music, and they also imported items from the North and Europe.[52]

In spite of its prominence, the Siegling Music House was not the only shop where Charlestonians could buy music: the 1849 city directory included several other places. Zogbaum's at the corner of Beaufain and King Streets provided music to Charleston residents, as did George Cole at 175 King Street and George Oates at 234 King Street.[53] Charleston's music teachers might have provided their pupils with music. Among these teachers were Elizabeth and Ann Sloman from England, who taught at 28 Meeting Street; Mrs. Hammerskold, a Swedish musician living in the United States, who taught at 1 State Street; and Victor Petit, a Belgian, whose instruction occurred at 30 Pinckney Street. This snapshot of Charleston in only one year illustrates the different options that young women who lived in the city would have had when it came to procuring new music.

Furthermore, more affluent families traveled widely in the United States, usually heading north, and purchased music in Philadelphia, New York, or Boston. These were the usual sources of music purchased by East Coast southerners if they did not buy locally. Another layer to add to this circulation process is that some firms, particularly in New York and New Orleans, imported music from Europe. These copies could also have been sent to Charleston for sale there.[54]

Surprisingly, given the inconsistent properties of many musical items from the first half of the nineteenth century, sheet music remained somewhat consistent in size and presentation. The earliest music examined for this study, Harriet Lowndes's personal collection, is uniform in size—approximately 12 × 9 inches—even when it includes music from a variety of publishers. Works from this period also tend to be shorter, requiring fewer sheets of paper. The pages owned by Henrietta Aiken and Louisa Rebecca McCord, dating from the middle decades of the century, are slightly larger—14.5 × 10.5 inches—and longer, especially those belonging to Henrietta.[55]

With the later collections of Louisa Rebecca and Henrietta, the move by publishers to pictorial titles (in which the title page is entirely taken up by an image) is in full evidence. As the nineteenth century progressed, they increasingly added images to music as a means to entice buyers. Publishers added pictures of famous singers who had made a particular composition popular, such as

Anna Bishop, in costume or posed for a formal picture. In other cases landscapes or other scenes depicting themes in the sheet music can be found on the first pages. Such images were used on sheet music on both sides of the Atlantic.[56] Merchants such as Siegling exploited this tactic by placing the latest, and probably most attractive, images on sheet music outside their stores.[57]

Charleston Belles Abroad: The Music Collections of Harriet Lowndes, Henrietta Aiken, and Louisa Rebecca McCord

Charleston Belles Abroad begins with a close examination of music in one of America's leading cities in the 1820s, questioning the meaning behind the influx of foreign composers and genres in the binder's volumes that belonged to Harriet Lowndes. The binder's volumes of two of Harriet's Charleston contemporaries and social equals represent more typical American collections, and they provide a standard for comparison in part 1. This interrogation of European culture continues as it pertains to her daughter Henrietta's music from the 1850s in part 2, interlacing it with the family's extensive visits overseas. In part 3 Louisa Rebecca's binder's volumes are contrasted with Henrietta's collection in order to demonstrate the impact of their mothers on their music. Louisa Rebecca's collection vividly reflects how the Civil War interrupted music in Charleston, and her daughter's volume allows for consideration of postwar repertory changes. The conclusion contextualizes the personal nature of and maternal influences on the music collections of Harriet, Henrietta, and Louisa Rebecca by contrasting them with music owned by other young women of the 1850s, as related to the Aiken-Lowndes-Rhett families.

The three main parts of *Charleston Belles Abroad* interrogate the individual music collections of Harriet Lowndes, Henrietta Aiken, and Louisa Rebecca McCord in considerable detail in order to situate the unique qualities of each in the more general narrative of women and music in the United States. Each presents a distinctive set of composers, genres, and data concerning the owner's time in Europe. These collections illustrate not only a wide variety of composers and genres but also a large number of them. To understand how each binder's volume reflects the personal interests of Harriet, Henrietta, or Louisa Rebecca, it is necessary to delve deeply into the contents and their contexts. To do otherwise would be to convey only part of the special qualities of these collections. To cut down on the sheer data presented within each part, appendix C includes a brief biographical account of many of the relevant composers.

Nevertheless, at times what may seem like an overindulgence of data is, in fact, necessary to appreciate the breadth of these collections. For example, in part 1, concerning Harriet Lowndes, the reader encounters a multitude of unfamiliar French composers, several of whose names do not appear in standard music encyclopedias, such as *Grove Music Online.* This element serves to underscore the reason for their inclusion: how did a young woman from Charleston obtain music that did not circulate anywhere in the United States? Similarly, in part 2, on Henrietta Aiken, the case is made for including a substantial number of uninscribed pieces in the Charleston Museum as hers. The justification for inclusion requires explanation. In part 3, concerning Louisa Rebecca McCord, a new set of European publishers is encountered: she appears to have bought most of her music in Britain, unlike the previous two women. This, in turn, demands further exploration of how Charlestonians interpreted their time abroad.

Furthermore, Harriet's diary of the 1857–58 European journey and details of Louisa Rebecca's 1858–59 tour in her "Recollections of Louisa McCord Smythe" make it possible to weave some of the music in this collection into their travelogues. This aids our understanding of what young women might have purchased while abroad; it also reveals where they spent time in places such as London and Paris. Such details do not typically accompany the biographies of young women from the antebellum period, but they fill out modern conceptions of material culture, education, and individuality.

A few related collections have been added where appropriate for comparison with the binder's volumes of these three women. Some of their contents appear within the text and others are in appendix A. One focus of the conclusion is to contextualize the collections of Harriet, Henrietta, and Louisa Rebecca as they relate to binder's volumes surviving in the Charleston Museum from other members of the extended Lowndes-Aiken-Rhett family or women who studied with the same music teacher. These, in turn, help to amplify further the significance of the music collections of this study's main subjects.

Charleston Belles Abroad examines the music collections of three elite white women who were at the top of the social ladder and spent time in Europe. Their musical experiences differed substantially, and these individual variations in cultural practice within such a limited circle are illustrated. Generalizations of women's musical experiences have marginalized their activities. Women's choices contributed to both local and foreign commerce and were a driving force in American musical tastes. In spite of this, the evidence of what and how they participated in music has yet to be understood fully. Standard textbooks of Western European music history that venture into American music typically mention only Stephen Foster in connection with "parlor music," but his music surfaces only twice in over six hundred individual pieces in the collections forming the basis of this book. One could even argue that most of the music performed in the United States during the mid–nineteenth century came from the sheets in binder's volumes. This study reminds us that composers who have long been forgotten once dominated music in many households. We cannot understand American music history until we know more about the music that was heard in benefit concerts, parlors, and music lessons.

PART ONE

CHAPTER I

The Lowndes Family and Harriet's Music Collection

Harriet Lowndes was the ninth of eleven children born to Thomas Lowndes (1766–1843) and Sarah Bond I'on (1777–1840). Little information survives concerning Sarah's early life and upbringing that might assist our understanding about her thoughts while she raised her own daughter. Sarah's father was a man of considerable wealth, owning more than two hundred slaves when he died in 1796. Sarah's portrait, painted by Gilbert Stuart circa 1803, depicts her in her mid-twenties, fashionably dressed in a white gown with pearl and lace accents.[1] Whether she was musical is unknown, but most women of her class and station would have received lessons on a keyboard instrument, harp, or voice. That her daughter attained some skill in each of these suggests that Sarah studied music as well.

Thomas Lowndes was a lawyer, a Federalist member of the South Carolina House of Representatives from 1796 to 1800, and a U.S. congressman from 1801 to 1805. The Lowndes family had arrived in South Carolina from Cheshire, England, in the 1720s.[2] Thomas's father, Rawlins Lowndes (1721/2–1800), was president of South Carolina in 1778–79. The Lowndes name resonated among South Carolina's elites, and they married among others of their class and influence. Harriet's family also had Huguenot roots, which further linked them to several families in the area.

In South Carolina members of Harriet's branch of the family divided their time between Oaklands Plantation, near Colleton, and a house in Charleston. They also spent some of her childhood summers in New Haven, Connecticut, where her brother Rawlins Lowndes was born in 1801.[3] Her parents' homes were scenes of many entertainments, as depicted by the Englishwoman Margaret Hunter Hall, who attended a party at the Lowndes home in Charleston in 1828. Her description of the women in attendance was much more generous than any of her other comments on women in South Carolina, noting "a greater number

of pretty women." Born in Edinburgh and brought up in Spain, Margaret
Hunter Hall moved among high society in London and Edinburgh. That she
included the Lowndes's plantation on her American itinerary testifies to the
family's social reputation.[4]

By nature of their "conspicuous social station," George B. Chase found that
the Lowndes home served as "the resort . . . of distinguished citizens of the state."
He further described Sarah as a lady "who united great charm of manner to a
handsome and distinguished presence."[5] Gilbert Stuart captured this presence in
his 1803 portrait of Sarah. Although little information survives to provide a sense
of her personality, she performed the duties as expected of a southern lady, as
the descriptions of parties at the home have attested.

The Lowndes's social position included the education of their children
according to the standards of the day. For Harriet, this meant extensive studies in
languages—she reportedly spoke four—and music, evidence for which endures
in her music collection, now housed in the Charleston Museum.[6] This collection consists of four binder's volumes amassed before her marriage in 1831 and
nine complete opera scores—piano-vocal arrangements—purchased after her
marriage.[7] Her legacy is closely tied to European arts and literature, and her pre-
nuptial music collection evinces remarkably strong French connections—as if
she had made the journey overseas. But nothing indicates that Harriet traveled
to Europe before her honeymoon, which renders this foreign music all the more
conspicuous.

The Lowndes family maintained several connections with Europe, probably
through a Huguenot network, and that may explain part of her devotion to all
things French. Most notable among these relations was her aunt by marriage,
Elizabeth Brewton Pinckney (d. 1857). Prior to her marriage to Harriet's uncle
in 1802, Elizabeth had lived for a time in England and then attended Madame
Campan's famous school for young women in Paris—Saint-Germain-en-Laye—
for two years.[8] As a married woman, she traveled with her husband, William
Jones Lowndes, who was a U.S. congressman on the Committee of Foreign
Affairs, and their daughter Rebecca Motte Lowndes to Europe in 1822. William
died before they arrived and was buried at sea.[9] Nonetheless, Elizabeth and
Rebecca continued on to France, where they stayed first with Jean-Pierre, Baron
Hyde de Neuville, and his wife, friends they had met in Washington, D.C.
De Neuville had briefly been exiled to the United States by Napoleon, but in
1816 Louis XVIII named him French ambassador. Another family member who
strengthened the bond with France was Elizabeth's cousin Pinckney Horry, who
married a Frenchwoman, Mademoiselle de la Faye de la Tour Maubourg. That
family remained in Paris instead of returning to South Carolina. In 1822 Elizabeth and Rebecca Lowndes stayed with them after they left the de Neuvilles.[10]

These examples illustrate the Lowndes family's robust contacts with France in the early nineteenth century.

When Elizabeth returned to the United States, she brought a number of items with her. Her granddaughter, Harriet Horry Rutledge (wife of Dr. St. Julien Ravenel and author of several books about Charleston and its inhabitants), provided a partial list of the books Elizabeth owned. These demonstrate a deeply held appreciation for French culture, an appreciation that continued through successive generations, extending to Harriet and her daughter, Henrietta.[11] An attraction to French language and cultural ideals was expected of elite young southern women, and Elizabeth's family had the economic means to allow her to pursue them, beginning in the late eighteenth century. Cultural historians such as Kilbride and O'Brien have found that southerners identified especially with English culture, but for the Lowndes family this seems not to have been the case.[12] Huguenot connections strengthened the family's association with France, and several other members of the extended Lowndes family made the journey across the Atlantic before the Civil War.

Harriet's surviving music collection reveals an astonishing amount of information, both in the context of this book and in the broader history of music in Charleston, the South, and the United States during the early nineteenth century. It is a large collection, and no other amateur American collection from the 1820s compares to it on several levels. First is its sheer size. In a few cases multiple binder's volumes survive from southern women who came of age before the Civil War. Those whose economic circumstances allowed for such expenses might have owned two volumes, but a collection of four volumes represents real luxury, interest, and perhaps talent.[13] That Harriet compiled hers essentially in the 1820s further distinguishes this collection.

Since all of Harriet's extant binder's volumes, cataloged as SMB 47–50 in the Charleston Museum, carry her maiden name stamped in gilt on their covers, they date from before her marriage to William Aiken Jr. on 3 February 1831. By the mid–nineteenth century most young women had their music bound before marriage, sometimes as "going-away" gifts from their parents. But the sheer size of binder's volumes from the 1850s—often with well over 250 pages of sheet music—seems to have precluded using them after they had been bound because such thick books simply could not remain open easily. In the 1820s, however, they tended to be smaller and could have been used in performance. Each of Harriet's volumes can easily lie open on a piano desk, even a smaller-sized forte-piano or spinet from this period.[14]

Even more important than the magnitude of the collection that Harriet owned, this group of binder's volumes stands out because it preserves two entirely distinct repertories, each illuminating in its own way. These volumes imply vibrant and varied musical experiences at the Lowndes home as well as familiarity with professional musicians in Charleston. Her music represents the highest cultural standards possible in the 1820s and a knowledge of French music that far exceeds the familiarity exemplified in contemporary southern collections. It also reminds us that the repertory that twenty-first-century historians associate with this period—composers such as Beethoven and Schubert—was not preferred by audiences in 1820s Charleston.[15] Moreover, Harriet's collection suggests that she, or her parents or teachers, wished to distinguish music in the Lowndes home from that of her contemporaries by emphasizing a French music repertory that was unusual in South Carolina, although it was quite the rage in Paris and Brussels.

This is not to say that French music was unknown in Charleston. Indeed, Nicholas Butler has described an influx of French musicians in 1804 when Saint Domingue proclaimed its independence from France, with the result that the St. Cecilia's Society's orchestra consisted mainly of French musicians during the 1804–5 concert season. Naturally they programmed music by their fellow countrymen, such as Étienne-Nicolas Méhul, André-Ernest-Modeste Grétry, and Nicolas-Marie Dalayrac—all leading opera composers of the late eighteenth and early nineteenth centuries. But by 1815 a repertory dominated by composers such as Handel and Haydn replaced much of this, and other musicians arrived in Charleston. Since Harriet was born in 1812, these French musicians in Charleston cannot have been the sole reason she turned to a repertory common in France but almost nowhere else. As Butler has noted, the 1820s marked "the end of an era" in Charleston's music.[16] This being the case, Harriet's collection does not represent the music frequently heard in the city during the 1820s but stands apart from contemporary trends.

All of Harriet's binder's volumes were bound with red leather on the spines and name plates on the covers, but this is where the similarities in the collection as a whole end. The earliest book appears to be SMB 49, a collection of English-language pieces published in the United States, some with solid connections to Charleston. Those labeled SMB 47 and SMB 50 belong together both in their physical details and in their contents. The final volume discussed here, SMB 48, stands alone in its provenance, publisher, and inclusion of manuscript music.

Vocal Music in English

SMB 49 exemplifies the music that would have been available in Charleston and other urban areas in the United States during the 1820s. William Estill (1800–1882), a bookbinder and seller in Charleston, bound the volume in marbled paper and red leather in 1825 and stamped "H L Lowndes" in gold on the cover.[1] Publication dates of 1823 and 1824 on several pieces signal that SMB 49 is the earliest of her books, and the repertory, typical for the United States, confirms these as probable dates for Harriet's music. Its adherence to popular sheet music preferences in early nineteenth-century America supports the likelihood that it was her first set of pieces, following the trends seen in the homes of her friends and acquaintances. On the first page she signed it "Harriet L. Lowndes 1825," when she would have been twelve or thirteen years old.[2] (See figure 2.1.) Moreover, that none of the other volumes includes a similarly familiar repertory suggests that it belongs first chronologically. It is reasonable to assume that Harriet began her music collection with music that was similar to that of her contemporaries. Table 2.1 provides the inventory for SMB 49.

Containing relatively simple songs in English, the works therein typify the repertory that a twelve-year-old girl in Charleston would have been expected to learn in the mid-1820s. The ballads and airs range from well-known songs from

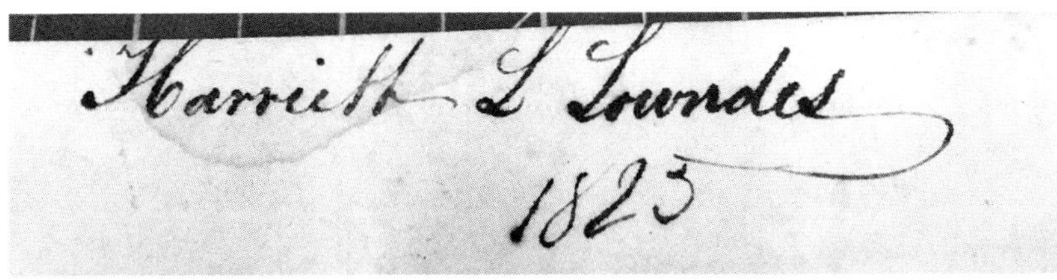

Figure 2.1. Harriet's signature in SMB 49

Table 2.1 Contents of SMB 49

No.	Title	Composer	Date	Notes
1	Oh tell me how from love to fly	A. Clifton		Charleston: H. Dunning. Markings
2	I left thee where I found thee love!	Charles Gilfert		NY: Dubois & Stodart. "as Sung with rapturour applause by Mrs. Holman at the Oratorio Given at the Park Theatre"
3	Allen A Dale / From Rokeby	Charles Gilfert		Charleston: Siegling
4	Believe me if all those endearing young charms			Charleston: Siegling. Duet
5	When e'er I see those smiling eyes	Charles Gilfert		NY: Dubois & Stodart
6	The Harper's Song	T. V. Wiesenthal		Charleston: Siegling
7	Melody Sketches No. 1 / The Castilian Maid	"Written by Moore"	4 Aug. 1823	Baltimore: Willig
8	Too late I staid / A favorite song	Charles Gilfert		Charleston: Siegling. Markings
9	'Tis love in the heart / The 'admired Rondo	Charles Horn		Charleston: Siegling.
10	My heart and lute / A new Ballad	Thomas Moore		Charleston: Siegling.
11	Home! Sweet home!	Henry R. Bishop		Charleston: Siegling. "Sung by Miss M. Tree in Clari, or The Maid of Milan at the Theatre Royal Covent Garden / Composed & partly founded on a Sicilian Air"
12	Donne l'amore / In Italian / Air			Philadelphia: Willig. English words above vocal line
13	The nosegay	Mr. Brenan		Charleston: Siegling. nearly opposite the Circular Church

14	Oh! Say not womans heart is bought / A favorite ballad	John Whitaker		Charleston: Siegling. "Sung . . . by Mrs. French" piano part is fingered and has alignments added
15	The plain gold ring / Adapted to an Air in Der Freischütz"	C.M. von Weber		Baltimore: Willig. *Der Freischütz*
16	Hurrah! Hurrah! / A celebrated German song / in the opera of "Sweedish Patriotism"	A. Clifton	6 Jan. 1823	Philadelphia: Willig
17	The maniac song!	C.F. von Bonnhorst, Esq.		Philadelphia: Blake
18	O swiftly glides the bonny boat / Scotch Air	J.F. Hance	3 Dec. 1824	NY: Dubois & Stodart
19	From the Third London Edition / The light guittar [*sic*] / A celebrated Serenade	John Barnett		Boston: Hewitt & Co. Sold J.J. Rickers, NY
20	Here we meet too soon to part / Adapted to Rossini's Air / Di tanti palpitti	G. Rossini; arr., T.B. Phipps		Charleston: Siegling
21	Forget me not / Favorite song / in the Comic Opera called Narensky, or The Road to Yaroslaf	Mr. Braham		NY: Dubois
22	I've been roaming / A Cavatina	C.E. Horn		Charleston: Siegling. "Sung by Mrs. Knight"
23	Today, dearest is ours	Thomas Moore		NY: Dubois & Stodart
24	Follow follow over mountain	S.T. Smith		Philadelphia: Klemm. "Sung by Madam Vestris"
25	Behold in his soft expressive face / In the Opera of The Devils Bridge			Philadelphia: Klemm. "Sung by Mr. Phillipps" Philadelphia: Klemm. "Sung by Mr. Phillipps"

Table 2.1 Contents of SMB 49 (*continued*)

No.	Title	Composer	Date	Notes
26	Let us haste to Kelvin grove / In the Opera of Guy Mannering	R.A. Smith		Baltimore: Cole. "Sung by Mr. Braham"
27	I'll watch for thee from my lonely bow'r / Ballad / Adapted to A German Air	John A. Stevenson		Philadelphia: Klemm
28	Tho' tis all but a dream / A French Air from Moore's National Airs	Henry R. Bishop, arr.		NY: Dubois & Stodart
29	American Musical Miscellany No. 7 / The Minstrel Song from The Queen's Wake	T.W. Wiesenthal		Philadelphia: Klemm
30	Come o'er the sea	John A. Stevenson		NY: J.A. & W. Geib
31	And ye shall walk in silk attire	Henry R. Bishop		NY: Dubois & Stodart. "Sung by Signorina Garcia"
32	Hinda's appeal to her lover	G. Kiallmark		NY: Dubois & Stodart
33	Painted butterfly / Ballad	J.F. Hance	10 Apr. 1823	NY: Dubois & Stodart. "Sung by Mrs. Hackett"
34	Isabel / A celebrated Spanish Serenade	Henry R. Bishop		Philadelphia: Willig. "Sung by Miss Stephens"
35	My native land good night!	Miss Fowler		NY: Dubois. "Sung by Mrs. French"
36	Follow follow thro' the sea / Mermaid song	Henry R. Bishop, arr.; Martini		NY: Dubois & Stodart. "Sung by Miss Kelly"
37	Haste idle time / The admired Polacca	J.F. Hance		Philadelphia: Klemm. "Sung by Miss Boudet"[1] [American Musical Miscellany No. 9]

38	Go my love / A Rondo	Henry R. Bishop	Philadelphia: Blake. Sold J.J. Rickers, NC "Sung by Miss Kelly"
39	Tho' you leave me now in sorry / The much admired Duetto . . . in Rob Roy Macgregor	John Davy	NY: Dubois. "Sung by Mrs. Holman & Mr. Howard"
40	Like the gloom of night retiring / with vocal embellishments	Henry R. Bishop	NY: Dubois & Stodart. Sold J.J. Rickers. "Sold Mrs. Holman"

Note:

1. "Dancing Academy" *Savannah Republican*, 14 October, 1820.

"Mr. Boudet, Professor of Dancing and Music, respectfully informs his friends and the pubic generally, that he will open his Dancing Academy in this city on the 1 of November next, having already a number of pupils subscribed to his Dancing School. Mr. Boudet and his family will consequently move to Savannah in October next, in hopes of receiving sufficient encouragement to enable them to make Savannah the place of their permanent residence.

"Miss VICTORIE BOUDET, Tutress of Harp, PianoForte, and Guitar, singing in English, French and Italian, also respectfully gives notice that she will open her MUSIC ACADEMY here for the reception of pupils at the time of the opening of the Dancing Academy. Miss Boudet hopes that her mode of teaching will please, as it is the same as used at the Conservatoire at Paris."

the Irish poet Thomas Moore's several publications—most notably "Believe Me If All Those Endearing Young Charms"—to excerpts from stage works. The latter include pieces from comic "operas" such as *Narensky, Guy Mannering, Rob Roy MacGregor,* and *Clari, or The Maid of Milan,* from whence the immensely popular song "Home! Sweet Home!" originates. This song, which became one of the most frequently encountered works in the United States before the Civil War, had its American debut in New York on 12 November 1823.[3] Harriet procured her copy early, including it in a volume bound in 1825.

Operas staged in America and Britain in the 1810s and 1820s differed significantly from what we today think of as "opera." In both places the term usually meant a light, somewhat satiric or comical play with strophic songs scattered throughout. The music might have been the work of a single composer or a combination of songs belonging to different composers—known as a pastiche—which were often tailored to a particular audience as defined by geographic area, politics, or other markers.[4] Such performances were popular in cities such as Charleston, a regular part of the concert circuit. They worked in tandem with publishers who made favorites available for local residents.

As the nineteenth century progressed, different types of operas found their way to the United States, as other excerpts in SMB 49 demonstrate. Included among its pages are two adaptations of arias from operas that conform closer to modern images of opera but differ substantially in style from each other: "The Plain Gold Ring" (no. 15), an adaptation from Carl Maria von Weber's German romantic opera *Der Freischütz* (1820); and "Here We Meet Too Soon to Part" (no. 20), T. B. Phipps's version of Rossini's immensely popular "Di tanti palpiti" from *Tancredi* (1813). The aria "Di tanti palpiti" exists in many antebellum binder's volumes, and several professional singers performed it in concerts in Charleston during this period. Excerpts from Weber's opera can be found in various guises in American binder's volumes from the first half of the nineteenth century. The latter work, either in Italian or fitted with English words, appears in many collections from the same period. Italian opera, in particular, experienced a rapid rise in popularity beginning in 1825 and truly flowered in the 1840s. Many southern binder's volumes contain excerpts from such works as Bellini's *Norma* and *La Sonnambula* (both 1831) or Rossini's *Otello* and *Il barbiere di Siviglia* (both 1816). Weber too rose to prominence in the 1820s. Having music by both Rossini and Weber bound into SMB 49 illustrates that whoever advised Harriet's music purchases followed current trends.[5]

Most of the music in SMB 49 was produced by publishers in Philadelphia: ten, including Willig, Blake, and Klemm; and New York: fourteen from Dubois & Stodart. Three came from publishers in Baltimore: Willig and Cole; and one came from Boston: Hewitt. Sheet music did not have to be procured directly from the publisher, however, and many music "warehouses" and "saloons" sold pieces that the proprietors received from others. For example, even though "The Light Guittar" was published in Boston, it bears the New York seller's stamp of J. J. Rickers. A family member may have purchased this music for Harriet while on business trips, or her music teacher may have had them and sold them to the Lowndes family, or they may have been available in shops in Charleston but lack the seller's stamp.

That Harriet owned music from northern publishers was natural given that in 1825 most American music businesses were located in Baltimore, Philadelphia, or cities farther north. Charleston's music sellers, printers, and musicians shine prominently in SMB 49, however, and testify to a growing music commerce there. The remaining twelve works in SMB 49 came from the Charleston publishers H. Dunning and John Siegling. Siegling's publications far outnumber those of Dunning.[6] Most of the Charleston imprints are located at the beginning, as if Estill chose to highlight the local merchants when he bound the volume. Other connections with Charleston exist in SMB 49, and these contribute further to its historical significance. One is Charles Gilfert (1787–1829), a composer who moved from New York to manage the Charleston Theater.[7] His career in Charleston began by 1807 when he performed in a benefit for himself on 3 March.[8] Gilfert also sold music in Charleston for a short period, played in the Philharmonic Society Orchestra, and unabashedly identified himself as the musical center of the city.[9] He was such a major force in Charleston's musical scene that it is possible Harriet met him.[10] As with any era, we are on firmer ground in identifying performers than we are knowing who was in the audience, and 1820s Charleston is no exception.

In an appeal to local music practitioners, Siegling advertised "Oh! Say Not Woman's Heart Is Bought" as having been sung by Mrs. French, formerly Ann Maria Mestayer Thorne, who had performed in Charleston in 1819. Other favored performers, according to SMB 49, included Miss M. Tree, Mrs. Holman, Mrs. Knight, Madam Vestriss, Mr. Phillipps (Phillips), Mr. Barham, Signorina Garcia (Maria Garcia), Miss Stephens, Miss Kelly, and Miss Boudet. The last of these came from nearby Savannah, Georgia, where her father taught dancing and music.[11]

Most of the pieces in SMB 49 lack publications or copyright dates, but Harriet's notation of "1825" helps to pinpoint the date by which it was bound. Three pieces—nos. 7, 16, and 33—bear copyright dates of 1823, and no. 18 was published in 1824. The opening work in SMB 49, "Oh Tell Me How" by Arthur Clifton, dates from 1820, according to copies of the work that exist in other archives.[12] Nicholas Tawa has given the date "ca. 1823" for Gilfert's "I Left Thee Where I Found Thee Love."[13] Gilfert's setting of "Allen-A-Dale," set to a text from Sir Walter Scott's *Rokeby,* was dated circa 1819 by William Burton Todd and Ann Bowden in their bibliographical history of Scott's works.[14] These provide a general dating of the late 1810s and early 1820s for the music in SMB 49. At age twelve at the beginning of 1825, Harriet would have been precisely the age when most affluent young women immersed themselves in their music studies in earnest.

Harriet left her imprint on SMB 49. Several clues, such as fingerings on songs such as "Oh Tell Me How from Love to Fly" and "Too Late I Staid [*sic*]," as well as breath marks, new texts, and hand alignments testify to her involvement with its pages. Someone, possibly Harriet herself, wrote the second verse of Gilfert's "I Left Thee Where I Found Thee Love" underneath the first. This annotation could mean either that its tune was not familiar enough to add it without looking at the melodic line or that she accompanied herself and needed to follow the piano part as well. In her copy of "Believe Me If All Your Endearing Young Charms," the piano part has been fingered and alignments between the right- and left-hand parts have been added. This sort of notation can be found in numerous binder's volumes from the period, because eighteenth- and early nineteenth-century printers usually did not vertically align the right- and left-hand parts, with the result that sheet music did not simultaneously present the parts as they were to be played.

Harriet's version of "Believe Me If All Your Endearing Young Charms," published by Siegling, is an arrangement for two voices. Duets occur in many binder's volumes and indicate that musical performances in the parlor could include more than one soloist. Duets and trios also figure prominently in the music in SMB 50, but nothing reveals the names of those with whom she might have performed them. Concerts from this period frequently included duets, and Harriet may have mimicked such performances with her sister, a friend, or even her teacher.[15]

Another binder's volume at the Charleston Museum, SMB 12, is contemporary with SMB 49 and helps illustrate the extent to which the latter characterizes collections owned by young women from prominent Charleston families. (See table 2.2.) The cover of SMB 12 bears the name "Miss Rose," and her first and last name appear inside on some of the music, confirming that it belonged to Rose Butler Drayton (1806–86), the daughter of John Drayton and Hester Rose Tidyman.[16] John was a judge, governor of South Carolina, and the founder of South Carolina College. Rose offers an excellent test case for comparison with Harriet because she was only slightly older and her family could boast considerable social prominence.

Like Harriet, Rose collected arrangements of familiar airs, but unlike Harriet's music, some of Rose's pieces are for piano solo. She included several sets of

Table 2.2. Contents of SMB 12, binder's volume belonging to Rose Butler Drayton, 1820s

No.	Title	Composer	Date	Notes
1	Chinese Rondo			Charleston: Siegling "Opposite the Circular Church," Used copy. Image of Chinese people on front
2	German Air	F.C. Hoffman		Charleston: Siegling "Opposite the Circular Church"
3	A Masonic Air with Variations	Jacob Eckhard Jr.		Charleston: Siegling
4	Robin Adair with Variations for harp or piano	S. Cristiani		Philadelphia: Blake
5	Air by Mozart	F.C. Hoffman		Charleston: Siegling. *Die Zauberflöte.* (Papageno's aria, instrumental arrangement)
6	A French Air with Variations			Charleston: Siegling
7	Musette de Nina with Variations for harp or piano	N. Dalayrac; arr., W.L. Hayden		Charleston: Siegling. Cadenza on p. 3 (p. 35 in SMB)
8	Select Airs arranged with Variations for Piano Solo ("Come rest in thy bosom")	Kiallmark		Charleston: Siegling
9	Select Airs arranged with Variations for Piano Solo ("Since then I am doomed")			Charleston: Siegling
10	A temple of friendship – Spanish Air with Variations for Piano Forte	Julius Metz		NY: Dubois & Stodart
11	Auld Lang Syne – The Favorite Scotch Air with Variations for the Pianoforte or Harp	D. Ross		Charleston: Siegling

Table 2.2. Contents of SMB 12, binder's volume belonging to Rose Butler Drayton, 1820s (*continued*)

No.	Title	Composer	Date	Notes
12	Tyrolesian Air with Variations for Pianoforte or Harp	F.J. Nadermann		Charleston: Siegling
13	Washington's March with Variations for Pianoforte	Jacob Eckhard Jr.		Charleston: Siegling
14	Auld Lang Syne with extra words by Mrs. A. Cambridge			Charleston: Siegling
15	Begone dull care with Variations for Pianoforte or Harp	D. Ross		Charleston: Siegling
16	[missing title and second piano part at the beginning] Latours Duett			
17	The peasant's joy – Rondo – A New Favorite Lesson	Mr. Blagrave		Charleston: Siegling
18	Yankee Doodle	Jacob Eckhard Jr.		Charleston: Siegling
19	Egyptian Air arranged as a Rondo for Pianoforte	T.H. Butler		Charleston: Siegling
20	La Danse du Shal arranged for Pianoforte			Charleston: Siegling
21	Miss Lettine's Favorite Dance arranged for Pianoforte	Charles E. Gilfert	Aug. 1823	Charleston: Siegling
22	The favorite serenading waltz, No. 1	Charles E. Gilfert		Charleston: Siegling
23	The Boston cadet's waltz			Charleston: Siegling

No.	Title	Composer	Date	Publication / Notes
24	The bird waltz for pianoforte or harp	Francis Panormo		Charleston: Siegling
25	The New York serenading waltz			Charleston: H. Dunning
26	The lovely rose-A new song for the piano forte and harp [not a duet]			Charleston: Siegling
27	The maniac	John Stevenson		n.p
28	Love but an April day for harp or pianoforte	Reeves		n.p
29	The bed of roses – Favorite song in the grand Historical Opera The Virgin of the Sun			n.p.
30	Home! Sweet home! Composed and partly founded on a Sicilian Air	Henry Bishop		Charleston: Siegling. "Sung by Miss M. Tree in Clari, or The Maid of Milan at the Theatre Royal, Covent Garden"
31	Robin Adair	Braham		London: Charles Christmas Opera Saloon, 36 Pall Mall. Same as #4, different arrangement, same key.
32	Oh 'tis love – Adapted from the French Air "C'est l'Amour"			Charleston: Siegling. Sung by Mr. Keene at the Charleston Theatre
33	I left thee where I found thee love!	Charles Gilfert		NY: Dubois & Stodart
34	Love thee dearest!	Charles Gilfert	Sept. 1823	NY: Dubois & Stodart
35	The heath this night must be my bed	J. Willson		NY: by the author. Sold NY: J & M Paff, J. Hewitt. From Scott's "Lady of the Lake." Top left "M.G. Porcher"
36	All things bright & fair are thine	O. Shaw		Providence, RI: O. Shaw. From Moore's Sacred Melodies. Duet

Table 2.2. Contents of SMB 12, binder's volume belonging to Rose Butler Drayton, 1820s (*continued*)

No.	Title	Composer	Date	Notes
37	Arrayed in chords of golden sunlight-Duett	O. Shaw		Providence, RI: O. Shaw
38	Strike the cymbal	V. Pucitta		Charleston: Siegling
39	Bonja song – A celebrated Negro	H. Wilberforce, M.P.		Charleston: Siegling
40	The pilgrim of love	Henry Bishop		Charleston: H. Dunning. "From the Noble Outlaw, Theatre Royal, Covent Garden"
41	Flora's wreath	T. Mazzinghi		Charleston: Siegling. "Sung by Mr. Brenan at the Oratorio given at the Charleston Theatre"
42	Dear woman, lovely woman	Henry Thomas Heathcote, Esq.		Charleston: Siegling
43	Love with doubt should never dwell			Charleston: Siegling. "From the Popular Drama Tom and Jerry"
44	Flow on thou shining river – Portugese Air	John Stevenson		Charleston: Siegling. From Moore's Popular National Melodies
45	A temple to friendship – Spanish Air			Charleston: Siegling
46	Blue-eyed Mary			Charleston: Siegling
47	Come rest in they bosom – Adapted to the Favorite Air "Fleuve de Tage"			Charleston: Siegling. French words are printed above the vocal line.
48	The harper's song	T. von Wiesenthal		Charleston: Siegling. "From Rokeby"
49	When e'er I see those smiling eyes	Charles Gilfert	Oct. 1823	NY: Dubois & Stodart. Moore
50	Ellen Aurien for pianoforte or harp			Charleston: Siegling. Missing all but the first page

variations on melodies such as "Auld Lang Syne" and "Robin Adair," including two versions of the latter, well-liked song. Such variations on well-known tunes formed a major part of the piano repertory performed by young women until at least 1870, although the melodies changed over time to suit popular taste. Another feature found in SMB 12 is that five of the songs—nos. 43 through 47—do not have separate lines printed for the voice parts, indicating that the right hand and the singer followed the same line. This notation also suggests an improvised (continuo) accompaniment by the right hand, a performance practice that began two centuries earlier. Songs published in the mid-century rarely appeared this way, since the practice of improvising accompaniments seems to have died out by then.

Like Harriet's SMB 49, Rose's binder's volume includes several Charleston connections. Seven of the forty-six pieces in SMB 12 came from Charleston publishers, and only two of these did not originate with Siegling. The composers represented in SMB 12 include Jacob Eckhard Jr. (1787–1832), a professional musician and son of Jacob Eckhard Sr., whose obituary described him as the "father of music" in Charleston.[17] Rose played and sang at least five pieces by Gilfert, which further establishes his popularity in Charleston. Taken as a whole, SMB 12 also represents the typical repertory of a young woman who lived in Charleston and came of age in the 1820s. She played pieces by local musicians that were sold in local shops and other popular tunes sold by American publishers.[18]

Through Harriet Lowndes's SMB 49 and Rose Drayton's SMB 12, a picture of the type of music young women in Charleston would have learned in the early 1820s emerges: English-language songs, many taken from contemporary stage works, with simple melodies of limited range and accompaniments for piano or harp. The most commonly featured composers either had Charleston connections, such as Gilfert, or were from the United Kingdom, for example, Moore/Stevenson or Bishop.[19] These collections also document the arrival of Italian opera in the United States.[20]

By itself, the music in SMB 49 would not have brought Harriet Lowndes's music into the spotlight, since it typifies what almost any young woman of means might have sung in the 1820s. It is the rest of her music that distinguishes this collection. These three binder's volumes—SMB 47, SMB 48, and SMB 50— share qualities that set them apart from other early nineteenth-century American music collections, even Harriet's own SMB 49. More significantly, they demonstrate a decided turn toward a European repertory that was not common in her immediate area or even in the United States as a whole in the 1820s.

The gradual influx of new foreign music during the 1820s can be seen in the Charleston Museum's SMB 25, which belonged to Emma Middleton Huger (1813–92), the daughter of Isabella Middleton and Daniel Elliott Huger. Like

Harriet, Emma descended from prominent families in the area, and she was well known among social circles. Her friend Eliza Middleton Fisher described her as "witty, direct and affectionate," even "imperial," and suspected that she might be "the greatest belle ever known in Charleston."[21] Only a year younger than Harriet, Emma was married at a slightly older age but still in the 1830s—to Joseph Allen Smith Jr. in 1838.

Emma's binder's volume contains a much wider array of pieces than those described in SMB 49, and this different repertory illustrates modifications in the music American women were performing in their parlors as the 1820s progressed.[22] (See table 2.3.) Melodies from Italian operas by Rossini, Donizetti, and Bellini began to infiltrate young women's music collections in arrangements for piano that often included several variations on the principal theme or in simplified versions often adapted to English texts. Frequently these modified versions had altered texts, rendering them unrecognizable from the originals. Moreover, arias sometimes were transposed down to make them easier for amateur voices, particularly as the century wore on and opera composers demanded more and more from singers.

Occasionally, though, these pieces appeared in Italian, and Emma's binder's volume exemplifies this possibility in its opening pages. It begins with Giovanni Paisiello's immensely popular "Nel cor piu non mi sento" (from his opera commonly known as *La molinara*), and among its first pages can be found "Batti, batti o bel Masetto" and "Deh vieni, non tardar" from Mozart's *Il nozze di Figaro;* as well as "Madamina!," "O statua gentilissima," and "La ci darem la mano" from his *Don Giovanni.*[23] That these last three pieces were for male characters does not seem to have been an issue, with modifications aided by the publisher's use of treble clefs for the bass-baritone vocal lines.[24] Emma also sang arias by Rossini, including his ever-popular "Una voce poco fa" from *Il barbiere di Siviglia,* an aria that numbered among the favorites of young women in both the United States and Great Britain.[25] Other Italian works follow, but on page 85 Emma's repertory turns to French vocal pieces, including opera arias by Méhul and Dalayrac. Overtures by these men could be heard in Charleston between 1805 and 1817, and Gilfert composed a set of variations on a theme from Dalayrac's popular opera *Nina.*[26]

Weber's "Huntsmen's Chorus," in choral arrangement, from *Der Freischütz* and C. M. Sola's popular "Brûlant d'amour / A Troubadour Song" also occur in her music book.[27] Indeed, if one were to take a poll of the public's favorite opera pieces from the 1820s, the pieces in Emma's binder's volume would rank among them. Less expected in her binder's volume is a manuscript of a "nocturne" (duet) by Felice Blangini, "Tintendo si mio Cor," and several pieces purchased in Europe. Her Mozart arias and duets were published by Robert Birchall in

Table 2.3. Contents of SMB 25, binder's volume belonging to Emma Middleton Huger, 1820s

No.	Title	Composer	Date	Notes
1	Nel cor piu non mi sento	G. Paësiello		guitar and voice MS. Amateur piano part on p. 3
2	El Bajelito, Sr Garcia			NY
3	Le Depart, Mme Clozel		1827	NY
4	Batti, Don Giovanni by Garcia	W.A. Mozart		
5	Una voce poco fa	G. Rossini		Havana, Siegling
6	Deh vieni, solo	W.A. Mozart		London: Robert Birchall, Music Circulating Library 133 New Bond St
7	Madamina	W.A. Mozart		London: Robert Birchall, Music Circulating Library 133 New Bond St. treble clef
8	O statua gentilissima, Don Giovanni, duet	W.A. Mozart		London: Robert Birchall, Music Circulating Library 133 New Bond St. treble clefs
9	La ci darem, Don Giovanni	W.A. Mozart		London: Robert Birchall, Music Circulating Library 133 New Bond St. "Zerlina, Masetto," latter crossed out and "Don Giovanni" treble clefs
10	Crudel perche fi nora, Figaro	W.A. Mozart		Brussels: Weissenbruch, Rue de Musée, No. 1085. "Huger" in pencil
11	Vorrei che il tuo pensiero, Otello	G. Rossini		NY: Dubois & Stodart
12	Deh calma, oh ciel	G. Rossini		NY: Dubois & Stodart
13	Air de la Molinara, Chanté par la Signora Strinesachi	G. Paësiello		Brussels: Weissenbruch, Rue de Musée, No. 1085, added notes
14	Degli augelletti al canto, Orlandi	arr. by Pacini		Paris: Pacini, for harp or piano (all this written in French) in Paris, and Bochsa

Table 2.3. Contents of SMB 25, binder's volume belonging to Emma Middleton Huger, 1820s (*continued*)

No.	Title	Composer	Date	Notes
15	Porche se mia tu sei? Canzonetta	H.N. Gilles		Baltimore: John Cole. "for his pupil Mrs. French."
16	Quand erran le Agnelle	H.N. Gilles		Baltimore: John Cole. ""for his pupil Miss Emily Chatard."
17	"Tintendo si mio Cor"	F. Blangini	MS	MS Nocturne. duet
19	Bolero Perles de Mr Leonard-Malibran "Idole de ma vie"	T. Seguri		NY: Dubois & Stodart
20	Trois Ais Suisses	Madame Stokhausen		Paris, Pacini, stamp "__ Royal Seine" (roman with a shield). German and French words
21	Le chant du printemps – du Canton de Lucerne			Paris: Pacini, stamp "__ Royal Seine" (roman with a shield). German and French words
22	Portrait Charmant – A Favorite French Song with New English words			Charleston: Siegling
23	No. 2 La journée aux aventures	É. Méhul		Brussels: Weissenbruch, Rue de Musée, No. 1085. Sung by Huet.
24	No. 7 La pavillon des fleurs	N. Dalayrac		Brussels: Weissenbruch, Rue de Musée, No. 1085. Belge stamp
25	L'Amandier	Music set by Louis Balochi, amateur		Brussels: Weissenbruch, Rue de Musée, No. 1085
26	Now at moonlight's fairy hour,	Tho. Thompson		NY, J.A. & W. Geib, 23 Maida Lane. duet

27	Hours there were	Jos. Ward, Esq.	Charleston: John Siegling Musical Warehouse, 109 Meeting St.
28	I'll watch for thee from my lonely bow'r, adapted to German air	John Stevenson, arr.	Charleston (109 Meeting St.) and Havana (Calle de la Obra pia No. 7), Siegling
29	When life has lost its greatest charm	Jacob Eckhard Jr.	Charleston (109 Meeting St.) and Havana (Calle de la Obra pia No. 7), Siegling
30	Meet me by moonlight	J. Augustine Wade, Esq.	
31	The chain & lute	John Barrett	NY: E.S. Meier. in ink "EM Huger"
32	Oh! Remember the time, A Spanish air	T. Moore	NY: Bourne
33	I've been roaming	C.E. Horn	Sung by Mrs. Knight. Charleston: John Siegling Musical Warehouse, 109 Meeting St.. "Emmanuell Huger" in ink
34	You don't exactly suit me	W.T. Parke	Sung by Miss Cramer at Niblo's Musical Festivals. NY: Mesier, 28 Wall St.
35			Music. Back side in pencil, Mesier list of pieces, Italian
36	Isabel, Spanish Serenade	H.R. Bishop	
37	I have fruit, I have flowers	J.A. Wade	Sung by Miss Mallet. Boston and NY: James L. Hewitt
38	Oh! No I'll never mention him	Henry Bishop	Sung by Miss George at Bowery Theatre. NY: A. Fleetwood, 47 Murray St.
39	Will you come where the sweetbriar grows	John Barnett	duet by Miss Moran and Mr Howard. NY: Mesier
40	Ah! I remember that sweet hour	Henry Bishop	Sung at Park Theatre by Miss Clara Fisher

Table 2.3. Contents of SMB 25, binder's volume belonging to Emma Middleton Huger, 1820s (*continued*)

No.	Title	Composer	Date	Notes
41	Honi soit qui mal y pense, Cavatina	A. Lee		NY: Mesier. Dedicated to Miss Fisher Alexandre.
42	Where roses wild were blowing, Venetian air	I.R. Planche		Charleston: Siegling
43	Strike the cymbal	Pucitta		Charleston: Siegling. Fingered trio. "Sabina E. Huger" in ink
44	Flow, on, thou shining river. Portuguese air from Moore's National Melodies	John Stevenson, arr.		Charleston: Siegling . "Sabina E. Huger" in ink
45	Huntsmens Chorus, Der Freischutz	C.M. von Weber		NY: Mesier. Choral work
46	I'd be a butterfly	T. Bayley		NY: A. Fleetwood, 47 Murray St. Sung by Mrs. Sharpe.
47	My love and lute	T. Moore		NY: A. Fleetwood, 47 Murray St. Sung by Mr. Pearman.
48	The light house	A. Remoussin		Charleston: Siegling. Guitar accompaniment
49	The sentinel			Charleston: Siegling. Harp, piano, and guitar accompaniments, No. 2 Miscellany, English and French
50	Oft in the stilly night	John Stevenson		Charleston: Siegling
51	Follow, follow over mountain	S.T. Smith		Charleston: Siegling. Sung by Mrs. Hackett.
52	Home! Sweet home!	H. Bishop		Charleston: Siegling. Sung by Miss M. Tree, Covent Garden, "Sabina E. Huger" in ink

53	O! Rest thee babe, rest thee	J. Whitaker		Charleston: Siegling (marked in)
54			MS	nothing except farther down on page: D E Huger in ink
55	Brulent d'amour, A Troubadour Song	C.M. Sola		Charleston: Siegling. No. 1 Miscellany
56	There's Nothing true but Heav'n	T. Moore		Providence: O. Shaw. Sacred Melodies.
57	Tyrolese air: Gentleman			Pages have been glued together; duet part
58	When thy bosom heaves the sigh			Philadelphia: Blake. Sung by Mrs. Dickons and Mr. Braham, Narensky comic opera, or Road to Varohslal[?], Drury Lane, Theatre Royal. "E M Huger" in ink
59	Non Giova il sospirar	N. Vaccai	MS	
60	Vecher kom krass . . . tiga tiga tiga tiga		MS	

London, two Swiss songs have stamps from Pacini in Paris, and three compositions were published by Weissenbruch in Brussels. The latter three include two popular opera composers, Méhul and Dalayrac, and the more obscure Louis Balochi. Since most of her other music came from Siegling's store, he might have been importing French music and making it available for Charleston musicians, or they could have arrived with an émigré music teacher.[28]

Although some unusual compositions number among Emma's pieces, her collection reflects both a typical American repertory of the period and changes that occurred in American practices during this period. Having foreign music first might have been some attempt at showing off Emma's modern music and familiarity with a European repertory. Other than these, SMB 25 continues with predominantly English fare, featuring the same composers found in the binder's volumes of Harriet (SMB 49) and Rose Drayton: Moore, Bishop, Wade, Horn, Barnett, Eckhard, Stevenson, and Whitaker. Her volume reflects stylistic trends such as "The Tyrolese Air: Gentleman," "Oft in the Stilly Night," and "Home! Sweet Home!" Like Rose, she included Pucitta's "Strike the Cymbal." The earlier English-ballad-style songs remained popular at least through the Civil War, and Emma owned her share of these. They were bound into the latter part of her book, and whether this was Emma's choice, her parents', or the binder's is unknown.

That there is overlap among the repertories in the binder's volumes of Harriet Lowndes, Rose Drayton, and Emma Huger is to be expected. Taken together, these three volumes represent the type of music young women learned as part of their music education in the 1820s. Favorite airs in English by Moore/Stevenson as well as popular tunes sung in American theaters still dominated the repertory. By this time music by Rossini began to take hold in concerts by professionals and in parlor entertainments by amateurs. French music declined in favor of Italian opera. Emma Huger's miscellany of works in Italian, English, French, and Spanish (one song only) typifies the music that affluent young women learned.

This being the case, the contents of Harriet's binder's volumes SMB 47, SMB 48, and SMB 50 do not follow the norms seen in the music collections of Emma, Rose, or in Harriet's own SMB 49. Each includes a predominantly French repertory, much of it obscure and most of it published in Brussels or Paris. The collection stands alone among women's music in the United States during the 1820s, a circumstance made even more amazing considering that Harriet had not yet traveled abroad. Such music preservation suggests that she had journeyed to Europe, bought this music, and brought it back to Charleston. But Harriet had not been to Paris or Brussels, so the fact that she had them in her possession before her marriage in 1831 renders them all the more remarkable.

CHAPTER 3

Vocal Music in French

With matching bindings and name plates—"Miss Harriet Lowndes" in gilt on red leather—and indexes in the same hand, SMB 47 and 50 clearly belong together. Neither volume contains an English song or ballad, and most of the lyrics, titles, and other information are in French. SMB 47 contains solo pieces, and SMB 50 consists mostly of duos and trios taken from the same repertory: French operas, mostly comic; romances; nocturnes; and related genres from the 1810s and 1820s. (See tables 3.1 and 3.2 for inventories of these binder's volumes.)

Both SMB 47 and 50 have indexes organized alphabetically. While this practice is not unknown, most indexes in binder's volumes reflect the order of pieces within or group them by genre—much rarer. Furthermore, whoever structured the volumes attempted to group works by the same composer together—another unusual feature. With contents arranged by composer, it is easier to see considerable overlap between the two books because both follow a similar order. For example, in both SMB 47 and SMB 50 the arias by François-Adrien Boieldieu follow one another, as do those of Nicolas Isouard, Antoine Romagnesi, Jean-Baptiste Roucourt, Henri-Mouton Berton fils, and so on. The works by Mozart, Rossini, and Ferdinando Päer appear at the end of each book, which implies that the person who organized the volume interpreted the music of these Italian opera composers to be related to each other yet distinct from the French repertory.

Of the two volumes, SMB 47 is the more homogeneous and cleanly organized. All of the pieces are in French only and for solo voice until no. 55 (of fifty-nine). The last four works (nos. 55–58) are Mozart's "Duo delle Nozze di Figaro" (as "Sull'aria" and "Sur air") and "Duo de Don Giovanni" (as "La ci darem la mano" and "La d'un doux marrage"), Rossini's "No. 3 Le Barbier de Séville" (as "All'idea di quel metallo" and "D'un metal si précieux"), and Paër's "Duo de l'Agnese" ("Come la nebbia al Vento," with Italian text only). The Rossini and the Mozart have both Italian and French texts, befitting their publication by

Table 3.1. Contents of SMB 47

No.	Title	Composer	Date	Notes
1	Valentine de Milan / Romance ("Vaillant genvier")	É. Mehul	[ca. 1822]	Brussels: H. Messemaeckers. "Chantée par Mme. Paul"
2	La journée aux aventures / Rondeau ("Francais et militaire")	É. Méhul	[1816]	Brussels: Weissenbruch. "Rondeau Chanté par Ponchard"
3	Ne pouvez vous l'ente[n?]dre / Rondo ("Lorsqu'un aman? Bien tendre")	Fabry Garat	[182-?]	Brussels: Weissenbruch
4	Le départ des jeunes guerriers ("L'ordre est dormé marches")	Fabry Garat		Brussels: Weissenbruch
5	Les soeurs jumelles / Opéra comique en un acte ("Il nous faut savoir en silence")	F.-J. Fétis	[1823]	Brussels: Weissenbruch
6	Les deux jaloux ("Il est vrai que Thibaut")	Mme. S. Gail	[?1813]	Brussels: Weissenbruch. "Avec accompagnement de Piano ou Harpe"
7	Air de Dardanus (Rec.: "Ah! Contre tant d'amour")	A. Sacchini	[ca. 1786]	Brussels: Weissenbruch
8	Air d'Œdipe ("Dieux! Ce n'est pas pour moi")	A. Sacchini; arr., L. Lachnith,	[ca. 1786]	Brussels: Weissenbruch. *Œdipe à Colone* [has keyboard part lining up correctly]. *Échos de France,* 2
9	Air d'Œdipe ("Votre cour devint mon asile")	A. Sacchini	[ca. 1786]	Brussels: Weissenbruch
10	Le Solitaire / Opéra en trois actes ("Vôtre coeur devint mon Asile")	L. Jadin, arr.; M. Carafa		Brussels: Weissenbruch

	Title	Composer/Arranger	Date	Publisher
11	Jenny / Ópera comique en trois actes, No. 7 ("J'arrose, J'arrose")	V. Rifaut, arr.; M. Carafa	[1829]	Paris: Madame V. Aug. Leduc
12	Jenny / Ópera comique en trois actes, No. 3 ("Eh bien qu'une epienvé")	V. Rifaut, arr.; M. Carafa	[1829]	Paris: Madame V. Aug. Leduc
13	Le billet de loterie / Scène et Rondo ("Non je ne veux pas chanter")	Nicolo Isouard	[1811]	Brussels: Weissenbruch. *Le Billet de Loterie*
14	Joconde ("Parmi les filles du Canton")	Nicolo Isouard	[1814–19]	Brussels: Weissenbruch. *Joconde* 1817
15	Aladin ou La Lampe merveilleuse / Romance ("Pour noble princesse")	Nicolo Isouard; arr., A. Piccini	[1822]	Brussels: Weissenbruch. "chantée par Mr. Nourrit père"
16	Romance ("Dans le desert une gazelle") / Dans l'opéra de Nadir et Sélim	A. Romagnesi	[1822]	Brussels: Weissenbruch. In *Collection des romances, chansonnettes et nocturnes* . . . [2e] volume
17	L'Amant timide / Romance ("Mon coeur soumis à vôtre")	A. Romagnesi		Brussels: Weissenbruch
18	No. 4 Cavatine / Dans l'Opéra Nadir et Sélim ("O des beaux arts douce puissance")	A. Romagnesi	[1822]	Brussels: Weissenbruch. "Chantée par Mr. Ponchard"
19	No. 5 Air / Dans l'Opéra Nadir et Sélim ("Un rossignol dont le ramage")	A. Romagnesi	[1822]	Brussels: Weissenbruch. "Chantée par Mr. Ponchard"
20	No. 3 Chanson Indienne / Dans l'Opéra Nadir et Sélim ("Dans le jardin de la beauté")	A. Romagnesi	[1822]	Brussels: Weissenbruch. "Chantée par Mr. Ponchard." In *Collection des romances, chansonnettes et nocturnes* . . . [2e] volume as "L'Amour oriental"

Table 3.1. Contents of SMB 47 (*continued*)

No.	Title	Composer	Date	Notes
21	No. 1 Romance / Dans l'Opéra Nadir et Sélim ("Loin de cette que j'aime")	A. Romagnesi	[1822]	Brussels: Weissenbruch. "Chantée par Mr. Alexis"
22	D'ici voyez ce beau domaine / Ballade	A. Boieldieu	[ca. 1826]	Philadelphia: Willig. *La dame blanche*. "Chantée par Madame Alexandre"
23	No. 5 *Le petit chaperon rouge* ("Depuis longtemps gentille Annette")	A. Boieldieu	[ca. 1818]	Brussels: Weissenbruch. "Rondo chantée par Mr. Théaulon"
24	No. 2 *Le petit chaperon rouge* ("Le noble éclat du diademe")	A. Boieldieu	[ca. 1818]	Brussels: Weissenbruch. "Romance chantée par Mr. Ponchard"
25	No. 12 *La dame blanche* Opéra comique ("Enfin je vous révois")	A. Boieldieu	[ca. 1818]	Brussels: Weissenbruch. "Air, chanté par Mme. Rigaut"
26	L'amoureux de quinze ans ("Tu me crois trop jeune Sylvie")	J.-B. Roucourt	[1808]	*Six Romances*
27	Romance d'Alfred ("Alfred un jour, banni de son domaine")	J.-B. Roucourt	April 1815	n.p. but looks like Brussels: Weissenbruch
28	Il est parti / Bollero	J.-B. Roucourt		n.p. but looks like Brussels: Weissenbruch
29	Chanson comme une autre ("Approchez une pretez l'oreille")	J.-B. Roucourt		n.p. but looks like Brussels: Weissenbruch
30	Souvenirs du soir / Romance ("L'ombre a remplacé la lumière")	J.-B. Roucourt		Brussels: Weissenbruch

31	A toi / Romance ("Ce que je désire que j'aime")	J.-B. Roucourt	n.p. but looks like Brussels: Weissenbruch
32	Fidélité, vaillance ("Chéri de la Victoire")	n.c.	n.p. but looks like Brussels: Weissenbruch
33	Sur une ecorse légère / Romance	J.-B. Roucourt	Same publisher font as #41
34	Le ménestrel abandonne ("Toi, que jadis charmais")	J.-B. Roucourt	n.p. but looks like Brussels: Weissenbruch
35	Le Songe d'amour / Romance	J.-B. Roucourt	n.p. but looks like Brussels: Weissenbruch
36	L'enfance / Romance ("Plaisirs naifs de l'innocence")	J.-B. Roucourt	n.p. but looks like Brussels: Weissenbruch
37	Le secret de ma vie / Romance ("Tu le sauras le secret de ma vie")	J.-B. Roucourt	n.p. but looks like Brussels: Weissenbruch
38	Romance / Eveille toi ma tendre Lyre	J.-B. Roucourt	*Six Romances*
39	A l'ombre d'un ?illeul	J.-B. Roucourt	n.p. but looks like Brussels: Weissenbruch. Traduite de Coweley, Poëte Anglais
40	Zoé ou La provencále / Romance ("Beau feu d'amour qui")	J.-B. Roucourt	n.p. but looks like Brussels: Weissenbruch
41	Beau feu d'amour / Romance	J.-B. Roucourt	n.p. but looks like Brussels: Weissenbruch. Not in index?
42	Le bon troubadour quelle melancolie / Romance	J.-B. Roucourt	Same publisher font as #32
43	Tendresse et mistere / Romance	J.-B. Roucourt	n.p. but looks like Brussels: Weissenbruch

Table 3.1. Contents of SMB 47 (*continued*)

No.	Title	Composer	Date	Notes
44	Le marechal de Saxe / Romance ("Noble chateau sombres forêts")	J.-B. Roucourt		n.p. but looks like Brussels: Weissenbruch. "Sur la mort de Mademoiselle Lecouvreur"
45	A Laurette / Romance ("Ce que j'aime en toi me Laurette")	Chaumas		Brussels: Weissenbruch
46	Voila le plaisir mesdames / Chanson ("L'amour courait cherchant")	[A. Marque]	[ca. 1810]	Brussels: Weissenbruch
47	No. 7 Le Pavillon des fleurs ("Sur ce rivage attachon")	N. Dalayrac	[1822]	Brussels: Weissenbruch. "Couplets chantés par Ponchard"
48	Air de Renaud ("Barbare amour!")	[A. Sacchini]	[from 1783]	Brussels: Weissenbruch. *Renaud,* 1783. *Échos de France* vol. 1
49	Le Caprice / Romance ("En viant., Amynte refuse")	M.C. Mansui		Brussels: Weissenbruch.
50	No. 6 Le premier vendu ou Six lieues de chemin ("Messieurs je rende grace")	F. Hérold		Brussels: Weissenbruch. "Rondo Chanté par Mme. Boulanger"
51	Je l'aimerai / Romance	Rigel		Brussels: Weissenbruch
52	No. 9 Aladin ou La lampe merveilleuse ("Venez charmantes bayaderas")	N. Isouard; arr., A. Piccini		Brussels: Weissenbruch. "Air chanté par Mlle. Javurek"

53	Le troubadour / Danes le Procès, Opéra comique en un Acte ("Aux vains désire qui trumentez")	Pacini, arr.		Brussels: Weissenbruch. "Romance chantée par Mr. Paul"
54	La sentinelle ("L'astre de nuits donc")	Jacques Strunz	[ca. 1810]	
55	Le bonjour / Romance ("La nuit l'eloique et fait")	D'Aubert, fils		Brussels: Weissenbruch
56	Duo delle Nozze di Figaro ("Sull'aria")	W.A. Mozart		Brussels: Weissenbruch. "Chanté par Mmes. Barilli et Bianchi." *Figaro,* duet Countess and Susanna" [in French also: "Sul'air"]
57	La ci darem la mano / Duo de Don Giovanni	W.A. Mozart	[182-?]	Brussels: Weissenbruch. "Chanté par Mme. Festa et Mr. Tacchniardi" [in French also: "La d'un doux marrage"]
58	No. 3 Le Barbier de Séville ("D'un metal si précieux")	G. Rossini		Brussels: Weissenbruch. "Duo chanté par MM. Damoreau et Derubelle." *Barber,* duet Figaro and Count [in Italian also: "All'idea di quel metallo"]
59	Come la nebbia al Vento / Duo de l'Agnese	F. Paër		Brussels: Weissenbruch. "Chanté par Mme. Mainvielle-Fodor et Mr. Pellegrini." *L'Agnese,* 1816, Uberto. [Italian only]

Table 3.2. Contents of SMB 50

No./Page[1]	Title	Composer	comments
1/1	Duo de *Montano et Stéphanie* ("Venez, Venez, aimable Stéphanie")	Henri-Moutan Berton	Brussels: Weissenbruch. *Montano e Stéphanie*, Théâtre de l'Opéra-Comique, 1799. "Chanté par Mme. Bouvier et Mr. Solié" [CP02-CMBV-Catalogue de l'oeuvre de Hyacinthe Jadin.pdf; Buffalo, FVM 130]
2/7	Duo *d'Aline* ("Tu m'aimeras toute la vie")	Henri-Moutan Berton	Brussels: Weissenbruch. *Duo d'Aline.* "Chanté par Mme. Gavaudan et Mr. Baptiste" [Buffalo, FVM 127]
3/19	*Les sœurs jumelles*, No. 7 / Opéra comique en un acte / Echo ("Le vieux berger Sylvandre")	F.-J. Fétis	Brussels: Weissenbruch. *Les sœurs jumelles.* Duo en Canon chanté par Mmes. Rigault et Casimir
4/27	*Les sœurs jumelles*, No. 2 / Opéra comique en un acte / Duo ("Les souvenirs de mon jeune âge")	F.-J. Fétis	*Les sœurs jumelles*
5/40	*Les deux jaloux* / Trio ("Tu fanchette est charmante")	Mme. S. Gail	Brussels: Weissenbruch. *Les deux jaloux.* Chanté par Mme. Gavaudan et Mrs. Lesage et Batiste [sic]
6/51	Duo d'*Œdipe* ("En ma faveur daigni attendrir")	A. Sacchini; arr., L. Lachnith, arr.	Brussels: Weissenbruch. *Œdipe à Colone*
7/57	*Joconde*, No. 2 / Trio ("Amour! Amour seconde mon courage")	Nicolo [Isouard]	Brussels: Weissenbruch. *Joconde.* Chanté par Mmes. Boulanger, Paul, et Mr. Roland [Buffalo, FVM 212]
8/68	Romance, No. 6 ("Combien j'ai douce souvenance")	A. Romagnesi;	Brussels: Weissenbruch. *Nader et Sélim*
9/71	*Le petit chaperon rouge* / Duo ("Mon doux Seigneur je vous en prie")	F.-A. Boieldieu	Brussels: Weissenbruch. *Le petit chaperon rouge.* Chanté par Mr. Martin et Mme Gavaudan

10/87	*Le Nouveau Seigneur du village*, No. 7 / Duo ("Je vais rester à cette place")	F.-A. Boieldieu	Brussels: Weissenbruch. 1816. Chanté par Mlle. Regnault et Mr. Martin
11/97	*Le Nouveau Seigneur du village*, No. 2 / Couplets ("Oh! vous avez des droits superbes")	F.-A. Boieldieu	Brussels: Weissenbruch. 1816. Chanté par Mlle. Regnault et Mr. Martin
12/104	Le depart / Romance a une ou deux voix ("Adieu vous que j'aimais")	J.-B. Roucourt	n.p.
13/108	Suite du Bon Troubadour / Romance ("Nymphe de a bocage")	J.-B. Roucourt	n.p.
14/112	*Milton* / Air ecossaise ("Quittez les riantes compagnes")	G. Spontini	Brussels: Weissenbruch. 1804. Chanté par Mrs. Gavaudan, Solié et Mme. Gavaudan
15/119	*Nephtali ou Les Ammonites* / Duo	F. Blangini	Brussels: Weissenbruch. Chanté par Roland et Mme. Branchu [Buffalo, FVM 133 as "Il est trop tard," romance]
16/130	*L'exilé* / Romance a deux voix ("Pourquoi me fair passagére hirondelle")	Madame Charlotte	Brussels: Weissenbruch
17/134	*La Neige ou Le nouvel Eginard* / Duo ("Oh ciel après trois mois d'absence")	D. Auber; arr., Auguste Pansenron	Brussels: Weissenbruch. *La Neige ou Le nouvel Eginard.* Chanté par Mme. Rigaut et Mr. Ponchard, 1823
18/148	Numi se giusti siete / Canzonetta	G. Crescentini	Brussels: Weissenbruch *Canzoni o sianno ariette a solo*, #8
19/152	Dal di ch'io vi mirai / Canzonetta	G. Crescentini	Brussels: Weissenbruch *Canzoni o sianno ariette a solo*, #6
20/156	Se spiegar potessi appieno / Canzonetta	G. Crescentini	Brussels: Weissenbruch *Canzoni o sianno ariette a solo*, #12
21/160	Non v'e pui barbaro / Canzonetta	G. Crescentini	Brussels: Weissenbruch *Canzoni o sianno ariette a solo*, #9
22/164	Per valli per boschi / Canzonetta	G. Crescentini	Brussels: Weissenbruch *Canzoni o sianno ariette a solo*, #11

Table 3.2. Contents of SMB 50 (*continued*)

No./Page[1]	Title	Composer	comments
23/168	Ecco quel fiero istante / Canzonetta	G. Crescentini	Brussels: Weissenbruch *Canzoni o sianno ariette a solo, #5*
24/172	O teneri pensieri / Canzonetta	G. Crescentini	Brussels: Weissenbruch *Canzoni o sianno ariette a solo, #4*
25/176	Tu mi chiedi O mio tesoro / Canzonetta	G. Crescentini	Brussels: Weissenbruch *Canzoni o sianno ariette a solo, #1*
26/179	Air de Mozart ("O dolce concento")	W.A. Mozart	Brussels: Weissenbruch. *Die Zauberflöte*
27/185	Batti, Batti, O bel Masetto / Aria	W.A. Mozart	Philadelphia: Blake. *Don Giovanni,* In English: Chide me chide me dear Masetto. "Sung by Signorina Garcia"
28/191	Tu che accendi questo core / Recitativo nel Tancredi	G. Rossini	Philadelphia: Willig. *Tancredi*
29/198	Deh calma, oh! Ciel / Aria	G. Rossini	NY: Dubois & Stodart. *Otello.* "Sung by Signorina Garcia"
30/202	*Guillaume Tell / Opéra in quatre Actes,* No. 10 / Romance ("Sombre forêt, désert triste et sauvage")	G. Rossini	Paris: Troupenas. *William Tell.* Chantée par Mme. Cinti Damoreau
31/207	*L'Agnese /* Scène et Air ("Ne che tu vivi o cara")	F. Paër	Brussels: Weissenbruch. *L'Agnese.* "Chanté par Mr. Bordogni"
32/219	*De la destruction de Jerusalem /* Cavatine avec Chœur ("Meste dolenti e supplici")	Nicola Antonio Zingarelli	Brussels: Weissenbruch. *De la destruction de Jerusalem,* 1804. "Chanté par Mr. Barilli"
33/228	Aria del Sig'r Bertoni nelle Gelosie villane ("La verginella come la rosa")	F. Bertoni	Paris: H. Naderman (rue d'Argenteuil à Appollon). *La governante,* 1780. In French: "Une bergére qu'amour inspire" under Italian words
34/232	Aria Della cosa rara / Cantata ("La mia crudele tiranna")	Signor Nozari	Brussels: Weissenbruch. In French: "J'aimais une cruelle"

35/235	Quando volt al patrio monte / Recitativo e duetto / Nell'Ifigenia in Aulide ("Ami tu dunque la sposa tua")	G. Simone Mayr; arr., A. Garaudé	Brussels: Weissenbruch. In French: "Te serai-je donc toujours" Nell'Ifigenia in Aulide
36/245	Rondo par Plantade ("E pure in mezza a ll' vie")	C.H. Plantade	Brussels: Weissenbruch
37/253	Polonaise ("Ah senti non partir")	V. Fiocchi	Brussels: Weissenbruch. Chantée par Mr. Garat. In French: "Elle vient de partir"
38/263	Cavatine ("Povero augusto rio")	M. Bolaffi	Brussels: Weissenbruch. In French: "O toi dont l'onde pure"
39/271	Rondeau de Garat ("Siami lascia mato")	N. Carbonel, arr.	Brussels: Weissenbruch. "Chanté par elle au Concert du Théâtre Feydeau." In French: "Si tu quittes ton Hélène"
40/280	Rondo ("Qu'il est duo ce premier délire")	Lambert	Brussels: Weissenbruch. In Italian: "Poverin intante"
41/287	*D'Aline* / Reine de Golconde / Opéra en trois actes ("Gio posi ognir canti")	A. Boieldieu	Paris: Cherubini, but pasted over "Se vend chez Weissenbruch . . . Bruxelles"). In French: Eh gaiment mes amis
42/291	La calme de Winter [Mon âme languissante]		Brussels: Weissenbruch
43/296	Donne l'amore / An Italian Air ("Lady if ever you hear young, love")	G. Simone Mayr	Philadelphia: Willig. In *Blake's Musical Miscellany.* In Italian: Donne l'amore é scattro parge
44/299	Vedrai carino / Aria . . . Il Don Giovanni	W.A. Mozart	NY: Dubois & Stodart. *Don Giovanni.* "Sung by Signorina Garcia"

Note

1. Both numbers and pages are given to illustrate the size of SMB 50.

French-speaking publishers. Rossini's popular *Il barbiere di Siviglia* (1816) was first performed in the United States in New Orleans (in French) in 1823, and Manuel Garcia and his opera troupe presented it in Italian in New York City— reportedly the first opera performed in Italian in the United States—in 1825.[1] Curiously, "D'un metal si précieux" was printed with the voice parts in the bass clef, which is logical, in that the male characters who sing the duet would have read from bass clefs, but seems odd in a young woman's volume.[2] This practice differs from the examples seen in Emma Huger's binder's volume (SMB 25), and it may reflect the publisher's choice.[3]

As the inventories in tables 1.3–4 illustrate, most of the sheet music in SMB 47 and SMB 50 was sold at "Chez Weissenbruch, éditeur et M[archan]d de Musique, Rue der Musée, No. 1085" in Brussels. Harriet's copy of "Votre cour devint mon asile" from Sacchini's *Œdipe à Colone* in SMB 47 has the *papier timbré* showing its sale in Brussels (see figure 3.1). Weissenbruch surfaces again in Harriet's music collection because it is where she purchased more scores on her honeymoon trip in 1831. That she owned a binder's volume with many pieces from this establishment in Brussels before her marriage and a number after it hints that she had some connection to it, although not a direct one because, again, she does not appear to have traveled to Europe before 1831. Emma's binder's volume includes only three Weissenbruch publications, which seems more representative of a local merchant's having imported some music from Europe. That the majority of Harriet's music is European suggests a different situation altogether.

Music by a wide range of composers populates these binder's volumes, of which Mozart and Rossini are the best-known composers today. Mozart's operas were just beginning to be performed in the United States at the time Harriet was singing excerpts from them. Rossini's operas represented in Harriet's collection include popular ones from the 1810s, such as *Tancredi* (1813) and *Il barbiere di Siviglia* and *Otello* (both from 1816). More surprising, however, is "Sombre forêt, désert trist et sauvage" from *Guillaume Tell,* which premiered in Paris in August 1829.[4] That Harriet had it in a binder's volume (SMB 50) marked with her maiden name indicates that she owned some of the latest European music available. The circulation of sheet music featuring popular excerpts could have been one way a young woman in Charleston became acquainted with the newest operas from Paris. A few enterprising American publishers made Rossini's music available at least as early as 1819, when George Willig printed "The Celebrated Overture to the Opera of *La Gazza Ladra*" in Philadelphia. The music from *Guillaume Tell* hit the American market with alacrity; undoubtedly publishers banked on his meteoric rise in popularity in the 1820s. In Philadelphia, the cultural center of the new country, Willig sold an American imprint of an aria from the opera in 1829, the same year it premiered in Paris.

Figure 3.1. Sacchini's "Votre cour devint mon asile" from *Œdipe à Colone* in SMB 47, Brussels publication

Unexpectedly, the remaining contents of SMB 47 are all in French except Paër's "Come la nebbia al Vento," but even this is subtitled "Duo de l'Agnese," and Weissenbruch advertised it as "Chanté par Mme. Mainvielle-Fodor et Mr. Pellegrini." Most of the composers' names did not grace Charleston music programs before 1825, or if they did, it was infrequently. The majority of the other composers whose pieces comprise SMB 47 and SMB 50 spent their careers in France and England, and their popularity, based on the contents of American collections, varied considerably but was usually nonexistent. Two of the more famous today are Méhul, a leading composer from the revolution to the Napoleonic era; and the Belgian musician François-Joseph Fétis, recognized as a leader in European music circles and beyond.

Harriet sang several pieces by Boieldieu, an influential opera composer in Paris known by the sobriquet "the French Mozart," who also worked for a time as the court composer to the czar in St. Petersburg. Boieldieu's music, especially excerpts from his opera *La dame blanche,* appears with some frequency in southern binder's volumes of the 1820s to the 1840s, although his popularity faded soon thereafter as bel canto operas by Bellini and Donizetti dominated American tastes.[5] Harriet owned arias from Boieldieu's *La dame blanche* (1825), *Le nouveau seigneur du village* (1813), and *Le petit chaperon rouge* (1818).[6] *La dame blanche* had its United States premiere at the Théâtre d'Orleans in New Orleans in 1827, which again suggests that Harriet's music collection contained the most au courant repertory possible, and her choices most often were from music popular in France.[7]

Boieldieu's pieces in Harriet's binder's volumes come from the type of opera known as opéra comique, which is French comic opera that incorporates spoken dialogue, performed in a theater, the Opéra Comique, designated specifically for the genre. It was one of three primary venues for opera in Paris at this time, the other two being the Opéra, for entirely sung works, and the Théâtre-Italien, for Italian-language operas. Harriet owned several other excerpts from opéras comique as well. Sophie Garre Gail published her first composition at age fourteen and had a career as a respected singer, accompanist, and *salonnière.*[8] Her *Les deux jaloux* was the first of four opéras comique she is known to have composed, and "Il est vrai que Thibaut" (SMB 47, no. 6) comes from this work. Some of her romances were included in *Échos de France,* a publication of French vocal pieces extending as far back as the sixteenth century that, significantly, Harriet later bought for her daughter, Henrietta Aiken.[9]

The Italian composer Antonio Sacchini's works appear four times in Harriet's collection. Sacchini specialized in serious opera—*tragédie lyrique,* in which all the words are sung—which establishes that Harriet was exposed to different types of French opera. Harriet's SMB 47 and SMB 50 include arias and a duet from his most famous operas, *Renaud* (1783) and *Œdipe à Colone* (1786).[10] Music from both of these had been performed in Charleston as early as 1805 when Miss La Roque performed "Dieu! Ce n'est pas pour moi" and "Le fils des Dieus" from *Œdipe,* and "Ciel injuste!" from *Renaud.*[11] By 1820, however, Sacchini's music had fallen out of favor with Charlestonians, and his works were no longer programmed. Thus, Harriet's performance of them at that time did not reflect current trends at home.

Among the remaining composers, certain points deserve further exploration, and two are particularly suggestive. In SMB 47, nos. 15 through 20 belong to Antoine-Joseph-Michael Romagnesi (1781–1850), a composer about whom we know very little.[12] He published *L'art de chanter les romances, les chansonnettes et les nocturnes et généralement toute la musique de salon* in 1846, and it is chiefly that genre, the romance, with which he is associated.[13] He also composed operas, and Harriet had four pieces from his opera *Nadir et Sélim,* which had been presented at the Théâtre Royal de l'Opéra Comique on 27 July 1822.[14] This date suggests that Harriet had access to somewhat obscure French music in a timely fashion, since SMB 47 had to have been bound by the time of her marriage in 1831.[15]

Even more enigmatic are eighteen pieces attributed, and probably one more unattributed, to Jean-Baptiste Roucourt (1780–1849), who participated in a campaign of raising the standard of music education and opened a singing school in Brussels that was patterned on the conservatory in Paris, at which he had been a student.[16] Several works in SMB 47 and SMB 50 are from his *Six Romances* (1808), and one of his pieces in SMB 47—no. 26, "Romance d'Alfred"—bears the date April 1815. Only once is the publisher, Weissenbruch in Brussels, listed for his compositions in Harriet's books, but the engraving and layout of most of them resemble others from this firm.[17] What makes Harriet's collection of pieces by Roucourt so special is that outside of Paris and Amsterdam, this may be the largest collection of his works.[18]

SMB 50 continues the trends seen in SMB 47 with its concentration on French romances and other works, usually culled from *opéras comique.* Most of the works in this volume are for two or three singers accompanied by harp or piano, and it may be that SMB 47 and SMB 50 were intended as a set of volumes, one for solo voice and the other for multiple voices. Composers and publishers tended to distinguish romances for solo voice from those for multiple voices by calling the latter "nocturnes."[19]

Several works of the same composers recur here, including Boieldieu, Fétis, Gail, Sacchini, Isouard, Romagnesi, and Paër. Excerpts from Mozart include "Batti, batti o bel Masetto," from *Don Giovanni,* which was also in Emma Huger's SMB 25. Rossini is represented with works from three operas: *Otello, Tancredi,* and *Guillaume Tell;* "Deh calma, oh ciel" from *Otello* became one of his most popular arias in the United States. Other composers included are Berton fils, Daniel Auber, and Girolamo Crescentini. Auber was another leading opera composer, and his *La neige ou Le nouvel Eginard* of 1823—from whence the composition on page 134 of SMB 49 derives—was one of his earliest works. Berton fils is a more obscure artist but of note because another work of his surfaces in SMB 49.

As in SMB 47, Italian music forms a part of SMB 50, and someone decided that it was "other"—it differed from the French repertory—and grouped it together, for the most part. The choices of pieces in Italian range from obscure songs to favorites from Mozart's operas. A series of eight songs by the castrato Crescentini, all taken from his *Dodici canzoni o sianno ariette a solo,* occupies the middle of the volume. It is one of the largest groupings found in any of Harriet's binder's volumes, the others being by Roucourt and Romagnesi. Crescentini stands out as the most unusual composer among the pieces with Italian texts. He was an Italian castrato who sang in Europe's best opera houses, including La Scala in Milan and La Fenice in Venice. In Paris, Napoleon conferred the Order of the Iron Crown of Lombardy on the singer and made him the singing master for the imperial family. Eight songs from his *Dodici canzoni o sianno ariette a solo* appear together as a group in SMB 50. For solo voice, these Italian pieces seem out of place in the middle of this binder's volume, but his having been a particular favorite of Napoleon most likely accounts for his inclusion in the French section. The canzonas apparently survive as a suite of twelve only in manuscript form, although Harriet's binder's volume has eight individually published pieces, which Weissenbruch brought out under the title *Canzoni o sianno arietta a solo,* without "Dodici."[20] Notably, Crescentini's works also appear in *Échos de France.*

After the Crescentini canzonettas come excerpts by Mozart, Rossini, and Paër—music by each of whom appears in SMB 47—as well as single specimens by Nicola Antonio Zingarelli, Ferdinando Bertoni, and Andrea Nozari.[21] Similarly, near the end of SMB 50 are two Italian compositions, one with an English translation: Giovanni Simone Mayr's "Donne l'amore." SMB 50 strays somewhat from the stricter organization of SMB 47, but the inclusion of several items by Crescentini may have thrown off the binder, if he indeed determined the ordering. Also noteworthy is that SMB 50 has five pieces published in the United States—three in Philadelphia and two in New York—and two from Paris. The remainder, however, came from Weissenbruch in Brussels. One published in Paris, "Eh gaiment mes amis," from Boieldieu's *D'Aline / Reine de Golconde / Opéra en trois actes* ("Gio posi ognir canti"), has a paper pasted at the bottom of the front page that reads "Se vend chez WEISSENBRUCH, Éditeur et Marchand de Musique, Imprimeur et Libraire, place de la Cour, section 7, no. 1085, à BRUXELLES." This addition substantiates connections between Harriet's music and Brussels: it confirms that whoever obtained almost all of these pieces did so in Belgium.

The organization of the binder's volumes reveals more about Harriet Lowndes's music collecting. As shown above, SMB 49 represents the first music she owned, and probably the music she received from her instructors during her earliest lessons or from her parents even before lessons began. Its Charleston connections are undeniable, and it reflects local trends in the area, as well as broader tastes in American parlors from Charleston to Boston. In contrast, SMB 47, SMB 48, and SMB 50 contain almost nothing in English nor anything like the English opera ballads found in SMB 49. Almost everything about SMB 47 and SMB 50 stands in contrast to other binder's volumes owned by young American women in the 1820s. They are clearly an unusual pair: their matching bindings, indexes, organization, emphasis on French vocal compositions, and reliance on music published by Weissenbruch in Brussels mark them as distinct from all others and connected to each other. The obvious questions that arise from this appraisal of their contents are, how and why did Harriet Lowndes come to own music that differed so dramatically from that of her Charleston contemporaries? The key to answering these questions lies in yet another of her binder's volumes: SMB 48.

Printed and Manuscript Music: SMB 48

The contents of SMB 47 and SMB 50 contrast with those in SMB 49 (the earliest volume) to such a degree that they suggest some catalyst for new repertory in Harriet's musical study. The repertory shifts from English songs, typical of American binder's volumes of the early nineteenth century, to French and Italian music. How and why did Harriet Lowndes turn from English songs sold in the United States to French romances and Italian arias sold in Brussels? SMB 48 may be the intermediate volume between the English-music SMB 49 and the printed foreign repertory in SMB 47 and SMB 50. It is the only one of her binder's volumes that includes manuscript music, the only one that includes inscriptions that identify the people who gave her music, and the only one of the foreign group that does not have an index. It is also a smaller volume, containing only twenty-eight pieces. (See table 3.3.)

The first fourteen pieces in SMB 48 are published sheet music. Dubois & Stodart in New York published the first one, and Simon Gaveaux in Paris published the last, but all of the pieces in between originated at Maison Pleyel in Paris. Of the remaining fourteen pieces, all but one are in manuscript form. The single exception is no. 24, "Brûlant d'amour" by C. M. Sola (1786–1857), which Siegling published in Charleston. It was a popular work that Emma too owned, in SMB 25.

Table 3.3. Contents of SMB 48

No.	Title	Composer	Hand	Notes
1	Arietta from Rossini's Otello, Assisa a piè d'un salice	G. Rossini		NY: Dubois & Stodart. J.J. Vickers stamp (NY). *Otello*
2	Fiez vous donc au Lendemain / Chansonette	Édouard Bruguiére		Paris: Pleyel
3	Le commencement du voyage / Chanson	Berton fils		Paris: Pleyel, and stamp
4	Tu ne sais pas que je t'aime / Romance	Camille Petit		Paris: Pleyel, and stamp
5	Les regrets / Romance	Mlle. Blanchet		Paris: Pleyel
6	Il m'attend	Mme. Du Chambge		Paris: Pleyel, and Mme. Neyts
7	Marie / Romance	Mme. Du Chambge		Paris: Pleyel
8	Les adieux / Romance	n.c.		Paris: Pleyel
9	La Marguerite / Chansonnette	Mlle. Blanchet		Paris: Pleyel
10	Ramène ton bateau / Nocturne a deux voix	'Ch'er Lagoanère		Paris: Pleyel
11	Le matelot	Mme. Du Chambge		Paris: Pleyel, and Mme. Neyts. [Buffalo, FVM 2–111]
12	La plainte / Romance	Édouard Bruguière		Paris: Pleyel, and stamp
13	Naïs ou La jeune grecque a Paris / Romance	Camille Petit		Paris: Pleyel
14	Dormez, dormez, cheres amours / Nocturne à une òu deux voix	Mr Amédée de Beauplan		Paris: S. Gaveaux. Gift of Madame Giraud

15/p. 59	Stay sweet Enchanter of the grove		1	Manuscript. Guitar accompaniment, fingerings in pencil
16/p. 60	Le baiser	[Félix Blangini]	2	Manuscript. From *Quinzième recueil de romances*
17/p. 62	Je ne sai plus ce que je veux	Acc. by B. Henry	3	Manuscript. Harp accompaniment
18/p. 64	Les adieux	?Castellacci	4	Manuscript
19/p. 65	Venez aux Champs / Romance		4	Manuscript
20/p. 67	La dernière fois	F. J. Nadermann	5	Manuscript. [Buffalo, FVM 2–111, #95]
21/p. 69	No text		5	Manuscript
22/p. 72	L'Amandier / Romance a deux voix	[Louise Balochi]	6/?2	Manuscript. [Buffalo, FVM 2–111, #111]
23/p. 75	Air des maris garcons		6	Manuscript. Down on page
24	Brulant d'amour / A Troubadour Song	C.M. Sola		Siegling, 109 Meeting Street (corrected place?)
25/p. 92	La Bergerette delaisée	Louis Jadin	7	Manuscript. Gift of Miss Bridon
26/p. 95	La dernière fois / Romance	P.-I. Bégre[t]z	8	Manuscript. Same as #20
27/p. 99	La Denouement [?]	P.-I. Bégre[t]z	8	MS
28	"Partant pour la Syrie"	La Reine de Hollande	9	MS

The main manuscript section, nos. 15–23, consists of a single gathering and was included as a complete fascicle when it was bound into the volume. (See figure 3.2.) In contrast, the final four manuscript pieces differ in paper size and seem to have been afterthoughts or bits gathered together when the music was sent to the bindery. All of the music is in French except the first manuscript entry: "Stay Sweet Enchanter of the Grove" (no. 15). This popular ballad by Reginald Spofforth and known as "Julia to the Wood Robin" appeared in print circa 1799 in London.[22] Nonetheless, it seems out of place among the French compositions in SMB 48. Of the several published versions of "Stay Sweet Enchanter" known to exist today, none has the same guitar accompaniment found in Harriet's book. Because all of the manuscript pieces in the Aiken-Rhett Collection begin music on the first page inside (verso) and not the outside, "Stay Sweet Enchanter" probably was a later addition to SMB 49. It may even be in Harriet's own hand, and one of the versions of "La dernière fois" may be as well.

As to the printed music in SMB 48, almost all of it came from Paris and most from Ignaz Pleyel. In this it differs from the French music in SMB 47 and SMB 50, which originated in Brussels. With its strong cultural ties to France, Brussels functioned almost like a suburb of Paris at this time, so the distinction between these two publishers is not as meaningful as the fact that a Charlestonian owned

Figure 3.2. Fascicle of manuscript paper bound into SMB 48

so many of their pieces. Many of the compositions bear Pleyel's stamp as well, suggesting that they were published and sold at his establishment. For example, in SMB 48, "Fiez vous donc au lendemain," a "Chansonette" by Edouard Bruguière (or Brugière), bears the name as publisher and in the stamp of "Pleyel et fils, aîné Boulevard Montmartre au coin de la rue Grange-Batelière." Pleyel opened his publishing firm in Paris in 1797 and was joined by his son Camille in 1815. Maison Pleyel remained in business until 1836 and was an integral part of the Paris music scene. In addition to Pleyel's piano manufacturing, he had a well-known salon that later included performances by the pianist Frédéric Chopin.[23] The most likely conjecture as to why Harriet owned twelve publications from Maison Pleyel is that she received all of these pieces from a single person who had brought them over from Paris.

Even though the publishers differ and so do some of the composers, the repertory in SMB 48 does not differ substantially from that in SMB 47 and SMB 50. It includes the same types of pieces—French romances and related songs—and taken together, the music in these three binder's volumes typifies what one might have heard in wealthy French and Belgian homes. Bruguière (1793–1863), a native of Lyon, was active in Paris from 1823, later in Lausanne, and back in Paris—at the Salon Fétis—in the 1830s.[24] Along with Romagnesi, Berton fils, and Panseron (one work in SMB 50), he is considered a significant composer of romances. Indeed, nine of the works in SMB 48 have this designation, including Bruguière's "La plainte," no. 12.

Several women composers' songs survive in SMB 48. "Mme. Du Chambge" is Pauline Montet Duchambge, who was born in the West Indies to noble parents and sent to a convent school in Paris. After losing both parents and divorcing her husband, Duchambge turned to music as a source of income. Between 1816 and 1840 she published almost four hundred romances, and two of these in SMB 48 list both Pleyel and "Mme. Neyts" as the publishers.[25] Harriet owned three songs by Duchambge, including "Le matelot," one of her best-known works, as well as compositions by Gail.[26] Another of the women composers is "Mlle Blanchet," Élisabeth-Antoinette Blanchet (Couperin), daughter of the harpsichord maker François-Étienne Blanchet. She composed "La Marguerite," according to Pleyel's publication. Her skills as a keyboard player (harpsichord and organ) were lauded by several French writers.[27] The manuscript portion of SMB 48 claims that "Partant pour la Syrie" was composed by "La Reine de Hollande." What she or her family may have thought about women composers is unknown, but music by other women too appears in Harriet's collection. The romance became a genre frequently associated with women in Paris, but Charleston was not Paris.

Harriet included the popular "Dormez donc, mes chères amours" by Amédée Rousseau de Beauplan in SMB 48. According to Olivier Fauveau, all of France sang this nocturne, and its presence in a Charleston binder's volume points to a familiarity with the most admired music in France.[28] Beauplan's obituary in the *Athenaeum,* while noting "his romances . . . which staid musicians despise, and simple amateurs delight in," mentioned the song in a description of his music by stating that "there has never been melody more widely welcomed than the air 'Dormez, donc, mes chers amours,' used with such picturesque skill and effect by M. Scribe in 'La Somnambule' [*sic*]."[29] Its presence in Harriet's collection is less easily explained, if she did not travel to Paris before 1831, although a Parisian musician newly arrived in Charleston might have assumed that the same repertory sung in Parisian salons would appropriately suit parlors in the South.

As demonstrated, the printed music in Harriet's SMB 48 is noteworthy for several reasons. It represents the most popular genres in early nineteenth-century Paris: romance, chanson and the related chansonette, and nocturne. These pieces formed the foundation of French salon music in the 1810s and 1820s, much as the Anglo-American music in Harriet's SMB 49 did for American parlors. The strophic songs demand little of the singer, having a limited range and a simple melody accompanied by a consistent guitar or piano part. All of the French pieces were printed by Pleyel in Paris except for "Dormez, dormez."

The manuscript pieces in SMB 48 were composed by people whose names are rarely encountered today, but Harriet's connection to them reveals a close association between musicians and at least one elite young woman in Charleston during the 1820s. A brief survey of some of the pieces here illustrates the breadth of this collection. "Air des maris garcons [*sic*]" is an arrangement of the opening material from Berton's intermezzo by that name. The original work was published in 1806 in Paris, and the arrangement for piano by "H. Berton fils"— which is the version in SMB 48—was published in Paris circa 1815 by Madame Duhan.[30] Harriet might have heard a "Mr. Aimé" when he performed this air in Charleston on 25 July 1823 in Fayolle's Long Room, 80 King Street. He also sang works by Dalayrac, Grétry, Boieldieu, and Méhul there during July and August of that year.[31] Peter Fayolle, a French émigré, local dancing instructor, and former professional dancer in France, leased the property from the Huguenot Church from 1801 until his death in 1837.[32] Fayolle might have had stronger ties to the French repertory, but there is too little information to say this definitively. A Huguenot connection encompasses several of the people in this narrative, as the Lowndes family were also Huguenots.

Another now-obscure musician's work can be found in the manuscript section of SMB 48. Pierre-Ignace Bégrez, author of "La dernière fois // Romance," left his native Belgium to work as a violinist in "l'orchestre de Théâtre italien in Paris."[33] He also had a career as a tenor and in 1815 sang in these roles at the Opéra:

Armide, Anacréon, and *Les Bayadères.*[34] He later moved to London to sing at the King's Theatre and retired from the stage soon thereafter, in 1821, but he continued to sing concerts and teach in England.[35] In July 1822 he traveled to New York City to perform, but he does not appear to have traveled to the South.[36] He published several pieces of music, but no other example of his music in antebellum southern sources has been located.[37]

Music designated specifically for guitar appears in SMB 48 only, and it is part of the manuscript section as well. "Stay Sweet Enchanter" has a guitar accompaniment, and this version appears to be a unicum. The version of "Venez aux Champs // Romance" here is a setting of a song by François-Joseph Naderman made for guitar by Ferdinando Carulli, one of the greatest guitar players of the early nineteenth century.[38] Carulli's guitar method of 1810 was frequently used in southern schools for young women throughout the antebellum period, and it is possible that Harriet had learned from it as well.[39] Bénigne Henry, a lyre and guitar professor active in Paris in the 1820s and 1830s, was responsible for the guitar accompaniment given for "Je ne sais plus ce que je veux" on page 62. The sole English piece in the manuscript section, "Stay Sweet Enchanter of the Grove," also has a guitar accompaniment. Taken together, it seems reasonable to suggest that Harriet played the guitar, as well as piano and harp, and may have accompanied herself when performing these songs.

Harriet received two songs in SMB 49 from women musicians, one in manuscript form and one a publication, and these provide the links needed to connect Harriet's French repertory to Charleston. On the top left of the manuscript song "La Bergerette," an inscription reads "Offert a Miss Lownds par son affectionnée P.[?] Bridon[e?]." Bridon almost certainly was the "Miss Bridon" who performed in several concerts in Charleston between 1815 and 1823. An announcement in the *Charleston Courier* in 1815 mentioned her arrival in the city and seemed to suggest that it was recent.[40]

Miss Bridon may have been Virginie Bridon (1794–1860), who was born in Paris and married Frederick Greuhm, the Prussian ambassador to Washington, D.C., in late 1819 (see, for example, the announcement in the *Rochester Telegraph,* 21 December 1819). A Charleston connection can be established in two ways. First, the marriage took place at the residence of Henry Middleton at Kalorama, near Washington, D.C., and several published accounts mentioned that the bride had been Middleton's governess. Second, Sarah Rutledge wrote from Charleston to her sister Elizabeth Lowndes in early 1820 that she was not surprised at "Mlle. Bridon's having become Mme. Greenhowe, for I knew of his attachment when at Washington." Moreover, Bridon had written to Sarah shortly after the marriage.[41] These ties to Charleston and to the Lowndes family are suggestive and seem to corroborate the identity of Miss Bridon, the named concert singer in Charleston, as being Virginie Bridon, later Baroness de Greuhm. There is further confirmation from a decade later, when, after Bridon de Greuhm married Col. Luke Edward Lawless, Charles Delassus recalled dining with the Lawlesses in 1836 and remembered her as an accomplished musician.[42] This connection, however, is not so simple. Appearances in the 1820s by "Miss Bridon" would seem to rule out that this was indeed Virginia Bridon de Greuhm, especially if she were the wife of a diplomat.[43]

Miss Bridon and Mme. Giraud

Miss Bridon, the professional singer and harpist who performed on the stage in Charleston and advertised such in local newspapers, and Harriet Lowndes, daughter of an upper-class Charleston family, may have met socially, a prospect strengthened by Sarah Rutledge's having corresponded with Bridon about intimate matters. Miss Bridon might have been a featured performer at a soiree in the Lowndes home, but no record of such an event has been located to date. However, Miss Bridon was a student of Mrs. Giraud, according to the *Charleston Courier,* and Mrs. Giraud gave Harriet a popular French song and inscribed it to Harriet: on p. 56 of SMB 48, "Dormez, dormez, chères amours" bears the inscription in French that it was a gift to Mademoiselle Lowndes from Madame Giraud.[44] Giraud was born Adelaide Alexandrina Fayolle in Bordeaux, France, in 1786, the daughter of Peter Fayolle, and she married François P. Giraud (1786–1856), also of Bordeaux, in Charleston on 4 March 1817 at St. Mary's Roman Catholic Church.[45] Mrs. Giraud was included in the Charleston city directory of 1828 as a teacher of music at 80 King Street, the same address as her father's Long Room where dancing and other concerts took place.[46] According to a notice in the *Charleston Courier,* she had studied in Paris with Naderman, who declared her to be a "first-rate artist." The *Charleston Courier* noted that she was now a Carolinian and had "transcendent talent."[47] In Paris, Naderman had published the version of "Aria del Sig'r Bertoni nelle Gelosie villane" ("La verginella come la rose") contained in SMB 50, one of the few pieces in that volume not from Brussels. This connection might explain its presence in Harriet's collection.

In November 1819 Mrs. Giraud played harp in a concert in Charleston. The program, reprinted in John Joseph Hindman's "Concert Life in Ante-Bellum Charleston," also included a "Quarteto" for violin by Rodes that was performed by E. B. Fayolle.[48] The *Savannah Daily Gazette* had advertised a concert late that month with the promise that Mrs. Giraud would be playing the harp and that Mr. Fayolle would accompany his daughter on the violin.[49] The early date for Mrs. Giraud's performances in Charleston and the appearance on stage with her sisters indicate that this must have been the French harpist, not a Polish violinist with the same last name who too lived in South Carolina.[50] As early as October

1815 Miss Bridon played a piano recital that included a sonata by Clementi, Wolfel's variations on "Life Let Us Cherish," and Steibelt's "Andante, with Variations" and "The Storm."[51] Harriet was almost certainly not at this performance, being only three years old at the time.

Several years later, however, Miss Bridon and Mrs. Giraud performed together in a series of concerts, and these concerts are of interest because it is likely that Harriet attended at least a few of them. At a benefit concert for Mrs. Giraud on 18 February 1823, Miss Bridon accompanied herself on Bégrez's "The Caroline." She also sang a song by "Romagnesie," and Mrs. Giraud accompanied her. Mrs. Giraud's specialty was the harp, and at this benefit she performed Naderman's "New Variations on 'Friend of My Soul.'" The program also included a trio for three harps by Naderman, played by Mrs. Giraud and, according to the program, two of her pupils: Miss Bridon and Miss Septima Fayolle.[52] That the repertory included some of the same obscure French composers whose music can be found in Harriet's unusual volumes avers a connection between Harriet and Miss Bridon and/or Mrs. Giraud.

Not long after this program, the women put on a benefit for the Misses Fayolle, assisted by their sister Mrs. Giraud and Miss Bridon. This time Bridon accompanied herself on a song by Romagnesi and Marez. Whether this was the same Romagnesi song as on the previous concert program is unknown. Mrs. Giraud again offered Naderman's "New Variations on 'Friend of My Soul,'" and she and her sister Septima played a "New Duett on Two Harps (the Tirolesian Air)" by Nicolas-Charles Bochsa, a harpist who later toured the United States. The trio repeated Naderman's trio for harp, and Mrs. Giraud included Bochsa's "Grand Fantaisie, with Variations on 'The Knight Errant.'"[53] As was the case with several other concerts from the early 1820s, Miss Bridon took the stage with the three sisters Adelaide Fayolle Giraud, Emma Fayolle, and Septima Fayolle.

Adelaide, Emma, and Septima were the daughters of the dancing master Peter Fayolle, and all appeared together in Charleston concerts in 1823. Emma played the piano; Septima played the harp; and Adelaide, now Mrs. Giraud, also played the harp. Moreover, they appeared with Miss Bridon, who sang and played the harp as well. In fact, these women gave several performances in Charleston. As if this connection were not enough to warrant such a detailed account here, they performed some of the same obscure repertory bound into Harriet Lowndes's binder's volumes.

The information on a program for the concert presented on 18 February 1823 ties together several strands of this story. The program, as it appeared in the *City Gazette and Commercial* on 12 February 1823, is given below.[54] The composers included Nicholas Bochsa—the most acknowledged harpist in the western world and one who had toured in the United States—and Bégrez and Naderman.

Concert and Ball

MRS. GIRAUD, respectfully informs her Friends and the Publick, that her Concert will take place at Concert Hall, Church-street (which has lately been repaired and carefully examined by faithful workmen) *This Evening,* [?] and the following pieces will be performed.

1st Part.

1 Duett on the Piano and Harp, executed by Misses Fayolle,   Bochsa
2 A Song (the Carolini) by Miss Bridon, accompanied on
    the Harp by herself,   Begrez
3 Variations on the Harp, by Miss Septima Fayolle,   Bochsa
4 A Song by Miss Bridon, accompanied on the Harp by
    Mrs. Giraud,   Romagnesi
5 New Variations (Friend of my Soul) on the Harp, by
    Mrs. Giraud,   Naderman

2nd Part.

1 Duett on two Harps (away with Melancholy) with variations,
    by Mrs. Giraud and Miss S. Fayolle,   Bochsa
2 A Song by Miss Bridon   Plantade
3 Solo on the Piano, by Miss Emma Fayolle   Gelinke
4 A Grand Morceau, with variations on the Harp, taken from
    an Italian Opera, by Mrs. Giraud   Bochsa
5 A new Trio for three Harps, by Mrs. Giraud, and her
    two pupils, Miss Bridon and Miss Septime Fayolle   Naderman

Managers:

Col. J. Bond I'on, Fred. Kinloch, James Rose, W. S. Pringle, Arthur M. Parker

Doors to be opened at 6 o'clock, and the Concert to begin precisely at seven. Tickets to be had at Mr. De Villier's Music Store, corner of Broad and King-streets, at Mr. Siegling's Music Ware-House, Broad-street, Mr. Charles Lacoste's store, King-street, P. Fayolle & Son, King-street, and at the Ticket Office, on the evening of the performance.

A review of the concert on 20 February noted that there were so many people in attendance that many were "shut out from . . . those female forms so harmonising with the music they gave forth. . . . While on all sides it could feast on long rows of beauties—of matron maturity and blushing youth." Was Harriet among them? Music by both Bégrez and Naderman is in SMB 49. The announcement in the *City Gazette* reveals a possible connection to her: one of the "Managers" of the concert was Col. J. Bond I'On, Harriet's uncle. Jacob's association with the concert of 18 February 1823 establishes a link between Harriet's family and the two women who gave her music, Miss Bridon and Mrs. Giraud. Miss Bridon's name appears on a manuscript piece, Mrs. Giraud's on a printed one. Since Adelaide Giraud (née Fayolle) had studied music in Paris before her arrival in Charleston, she may have owned the music that Harriet acquired for her binder's volumes. She may even have brought it with her when she immigrated to South Carolina. The hand that copied most of the manuscript music might indeed be that of Miss Bridon, providing Harriet with musical selections copied from her personal collection.[55]

Mrs. Giraud departed Charleston in 1830; her farewell concert was announced in several papers. The advertisement mentioned her study in Paris and her taste in music, and it promised that this would be her final concert—no postponement was possible. Her repertory on that concert again included Bochsa's "Knight Errant," one of the harpist's most popular pieces and one she had played in Charleston previously. She then moved to San Antonio with her husband. Nothing else is known of Miss Bridon, who disappeared from newspaper announcements and other reviews.[56]

Possibly, Harriet studied music with Mrs. Giraud in Charleston during the 1820s. All of the newspaper commentaries declared that Miss Bridon was a student of Mrs. Giraud, and as such she probably would not have taught Harriet. The two younger women may have become acquainted through Mrs. Giraud. Miss P. Bridon gifted Harriet with "La Bergerette délaisée" by Louis-Emmanuel Jadin, a piece for solo work that resembles other romances in her collection. (See figure 3.3a.) Bridon's hand appears twice in SMB 48, and one piece, "La dernière fois," occurs twice in the same volume: once in Bridon's hand and once in someone else's. (See figures 3.3b and 3.3c.)

One version of Bégrez's "La dernière fois" was published in London as "La dernière fois / A French Song . . . by Mr. Bégrez" and dedicated to Lady Flint. The publication information says that it was published for the author at 22, Gerrard Street in Soho, and could be purchased at Chappell & Co. on Bond Street, as well as "all the Principal Music Shops." This setting is in G minor, and both of Harriet's versions are in A minor. Otherwise the three versions resemble each other in both vocal line and accompaniment. That the accompaniments

Figure 3.3a. Inscription from Miss Bridon on "La Bergerette délaisée" in SMB 48

Figure 3.3b. "La dernière fois" in Bridon's hand (Fig. 1.1a), SMB 48

Figure 3.3c. "La dernière fois" in a different hand, SMB 48

seem to be the same settings suggests a common version that circulated and was used by the copyists, one of whom could have been Mrs. Giraud, of SMB 48.[57]

How did Harriet—or one of her parents, who would have arranged for the lessons—and Mrs. Giraud meet? Perhaps they could have done so through Harriet's uncle, who managed the February 1823 concert. Harriet had turned eleven the previous month—an appropriate age to be studying music with an instructor. SMB 48 might be the result of such interactions: the ties to Parisian music made possible by a French music teacher who came to Charleston and made a name for herself as a harpist, and her student who might have been a friend or older mentor of Harriet. They were not of the same class, of course, and would not have mingled socially, but they may have spent time making music together. That Miss Bridon was of a different social class from Harriet's can be shown by the fact that her name appeared in the newspaper, whereas Harriet's never would have done so.

French Connections

As unique as it seems, Harriet's was not the only collection in Charleston to include French romances. Yet another binder's volume in the Charleston Museum, SMB 218, provides some crucial clues as to how Harriet might have encountered such unfamiliar French music.[1] SMB 218 substantiates her connection to members of the Fayolle family and broadens our understanding of musical culture in 1820s Charleston because it dates from the same period and includes some of the same unusual composers.

SMB 218 consists of sixty-two pieces, all in manuscript. All except for the third work—"My Henry Is Gone" by E. E. Ulmo—are in French.[2] The accompaniments are for guitar, harp, and/or piano. Two sections where intervals are explained in details—the half-steps between them are written out—imply a didactic purpose behind this binder's volume. No. 14 is a "Walse" for a solo instrument that was added after someone had connected two staves together. At least five hands can be discerned, with the bulk of the music being copied by hand C and hand E. Copyists wrote in the manuscript from both ends, a common practice for music sources dating back to at least 1600.[3] In spite of the number of hands, the repertory stays the same.

SMB 218 relates to SMB 48 in several ways. Most of SMB 218 comprises similar types of music, particularly French romances and nocturnes, encountered in SMB 47, SMB 48, and SMB 50. Moreover, some of the same rare—at least in the United States—composers are found here as well, such as Berton and Romagnesi, as well as more familiar ones, such as Boieldieu and Dalayrac. In fact, SMB 218 has twelve attributed songs by Romagnesi (and at least one other not credited to him in the volume), some of which can be found among the three volumes of his *Collection des romances, chansonnettes, et nocturnes,* published by the author in Paris in 1807, 1819, and 1828.[4]

Accompaniments explicitly for the harp further connect SMB 218 and SMB 48. SMB 218 contains several accompaniments specifically for harp and a work,

"Le diable, couleur et Rose [*sic*]," by Pierre Gaveaux. Gaveaux wrote a harp tutorial and several pieces for harp, and many of the Pleyel publications in SMB 48 are described as accompaniment with piano or harp. Harriet may have played the harp as did many other women of her social class, and these connections point to the likelihood that she was acquainted with the person who either copied or owned SMB 218.

The strongest connection between SMB 218 and SMB 48 is that they contain at least one of the same hands. Whoever entered "Le baiser" (no. 16) and possibly "L'Amandier" (no. 22) in SMB 48 copied two pieces into SMB 218 (on pages 2 and 40).[5] Other similarities in hands between the two volumes indicate that Harriet's volume originated from the same circle as did SMB 218. Furthermore, in SMB 218 particularly and to a lesser degree in SMB 48, the headings reproduce the visual placement of title, author, and lyricist (if given) found in European publications, which suggests that the copyists either copied directly from Belgian and French printed music or were so familiar with it that they adopted these physical placements in handwritten copies. (See figure 3.1, above.)

While it is tempting to think that Harriet may have copied some of the music in SMB 218 and that the manuscript belonged to her, too little information can be gleaned from its pages to say one way or the other: we have no confirmed sample of her music handwriting, and her name does not appear in the volume. Did the Fayolle family or Bridon copy both SMB 218 and SMB 48? It is plausible that they brought music with them to Charleston from France and copied from their personal library for their pupils. They may have continued to receive music via post for these purposes as well. The printed pieces in SMB 48 have only Parisian publisher and dealer stamps as well as *les papiérs timbres,* which convincingly advocates that Harriet did not buy them from a local importer of foreign music but rather procured them in some other manner. If Madame Giraud (née Fayolle) was her teacher, this means of transmission best answers the questions posed by SMB 48. Additionally, this connection also explains the obscure repertory of French romances in SMB 47 and SMB 50.

Most scholars stress Charlestonians' identification with Great Britain, stemming from close familial ties in the eighteenth century to education and commerce in the nineteenth century.[6] This may be the case, but Harriet's sheet music collection argues for a more continental emphasis. After SMB 47 she seemingly abandoned the English and American composers that her contemporaries favored and studied a decidedly French repertory that included romances by composers whose works were heard in Parisian salons. Indeed, the extant collection that most resembles Harriet's belonged to Mme. la Comtesse Caroline de Saint Didier (1790–after 1820), now housed in Buffalo, New York.[7] Saint Didier was an amateur singer and composer, and her binder's volume includes sixty-one French romances for solo or duet with accompaniments, some of which she composed.[8] The composers include Saint Didier as well as Bruguière, Panseron, Duchambge, Romagnesi, Berton fils, Beauplan, Paër, and Plantade—each of whom also exists in Harriet's collection.[9] Housed in the same collection are several other groups of pieces with similar names. One may have belonged to a family of musicians in Paris by the name of Le Carpentier and consists of both printed and manuscript romances. It too includes many of the same names and some of the same pieces as those in SMB 48, such as "Venez les Champs" by Naderman.[10] Like Harriet's, many of these pieces are for piano or harp accompaniment. The Buffalo collection, however, originated in France and belonged to a French musician. That Harriet Lowndes owned a similar collection confirms that her music was closer to that sung in French salons than that performed in Charleston parlors in the 1820s.

Several factors might explain Harriet's attraction to French music. Certainly, the influence of French music teachers heightened her awareness of an alternative to the English-language songs she had in SMB 49. In addition, French musicians immigrated to the United States during the eighteenth and nineteenth centuries, and many taught young southern women. They tended to assign a repertory such as that found in SMB 49, so this in and of itself is not a persuasive argument for the romances in SMB 47, SMB 48, and SMB 50. Moreover, southern women studied with Italian, German, and British music professors, but these teachers tended not to deviate from a standard repertory of English and American songs, and they favored opera arias and familiar tunes.[11] The unfamiliar French music demands another explanation, of which a Huguenot connection offers a small degree. Descendants of Huguenot families formed a significant part of Charleston's population, and this association may have drawn French musicians such as Peter Fayolle and his family to the city.[12] Charleston's reputation as a cultural center also contributed to its attractions. French cultural connections in Charleston deepened after refugees from Saint-Domingue arrived following the revolution of 1804.[13]

Taken together, these influences may have sparked Harriet's interest in French culture. Other stimuli, such as her extended family, might also have influenced her collection. Perhaps she longed for opportunities to live in France, as her aunt and other relations had done.[14] Others in her acquaintance, such as the Hugers, Middletons, Manigaults, and Izards, did likewise. Southerners with the means to do so spent considerable time in Paris, and Harriet Lowndes Aiken would travel with her husband and daughter there on several occasions. She unquestionably seems to have been more enamored with the city of light than most of her contemporaries were, or at least could afford more than a passing acquaintance with it, as a discussion of her family's later journeys there illuminates.[15]

Thus far the discussion has focused on what was in Harriet's music collection and how she might have acquired it, but other questions remain. How well did Harriet sing? What instruments did she play? Vocal music dominates her collection—there is only one keyboard piece—and the preponderance of songs and arias suggests that singing was her strong suit. That she may have also played the guitar, harp, and piano signifies that her parents ensured that she was accomplished according to the standards of the day, although doing all four promotes the idea of a young woman who was more accomplished than many others.

The pieces in these three binder's volumes range from simple songs to opera arias that employ the latest expectations of the singer. The technique required in the simple songs will not suffice for the bel canto arias, nor for those from grand opera. This is not to say that Harriet's progression in her music studies resulted in a different style, but it reflects changes in the professional repertory as well. Thus, the arias in her binder's volumes demonstrate an evolving style in singing. For example, the Italian arias, even though they range from expressive sadness to graceful simplicity to agile playfulness, fall in the same pitch range, which may suggest Harriet's preferred tessitura.[16] Most of Rossini's "Assisa a piè d'un salice" (now known as "The Willow Song") keeps to a range of an octave (G4 to G5), but it does require facile singing of thirty-second and even sixty-fourth notes. As seen in SMB 50, Harriet also owned the music that follows "Assisa a piè d'un salice" in *Otello:* the aria "Deh calma ciel bel sonno." Both are relatively short works that would have been appropriate for performance in the parlor.[17] In contrast, Boieldieu's dramatic arias have declamatory recitatives that require the singer to negotiate arpeggiated vocal lines and are, generally speaking, bigger pieces.[18] Rossini's later "Sombre forêt, désert triste et sauvage" requires more bel canto technique than the earlier pieces do.

More surprising in Harriet's collection is an operatic piece assigned to a male character, in this case the duet between the two men, the Count and Figaro, "D'un metal si précieux" ("All'idea di quel metallo") from *Il barbiere di Siviglia.* The vocal parts are printed in the bass clef, which seems odd in a young woman's music collection, given the binder's volume's role in cultivating feminine accomplishment.[19] Perhaps the editors realized their consumers would have known that this music was originally written for male voices and to try to pretend otherwise would not make good business sense. However, some of the same operatic works for male characters in Emma's binder's volume, SMB 25, were printed with treble clefs.

Sacchini's aria "Barbare amour!" contains the same tessitura as the Rossini pieces, as does "Dieux! Ce n'est pas pour moi" and "Votre cœur devint mon azile." The Mozart arias and duets too essentially encompass this vocal range. Zerlina's "Vedrai, carino," "Batti, batti, o bel Masetto," and the duet "La ci darem la mano" follow the same pattern—with some brief high B-flats in "Batti, batti." The duet from *Figaro* "Sull'aria" extends to B-flats in Susanna's part but only to G5 in that of the Contessa. How much information Harriet, or her parents, had about some of the characters whose music she sang, such as the flirtatious Zerlina from *Don Giovanni,* is unknown, but "La ci darem la mano" remained popular with southerners until at least the Civil War.[20]

CHAPTER 5

Harriet Lowndes Aiken's Opera Collection

While the obscure European music in Harriet Lowndes's binder's volumes distinguishes her music collection from that of other unmarried women of similar social status in the American South, her collection of complete operas in foreign languages stamps it as unique. Nine of these survive in the Charleston Museum, including six operas by Rossini and Mozart's *Le nozze di Figaro*. She already owned selections from Rossini and Mozart in her binder's volumes, but she chose to augment her collection with copies of their complete operas. She bought these opera scores on her extended honeymoon in order to confirm that she cultivated sensibility and taste, similar to the objets d'art that she also selected while in Europe. Displayed in the parlor so that anyone entering the room might examine the owner's musical tastes, books such as these were on exhibit when young women performed the rituals that signified culture. The books served as both public and private artifacts to be displayed for their many visitors.[1]

Both Harriet and her husband had a passionate interest in European culture, and their home reflected such. When Harriet Lowndes married William Aiken in 1831, she wed a man whose acquaintance with Europe, at least England, was extensive. His father came to the United States from Ireland as a young boy, and he brought William to South Carolina when his son was only ten years old. By the time he married Harriet, William had traversed the Atlantic several times. Passenger records indicate that he traveled from London to Charleston, arriving on 16 November 1820 on the ship *Issabella*.[2] At this time he was in the company of his parents and brother James, and his father was listed as a merchant.[3] As he was a "gentleman," William's name appeared again when he arrived in New York from Liverpool on 31 July 1829. He was twenty-three at the time and had had a bust-length miniature made during this trip.[4]

After their wedding in 1831, Harriet and William embarked on a honeymoon to Europe.[5] During this journey Harriet took the opportunity to buy many things for her home, including several almost-complete opera scores. These are fascinating artifacts because they reveal nuances about her approach to culture and cultural representation. Among the most surprising artifacts that she purchased were several volumes of complete operas.[6] Why she felt the need to purchase these scores remains an enigma. They may be something of a souvenir of her honeymoon. These books were all purchased in Europe and brought back to Charleston, and Harriet signed her name "H Lowndes Aiken 1831" in them, as if celebrating her new last name. The date is important as well because it demonstrates how up-to-date her choices were. By writing it in the front of the books, Harriet may have been creating a memento of her wedding trip. Habitually both Harriet and William wrote their names and dates, and sometimes places, in many of the books they purchased in Europe.

The operas Harriet chose reflect the popular trends in northern Europe in the early 1830s. The earliest of these by far is Mozart's *Le nozze di Figaro* (SMB 224), which premiered in 1786. This date, however, is deceptive, for Mozart's complete operas were not well known in the United States, even if individual excerpts were. All of the other operas in this collection date from 1813 or later. Four by Rossini had first performances in the 1810s: Rossini's *L'italiana in Algieri* (1813, SMB 221); *Il turco in Italia* (1814, SMB 220); *Il Barbiere di Seviglia* [*sic*] (1816, SMB 227); and *La Donna del Lago* (1819, SMB 223). The remainder are from the 1820s and represent much more diverse styles: Weber's *Der Freischütz* (1821, SMB 190); Giacomo Meyerbeer's *Il Crociato in Egitto* (1824, SMB 225); Rossini's *Le Siège de Corinthe* (1826, SMB 226); and Vincenzo Bellini's *Il pirata* (also 1826, SMB 222). This is a remarkably varied selection from the 1820s, even if all were undeniably popular. Harriet added a German romantic opera, bel canto works, and the beginnings of French grand opera to the shelves at the Aiken-Rhett House—which is surely where they must have remained as there were no performance options for complete operas in 1830s Charleston homes.[7]

The title page of SMB 227 describes it as *Il Barbiere di Seviglia,* an "Opera Buffa" in two acts, "Composta e Ridotta per il Cembalo da G. Rossini." Availability was "À Paris // Chez Maurice Schlesinger, Md de Musique de ROI // Éditeur des Opéras de Mozart, Rossini, Mayerbeer [*sic*], et des Œuvres de Hummel, Moscheles, Mayseder, &c.," for thirty-six francs, at 97, rue de Richelieu. It also bears his stamp. This edition includes the famous overture, arranged for piano solo, and does not include many of the recitatives.

Rossini's operas were popular throughout the United States well into the nineteenth century, and his works among Harriet's collection reflect her familiarity with his music. But the other opera choices show astounding prescience, for she purchased operas by composers whose works would dominate the repertory in the decades after 1830. One of these is Weber, the first architect of

German romantic opera whose creative treatment of motive and imaginative instrumentation influenced such composers as Mendelssohn and Wagner. *Der Freischütz* was an immediate success after its premiere in Berlin in 1821, and the first Parisian performance, as *Robin des bois,* occurred in 1824. The edition that Harriet owned, her SMB 190, had been purchased in Paris under the name *Robin des bois // Freischütz // Opera romantique en trois actes composé et arrange pour le forte piano.* Like *Il Barbiere di Seviglia,* it came from Schlesinger's, with his stamp. This edition includes seventeen pieces and has French text, with German beneath. SMB 190 is bound plain, beige, with no plate or embossed name, and has a hand-sewn cover in linen. She wrote "H Lowndes Aiken // 1831" inside.

Bellini too experienced a meteoric rise in popularity with the premiere of *Il pirata* in 1827, but he did not live long after he wrote his more famous operas. His *Norma* (1831) was particularly popular in the United States and can be found in arrangements in many southern binder's volumes. Bellini and Gaetano Donizetti are today the best-known composers of the style of opera known as bel canto. The long, flowing melodies from their operas formed the basis for numerous settings and arrangements throughout the nineteenth century.

Il Crociato in Egittto was the first of many successful operas by Meyerbeer, one of the doyens of French grand opera. Arias and choruses from his *Les Huguenots* populate southern binder's volumes from the antebellum period and may have particularly resonated with Charleston Huguenot families. His *Robert le diable* (1831) had similar success, gauging by excerpts in binder's volumes. In contrast to the melody-driven Italian bel canto operas of Bellini, and to a certain extent Rossini, Meyerbeer specialized in French operas that depended on lavish sets, large casts and orchestras, melodrama, and spectacle. His *Robert le diable* represents his first foray into the genre. Rossini's last opera, *Guillaume Tell,* too falls into this category of opera.

If Meyerbeer and Bellini represented new styles of opera that emerged in Europe in the late 1820s and early 1830s, and Rossini's Italian operas were the height of fashion, then Harriet Lowndes, now Aiken, brought the most stylish music available back to Charleston. With a few exceptions, most of the music in her binder's volumes was in vogue between 1780 and 1820, a period that coincided with the golden age of the St. Cecelia Society's concerts.[8] But only a few of the composers whose music she owned—such as Rossini and Boieldieu—had real staying power once the music of Meyerbeer and Bellini arrived in the United States.

Harriet's copy of *L'italiana in Algieri,* purchased in Paris, has a bookplate from New York City on the inside. It seems likely that Harriet purchased the volumes while in Europe and then had them bound once she returned to New York.[9] The operas would have looked much more impressive on the shelf in the

Aiken home if they were uniformly bound—they would resemble other sets of books that her husband owned. These were complete operas, an unusual find in a home of a lady of leisure. They differed substantially from her other binder's volumes. Almost all the young women of Harriet's acquaintance had binder's volumes, but few, if any, owned complete opera editions. This leaves us to ponder why she bought opera scores while on her honeymoon.

In the decades after Harriet's honeymoon, some young Charleston women deliberately sought opera scores. In 1848 Emily Wharton Sinkler wrote to Thomas Wharton that she wished her sister Mary to find some music for her while in Philadelphia. She requested "either *Anna Bolena*[,] *Puritani* [Donizetti, 1831], *La Muette di Portici* [Auber, 1838] or *Otello* [Rossini, 1817]," and if these were not available, "Mary can choose what she thinks best with the exception of *Norma* [Bellini, 1831] and *Somnambula* [*sic*; Bellini, 1833]."[10] Of course, she may have been referring to only a single aria from one of these operas, as Harriet would do when she described Henrietta singing *Il trovatore* in 1858.[11] This comment leads to another question: did southern women such as Harriet and Emily hear these operas in person? Emily wrote, "Oh Hen how I felt when I read that you had heard the Havanna Opera troupe in *Lucia*. Of all Operas I should prefer hearing that" (letter, 21 May 1850), which implies that "Hen" had heard this opera in person.[12]

Emily wrote often about music at Charleston gatherings in the 1840s. At The Eutaw, her family's plantation, she entertained guests, including the Kinlochs, from Charleston: "In the evening we have some very good music. Anna and I have some nice duets and Tom Kinloch has brought up his flute. To be sure he will harp on the hearts affections, the forsaken and twilight dews but everyone is so used to his singing them that it would not seem natural for him not to send them every evening. Seaman has given Anna and myself each an opera (the music I mean) and I am determined this winter to practice so that when I come on I will surprise you."[13] She did not like the sentimental songs such as "Twilight Dews," and apparently neither did Harriet. In the same year, 1845, Emily mentioned that the family had Steinway pianos at both The Eutaw and Belvidere plantations. She wanted a new one in 1845, but her "beau pere" was unwilling to put forth $580; he capped his limit at $400. Elizabeth Waties Allston Pringle too mentioned owning Steinways—six over the course of her life.[14] We do not know what type of piano the Aikens had before their 1867 Chickering, which remains in the Aiken-Rhett House today.

Emily's 30 November 1848 correspondence with her sister Mary Wharton indicated something about taste: "Anna and I are practicing to need duets for your special edification. I hope you're getting ready some pieces [for] persons who are not quite *au fait* to intricate music. 'La Coupe' I know will be liked. By the bye did you get the music book I sent you by Dr. Huger and did you see him?"[15] She played down her knowledge of current trends and insinuated that Mary had been exposed to better—"intricate"—music. Later, Emily's oldest daughter, Lizzie, wrote about evenings at The Eutaw: "Mamma and Aunt Anna entertained the guests in the drawing room by singing duets which sounded to me like the songs of angels. Their voices were so lovely and so well trained, and soprano and one contralto, and they were fascinated with Jenny Lind's songs of which they had a number." They sang in Italian and German. In addition to the Steinway, Emily had a guitar that came from Spain.[16]

Harriet spoke four languages, played several musical instruments, and, like other Charlestonians, traveled to Europe for pleasure as well as intellectual and cultural enrichment. She demonstrated the desire to acquire cultural artifacts in Paris and show them off at home, as Kilbride suggested when he wrote that Americans traveled to Europe to acquire items and behaviors that could "testify to the significance of display and genteel culture," employing "the most of attention-grabbing demonstrations of their refinement."[17] By accumulating a large number of tangible goods, she deliberately sought to bring French culture back to Charleston, South Carolina, from each of the three trips she took to Europe. The tactic worked, for the Aiken-Rhett House, as it is now known, became a seat of cultural sophistication in a city that prided itself on such. Considered to be "connoisseurs as collectors," Harriet and William supported the new Carolina Art Association because they understood an art gallery to be a modern expression of life in the city. In 1858 the Aikens installed an art gallery in their house in order to display their European treasures, and some of these remain in the gallery today. That year George W. Flagg, a native of Connecticut who studied painting abroad and later moved to South Carolina, produced a famous full-length portrait of Harriet. These items served to underpin a self-perception that in Charleston the representation of a French home, with all its accoutrements, indicated superior culture.

How many times did Harriet travel to Europe? According to Ann Ratliff Russell, she and William went to Paris for the first time two years after their marriage in 1831.[18] The inscriptions in her operas, bought in Brussels and Paris, suggest that they were there in 1831. Russell did not indicate the evidence for a journey in 1835. Two books purchased by Harriet in Paris bear the date 1837, which could mean that the Aikens were there in 1835 and 1837.[19] Harriet was back in Charleston when Henrietta was born in 1836. The Aikens returned in 1848, 1850, 1854, and 1857; these journeys are examined in detail in part 2. Moreover, during the 1850s an art gallery in ornate rococo-revival style was added to their house, and floor plans were mailed to them abroad so they could purchase appropriate items.[20] Elizabeth Garrett has interpreted the Aikens' collection of paintings as a way for them to create an "artistic history" as the artworks show that they were aware of current styles and artists as well as Renaissance masters.[21] This idea can be extended to the music owned by both Harriet and her daughter, Henrietta, which included older French composers as well as some of the latest music available.

When Charleston residents visited the Aikens, the opulent surroundings were not lost on them. A letter written to Francis Kinloch Middleton by an unknown author described a social event that took place at the Aiken-Rhett House in 1839: "last night I was at the handsomest ball I have ever seen—given by Mrs. Aiken—Miss Lowndes that was—they live near Boundary Street in the house he has added to, & furnished very handsomely—2 floors were entirely thrown open—the orchestra from the theatre played for the dances—and the supper table was covered with a rich service of silver—light in profusion, a crowded handsomely draped assembly."[22] Undoubtedly some of the riches from their time in Paris graced the home during this event. Notably, they allowed people access to two floors of their home, which was unusual, and hired an "orchestra" to provide music for dancing—not a band or small group of performers. Garrett has summarized the Aikens by saying that "to them, entertainment was an art form." Indeed, it continued to be so up until the Civil War, extending to their daughter's comparatively extravagant wedding in Flat Rock, North Carolina, in 1863. Those who taught Harriet early on to emulate French tastes and habits would have been proud of how she demonstrated these in adulthood.

PART TWO

CHAPTER 6

The Aiken Family and Henrietta's Music Collection

The story of Henrietta Aiken begins where that of Harriet Lowndes left off, in the same house at 48 Elizabeth Street in the Wraggborough district of Charleston. Born on 17 July 1836, "Etta" was the only child of Harriet and William to survive to adulthood. Harriet's desire to instill European culture, particularly French, in her home in Charleston has been documented. Her husband, it seems, was equally captivated by the possibility of experiencing life abroad. Henrietta benefited from her parents' interests by accompanying them to Europe four times before her twenty-second birthday.

William engaged with politics as did other prosperous South Carolinians in his social circle: he was governor of South Carolina from 1844 to 1846 and later served in the state and federal legislature. He retired from politics in 1857. However, his ties to the British Isles and elsewhere in Europe ran deep and contributed to his financial success, even during and after the Civil War. His father, also named William Aiken, came to the United States from Ballymenagh, County Antrum, Ulster Province, (now) Northern Ireland, in 1775. He returned to Ireland to marry Elizabeth Reid—whose sister was a music teacher—and later brought his ten-year-old son, William Jr., to South Carolina. William Sr. left his son with a Mr. Blaney to learn the cotton trade and went back to Ireland.[1] William Jr. traveled to Europe on several occasions, particularly England. His connections to England most likely descended from his father's commercial enterprises in Great Britain.[2] His wife did not share the same enthusiasm for England and spent comparatively little time there.

Their social station demanded that the Aikens host parties, soirees, and other entertainments. Governor Aiken's inaugural celebration was certainly lavish: one thousand guests drank eighteen hundred bottles of champagne, in addition to wine and brandy.[3] In 1853 the Swedish writer Fredrika Bremer described a May 1850 party given by Governor Aiken "and his lovely wife" with five hundred guests: "There was beautiful music . . . the entertainment was one of the most beautiful I have been present at in this country."[4] Henrietta probably would not have made much of an impression—if she were even present at this party—being only thirteen at the time and presumably not "out" in society yet.

When the Aikens were not in Charleston or at Jehossee—their island plantation near the city—they visited Paris, where William maintained an apartment at least in the 1840s, or lived in Washington, D.C., while William served there. They also traveled to New York and popular spas, as befit their social station. Most impressively, the Aikens made six visits to Europe between 1831 and 1857, touring extensively during some of them.[5] This recurrent travel served as a fulfillment of Henrietta's parents' desire to immerse the family in European culture and to surround themselves with many of its accoutrements back home in Charleston. Today the Aiken-Rhett House retains many of the architectural features, the chandeliers, much of the artwork, a *potager,* and some of the silver and wallpaper that the Aikens imported from France.

Henrietta's education during this time seems to have been simultaneously deliberate and haphazard. None of the Aiken-Rhett family papers indicate that she attended school, but William Porcher Miles wrote to Harriet that he was sorry to have missed Henrietta's French recitation. He called her "Little Heart," Harriet being known as "Heart"; even so, he seemed to know that "she did not show too much 'cheek';—but was diffident and modest; — + a little timid;—as little girls ought to be on such occasions."[6] Where she performed this recitation or how "little" she was remains a mystery, but it suggests that she may have been in a school somewhere. Most of her surviving textbooks in the Charleston Library Society cover a variety of subjects and are in French, and they were purchased abroad. The Aikens engaged at least one governess for Henrietta in 1850, a Frenchwoman named Pauline Boudet.[7] She arrived in Charleston via New York in November 1848 and did not stay with the Aikens long.[8] The name "Marmiez" appears on a few pieces of music owned by Elise Rhett and Henrietta, but nothing points to this woman instructing Henrietta. No other details survive to indicate other teachers or instruction in general education. Her music constitutes the surest evidence of her teenage years.

Henrietta was rarely mentioned in letters or diaries of her contemporaries that have been published in modern times, and her primary correspondence seems to have been confined to family members. Her personality during her younger years remains somewhat of an enigma, but her books and music evince that she was a wealthy and accomplished young woman, befitting Mary Chesnut's comment that she was "the greatest heiress in the state."[9] One letter to Henrietta from "Helie" [Helen], a cousin in Columbia, mentioned a musical gathering "in the shape of a very pleasant serenade—The music was really very good," but this hardly accounts for the vibrant musical household that the Aikens must have had. After a reference to Dr. [Lingard] Frampton, another cousin, Helie continued, "The other night at the musical club [I] actually summoned up the courage to plan an accompaniment for [Mr.] Heyward. I think I must practice hard so that one of these days you could let me play for you." This letter implied that there was a local musical club meeting, perhaps regularly, in Columbia. She asked Henrietta to give her love to Burnet, which suggests a date after Henrietta's marriage in 1862. It also connotes that her contemporaries admired Henrietta's talent, since her cousin had to prepare specifically to play the piano for her.[10]

Henrietta's Music Collection

Henrietta's music collection at the Charleston Museum and her books now in the Charleston Library Society prove that her parents made sure she had access to and training in all of the necessary accomplishments, and that she achieved fluency in French and became an admired vocalist. Her substantial collection of French-language textbooks indicates that she studied the language assiduously. Music was not a mere decoration in the house—although Harriet's opera collection must have been. Her music, some of which requires considerable skill to perform, contains many penciled-in additions, such as noting where to breathe in vocal pieces and how to finger passages in piano music. Such markings confirm its use. We might also infer that she had stylish clothes, dancing lessons, deportment practice, and all of the other lessons dictated by mid-century etiquette books, because her family's status among Charleston's elite would have demanded such.

This is only a guess, however. References to Henrietta are fewer than those to her parents. Fleeting comments in letters or diaries are uncommon, perhaps because the city's numerous fires and the devastation brought about by the Civil War destroyed such documentation, or because of the Aikens' frequent absences from the area. In June 1861 Meta Morris Grimball (1810–81) recorded in her diary that Miss Aiken; Mrs. Vanderhorst, Henrietta's eventual sister-in-law Mary Rhett; and the Manigaults came to tea. Binder's volumes belonging to these women now reside in the Charleston Museum.[11] The women shared a social life reserved for Charleston's elites that might explain how the binder's volumes of other women such as Elizabeth Waties Allston Pringle and Meta Morris Grimball came to be in the Aiken-Rhett House.[12]

Despite the paucity of letters and diaries, Henrietta's story can be gleaned from her music and books. Her music collection consists of unusual binder's volumes, individual pieces of sheet music, and pedagogical materials. Henrietta's extensive music collection provides more clues to her biography than does any other identified material. She was a talented singer with a lower vocal range, mezzo-soprano or even contralto, and a solid pianist. She had several music teachers, at least one of whom wrote a composition for her and coached her in its performance. Her family members continued to write of her love of music and considerable talent in letters of the 1860s and 1870s.

Furthermore, the Charleston Museum collection reveals that the Aikens made four separate trips to Europe, a number not given in accounts of the family in modern literature.[13] Most writers have listed two, in 1848 and 1857–58, and some have acknowledged three, including in 1851. There was yet another voyage across the Atlantic, however, in 1854. These have been validated by nonmusic books purchased by the family in Europe on the same journeys. Like her mother, Henrietta collected music while traveling abroad.

Vocal music features much more prominently in Henrietta's collection than does that for the piano. Henrietta Aiken was demonstrably a capable singer; many of her pieces include breath marks, added ornamentation, or other indications of use. In fact, there are more added notations in her music than in most other surviving pieces from the period, as is the case with her mother's music of a generation earlier. Whether this is because she truly enjoyed singing and practiced diligently, or because she had been exposed to more professional performances and therefore knew the level of achievement expected beyond her native city, or because it was a practice demanded by her mother or strict music teachers is unknown.

As much as Henrietta's music collection reveals, it also perplexes. It deviates substantially from standard practices in that most of it remains unbound. Only three are cataloged as bound sheet music—SMB 19, SMB 189, and SMB 228—and even these do not follow the usual pattern of popular pieces bound together into a single volume because they were published as books, not individual sheets of music.[14] I am aware of no other southern music collection of such breadth that was not bound during the antebellum period. This physical state, of course, renders the identification of all of her music impossible. Young women often inscribed their names on pieces of sheet music, but rarely did they always do so. It would be unreasonable to expect that Henrietta wrote her name on each piece she owned. In the Charleston Museum, there are fifty pieces with her maiden name and thirteen with her married name on them. These we can be sure were hers. Table 6.1 comprises the single sheet music pieces in the Charleston Museum with some form of Henrietta's name on them.

But there are others that almost certainly belonged to her and still others that might have. All of these pieces of sheet music are cataloged as "SMS" for "sheet music single." The Charleston Museum owns well over a thousand of these. It seems, however, that everything that belonged to the Aiken-Rhett House,

Table 6.1. Music with Henrietta Aiken's name in the Charleston Museum

SMS	Title	Composer	Inscription	Date	Notes
292	Carnaval in Washington-Willard's Polka	M. Strakosch	Miss Aiken with the Misses Mallards Compliments	1854	NY: Hall & Son
310	Zephyrs from Newport	F.B. Helmsmuller	H.A. Rhett [ink]		Boston: Ditson
328	Orphée	C. von Gluck, arr. by É. Prudent	Henrietta Aiken		Mayence: Schott. Sold by NY: Breusing; Baltimore: Beacham. *Orphée et Eurydice*
352	The Germania-Thou art so near	A. Reichardt	Henrietta Aiken Rhett	1860	Ditson
354	Grande valse chantée dans Le Barbier de Séville	G. Rossini; arr., Luigi Vinzano	H.A. Aiken / Paris / 1858	ca. 1833–35	Paris: Ménestral. *Il barbiere di Siviglia*
356	Collezione complete della canzoncine nazionale Napoletane (Santa Lucia)		"H.A. Aiken / [?]" – place illegible. McCord has same edition. Italian.		
359	Les plaintes de la jeune fille, op. 58, no. 3	"François" Schubert	H.A. Aiken / Paris [Des Mädchens Klage]	Ca. 1845 [Tunley give ca. 1836]	Paris: Richault
367	Gems from the German: Serenade	F. Schubert	H.A. Aiken		Boston: Clapp. Sold Charleston: Siegling
369	Romanza di Sm^eion [?Smeeton] dans Anna Bolena ("Deh! non voler constringere")		Paris / H.A. Rhett		

Table 6.1. Music with Henrietta Aiken's name in the Charleston Museum (*continued*)

SMS	Title	Composer	Inscription	Date	Notes
372	In the eye there lies a heart	F. Abt	Henrietta Aiken		Boston: Ditson. Sold NY: Breusing
373	Mon âme à dieu . . . mon coeur à toi!	L. Clapisson	H.A. Aiken / from / Mrs. Monck	1847?	Mayence: Schott
383	La brune Thérèse	Prosper Guion	H.A. Aiken / from / Mlle M[armiez?]		Mayence: Schott
384	Iodler		H.A. Aiken / Interlocken		
392	Je t'aimerai	F. Besanzoni	H.A. Aiken / Paris	1852	Paris: L. Parent
395	Lord, teach me how to pray	W.V. Wallace	H.A. Rhett / 1885	1876	Charleston: C. Gill stamp
397	Iodler		H.A. Aiken / Interlocken		
416	Numi, che tesi mai / Si m'abandonni	S. Mercadante	[Henrietta Aiken]		
418	Old black Joe	Dan Bryant	H.A. Rhett	1860	William A. Pond
424	O thou omnipotent (Sacred Song)	Henry C. Watson	Henrietta A. Aiken	1853	NY: Hall & Son. Sold NY: Breusing
425	This kiss I offer (Lu Vasillo) / Canzonetta Napolitana di Sarimento		Henrietta Aiken Rhett	1867	NY: Schirmer
429	For thee love! Only thee / From Linda di Chamounix	G. Donizetti	Henrietta Aiken Rhett	1847	Boston: G.P. Reed. *Linda di Chamounix*
430	L'Étranger	Guilio Alary	H.A. Aiken / Paris	[?1857]	Paris: Flaxland
431a	Ahi! Fu Sogno Ingannatore	Basvecchi	dedicated to Henrietta Aiken, has green cover		

431b	Ahi! Fu Sogno Ingannatore	Basvecchi	dedicated to Henrietta Aiken		
437	Dearest – I think of thee	C. Krebs	H.A. Aiken from Marion Monck [or Marie Cottonet Monck?]		Philadelphia: Willig
446	Airs suisses / Der Vertrauen, no. 20		H.A. Aiken / Interlocken		Basel: Hegar
447	Airs suisses / Schweizer Heimweh, no. 19		H.A. Aiken / Interlocken		Basel: Hegar
451	Then you'll remember me	Balfe	H.A. Rhett [late for this piece?]		NY: Firth, Pond & Co
460	Napolitaine-I am dreaming of thee[1]	A. Lee	as sung by Madam [Eliza Ostenelli] Biscaccianti. H. A. Aiken		Boston: Diston. Sold Charleston: Siegling
464	La Fidanzata del Marinajo / Des Seemanns Braut / Scene ed Aria	J. Concone	H. A. Aiken. Spanish and German; breath marks p. 9 photo. Has been sewn together	[1854 per Hofmeister]	Mayence: Schott. Sold NY: Breusing
465	La traviata, no. 10 (Romanza) / Addio del passato	G. Verdi	H.A. Rhett / Paris [opera in 1853; high A's but not too high—part of ending]	[ca. 1855]	Paris. Stamp Léon Escudier. *La traviata*
468	We met by chance	Kucken	H.A. Aiken. Beethoven's "Adelaide" also in this series, Erlking, Wanderer, etc. [key? A-flat is high]	?1858	Boston: Ditson

Table 6.1. Music with Henrietta Aiken's name in the Charleston Museum (*continued*)

SMS	Title	Composer	Inscription	Date	Notes
482	Di due figli from Il Trovatore	G. Verdi	H.A. Aiken. mentioned in Harriet Lowndes Aiken letter from Jehossee. Publisher's note that originally in bass clef but printed in treble so a contralto [HAA] could use it more easily	1856	NY: Firth, Pond & Co. *Il trovatore*
484	L'Africaine / Romance No. 1 / Adieu mon doux rivage	G. Meyerbeer	H.A. Aiken "from" Marie Mon? Could be Marie Cottenet/Mary L. Monck		Paris: Brandus & Cie. Sold NY: Scharfenberg & Luis. *L'Africaine*
486	When in hours of anxious sadness	John B. Müller	H.A. Aiken	1854	Philadelphia: Couenhoven
496	Operatic Gems: Like the Dawn / M'appari tall amor from Martha	F. von Flotow	Henrietta Aiken Rhett [in F? High B-flat at end] Lionel's aria		NY: Dressler. Sold Charleston: Cole. *Martha*
516	Kathleen Mavourneen	F. Crouch	H.A. Aiken		NY: Firth, Pond & Co. Sold Charleston: Zogbaum
518	When the swallows homeward fly from Agathe	Abt	H.A. Aiken from M.H.[?]		NY: Tyler & Hewitt. Sold Baltimore: Willig
519	Ah, Wherefore? (Si vous n'avez rien a me dire) / Romance	Mme la Baronne Willy de Rothschild	Henrietta Aiken Rhett	1866	NY: Schirmer

520	Airs suisses avec accompagnment/ Schweizerlieder etc.: Die Alpenrösle, no. 16		H.A. Aiken / Interlocken		Hegar
521	Airs suisses avec accompagnment/ Schweizerlieder etc.: Der Gemsjäger, no. 17	F. Huber	H.A. Aiken / Interlocken		Hegar
526	Drift, my boat	F. Kücken	Henrietta A. Aiken from Dr. Lingard. Soprano and contralto duet	1853	NY: P.K. Weizel
529	Déjà la nuit s'avance from Marie Stuart	L. Niedermeyer	Henrietta A. Aiken / Paris / 1858. RH in accompanimentis sewn in with different pattern		Paris: Legoux, and stamp. *Marie Stuart*
535	Oh, think not less I love thee / An Alpine melody	H. Proch	H.A. Aiken	1847	Baltimore: W.C. Peters
537	Oh! Tell him all		H.A. Rhett from Marie H. Cottenet	1860	NY: Beer & Schirmer
539	Think of me! (Pense á me)	A[lfonso] Guercia	Henrietta Aiken Rhett	1867	NY: Schirmer
562	La mer se plaint toujours!	Jacques Potharst	H.A. Aiken / Paris	[1847]	Paris: Meissonnier-Heugel. Ménestral stamp
566	Airs suisses avec accompagnment/ Schweizerlieder etc.: Uf-fern Bergli, no. 21		H.A. Aiken / Interlocken		Basel: Hegar
574	Gems of German Song with English Words: Cradle Song	F. Mendelssohn	H.A. Aiken [one of the Songs without Words?]		NY: Hall & Son. Sold NY: Breusing
582a	Ahi! Fu Sogno Ingannatore[2]	P. Basvecchi	dedicated to Henrietta Aiken. Same as earlier ones		1857

Table 6.1. Music with Henrietta Aiken's name in the Charleston Museum (*continued*)

SMS	Title	Composer	Inscription	Date	Notes
582b	Ahi! Fa Sogno Ingannatore	P. Basvecchi			
583	The two nightingales / The swallows' farewell	F. Kücken	Henrietta Aiken from Dr. Lynah [Lingard]		NY: Dressler & Clayton. Sold NY: Breusing
584	Flowers of the Opera: O Whisper what Thou feelest from Crown of Jewels		H.A. Aiken from Marion Monck		Philadelphia: Lee & Walker
606	Ecole de Garcia, Traite complet de l'Art du Chant par Manuel Garcia fils	M. Garcia	Henrietta A. Aiken / Charleston. in French and German not in English. Preface only		Mayence: Schott. Sold NY: Kerkstieg & Breusing
614	Ahi! Fu Sogno Ingannatore	P. Basvecchi	print dedicated to Henrietta Aiken, autograph to her by composer; only p. 9 of music here	1857	see 431a and 582a
617	Softly ye night winds / Ballad / Companion to Sleeping I dreamed of love	W.V. Wallace/ Mary E. Hewitt	H. A. Aiken	1853	NY: Hall & Son
623	Tears, Idle Tears	P. Basvecchi	"To Miss Henrietta A Aiken / With the Respects of the Composer." Sung for dedication of Calhoun Monument, 41 May 1856. Dedicated to Miss S.F. Elmore of SC		Charleston: Cole

625	Massa's in de cold ground, 5th ed.	S.C. Foster	To Etta / from / May [date is too faint to read]	NY: Firth, Pond & Co.
626	My old Kentucky home, good night	S.C. Foster	To Etta / from / May 1853	NY: Firth, Pond & Co.
655	[piano score, AM with trio section in Am]		"H.A. Aiken."	
656	La Siciliana Ballo Marzionale		"Henrietta A. Aiken." MS, Venice May 15 1848, easy piano solo; sewn, 3 ruled blank pages at the end; ink blotches; no clefs after p. 1	
662	Kalkbrenner's Exercises for the Piano Forte #3	F. Kalkbrenner	Mlle H.A. Aiken	
663	Kalkbrenner's Exercises for the Piano Forte #1	F. Kalkbrenner	Mlle H.A. Aiken	
664	Kalkbrenner's Exercises for the Piano Forte #2	F. Kalkbrenner	Mlle H.A. Aiken	
667a	Souvenir de Charleston	Marie Siegling	Dedicated to Harriet Aiken. Some markings in pencil	
667b	Souvenir de Charleston	Marie Siegling	Dedicated to Harriet Aiken. Has original green cover	

Notes

1. Various copies, different publishes. Duke has. LOC M1 .A15 vol. 9 Case; M1 .A13 L
2. SMS 582c is the same. SMS 582d is the same and is inscribed by the composer "To Miss Henrietta Aiken with the respects of the Composer."

including those of the owners' extended family, came to the museum in Frances Dill Rhett's bequest. Because of the way the sheet music ended up in the museum, almost all of the pieces between SMS 241 and SMS 667b have some association with members of the Lowndes or Rhett families, if they did not belong to Henrietta.

Clues to identifying which music belonged to Henrietta exist in the bequest's physical state. The music falls into groups, some of which are plainer than others. Most of Henrietta's piano music appears between SMS 241 and SMS 253 and then after SMS 629. Other clusters also seem to be how the music was kept for decades. For example, SMS 359 through SMS 396 include pieces with "H. A. Aiken" or something similar written on them.[15] It is likely that the pieces without such indication between these numbers belonged to her as well. The works that make the best case for being Henrietta's are listed in table 6.2.[16] A note of caution is needed concerning the dating of materials. Many of these works do not have publication dates or the dates when she acquired them, although some do. For these, circumstantial evidence assists in assigning approximate dates when Henrietta used them.

Henrietta was an accomplished musician, both as a pianist and as a vocalist, but she may have shone brighter as a singer, as indicated by the fact that an overwhelming percentage of her surviving music is for voice. What remains of her piano music is largely pedagogical—which further suggests that some of her music is missing.[17] Moreover, all of the piano music dates from before 1858.

Table 6.2. Pieces that likely belonged to Henrietta Aiken, now in the Charleston Museum

SMS	Title	Composer	Inscription	Date	Notes
250	Rouge et noire	Gaston de Lille			Mayence: Schott. Sold NY: Breusing. *Romance*
251	Six Romances sans paroles	É. Prudent		[1856]	Paris: Ledentu. *Romance*
350	Cavatina nell'Opera L'Adelia (Me perduta!)	G. Donizetti; arr., [Altrocchi]			MS. (See Appendix B) *L'Adelia*
351	Le Pré aux Clercs	L. Hérold	[premiered same time as Les Huguenots, both have Le Pré aux Clercs]	[1833–35]	Paris: Troupenas
353	Romanza nell'Opera Il templario	Nicolai [Isouard]; arr., [Altrocchi]			MS. (See Appendix B) *Il templario*
356	Collezione complete della canzoncine nazionale Napoletane (Santa Lucia)				McCord has same edition. Italian.
357	Air a la Tyrolienne	J. Hummel			Sold: Willig's Musical Repository, London Edition
362	Cavatina nell'Opera Semiramide per Piano Forte	G. Rossini, arr. Bagioli			
393	The winds that waft my sighs to thee	W.V. Wallace		1856	
396	Miserere nell'Opera Il trovatore di G. Verdi	G. Verdi; arr., [Altrocchi]		1853	MS. (See Appendix B) *Il trovatore*
402	Cavatina nell'Opera Maria Padilla	G. Donizetti; arr., [Altrocchi]		1841	MS. (See Appendix B) *Maria Padilla*

Table 6.2. Pieces that likely belonged to Henrietta Aiken, now in the Charleston Museum (*continued*)

SMS	Title	Composer	Inscription	Date	Notes
406	Barcarole del Maestro Mercadante	S. Mercadante; arr., [Altrocchi]			MS. (See Appendix B)
407	Barcarole del Maestro Donizetti	G. Donizetti; arr., [Altrocchi]			MS. (See Appendix B)
412	Romanza nell'Opera la Regina di Cipro, Halèvy	Halèvy; arr., [Altrocchi]			MS. (See Appendix B) *La Regina di Cipro*
413	Aria nell'Opera i due Figaro, Mercadante	S. Mercadante; arr., [Altrocchi]			MS. (See Appendix B) *I due Figaro*
419	In the morning by the bright light	James A. Bland		1879	Charleston: Gill [cover has two African-Americans]
426	Gems of German Song: Good night, farewell, no. 32	F. Kücken		1861	
427	Ah! mon fils / Le Prophète arioso	G. Meyerbeer			Paris: Brandus. Sold NY: Breusing
428	Les feuilles mortes!	Louis Abade			Mayence: Schott. Sold NY: Breusing
432	Salut à la France / Fille du Regiment	G. Donizetti		1845	NY: Firth, Hall & Pond
436	Mon ange / Melodie für alto, baritone, bass	H. Esser		[1845]	Mayence: Schott. Sold NY: Scharfenberg & Luis [Paris: Richault]
438	Tout pour toi! (Alles für Dich!)	L. Puget		[1839]	Mayence et Anvers: Schott. Sold Baltimore: C.F. Hoyer [1839 and 1840 by Meissonnier]

439	Je crois en toi (Ich glaube an dich)	L. Puget			Mayence et Anvers: Schott. Sold NY: C.F. Hoyer [several editions, none by Schott]
440	Veux-tu mon nom	F. Masini			Mayence: Schott. Sold NY: Scharfenberg & Luis
442	Would we'd never met	P. Basvecchi			NY: Firth, Pond & Co. "Sung by Mad^lle Teresa Parodi"
448	Cavatina nell'Opera i Capaleti, e Montecchi [sic], Bellini	V. Bellini; arr., [Altrocchi]			MS. (See Appendix B) *I Capuleti e i Montecchi*
449	Scena e Romanza nell'Opera i Capaleti, e Montecchi [sic], Bellini	V. Bellini; arr., [Altrocchi]			MS. (See Appendix B) *I Capuleti e i Montecchi*
450	Je veux	L. Puget		[ca. 1840]	Mayence et Anvers: Schott
452	Consider the lilies	R. Topliff			NY: Hewitt & Jaques
453	La mouette de Saint Marcou	Paul Henrion		[1850s]	Mayence: Schott. Sold NY: Scharfenberg & Luis
454	Little robin tell kitty I'm coming	Geo. W. Persley		[?after 1865]	Cleveland: Brainard & Sons. Sold Charleston: Gill & Son
456	Der Wanderer	F. Schubert	Hillseide, September 13th 59		MS. German with English underneath. Transposed to C minor (from C# minor)
457	Collection of operatic songs & ballads: Ever of the[e]	G. Linley			Charleston: Cole. No music
458	La Zingara / Ballata	G. Donizetti		1858	Paris: Schonenberger, and stamp. *La Zingara*

Table 6.2. Pieces that likely belonged to Henrietta Aiken, now in the Charleston Museum (*continued*)

SMS	Title	Composer	Inscription	Date	Notes
459	Mon amour – Ton coeur à moi	?Leonar			MS, in French on blue paper, bass clef for voice
461	Homeward love, homeward	G. Rossini			NY: Dubois & Stodart
462	Le lac: Mèditation poëtique / Der See eine Abend empfindung	L. Niedermeyer		[ca. 1840]	[Schott] Pacini published. French on top of German. "Aurora no. 95" at the bottom of the first page
463	The tribute of a tear	Jos. Philip Knight	Wm Ogilby [ink] see 479[1]		London: Charles Ollivier, 41 Old Bond St. (there from 1838 until death in 1878)
466	L'anima nutrita dal dolre / Anacreontica	Angelo Ciccarelli			Mainz, Antwerp, Brussels: Schott's Söhnen. Sold NY: C.F. Hoyer
467	Songs and duets by Handel: Angels ever bright and fair	G. Handel			Boston: Ditson. Sold NY: Breusing. *Theodora*
476	The nightingale (Oh, summer morn) / Jenny Lind	G. Meyerbeer		1850	NY: Vanderbeck, and stamp. Sold Charleston: Cole
478	Fortune! Queen of joys o'er flowing!	G. Meyerbeer			NY: Dubois & Stodart. *Robert le Diable*
479	Oh! The merry days	C[harles] S. W[hitmore]	Wm Ogilby [see 463]		London: Willis & Co. and Plymouth: P.E. Rowe
481	Vocal Beauties from the opera I Puritani	V. Bellini			NY: Hall & Son. *I Puritani*
483	*Flowers of Italian* / Plighted faith! (O luce quest'anima)	G. Donizetti		1857	Boston: Ditson. *Linda di Chamounix*
485	*Gems from German:* First violet	F. Mendelssohn			Boston: Ditson

502	Aria nell'Opera Saffo, Pacini	G. Pacini; arr., [Altrocchi]		MS. (See Appendix B) *Saffo*
503	Cavatina nell'Opera Gemma di Vergey, Donizetti	G. Donizetti; arr., [Altrocchi]		MS. (See Appendix B) *Gemma di Vergy*
557	To thee my God, to thee I call	P.O. Basvecchi	1857	NY: Firth, Pond & Co.
563	Une fleur pour réponse	F. Masini	[1847; US editions 1849]	Mayence: Schott. Sold NY: Scharfenberg & Luis
564	In tears I pine for thee (La mia Letizia infandere)	G. Verdi	[?1840]	Boston: Ditson. *I Lombardi*
565	Adieu faviland	W.V. Wallace	1847	NY: Firth & Hall. Matilda
567	Barcarola nell'Opera Marino Falliero, Donizetti	G. Donizetti; arr., [Altrocchi]		MS. (See Appendix B) *Marino Faliero*
570	La fille de l'exilé (Du tochter des Verbannten) / Scène	F. Burgmüller	[ca. 1840]	Mayence: Schott. Sold NY: Breusing
571	Petite fleur des bois / Chansonnette	F. Masini	[ca. 1820]	Mayence: Schott. Sold NY: Scharfenberg & Luis
572	[Helas!] Le verras-tu jamais	August Panseron[2]	[ca. 1820]	Paris: Petit. Paris: Letitz, stamp
573	*Semiramide:* Serbami ognor si frato	G. Rossini		Paris: Pacini. J.F. Sold Habana: Edelmann. Duet, Italian only
576	Au revoir Louise / Romance	A. Panseron		Philadelphia: Fiot, Meignen & Co.
577	L'Attente (Why com'st thou not)	Leo. Meignen	[before 1839 when Skinner married]	Philadelphia: Fiot, Meignen & Co. Sold Philadelphia: Oates. Dedicated to Miss P. Skinner of North Carolina

Table 6.2. Pieces that likely belonged to Henrietta Aiken, now in the Charleston Museum (*continued*)

SMS	Title	Composer	Inscription	Date	Notes
578	Son nom!	L. Puget			Mayence et Anvers: Schott. Sold NY: C.F. Hoyer
579	Vivi tu, te ne scongiuro	G. Donizetti			Philadelphia: Fiot, Meignen & Co. *Anna Bolena*
580	Comin' thro' the rye as sung by Jenny Lind				Baltimore: Benteen; NO: Mayo
581	J'ai cru le revoir	A. Panseron[3]			Paris: Petit
585	Ma mère et mes amours	L. Puget		[1838]	Paris: Lemoine
586	*A.F. Lindblad's Schwedische Lieder*				Hamburg and Leipzig: Schuberth u. Co. Sold NY: Kerksig & Breusing
587	The grave of Bonaparte	L. Heath		184[?]	Boston: Ditson
588	Italy / 3 Favorite Airs arranged in Duetts / Lucia di Lammermoor, La sonnambula, il Bravo	C.T. Brunner		[?1844–62]	Philadelphia: Fiot. Sold Charleston: Zogbaum. *Lucia di Lammermoor, La sonnambula, Il Bravo*
601	Di gemme de stele /Romanza	Sig. Carlo Salvioni			NY: Allen R. Jolli
603	Lungi del caro ben / La spoca fedele	G. Pacini		[1827]	
604	Una voce al cor	Donizetti, arr. Pacini			*Gemma di Vergy*
611	*Collection Complète des Lieder du Schubert:* Le roi des Aulnes	F. Schubert			Paris: Schonenberger. Sold NY: Scharfenberg & Luis

612	*Fifty Lessons in Singing for the Middle Register of the Voice*	J. Concone			Philadelphia: J. E. Gould & Co., Successors to Fiot. In French and English
615	L'Automne (Der Herbst)	L. Niedermeyer		[ca. 1840]	Mayence et Anvers: Schott. Sold NY: Breusing
616	*Gems of German Song with English Words:* Wanderer	F. Schubert			Boston: Reed
624	Jeannette & Jeannot	Charles Glover			NY: Hall & Son. Sold Charleston: Zogbaum
628	Table Thematique De' Capuleti et i Montechi: Ne alcun ritorna / Scena ed Aria de Giulietta	V. Bellini			Paris: Richault; Habana: Edelmann. *I Capuleti e i Montecchi*
629	Potpourri élégants	Henri Cramer	Faint writing on the title page		Paris: Offenbach. Sold NY: Breusing
630	Matheline	Paul Henrion		[before 1850]	Paris: Colombier, and stamp

Notes

1. British consul in Charleston, has 1830 Diary in South Carolina Historical Society, Charleston. See Butler.

2. Lazare Carnot Hippolyte, *Revue encyclopedia on analyse raisonée des prod.* V. 52, p. 510, includes Panseron (some of these pieces), Pacini, Masini, Romagnesi.

3. Reviewed in Hippolyte-Lazare Carnot, Auguste Jullien, Pierre Leroux, Anselme Petetin *Revue encyclopedique ou analyse raisonnee des productions les plus remarquables dans la litterature, les sciences et les arts, par une reunion de membres de l'institut et d'autres hommes de lettres. Ann. 1819-1833*, V. 52 (Paris: Baudouin, 1831), 510.

CHAPTER 7

Henrietta's Earliest Music and First European Journey

Her parents' fondness for and experience with travel overseas, combined with elite Charlestonians' penchant for European culture, resulted in a journey to Europe when Henrietta was eleven years old (1847). Passport and immigration records reveal that William, Harriet, and Henrietta Aiken returned from Europe in 1848, traveling directly from Le Havre to New York. This was a popular route, as was the alternative of stopping off in Liverpool and making one's way to the Continent via London. William's mother, Henrietta Wyatt Aiken (b. 1785), traveled with them. She died in Paris on 7 September 1848, while the family was still there. The Aikens arrived back in New York City on 26 October, having sailed from Le Havre via Southampton.

Prior to their journey, William Aiken had requested letters of introduction from John C. Calhoun, and these reflect the circles within which the South Carolinians moved. William specifically requested introductions to Sir Robert Peel, the former prime minister, and Richard Cobden, an influential manufacturer and liberal MP, in London; and Marshall Soult, François Guizot, and Adolphe Thiers in Paris.[1] The three Frenchmen had participated actively in governmental affairs in Paris, as prime minister, ambassador to London, and other positions of consequence. The Aikens may have developed relationships with these men or their acquaintances, which presumably brought them elevated status above mere tourists.

According to Gabriel Manigault, once in Paris the Aikens took an apartment on rue Castiglion, near the Jardin des Tuileries in the first arrondissement, and socialized with other Charlestonians, particularly members of the Manigault and Cheves families, until at least February 1848. The family found this residence too noisy and opted for a "perfectly quiet place" on rue St. Dominique, Faubourg Saint-Germain, seventh arrondissement, near the Chamber of Deputies. Faubourg Saint-Germain was a favorite neighborhood of the French nobility, and by establishing themselves there, the Aikens clearly defined the social group with which they identified. The Aikens moved into the basement level of the Hôtel de la Rochefoucauld, and they eventually rented out two entire floors for one thousand francs per month.[2] Manigault's description depicted the Aiken family's desire not only to see French culture firsthand but also to immerse themselves in it: "It was a typical residence of the French nobility under the old régime, being 'entre cour et jardin'; which means a great deal, as indicating wealth and the elbow room that a distinguished title required, when the noble had position very near to royalty."[3] That a Manigault would write about the Aikens' social positioning in such a way indicates that he understood precisely what they were doing. They wished to be seen not as typical Americans on the grand tour but rather as being as close to Parisian as was possible for these South Carolinians.

This attitude is confirmed by remarks made by Harriet during some of the upheavals of 1848. The family lived in Paris during the revolution that ended the Orleans monarchy in February of that year. While William was "enthusiastic about a new French republic," Harriet undoubtedly was not. Gabriel Manigault mentioned that Harriet, annoyed with having to walk through and around the barricades erected throughout the city, remarked "freely" and "emphatically" that she "had not come to Paris to live under a republic. She had enough of that sort of thing at home."[4] Harriet unmistakably did not wish to reside in a place where people of different social classes were seen as equal. This remark speaks to the heart of Harriet's attraction to Europe. She sought to elevate her family's social station above that which was available in the United States. Since there was no aristocracy there, Harriet consciously aligned the Aiken family with French nobility, an action expressed most tangibly in their choices of residence.

Evidence for Henrietta's first trip to Europe can be found in books and music purchased while there. Before the journey her parents purchased books that suggest an extensive tour including Greece, Spain, Malta, and Turkey.[5] (See table 7.2.) They bought the necessary items for Paris too, such as William's copy of the popular *Galignani's New Paris Guide*.[6] He signed and dated this book 10 September 1847, adding "Paris." Henrietta's copy of Maria Edgeworth's *The Parent's Assistant; or, Stories for Children* is noteworthy because it includes her name and "Cheltenham / 1847" inside. This is the only evidence that the family was in Cheltenham, a spa town in the English Cotswolds. Other books for Henrietta include a charming and beautifully bound set of children's stories, *Le livre des enfants*, which are inscribed "Henrietta A. Aiken" and "Paris / Octobre 1848." This is Harriet's handwriting, and the French spelling of the month typifies her desire to be seen as cosmopolitan, well traveled, and elite. William had similar tendencies, writing "Guillaume" for his name in one of his earlier books. Henrietta's *Nouveau dictionnaire portative Anglais-Français* includes terms used in the

Table 7.2. Books from the Aikens' 1847–48 journey

Title	Inscription	Date	Notes
WILLIAM AND HARRIET:			
Galignani's New Paris Guide	William Aiken / Paris / Sept. 10th 1847	1845	
Hand-Book for Travellers in the Ionian Islands, Greece, Turkey, Asia Minor, and Constantinople, Being a Guide to The Principal Routes in Those Countries, including A Description of Malta; with Maxims and Hints for the Travellers in the East, with Index Maps and Plans	William Aiken / 1846	1840	London
Incidents of Travel in Greece, Turkey, Russia, and Poland, with a Map and Engravings, 2 vols.	H.L. Aiken	1838	NY
Handbook for Travellers in Switzerland and the Alps of Savoy and Piedmont	William Aiken / Paris – July / 1848	1846	London
Le Menétrier, ou une Insurrection en Suisse, 4 vols	Harriet L. Aiken / Paris / Octobre 1848		Henry Zschokke
La Presbytère, 2 vols.	signed Harriet L. Aiken / Paris / Octobre 1848	1846	R. Töppfer, Paris
Set of Dumas volumes, including *Le Comte de Monte Cristo*	Harriet L. Aiken / Paris / Octobre 1848		
HENRIETTA:			
Dictionnaire universel d'histoire et de géographie	Mlle Henrietta A. Aiken / Paris / 18 October 1848	1847	Paris

Leçons de mythologie	Mlle. H.A. Aiken / Paris / 18 Octobre 1848		Includes fold-out images of Greek goddesses
Le livre des enfants, 4 vols	Henrietta A. Aiken; two have "Paris / Octobre 1848"	1837	Paris. Drawings in red crayon in the back of one, beautiful covers
Nouveau dictionnaire portative Anglais-Français	Henrietta A. Aiken / Paris / Oct. 28th 1847	1844	Paris
The Parent's Assistant; of, Stories for Children by Maria Edgeworth	Henrietta A. Aiken / Cheltenham / 1847	1845	London
Matched set including: *Le Vicaire Wakefield*, Charles Nodieu; *Esquisses Historiques*, Lévi; *Contes offerts aux enfants de France*, 2 vols	Henrietta A. Aiken / Paris / Octobre 1848 [all signed thus]	1843–44	Brussels
Matched set of eleven volumes by L'Abbé Gaultier (including *Exercises gradués sur la Composition française*, 1: Cahier de l'élève; *Leçons d'Arithmétique; Nouveau Guide de Conversations Modernes en français et en Italien; Grammaire française; Géographie*, etc.)	Mlle H.A. Aiken / Paris / 18 Octobre 1848	1838	Paris

arts and sciences, special vocabulary used in railways and other machines, geography, and English proverbs—all of which would have assisted her in maneuvering around Paris. It must have been an early purchase, because in addition to her name and the place, it is inscribed "Oct. 28th 1847."[7]

The Charleston Library Society now holds eleven books by L'Abbé Gaultier (1746–1818) that are inscribed with Henrietta's name and have matching bindings.[8] These address subjects such as geography, arithmetic, history, and French grammar and conversation. Henrietta used them, for several have markings befitting a student's preparation. In *Géographie,* Henrietta made notations concerning the names of mountain ranges, volcanoes, and European rivers. In her *Grammaire française* she marked issues of French grammar on pages 35 and 236–37. In the back of one of the history volumes, she made a list of the queens of France. These suggest that she was not only touring Paris but studying there as well. Her tutors probably included a music teacher, but no evidence confirms this.

Three of Henrietta's books contain the specific date 18 October 1848 and are marked "Paris." As the family arrived back in New York on the 26th and the sea voyage took at least ten days, the date 18 October remains a puzzle. Henrietta's other books suggest that she was undertaking some sort of education while the family was in France, and if she were, why were the books dated on the last possible (even improbable) date? Possibly her mother marked them as they were leaving as a sort of memento. That Harriet mistook dates can be found in other items, discussed below, so she may have simply written the wrong date here. Nonetheless, the books in question are definitely of Parisian or Belgian origin and may have been purchased before October 1848, possibly even 1847. An alternative explanation may be that Harriet intended them to be used in Henrietta's education once they arrived back in Charleston. Being "real" French books, they would have elevated Henrietta's study of the language and culture over that of her Charleston acquaintances.

One curious selection among Henrietta's books from this period is Oliver Goldsmith's *The Vicar of Wakefield* (1761–62, published 1766) in a French translation. This outdated novel had been extremely popular in the previous century, but in the middle of the nineteenth century something more modern could be expected. As a possible explanation, *The Vicar of Wakefield* may have been her mother's choice, a suggestion made plausible by several of Henrietta's music pieces that were old-fashioned as well and appear to have been chosen by Harriet.[9] Another Charleston acquaintance of the Aikens who visited while in Paris was Dr. Lingard Frampton, William's cousin, who was present at the Columbia music club described by Helie (above). At some point Lingard gave Henrietta a copy of Kücken's "Drift My Back," a duet for soprano and contralto (SMS 526), and the same composer's "The Two Nightingales / The Swallows' Farewell" (SMS 583). Frampton could have presented these to Henrietta in 1848, but since they are in English he most likely offered them to her back in Charleston, or at least in the United States.

The only piece of music that can be definitively associated with this voyage is "La Siciliana Ballo Nazionale / Eseguito delli Sig. F. Cerito e S. Leone" (SMS 656). It bears the inscription "Henrietta A. Aiken. Venice May 15th 1848, Florian." "La Siciliana" is also the earliest work for solo piano that is not intended as pedagogy in Henrietta's sheet music. She owned it in manuscript form, which was a rather unusual medium for the 1840s. The manuscript consists of two folios sewn together in the middle. Three blank-ruled pages remain at the end. The treble and bass clefs appear only on the first page, a common practice exhibited in several manuscripts in the Charleston Museum.

Three different hands copied this manuscript. Hand 1 wrote the title with what looks like the handwriting of a professional musician; it could have been that of a copyist, composer, or instructor. Hand 2 wrote "Florian" and "Venice // May 15 1848." It appears that hand 1 copied the music for hand 2, and the seller or the person who gave it to Henrietta wrote the date and "Florian" on it. "Florian" might have a connection with Caffé Florian in St. Mark's Square, Venice, although any such connection remains a mystery. Hand 3 is Henrietta's; she added her name twice at the top of the title page.

The piece is an easy piano solo in compound meter, befitting a Siciliana, but there is much more to its story. Fanny Cerito (1817–1909) was a famous dancer whom nineteenth-century critics ranked with Fanny Essler and Marie Taglioni, two dancers whose names are more familiar today.[10] She married Arthur Saint-Léon—also a dancer and named on the cover of SMS 656 "S. Leone"—in 1845 and remained with him for six years, which coincides with the date of 1848 for Henrietta's copy of "La Siciliana, Ballo Nazionale." Cerito's primary engagements were with Her Majesty's Theatre in London in the 1840s, but she made her way back to the Teatro La Fenice in Venice in 1848.[11] On 6 January 1848 at Teatro La Fenice, Cerito famously danced in a spectacle, called *La Siciliana,* designed to inflame anti-Austrian and pro-Sicilian fervor. The performance had its desired effect, and Austrian officials issued notice that all merchants were to cease making and selling patriotic—Sicilian—goods.[12] This political directive explains why Henrietta's copy of "La Siciliana, Ballo Nazionale" exists in manuscript form: music printers were under orders not to print inflammatory materials. The Aikens' awareness of the potential danger of owning such a piece is unknown.

This is not the only controversial sheet music to have political significance regarding Italian unification efforts in the collections discussed here, but it would be wrong to read too much into their presence in southern binder's volumes since none of the women expressed an opinion about the political situation in Italy, except annoyance at having to leave unexpectedly.[13] This manuscript suggests that the Aikens, Henrietta included, were in Venice in 1848, even though the other evidence points only to Paris on this journey. Regrettably, no other music in her collection has concrete European associations with this date. A few other items might belong to this period, but Henrietta acquired some of them while in Paris.

One of the earliest datable print items in Henrietta's collection is SMB 219, her copy of the *Encyclopédie du pianiste compositeur, dédiée à J. Cramer par J. Zimmerman.*[14] This Parisian publication has two dates: the publication date of 1832 on the cover and the dedication date 1840 on the inside. It contains a lithographed image of Zimmerman, "Professeur au Conservatoire de Musique." Pierre-Joseph-Guillaume Zimmerman (1785–1853) was a famous pianist and teacher whose salon was renowned for its music, which included salon operas.[15] At this salon, which was located in an artistic center of Paris nicknamed "cité d'Orléans," Zimmerman and his wife regularly featured opera stars and pianists, including Clara Schumann. Whether Harriet knew of his salon from her earlier journey to Paris or learned about it at this time or at all is unknown.[16] Several celebrated pianists studied with Zimmerman, and his reputation would have been familiar to Americans visiting Paris. Whether they were lucky enough to have been invited to the salon remains yet another mystery, but it is unlikely that they would have had the connections that brought them into the artistic community. The Aikens' tastes ran in a decidedly different direction, evinced by their choices in housing—for example in Saint-Germain—while in Paris. Had they asked about music, however, Zimmerman's name likely would have been mentioned.

The *Encyclopédie du pianiste* is a graduated piano tutorial entirely in French, and Henrietta obtained her copy in Paris. Because of its methodological trajectory—from the most basic rudiments of music to significantly more difficult exercises—it might have been one of her first books of music. As such, it is quite possible that she obtained it while there in the 1840s. Zimmerman provided three parts that take the pupil from the first lessons in piano study to reading open score, figured bass, and difficult technical exercises. Henrietta owned the complete set. Part 1 begins with the basics, such as note names, including solfège, and intervals. It also illustrates how to read music with C clefs, something rarely encountered by young women such as Henrietta, because music published for piano and voice in the United States used either treble (G) or bass (F) clefs, not the C clefs demonstrated here. The inclusion of C clefs might be significant because several manuscripts of vocal exercises in the Charleston Museum collection are written in C clefs, and these may have belonged to Henrietta.[17] After explanations of scales, rhythm and meter, and the placement of notes on the keyboard, Zimmerman provided exercises for five fingers, much like those of piano tutorials today.

Zimmerman required the player to progress quickly. The trill is introduced on page 9, which seems early by today's standards, as are the examples of double trills in a single hand in thirds and fourths on page 10.[18] Similarly, after the introduction of chromatic scales and fingerings, the pianist moves to playing them in thirds, sixths, and tenths. Then octave scales follow. These types of exercises demonstrate that this is not a piano tutorial for the slower student. Its requirements demand that the pupil progress rapidly through technically challenging aspects of piano performance.

Zimmerman took his examples from composers whose works are well known today, but the repertory includes some surprises. The first melody (page 27), for example, is from Schubert's "Die Forelle," transposed here to C major. Isolated settings of songs by Schubert exist in some southern binder's volumes, but these are almost invariably based on "Der Erlkönig" or "Ständchen," not "Die Forelle." Other arrangements of popular tunes follow, and these typify what Henrietta's Charleston contemporaries would have played. "Thême de Norma" by Bellini is used to practice expression, a waltz by Strauss for articulation. A passage from Mozart's *Magic Flute* has the student play in a new key, G major, and introduces the concept of two notes played simultaneously in the same hand. Familiar opera melodies by Rossini—from *Semiramide, La cenerentola, Zelmire,* and *Tancredi*—and from *Der Freischütz* by Weber appear as well. Indeed, the collection's attraction probably lay in its use of well-known opera pieces, extending to recent works by Boieldieu and even Meyerbeer's *Les Huguenots,* which had debuted in Paris in 1836.

Part 2 is significantly more difficult than part 1, with numerous exercises intended to increase facility and independence of fingers. Studies by Beethoven and Robert Schumann can be found alongside those of famous nineteenth-century pedagogues such as Kalkbrenner, Cramer, Bertini, Czerny, and Clementi. Short essays toward the end of the part instruct the student in touch, pedaling, and transposition—by substituting the aforementioned C clefs. Zimmerman recommended four hours of practice a day and provided a schedule for how to spend the practice time (page 68). This section of part 2 concludes with advice on how to choose "professeurs" for piano instruction.

Curiously, Zimmerman drew upon Beethoven's piano music for several examples. These examples do not reference the music that most young women would have known, although they may have been familiar with Beethoven's name from music journals. Zimmerman relied on the second movement of Beethoven's Seventh Symphony to teach the pupil how to bring out a melody while playing other notes in the same hand. He noted that playing arpeggios as ornaments is necessary in both Beethoven and especially Chopin, and he used Beethoven's *Sonata pathétique* (op. 13, first movement) in a footnote during his discussion of taste. Here he demonstrated how to change music that requires more pitches than the player might have available on a given keyboard, which reminds us that before the mid-nineteenth-century pianos were available with different numbers of keys.[19]

Zimmerman prized the symphonies of Beethoven, Haydn, and Mozart, as well as a few others, for duets.[20] Audiences in Paris readily took to Beethoven's symphonies in the 1830s and 1840s, as the painter Delacroix remarked to the writer George Sand that "he [Beethoven] is the man of our time."[21] The same cannot be said for the American South. Binder's volumes and graduation recital programs in southern women's schools did not include symphonic works such as these. They appeared in the South only after the Civil War, and Henrietta would not have encountered them at home until that time.[22]

The second section of part 2 includes an interesting assortment of pieces, such as an extract from Beethoven's First Piano Concerto on page 22. The volume ends with a collection of pieces for study, beginning with a nocturne by Zimmerman that is complete with an example of how a pupil might ornament the right hand.[23] Other etudes follow, with authors as diverse as Alkan, Ravina, and Czerny. Zimmerman then introduces students to fugues, beginning with "Fugue du chat" (K. 30) by Domenico Scarlatti, composed in 1739. As with other composers encountered in this collection, Scarlatti is a popular choice today but was not an option in southern publications of this period. Similarly, the inclusion of the "Fugue du Requiem de Mozart," the allegro double fugue (Kyrie eleison/Christe eleison) from the composer's famous Requiem Mass, distinguishes this piano tutorial. Henrietta's South Carolinian contemporaries did not play music by Scarlatti, or from Mozart's *Requiem,* or fugues. Scarlatti's music was essentially unknown, and as a genre, the fugue belonged to a more scientific, and less frequently encountered, music study.[24]

There is no evidence of use in this book, but that does not necessarily mean that Henrietta did not play the pieces. In the past, musicologists have suggested that music could have been purchased for the sole purpose of impressing visitors with the musical taste and skill of the inhabitants, without the owners actually being able to play the music. Their chief evidence for this practice is a lack of marking in the scores. However, most musicians own music that they read from but do not write in, and Henrietta almost certainly would have done the same.

In his tutorial, part 2, page 62, Zimmerman listed the "auteurs classics" that pianists should know: Handel, J. S. and C. P. E. Bach, Domenico and Alessandro Scarlatti, Haydn, Mozart, Beethoven, Weber, Clementi, Dussek, Johann Baptist

Cramer, Hummel, and John Field, followed by "etc." He mentioned learning duos (by which he meant sonatas), trios, quartets, and quintets by Beethoven, Mozart, and Mendelssohn, among others. He warned the student that Bach's fugues, Alkan's third book of capriccios, and various pieces by Chopin and Liszt challenge pianists the most. These recommendations are noteworthy because, at the time Henrietta owned this book, very little piano music by most of these composers was available in the United States. As such, Zimmerman's tutorial represented something from Europe and a different standard from what young women played in Charleston. Tellingly, in American publications that advertised available piano instruction books, such as the *American Publishers' Circular and Literary Gazette,* Zimmerman was not to be found.[25] This further marks Henrietta's use of his piano method as special, foreign, and—most importantly—French.

Both the repertory presented for practice and the range of difficulty seen in Zimmerman's piano tutorial surpass those used by American girls who studied piano during the 1840s and 1850s. *J. B. Cramer's Instructions for the Pianoforte* and Henri Bertini's *Progressive and Complete Method for the Piano-Forte,* both in various American editions, were popular choices and provide illuminating comparisons with the books purchased for Henrietta's piano study.[26] Johann Baptist Cramer (1771–1858) was a performer, composer, and pedagogue who spent much of his life in London. He began publishing piano methods as early as 1804 and continued through his *New Practical School,* op. 100, of 1844. American editions of his "instructions," given several different titles, were published by Dubois in New York (1820s), Firth & Hall in New York (around 1846), Fiot in Philadelphia (1840s), and Ditson in Boston (1859?). *J. B. Cramer's Instructions for the Pianoforte* can be found in southern collections, such as that once owned by Eliza Fisk Harwood Skinner of Williamsburg, Virginia.[27] Cramer did not include C clefs in his explanation of the notes, clefs, and keys. The last piece in his book is "Scotch Air: She Rose and Let Me In." Indeed, many of his pieces for playing are short, simple versions of popular tunes, which mirror the repertory seen in most binder's volumes of the period.

Bertini's *Progressive and Complete Method for the Piano-Forte* was perhaps the most popular piano instruction book in the United States during the mid–nineteenth century, and almost every catalog from a southern girls' school or local music seller included it.[28] American editions from the 1840s through the end of the century can be found. While Bertini's book covers much more technique than does Cramer's, it does not use music by other composers for practice pieces. Henrietta's use of Zimmerman's tutorial instead of Cramer's or Bertini's distinguishes her musical training from that of her contemporaries.

Zimmerman's method may not be the earliest piano music that survives in Henrietta's collection. An earlier publication is *Kalkbrenner's Exercises for the*

Piano Forte, Perfected by C. Thibault, volumes 1–3 (SMS 662–664, published in New York by J. L. Hewitt at 137 Broadway). During the 1830s Kalkbrenner toured frequently as a pianist and also became a partner in piano manufacturing with Pleyel. All three volumes are marked "Mlle H. A. Aiken," possibly by her teacher. They are unusual because they were developed to be used with Kalkbrenner's *guide-mains* (hand-guides), which resembled Johann Bernhard Logier's Chiroplast, another infamous invention of the early nineteenth century. This mechanism forced the hands to remain in a "correct" position while playing the piano. The composer Camille Saint-Saëns described it: "This invention consisted of a rod placed in front of the keyboard. The forearm rested on this rod in such a way that all muscular action save that of the hand was suppressed. This system is excellent for teaching the young pianist how to play pieces written for the harpsichord or the first pianofortes where the keys responded to slight pressure; but it is inadequate for modern works and instruments."[29] Kalkbrenner and Logier became partners in marketing these devices for young pianists at an academy in London.[30]

Nothing indicates that Henrietta used one of these devices, but that she owned these three volumes written expressly for its use is suggestive. Charles Thibault (1792–ca. 1853), editor of the American version of Kalkbrenner's work, was active in New York City between 1818 and 1850. Born in Nantes, France, Thibault published piano music in both the United States and Europe.[31] This edition distinguishes Kalkbrenner's hand-guide from the Chiroplast of Logier: the former supported the arm—"recommended for persons of delicate constitution" and "those who live in the Country without a teacher nearby"—whereas the Chiroplast merely helped one "learn the notes," after which the device was removed.[32] It is not a stretch to imagine that the southern woman's presumed "delicate constitution" was a selling point to families such as the Aikens. When Henrietta acquired it is unknown, but her edition is an American one. Like Zimmerman, Kalkbrenner figured among the featured pianists in Parisian salons when Harriet was in France during the 1830s, and she may have been the guiding force behind Henrietta's acquisition of Kalkbrenner's books.

Another work that Henrietta probably owned before 1850 is Marie Siegling's piano solo "Souvenir de Charleston," two copies of which exist in the Aiken-Rhett music collection (SMS 667a and 667b). One of these, SMS 667b, retains its original green cover, which is a rare feature for antebellum sheet music in general and Henrietta's collection specifically. The composer, a native of Charleston, dedicated the work to "Madame William Aiken De Charleston" in 1846. Her story further explicates women's musical lives in antebellum Charleston because she was a professional female musician—singer, composer, and teacher—who also participated in the cultural life of the city.

Marie Siegling

One of the copies of Marie Siegling's "Souvenir de Charleston" in the Charleston Museum might be a dedication copy—the one retaining its original green cover—given to Harriet, the dedicatee, and the other one used at the piano by Henrietta. SMS 667a has markings that suggest use, and more than likely Harriet would have received a copy of the work at about the time it was published. She may have played it then, but only one piano arrangement, Berton fils's "Air de maris garcons" in SMB 48, survives in her collection. A more likely candidate is Henrietta. The waltz typifies others from the period, beginning with an introduction based on arpeggios and elaborations on the dominant (G7) that set up the waltz proper. "Souvenir de Charleston" is an extended work consisting of seven pages of music that includes bravura flourishes typical of the era.

Marie (Mary) Regina Siegling Schuman-LeClerq (1824–1920) was the daughter of the most successful southern music merchant outside of New Orleans: her father was John Siegling, who ran a successful music store and publishing company in Charleston and Havana.[33] Marie's mother, Anna Mary Regina Schnierle (1805–96), was an accomplished musician who studied at the Moravian Seminary in Bethlehem, Pennsylvania.[34] The family's musical life in Charleston paralleled that of Harriet Lowndes and Henrietta Aiken, running simultaneously but in different social circles. While Harriet was learning the songs examined in part 2 of this book, Mary Schnierle was studying harp with Moravian instructors. Marie recorded in her *Memoirs of a Dowager* (1908) that her maternal grandfather sent a Broadwood piano from London to Charleston for her mother's (presumably musical) debut. Slightly older than Harriet, she married John Siegling in 1823. Both Harriet and Mary had musical daughters who traveled extensively but, again, in entirely different social circles.

Marie Siegling was both a performer and a composer in her own right. Her music studies included voice with Signor Gambatto, probably Alessandro Gambati, "an associate of Malibran" who had been a member of the Italian Opera in New York during the 1830s. He was also a brass player who taught in Charleston. She played the harp as well as sang and probably played the piano, since her publications are for piano solo. Marie traveled to New York City for "lessons," unspecified but probably voice, in 1842. Two years later she accompanied her father on a visit to his business in Cuba and sang a series of performances for which she was dubbed "Charleston's Jenny Lind." One notice for her debut stated, "A new candidate for musical honors, has appeared in Havana, a beautiful young countrywoman of ours, Miss Siegling, of Charleston. She lately made her *debut* in Lucia, in the 'Lucia di Lammermoor,' with the greatest applause. She is lauded as inferior only to artists like Malibran."[35] Almost twenty years old at this time, she seemed destined for a career as a professional singer. While in

Havana she visited a salon given by Countess Fernandina, a cousin of Countess Merlin in Paris.[36]

Harriet's own experience in Paris or with Parisian singers could have provided a model of the semiprofessional aristocratic musician such as Countess Merlin. Countess Merlin was one of the "amateurs of the musical aristocracy," and her name was the most frequently mentioned in French musical journals of the 1830s and 1840s.[37] An amateur musical aristocracy might have been the model for the type of social circle Harriet wished to implement in Charleston. Harriet might even have intended Henrietta to have a similar reputation in Charleston, and a connection between Marie Siegling and Countess Merlin could have held an attraction for her.

Later that same year, 1844, Marie went to Europe to study music, and while there she was exposed to musical circles that included prominent professional European musicians. For example, she remembered that she heard Liszt improvise in "a private circle" and attended the premieres of Wagner's *Tannhäuser* and *Lohengrin*. She also met Wagner and, through him, the foster brother of the Queen of Saxony, to whom she later dedicated a piano work, "Souvenir de la Saxe" (1849).[38] Returning to Charleston, Marie attempted to emulate the European salons she had visited by holding musicales in her home between 1848 and 1850. According to her *Memoirs of a Dowager,* these musicales included harps, pianos, violins, and singing, and they were popular in the city. Unfortunately, she did not record who performed or the type of music heard; however, the musicales probably featured a parlor repertory stylistically similar to her own publications. Many music teachers held such events, and they often featured their own students performing pieces. There is no indication that she introduced Charlestonians to the music of Liszt or any of the German composers she met.

"Souvenir de Charleston," dedicated to Harriet Lowndes Aiken, might have been an attempt by Marie Siegling to establish a relationship with the powerful Aiken family, perhaps capitalizing on an association with them to further her career as a music teacher in Charleston. Both the Aiken family and Marie were in town between 1848 and 1850. In her *Memoirs of a Dowager,* Marie hinted that she sought such connections but her actions were mitigated somewhat by her engagement to a German she had met while overseas—or at least that is how, in retrospect, she perceived her social isolation in the late 1840s. While in Europe in 1844, Marie met her future husband, Eduard Schuman LeClercq, but she returned to South Carolina before they married. She wrote that news of her engagement made her "very unwelcome" in Charleston homes. However, "as an eleve [*sic*] of [Manuel] Garcia," she gave lessons in his "world renowned method" and "made a great deal of money."[39] One of her students may have been Henrietta, whose copy of Garcia's *École de Garcia* exists as Charleston Museum SMS 606.

In *Bel Canto: A History of Vocal Pedagogy*, James Stark has claimed that Garcia was "one of those seminal historical figures whose career marked a watershed between the past and the future," and Garcia's fame as a voice teacher was such that in Charleston, Marie Siegling professed that she taught according to his method.[40] He took a post as professor of singing at the Paris Conservatoire in 1835, and his *Traité complet de L'Art du Chant* (complete, in two parts) first appeared in print in 1847. Henrietta owned his *École de Garcia / Traité complet de L'Art du Chant per Manuel Garcia fils, 1 Partie,* published in Mainz, Anvers, and Brussels by Schott in 1840. Her copy (SMS 606) is marked "Henrietta A. Aiken Charleston" and today consists only of the table of contents and foreword. Henrietta's copy is the first part only, which suggests that hers was printed after the method book had two distinct parts (1847).[41] The edition she owned was sold by proprietors in Mainz, Anvers, and Brussels (where the publisher owned stores); Paris (where Garcia provided them); and in London at the house of Cramer, Addison, and Beals. Henrietta's copy, however, came from Carl Breusing's music store at 701 Broadway, New York City, according to the bookseller's stamp on the front page. Breusing opened his establishment in 1848.[42] It is entirely possible that the Aikens purchased this book while in New York on their return from their first European journey, which would mean that the edition came to Breusing early. They could have bought it at another time, though, since they sailed from New York on three other occasions.

Direct connections between Henrietta and music teachers before 1857 do not survive. Marie Siegling may have been one, and she may have learned from the aforementioned Pauline Boudet, a Frenchwoman who was living with the family in 1850. The Aikens may have met her while in Europe in 1847–48 and hired her to be Henrietta's governess as a way to further surround the child with French culture. Pauline married in 1850 and left the Aiken family.[43]

CHAPTER 8

Henrietta's Music, 1850–1857

The Aiken family traveled again to Europe in 1850 and 1854. The exact date of their departure is unknown, but Harriet's mail had been forwarded to London by at least 5 July 1851. Garrett has proposed that the purpose of this journey was to see the Crystal Palace Exhibition, including Hiram Powers's *The Greek Slave*.[1] Ship passenger data reveal that William, Harriet, and Henrietta traveled with Harriet Randolph, who was a "servant" from South America, and Mary Lowndes on this journey and returned to New York from Liverpool on 25 October 1851.[2] Henrietta was fifteen at the time. Other evidence for Henrietta's participation in this venture is a book, *Nouveau dictionnaire portatif, Anglais–Français et Français–Anglais,* signed "H. A. Aiken / Paris / 1851," now in the Charleston Library Society collection. Moreover, it appears that Harriet deliberately planned for this expedition by buying *European Life and Manners* by Henry Colman (2 volumes), which she signed "Harriet L. Aiken / 1850."

Before the Aikens next sailed for Europe, Henrietta spent time in Washington, D.C., because her father had been elected to the U.S. Congress in 1851. Here she purchased *A Lady's Voyage round the World: A Selected Translation from the German of Ida Pfeiffer by Mrs. Percy Sinnett* (New York, 1852), signing it both "H. A. Aiken / Washington / 6 February 1852" and "Henrietta A. Aiken." Another item of hers associated with their time in this city is a single piece entitled "Carnival in Washington—Willard's Polka" (SMS 292) by Maurice Strakosch (1825–87), published in 1854. A note on the first page says that she received it from the "Misses Mallards." The image on the title page depicts the fashionable Willard's Hotel and Pennsylvania Avenue in Washington, D.C.[3]

The Aikens set sail for Europe again in 1854, as shown by SMB 19, a complete copy of *Échos* [sic] *de France,* a book of vocal music, marked "Henrietta A. Aiken / Paris / 1854." Henrietta obtained her copy from the publisher, G (Gustave-Alexandre) Flaxland at 4, place de la Madeleine, Paris. This location was near where the Aikens first lived in 1847 and was not far from the stylish Hôtel Meurice, where many Americans stayed. She signed "Henrietta A. Aiken" in the top right corner of the title page. Flaxland was a well-respected music-publishing house that specialized in vocal anthologies, and several southern women purchased music there, notably Henrietta and Louisa Rebecca McCord.

Henrietta's volume is the first in the series known as *Échos de France,* published in the mid–nineteenth century, and it is one of the few items that she had bound.[4] This curious book contains arias from the seventeenth century to the early nineteenth century but is primarily retrospective.[5] The earliest work in *Échos de France* belongs to Pierre Guédron, a composer and singer of the late sixteenth and early seventeenth centuries noted for his *airs de cour.* Other notable pieces include Lully's "Bois épais" and "Suivons l'amour" from the 1684 *Amadis* and his "Le héros que j'attends" from *Alceste* (1674); and Rameau's "Arrachez de mon coeur" from *Dardanus* (1739) and "A l'amour rendez les armes" from his first opera, *Hippolite et Aricie* (1733). These two composers represented the epitome of early French opera, but their works do not exist in other Charlestonians' binder's volumes. Even in France their music was rare in the nineteenth century, certainly in the 1850s.[6] Other composers whose music figures in *Échos de France* include Dalayrac, Grétry, Gluck, Paër, Piccini, Sacchini, Martini, Garat, Monsigny, Méhul, Gaveaux, and Gail. Most of these names appear in Harriet's binder's volumes and belong properly to the 1820s.

The more modern opera excerpts by Dalayrac, Grétry, Monsigny, and Méhul in *Échos de France* can occasionally be found in some other collections from the antebellum South. The latest pieces in *Échos de France* are by Mme. Gail, dating from 1813 and 1815. The earliest, Guédron's *air de cour* "Aux plaisirs, aux délices," reaches back to 1614. The retrospective nature of Henrietta's *Échos de France* singles it out as unusual among the repertory sung by young women in Charleston, or even the entire United States. Certainly, having the most up-to-date music was not necessarily an aim of young women's music collecting, and older pieces, particularly familiar settings of "Old World" tunes, figure prominently in many binder's volumes. Moore's works, arranged by John Stevenson, such as "The Last Rose of Summer" (1813), represent the typical repertory one might find in volumes from the 1820s and 1830s. Operatic pieces in American collections tended to depend heavily on arias by Bishop, such as "Home! Sweet Home!" (1823), and from the 1840s to the Civil War, Balfe's music, featuring such famous songs as "I Dreamt That I Dwelt in Marble Halls," frequently occurs. There must be some other explanation for the peculiar French works in Henrietta's collection.

Music by several of the composers in Henrietta's copy of *Échos de France,* as well as in her single sheet music collection, hearkens back to the unusual repertory that Harriet sang when she was Henrietta's age. In fact, there is some overlap between the music in Harriet's binder's volumes and Henrietta's pieces. Sacchini composed both "Dieux ce n'est pas pour moi" and "Vôtre coeur devint mon Asile" for his final and most successful work, *Œdipe à Colone,* and each appears in the collections of both Harriet and Henrietta. These arias and "Il est vrai que Thibaut"—which is also in Harriet's collection—appear in the second part of *Échos de France,* published in 1861.[7] Similarly, another pair of undated pieces might belong to one of the pre-1857 Paris trips because they too belong to an earlier style: "La mer se plaint toujours!," a "Romance dramatique chanté par Mme Iweins-d'Hennen" by the composer Jacques Potharst; and "Il me l'a dit cent fois! Mélodie," a romance associated with Madame Emilie Gaveaux-Sabatier (née Bénazet) was a popular Parisian salon singer and the dedicatee of more than thirty songs. Both were published in Paris au Ménestral, at the Maison Meissonnier-Heugel located at 2 bis, rue Vivienne, around 1842. Henrietta's name is inscribed on the top of each, and the Potharst work also has the addition of "Paris." The women mentioned on the sheet music were popular singers in Parisian salons. Ferdinando Besanzoni's romance "Je t'aimerai," published in Paris by L. Parent in 1852, might also belong to the 1854 trip. It too has "H. A. Aiken / Paris" at the top.

Henrietta's *Échos de France* and some of the isolated romances in the Charleston Museum collection point to Harriet's imprint on her daughter's music. A decided preference for French songs at a time when Italian bel canto was all the rage further suggests her mother's ideas of the proper music a well-traveled young woman should know in this period. Harriet's influence on her daughter can be found in other places too. Henrietta and her husband, Burnet Rhett, lived with Harriet in the house on Elizabeth Street. Burnet died in 1879, and Harriet outlived him by a number of years. After her mother died, Henrietta reportedly closed her room and vowed never to touch any of Harriet's things. Harriet continued to hold sway over her daughter.[8]

Washington, D.C., and Basvecchi: 1855–57

The Aikens traveled to New York and Washington several times before the Civil War, and some of Henrietta's music may have been purchased during these trips. For several works, such as "La Fidanzata del Marinajo-Des Seemanns Braut. Scena ed Aria per Soprano" by J. Concone, we cannot be sure when she acquired them. Her copy of "La Fidanzata" (SMS 464) came from Breusing's on Broadway, a firm that specialized in importing music from Europe, particularly Schott in Mainz, from whence her copy came.[9] She wrote "H. A. Aiken" in ink on the first page. This edition is undated, but it was listed in Friedrich Hofmeister's *Handbuch der musikalischen Literatur* of 1854.[10] It is yet another vocal composition that includes markings reminding the singer where to breathe.

Henrietta may have acquired the copy of Concone's vocal method, *Fifty Lessons in Singing for the Middle Register of the Voice* (SMS 612) that is in the Charleston Museum at the same time she sang his "La Fidanzata." "J. Concone" was the anglicized name for Paolo Giuseppe Gioacchino Concone, a singing teacher and choirmaster who was born in Turin in 1801 and died there in 1861. His voice tutorial *Fifty Lessons for Medium Voice,* published by Ditson, or *50 leçons de chant,* op. 9, was particularly popular in the United States.[11] This copy is in English and French and is for mezzo-soprano; both of these aspects point to Henrietta as the owner. She owned two other vocal tutorials, only one of which, *Lablache's Complete Method of Singing* (SMB 148), was purchased in Charleston.[12]

One other volume can be assigned to the Aikens' time in Washington, D.C., and it too shows Harriet's influence: a copy of Rossini's *La Semiramide* (SMB 228). Inside the front cover she wrote in pencil, "Henrietta A. Aiken / Washington / ~ 1856 ~," and the hand matches that in SMB 19. The title page reads, "Semiramide / Opera Seria / Musica del Maestro / rossini / Ridotta con accompagnamento di / Piano Forte / No. 11 / de la Collection / Prix 36r / Paris / Au magazine de Musique de Pacini Editeur des Operas de Rossini / Boulevard des Italians No. 11." The thematic table lists twenty pieces; as in Harriet's opera scores, recitatives are sometimes omitted. While her mother purchased several volumes of complete operas while in Europe, it appears that Henrietta obtained only this one. Of course it is possible that she owned others now lost or at least unavailable to the public. Henrietta wrote, "Henrietta A. Aiken / Washington / 1856," which may suggest that she purchased it there, although it is equally likely that she got it in Paris in 1854 and had it bound while in Washington in 1856. By 1856 Rossini's opera was hardly new, even though it maintained popularity throughout the century. This might be another case where Harriet's musical choices inflected those of Henrietta, or more directly that Harriet bought it for her because she believed it appropriate from her own experience. As is the case with Harriet's opera volumes, SMB 228 shows no sign of use. This fact is noteworthy because most of Henrietta's vocal music has markings of some sort throughout, usually breath marks and phrasing.

The most direct evidence for Henrietta's music instruction is her connection to the teacher and composer Pietro O. Basvecchi, who became acquainted with her between the family's trips to Europe in 1854 and 1857. Basvecchi was in Charleston perhaps as early as 1848, and he played violin in several performances there in 1855.[13] On 13 February he performed the "Carnival of Venice" with the Charleston Philharmonic Society during its first concert of the season, in South Carolina Institute Hall.[14] In March a benefit concert at Hibernian Hall for Gambati—Marie Siegling's former teacher—featured Basvecchi as well. By the end of the year (December), he produced his own concerts, and that of

20 December featured a heavy dose of melodies from popular Italian operas, performed with "A Youthful Amateur," Ludwig Eckel (piano), M. S. Reeves, and a "Full Orchestra." This event included Verdi's overture to *Nabucco*, Goria's "Étude de concert," Aladd's "Grand fantasia sur la favorita" (played by "The Amateur"), the overture to Rossini's *La gazza ladra*, and Prudent's "Grand fantasie sur des motives de Lucia di Lammermoor." Basvecchi also played "Air Varie" by de Bériot. A review on 22 December pronounced the performance "delightful." As is the case for all of the performances described here, the "Amateur" and "Lady" (below) remain anonymous.

Basvecchi was involved with other Charleston performances in 1856 and 1857, including one on 10 May 1856 for which he composed a dirge for the Calhoun Monument Association. The famed Norwegian violinist Ole Bule too played at this concert.[15] In the early summer, Basvecchi and his male students traveled to Aiken for a concert. In March 1857 his "Calhoun Dirge" was again played for the Calhoun Monument Association. This concert also included Beethoven's "Adelaide," sung by "a Lady"; followed by "Briganti"—surely an excerpt from the opera of that name—by Mercadante, sung by "a Lady (Amateur)"; Basvecchi's "The Parting Kiss," sung by a "Lady Amateur" and M. S. Reeves; and a duo and chorus from Haydn's *Creation*, sung by "a Lady," H. W. Greatorex, and a chorus. The second part contained a similar repertory: overture from Verdi's *Nabucco;* "Song: Variations Composed for Madame Sontag by Kücken," sung by a "Lady (Amateur)"; an unnamed piano solo; "O mio Fernando" from Donizetti's *La Favorite,* sung by a "Lady"; and Haydn's "The Heavens Are Telling," from *The Creation.*[16]

The Italian and German emphasis of this performance and others reflected changing tastes in 1850s Charleston. Notably, nothing in French appeared on the program. Styles transformed considerably between the concerts Harriet would have heard in Charleston in the 1820s and those Henrietta might have attended in the 1850s, and those changes confirmed trends throughout much of the United States. The newer styles also imprint Henrietta's music purchases from the family's final trip to Europe in 1857–58. On 13 March 1858 Basvecchi, a "Professor of Music," was made a naturalized citizen in Charleston; his country of origin was given as Italy, and his age was twenty-nine at that time.[17]

In addition to his public performances, Basvecchi published several songs with Firth, Pond & Co. in New York, all of which date from 1856–57: "To Thee My God, to Thee I Call" (SMS 557); "The Parting Kiss" (SMS 549, a duet); "Tears, Idle Tears"; "I Live for Thee Alone"; "Would We'd Never Met" (SMS 442, which Teresa Parodi sang in concerts); and "Ahi! Fu sogno inganntore" (five copies of which are now in the Charleston Museum). His "Liverpool Polka" was published in London in 1863, which strongly suggests that he spent the war years back in Europe.

Two of these songs have special connections to Charleston, and both indicate that Basvecchi knew Henrietta personally. The cover of "Tears, Idle Tears" describes it as a "Cavatina Sung with great applause by a Distinguished Lady Amateur at the Grand Concert of the Calhoun Monument Association on May 14th 1856" and at a concert on 20 May 1857.[18] Henrietta's copy (SMS 623) is an 1856 imprint that includes a dedication to "Miss S. F. Elmore of South Carolina by P. O. Bassavecchi [*sic*]" and lists places where one could obtain this music: Charleston, New York, Philadelphia, Baltimore, Cincinnati, Boston, and New Orleans. This was clearly Basvecchi's most popular composition, and it appeared on concert programs as late as 1883, when it was performed by the Macon Harmonic Society in Georgia.[19]

It appears that the composer knew Henrietta well enough to give her an inscribed copy of "Tears, Idle Tears," because he wrote "To Miss Henrietta A. Aiken With the respects of the Composer" on the top right title page of her copy (SMS 623). She may have been a student of his by 1856. Although it is tempting to consider the possibility that Henrietta was the "Distinguished Lady Amateur" at the Calhoun Monument Association's concert in 1856, she probably was not the singer even though her father was a patron. She may have attended this performance.

The surest evidence that Basvecchi taught Henrietta is a dramatic song, "Ahi! Fu Sogno Ingannatore," that he dedicated to her in 1857. The published version reads, "Romanza 'Ahi! Fu Sogno Ingannatore' composed for and dedicated to Miss Henrietta A. Aiken of Charleston, South Carolina by P. O. Basvecchi" and locates the publication in New York by Firth, Pond & Co. and also available in Charleston and St. Louis. Four copies—SMS 431a, 582a, 582b, and SMS 614—of the published version of this song can be found among the Charleston Museum collection, all seemingly owned by Henrietta Aiken. On SMS 614 Basvecchi wrote, "To Miss Henrietta A. Aiken/With the respects of the Composer" in pencil on the title page. SMS 431a still has its original green cover.

Even more significantly, a manuscript of this *romanza,* in the composer's hand and dated 8 May 1857/Charleston, belonged to Henrietta and remains in the Charleston Museum (SMS 431b). This makes for a remarkable case in which the composer's autograph score and published versions of the same piece created for a young southern woman exist. Moreover, SMS 431b is not only a manuscript but also the score from which Basvecchi taught Henrietta. It provides documentation as to the seriousness with which this southern woman took her music studies, and when combined with other marked pages in Henrietta's music collection, it relates something about the detailed application of ornamentation, improvised cadenzas, and other pertinent information regarding performance practice in 1850s Charleston.

"Ahi! Fu Sogno Ingannatore" is a dramatic work for mezzo-soprano that stylistically resembles Verdi's middle-period operas, such as *La traviata*. The *romanza* resembles in no way the Parisian romances her mother sang. It consists of three main parts, beginning with *Recitativo cantando* (marked [A] in the translation).[20] The text replicates the passion and emotion typical of Italian operas of the 1850s and also draws on the idea of delirious dreams, à la *Lucia di Lammermoor* and other operas popular at that time:

Recitative [A]:
Qui ogn'ora a me d'accanto,
Ei piangeva, al pianto mio,
Cento volte innanzi a Dio,
I suoi voli ripeté. [repeated]
[Always here next to me he wept at my weeping / he wept with me,
A hundred times before God he repeated his promises.]

[B]
Mi chiamò coi dolci nomi,
Di sua speme e suo Tesoro
La sua cetra, il sacro alloro
Qui depose innanzi a me, si,
Qui depose innanzi a me.
[He called with the sweet names of his hope and treasure. He placed right before me his lyre and the sacred laurel, yes, he placed them before me.]

[C]
Mi credetti allor felice
Mi sentii, di me maggiore,
Ahi! Fu sogno ingannatore
Fu delirio fu de lirio il mio gioir
Ahi! fu sogno ingannator,
Ahi! fu sogno ingannatore
Fu delirio il mio gior
[Then I believed myself happy, I felt better than ever. Alas! My joy was a deceitful dream, it was delirium.]

Ahi! fu sogno ingannator,
Ahi! fu sogno ingannatore

Fu delirio fu de lirio il mio gioir
Ahi! fu sogno ingannatore
Fu delirio fu de lirio il mio gioir
Fu delirio fu de lirio il mio gioir[.]

Basvecchi matched his music to this forlorn text, carefully contrasting each part through closely related keys marked by expansive vocal phrases. For example, in the recitative (the first fifteen measures of vocal music), the singer covers a wide range (A4 to G5), modulates from A minor to C major, and concludes with a flourish. The next part [B], marked agitato non troppo, presents a new idea (C major in 6/8 meter), that is more harmonically stable than the opening recitative, before concluding with yet another flourish (this time touching B6), that outlines the dominant of A, E7. The concluding section [C] is in A major and is marked andante con passione. The music moves forward fervently, reaching a held fortissimo A6 and then falling softly to a lower register.

The differences between the two versions, printed and manuscript, of "Ahi! Fu Sogno Ingannatore" are minor, mostly dotted rhythms and slight changes in the accompaniment. The manuscript version does not include the ossia given in the publication, which suggests that either Henrietta did not need it or Henrietta's difficulty with the passage prompted Basvecchi to publish an easier option.[21] Thus, the published version probably came after the manuscript presentation copy made for Henrietta.

"Ahi! Fu Sogno Ingannatore" demands more of the young singer than contemporary "ballads," such as those of Stephen Foster, and gives the impression that Henrietta must have been talented indeed. As in other bel canto works, the soprano must navigate fast runs through the entire vocal range, encompassing over three octaves—A4 to B6. This is a far cry from the limited range of her mother's French romances and such technical demands reflect one effect that the meteoric rise of Italian opera had on many parlor performances in the United States. Granted, many but not all of the Italian arias sung by young amateurs in the early nineteenth century had been simplified, shortened, given new texts, and transposed down to make them easier to sing. By the 1850s, however, such alterations were less frequent.

Perhaps the most informative aspect of Henrietta's manuscript copy of "Ahi! Fu Sogno Ingannatore" is what it reveals concerning performance practice and instruction for an amateur singer in 1850s Charleston. The score is awash with dynamics, breath marks, accents, alignments between piano and vocal parts, and accidentals—proving that Henrietta studied this piece carefully, almost certainly with Basvecchi.[22] For example, in mm. 53–54, he added a breath mark before "fu de lirio," an accidental, accents, a mark to ensure "de" on the correct beat, and the pianissimo. (See figure 8.1a.) Particularly illustrative is an image above m. 48, replete with beribboned hair, drawn above the first outcry "Ahi!," which falls on a held high F. Henrietta apparently needed to open her mouth wider and move her tongue forward, because her teacher drew an image on the music for her to emulate (figure 8.1b).

Such an image would never appear as a serious endeavor on sheet music for a number of reasons but primarily because it is difficult to draw someone in the act of singing and still maintain the discreet, demure appearance of a lady. This is why most sheet music images show singers posed rather than singing. Moreover, the image in "Ahi! Fu Sogno Ingannatore" indicates work, practice, imperfection. Those are not the qualities a young lady must display in public.[23] More than likely, Henrietta studied from SMS 431b but sang in front of others from one of the other copies of "Ahi! Fu Sogno Ingannatore" that she owned—if she used one at all.

In addition to learning "Ahi! Fa Sogno Ingannatore," Henrietta sought out music by Verdi in 1857. Indeed, Henrietta's acquisition of "Di due figli" from Verdi's *Il trovatore* (SMS 482) demonstrated yet another way young women

Figure 8.1a. Basvecchi manuscript copy, "Ahi! Fu Sogno Ingannatore," SMS 431b, mm. 53–54

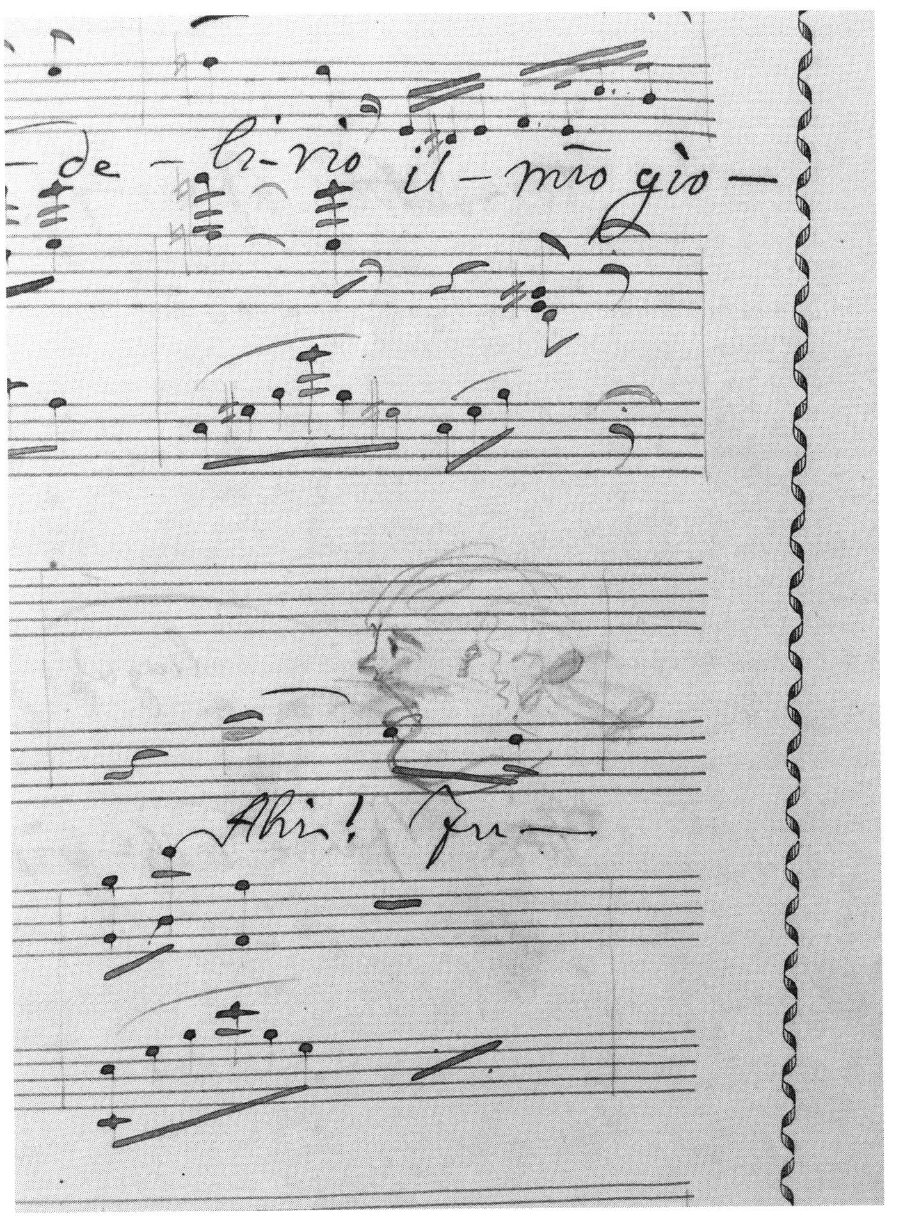

Figure 8.1b. Basvecchi manuscript copy, "Ahi! Fu Sogno Ingannatore," SMS 431b, m. 48

acquired music during the antebellum period. On 2 April 1857 her mother wrote to Mr. Heywood from Jehossee Island, a vast plantation south of Charleston where the Aiken family escaped to avoid the stifling summer heat in town. Harriet wrote, "My daughter begs me to thank you for the Trovatore which reached her quite safely—she sings it & I like it very much." At the conclusion of this letter, she added a postscript: "Henrietta has just asked to see my letter & says I have talked so much of my own affairs that I appear to have lost sight of her's—& she begs me to say for her that she is very much obliged to you for the trouble you have taken in sending the music she expresses a wish to have."[24] Unfortunately, there is no dealer's stamp on the music to indicate where Heywood bought it; this version was published in New York by Firth, Pond & Co. in 1856, but a Charleston dealer may have sold it to Heywood.

Henrietta's copy of "Di due figli" (SMS 482) survives in the Charleston Museum collection. In the opera Verdi assigned the role of Ferrando, the captain of the guards who sings this aria, to a bass voice.[25] This particular piece seems like an odd choice for a young woman, although Charles W. Glover and William Dressler, the arrangers, clearly intended it for parlor use by young women: its title page declares that "Di due figli / Two rosy children," taken from "The Vocal Beauties of Il Trovatore by G. Verdi," has been "Selected, Arranged Expressly for Parlour or Concert Use."[26] *Il trovatore* was an enormously successful opera, and Henrietta, pursuing the latest fashionable music from Italy, must have thought it necessary to sing something from it. We can imagine her sitting at the piano at Jehossee in the summer of 1857 practicing Verdi arias as the family prepared for yet another extended European tour.

CHAPTER 9

After 1857

Paris (again), Germany, and Switzerland

Thanks to a small travel diary of twenty-four pages that Harriet compiled, the movements of the Aiken family on their last antebellum visit to Europe in 1857–58 can be followed more precisely.[1] Books purchased by the Aikens while in Europe and some music of Henrietta's containing places and dates contribute to the documentation of this voyage. In fact, more books from the Aiken family survive from this trip to Europe than from any of the previous ones, as table 2.4 shows.

The Aikens left New York on 19 August 1857 and sailed for ten days on the *Persia* before arriving in Liverpool. They stopped first at the Queen's Hotel in Manchester and attended the Art Treasures Exhibition there.[2] While in Manchester, Harriet bought a copy of *Companion to the Most Celebrated Private Galleries of Art in London* by Mrs. Jameson (London, 1844), signing it and noting the place and date, "Sept. 2nd 1857." The family's interest in this exhibition confirms Harriet's search for art and knowledge of such an event. The Aikens spent only one day in London and lodged at Fenton's Hotel, St. James's. This establishment was in keeping with the other hotels they frequented; other guests at Fenton's included Napoleon I's stepdaughter and Charles Eliot Norton.[3] From London they went to Brighton for the day, then on to New Haven to travel by steamer to Dieppe—"a sea bathing place" where Harriet noted that they were amused by the "Country people." None of Henrietta's music seems to have been purchased as of this point in the trip—they were too busy heading to Paris and did not tarry long enough in London to visit Bond or Oxford Street, where most Americans shopped for music when in England.

The train took them to Paris, where they spent two weeks in mid-September 1857 at the Hôtel du Louvre. Harriet commented that the women required three carriages to carry their "ridiculous quantity" of trunks, and she was disappointed not to have a French maid while in Paris. That she desired a French maid attests to her desire to live like a Parisian, and no doubt she wished Henrietta to acquire

Table 9.1. Books published abroad, 1857–1858

Title	Inscription	Date	Notes
Briccolani Dictionnaire Français-Italien	Henrietta Aiken / Paris / 1858		
La Cenci	H.A. Aiken / Rome / 1858		In Italian
Companion to the Most Celebrated Private Galleries of Art in London, by Mrs. Jameson	Harriet L. Aiken / Manchester / Sept. 2nd 1857	1844	
Complément du Dictionnaire de l'Académie franćaise	Henrietta A. Aiken / Paris / 1858	1856	Paris
Dictionnaire des Synonyms de la langue français	Henrietta A. Aiken / Paris / 1858	1843	Paris
Dictionnaire universel d'histoire et de géographie	Henrietta A. Aiken / Paris / 1858	1858	Paris
Handbook for Travellers in Switzerland and the Àlps of Savoy and Piedmont	[unsigned but in this collection]	1858	London
Hillard's Six Months in Italy	Henrietta A. Aiken / Venice / October 26th 1857	1856	Boston
L'histoire de France, Thomas Lavallée, vol. 2	H.L. Aiken / Paris / 1858	1858	Paris
L'histoire de Marie Stuart (2 vols), by M. Mignot	H.L. Aiken / Paris / 1857	1854	Paris
Institut de France Dictionnaire de l'Académie franćaise, 6e ed., vols. 1 and 2	Henrietta A. Aiken / Paris / 1858	1856	Paris
London in 1857	William Aiken	1857	London
Lord Byron's Works	Henrietta A. Aiken / Venice / October 26th 1857	1852	Venice
Murray's Hand-Book for France	William Aiken	1857	
Un Philosophe sois les touts, by Souvestre	H.L. Aiken / Paris / 185[illegible]	1851	Paris

The Poetry of Sacred and Legendary Art, by Mrs. Jameson, 2 vols	Henrietta A. Aiken / Rome / June 1858		
Spiers Dictionnaire Français-Anglais (and 2nd vol., *Anglais-Français*) *ouvage adoptée par l'Université*	Harriet L. Aiken / Paris / June 1858		
Le Veritable Manuel des Conjugasions	Henrietta A. Aiken / Paris / 1858	1853	Paris. 8000 verbs

similar tastes. Once in Paris they again met with many American acquaintances, along with the U.S. minister John Mason. To this point the Aikens socialized only with those in their class, and all indications confirm that these people were Americans.

On 19 September the family departed for Cologne, the first stop as they made their way to Berlin. In Cologne, Harriet picked up a map of middle Europe at the Hôtel Disch. Another map that belonged to Harriet, now in the Aiken-Rhett Papers at the Charleston Museum, shows the probable journey the family took from Paris to Berlin. (See figure 9.1.) Additionally, two similar documents in that archive provide a map of middle Europe. The Aikens toured Berlin for seven days, seeing the U.S. minister in Berlin, Joseph A. Wright. He introduced them to Count Datzfeldt, a member of the nobility—precisely the type of connections they wished to make. The company then set out for Leipzig. At the Hôtel de Pologue they heard a band of musicians while dining. This particular hotel was not one especially given to American tourists, but in May 1859 Franz Liszt made it his residence.[4]

Leaving Leipzig, the Aikens traveled to Dresden, where they stayed at the Hotel Bellevue. In the gallery of paintings at the hotel, they met several Charleston families, including members of the Izard and Preston families. The Prestons' widowed sister-in-law, Ann Fitzsimmons Hampton, too was in attendance. The Aiken and Preston families had cofounded the Charleston Art Association, and in Dresden they were pursuing common interests in art. John Preston had sold his Houmas sugar plantation so that the family could live in Europe for a few years.[5] The Aikens remained in Dresden for ten days before going by rail to Prague. Murray, the family dog, was lost there, possibly stolen. That they traveled with their dog is yet another conspicuous display of wealth and connection.

The next city on the itinerary was Vienna, beginning on 10 October, where their address was the Hôtel de l'Impératrice Elisabeth. There, Harriet commented, they dined with U.S. Minister Henry R. Jackson and later attended the ballet and Meyerbeer's *Le prophète,* probably hearing Róza Csillag in the mezzo-soprano lead. Why Harriet specially noted this performance remains unknown. She did not mention attending other operas and yet almost certainly did so. She rarely recorded any specific activities, so it is not unreasonable to assume that the Aikens found the time to see various operas in the cities they visited.[6]

Ten days later they headed to Venice on a train journey that took them through Graz and Trieste. They had to cross the Adriatic Sea at night, arriving in Venice on 23 October. After a week sightseeing in Venice, the family headed to Verona, taking a quick trip to Mantua and Milan. After stopping in Milan for a week, the Aikens made their way south to Florence, stopping in Lodi, Piacenza, Parma, Modena, Bologna, and Pianoro on the way. They remained at

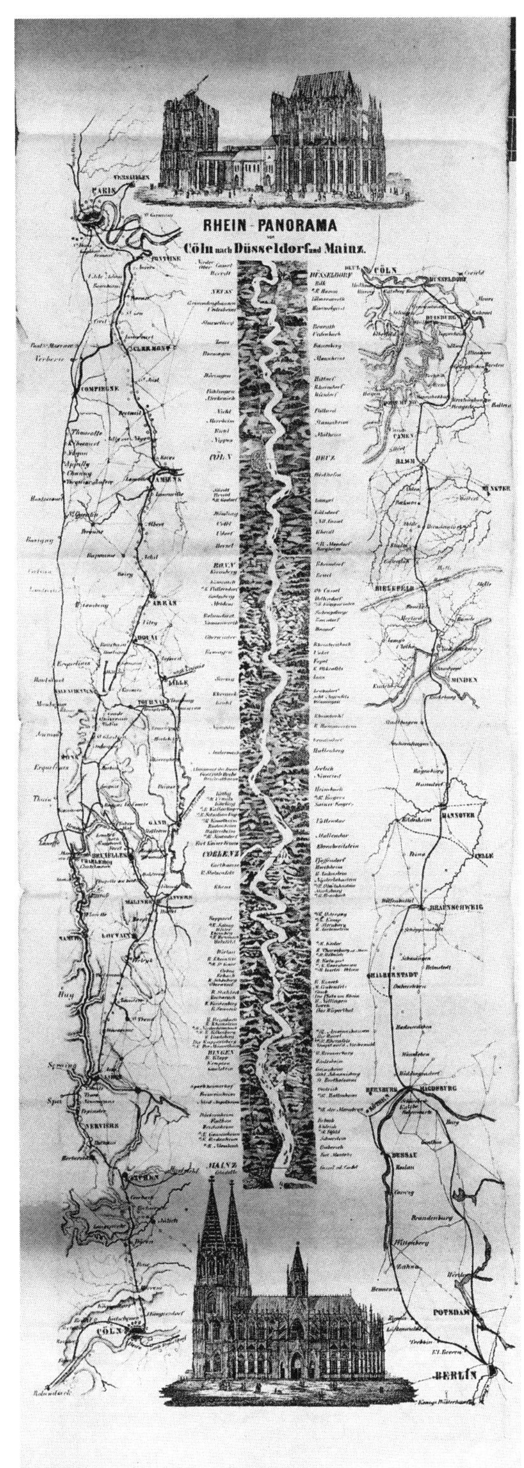

Figure 9.1. Map of
the journey taken
by the Aikens, from
the Hôtel Disch

the Hôtel d'Italie—one of those recommended in Francis Coghlan's 1845 *Handbook for Italy*[7]—in Florence for six weeks. There Henrietta had Italian lessons, though there was no mention of music lessons. Harriet also attended a reception, which she described as "very stupid," given by Mrs. Lewis Cass, the U.S. minister in Florence. Cass had been there when they visited in 1848.

At the end of February the family left by coach for Naples, taking in Pompeii and Mount Vesuvius. Remaining in Naples for a month, the family visited the nearby towns of Sorrento, Salerno, and Pestum. By Holy Week they were in Rome, and they attended Palm Sunday services at St. Peter's Basilica. They left Rome on 8 April and traveled by carriage to Siena. By May the family had made their way back to Paris by way of Pisa, Genoa, Turin, and Nice.

They also visited the spa town of Interlaken, Switzerland. The spa would have been a practical choice for Harriet's poor health. Because she gave a detailed account of their journey from Berlin to Dresden, Prague, and Vienna, it is likely that they went into Switzerland on their return. While in Interlaken, Henrietta—or Harriet—bought at least four pieces of music and signed them "H. A. Aiken / Interlochen." Five were published in Basel by Hegar and belong to the set *Airs Suisses avec accompagnement de piano ou guitarre. Schweizerlieder mit Begleitung des Piano oder Guitarre.* "Die Alpenrösle" (no. 16, SMS 520), "Schweizer Heimweh" (no. 19, SMS 447), "Der Vertrauen" (no. 20, SMS 446), and "Uf-fern Bergli" (no. 21, SMS 566) are anonymous, and "Der Gemsjäger" (no. 17, SMS 521) has F. Huber as composer. Additionally, she had two copies of "Iodler" (SMS 384 and SMS 397), which give neither composer nor publisher. Both are signed "H. A. Aiken / Interlochen."

These Swiss songs include French and German texts, except SMS 566, which has only German.[8] Most southern women did not sing in German unless there were overriding reasons, and the scant amount of German-language music in Henrietta's collection testifies to her time in German-speaking lands.[9] Moreover, while "Tyrolian" songs were popular in the United States, women rarely sang songs that had actually been published in Switzerland. Henrietta's ownership of these pieces attests to her acquisition of European goods, such as the furniture and artwork her parents chose, that were "the real thing."

On the Aiken family's return to Paris, Henrietta acquired several pieces of sheet music. Like her southern contemporaries—such as Louisa Rebecca McCord (see chapter 13 below)—Henrietta shopped at Flaxland in the late 1850s. Her copy of Guilio Alary's "L'étranger" (SMS 430), which is marked "H. A. Aiken / Paris," must belong to this trip since Flaxland did not publish the work until 1857.[10] Instead of the earlier romances that connect the music collections of mother and daughter from earlier trips, opera excerpts figured prominently in 1858. She sang "Déjà la nuit s'avance" (SMB 529) from *Marie Stuart* by Louis

Niedermeyer, which the publisher, Legouix, advertised as sung by Madame Stoltz. "H. A. Aiken / Paris / 1858" appears on the first page. The opera premiered with Rosina Stoltz in the leading role more than a decade earlier (December 1844) at the Théâtre de l'Académie Royale de Musique. The interest in Mary Stuart may have been directed by Harriet. She had purchased a two-volume *L'histoire de Marie Stuart* by M. Mignot (Paris, 1854) when the family was in Paris the previous autumn. This particular piece of sheet music proves that Henrietta's interest was not merely in collecting music but also in using it. Curiously, "Déjà la nuit s'avance" has an unusual feature in that the right-hand part of the accompaniment has been painstakingly revised by sewing in an alternative pattern. (See figure 9.2.) Only minor differences exist between the new version and that which lies underneath—the original has the pattern beginning with a sixteenth-note rest on each beat. It is not known who made this alteration, but it was obviously someone who thought that the accompaniment part required such attention.

Another opera aria that Henrietta bought in Paris in 1858 is "Grande valse chantée dans le barbier de Séville," which could be interpreted as another nod perhaps to her mother's older preferences, although *Il barbiere di Siviglia* remained popular throughout the nineteenth century. Léon Éscudier's edition of "Addio del passato bei sogni: La traviata, no. 10 bis: romanza" (SMB 465) can probably be assigned to the 1857–58 sojourn in Paris because Verdi's *La traviata* premiered in Venice in 1853. Furthermore, the aria resembles other music she began singing at about this time, including "I due figli" from *Il trovatore* (see above).

The Aikens returned to the United States in the fall, arriving in New York on 30 November 1858. Determining if any other pieces fit into this or any other journey requires a case to be made for each of the more than sixty pieces marked with her name, as well as those that probably belonged to her and those that might have. It is doubtful whether such speculation would add to the picture painted here. Henrietta acquired music from her various travels, including the European ventures. In all likelihood, she probably had French music teachers while in Paris for extended periods. She left no other records of her time overseas or her musical experiences during the 1840s and 1850s.

In her travel diary from the 1857 trip, Harriet mentioned music only twice, when she heard a band outside the Hôtel de Pologue in Berlin on 20 September and when she attended *Le prophète* in Vienna on 12 October. No other recollections of music during these trips have yet come to light, and the impression forms that Harriet and Henrietta engaged in musical activity frequently but did not see the need to write about it. They purchased music in Europe partly as souvenirs and partly for personal study, just as they bought French textbooks and other materials. Henrietta's music functioned as souvenirs and, more to the point here, as physical reminders to those who visited the Aikens that these

Figure 9.2. Sewn accompaniment in "Déjà la nuit s'avance," SMB 529

women were accomplished and cosmopolitan. These and other items adorned the Aiken home. Undoubtedly, they left these artifacts out for visitors to notice: they were silent testimonies to the European journeys these women undertook to extend their cultural knowledge beyond the limits of antebellum Charleston.

Henrietta continued her music practice throughout her life, although evidence of this after 1861 is scant. The family suffered in unusual ways during the conflict, most notably because William, a staunch Unionist, was imprisoned in 1862 for refusing to take the oath of loyalty to the Confederacy and then again in 1865 for refusing to take the oath of allegiance to the Union.[11] This upheaval may explain why so little was recorded of Henrietta's musical experiences during this time. Opera continued to figure among her later pieces, several of which she received from her first cousin Marie Cottenet or Cottenet's daughter. These included a copy of Auber's "Oh, Whisper What Thou Feelest" (from Auber's *Crown of Diamonds*), in the series "The Flowers of the Opera," from "Marie Monck," likely Marie Cottenet's daughter (SMS 584).[12] She also received Meyerbeer's "L'Africaine / Romance no. 1 / Adieu mon doux ravage" (SMS 484) and Niedermeyer's "Oh! Tell Him All" (SMS 537) from Marie Cottenet, which she marked "H. A. Rhett." This last piece was not published until 1860, by Beer & Schirmer in New York, so it is possible that Henrietta received it after her wedding in 1862. Two other items from Marie—familiarly called "May"—to "Etta" in the Charleston Museum are some of Stephen Foster's most famous pieces: "Massa's in de Cold Ground" (SMS 625) and "My Old Kentucky Home, Good Night" (SMS 626).[13] One other piece, Abt's popular "When the Swallows Fly Homeward" (SMS 518, also known as "Agathe"), is marked "H. A. Aiken from M. H.," with the final bit cut off. It was probably a gift from Marie Huger Cottenet as well.

Marie "May" Huger Lowndes (1832–1915) married Edward Laight Cottenet in 1848. Their daughter was Marie Monck, née Cottenet, who may be the "Marie" referred to as "Marie Monck" on some of Henrietta's music. Since Marie H. Cottenet sometimes went by "May," just as Henrietta was called "Etta" by family and friends, we cannot always be certain which one of the women is "Marie Cottenet." The compositions that Henrietta received from Marie indicate that the latter's tastes ran from the most familiar songs published in the United States to less common opera arias imported by Scharfenberg & Luis in New York. Marie's own binder's volume, SMB 32, features difficult piano music by composers such as Thalberg, Rosellen, and Beyer.[14] It is easy to imagine that the two performed music together frequently, most likely with Marie accompanying Henrietta's singing. The date this music exchanged hands and whether such musicking continued later in life are not known.

Of the fourteen pieces in the Charleston Museum that have either "H. A. Rhett" or "Henrietta A. Rhett" written on them, only four were published after her marriage to Andrew Burnet Rhett on 25 September 1862: Wallace's "Lord, Teach Me How to Pray" (SMS 395), which she dated 1885; "This Kiss I Offer (Lu Vasillo) / Canzonetta Napolitana di Sarimento" (SMS 425); Mme la Baronne Willy de Rothschild's romance "Ah, Wherefore? (Si vous n'avez rien a me dire)" (SMS 519); and Alfonso Guercia's "Think of Me! (Pense á me)" (SMS 539). Three of these resemble the type of music she purchased while in Paris in the 1850s, but "Lord, Teach Me How to Pray" does not.[15]

All of the others (see table 6.1, above) could have been part of the collection before she became Mrs. A. B. Rhett. Several of the earlier works likely were purchased before the Civil War, particularly Balfe's popular "Then You'll Remember Me" from *The Bohemian Girl*, which graces many binder's volumes from the decades before the war. Blackmar published the song during the war while he was in Macon, Georgia, but Henrietta's copy came from Firth, Pond & Co. in New York in 1847. Since her music remains unbound, it might be that she added her name later to some of the pieces in order to make sure they stayed at the Aiken-Rhett House.[16] "Kathleen Mauvorneen as sung by the Composer, The Plymouth Concerts, Words Mrs. Crawford; Music F. N. Crouch, Member of the Royal Academy" (SMS 516) represents a more typical repertory for southern women during the antebellum period. Henrietta's version, marked "H. A. Aiken" and purchased at Zogbaum's store in Charleston, can be found in several volumes bound before the war.[17] Her version of "Robert, Robert, Thou Whom I Love" from Meyerbeer's *Robert le diable*, from "Jenny Lind's Operatic Songs" of 1850 (SMS 491, and again inscribed with "H. A. Aiken"), was another favorite in American parlors.

Henrietta's wedding to Burnet Rhett took place in Flat Rock, North Carolina, away from the military action that threatened the coast. They married at Hillside, the residence of Martha Rutledge Kinloch Singleton (widow of Matthew R. Singleton). A handwritten copy of Schuber's "Der Wanderer," an admired lied among southern collections, with "Hillside, September 13th [18]59" written on it, exists in the Aiken-Rhett Collection (SMS 456).[18] The song was transposed from C-sharp minor to C minor and has the German text written beneath the English. It could be Henrietta's music, transposed down a half-step to suit her lower voice. She owned other music with German texts brought back from Europe the previous year. Of the composers of lieder, the most popular in the United States during the antebellum period was Franz Abt. His songs can be found in many collections, almost always in translation. Henrietta owned his "When the Swallows Homeward Fly // Agathe"[19] (SMS 518). Another lied in her music was featured in the popular series *Gems from the German:* "We Met by Chance" by Kücken (marked "H. A. Aiken"). This series also advertised that Beethoven's

"Adelaide" as well as Schubert's "Erlking" and "Wanderer" were available as well. Henrietta also owned at least one of Schubert's lieder in French translation: "Les plaintes de la jeune fille," op. 55/3, published in Paris by Richault (SMS 359).[20] These compositions figure as the best-known examples of the genre in the antebellum United States. That Henrietta owned a Schubert lied in French constitutes yet another example of the Aikens' preference for French culture in their home.

Nothing specifically suggests that Henrietta bought music during the Civil War, but it would have been unusual not to have done so. Many southern binder's volumes include Confederate imprints and even music published in other places and purchased between 1861 and 1865. In Boston, Ditson published Alexander Reichardt's "Thou Are So Near" from the Germania series in 1860, and Henrietta marked her copy (SMS 352) "Henrietta Aiken Rhett." She may have purchased it after the war, or there could be some other explanation.

Henrietta lived in the western part of South Carolina during the last year of the war. A letter from V. C. Aiken was addressed to her, care of "Mr. [?]andale, Mansion House, Greenville [South Carolina], 22 March 1865."[21] In early 1866 Emma Taber (1836–1911) wrote to Burnet that she hoped to sing for him if he would visit her in Columbia and that perhaps one day he would "have the pleasure" of hearing her sing with Henrietta.[22] In March of the same year, Henrietta's sister-in-law Elise wrote from Zahara, a plantation in Aiken County, South Carolina:

Dear Etta,

. . .

The little piano we have here is quite sweet toned, and pleasant for singing though it has gone down so far below concert pitch that I expect you will take my voice for a powerful bass the first time you hear me sing; I shall have to train it up, when I get to town. Col. P . . . man sent me quite a roll of music last month, but it is almost all little french songs, and I don't fancy any of them much. I hear that you don't sing much now, I am so sorry; we might learn some duets together in the spring; do you like duets? I did know some beautiful ones with Marie Legare.[23]

Your affectionate sister Elise[24]

What is this "roll of music"? Are the "little" French songs similar to the romances in the Frances Dill Rhett bequest that do not have names attached? Several items in the Charleston Museum may be part of what Elise described. In particular, Émile Prudent's *Six romances sans paroles,* published by Ledentu in Paris in 1856 (SMS 251), might be what Elise meant by a "roll" of music. It is the only group of pieces in the collection that fits this description. Elise may not have liked them, but Henrietta owned quite a few, in the spirit of her mother having done the same.[25]

Also noteworthy in this letter is that Henrietta no longer sang as she had done previously. The circumstances of her daily existence in the months following the war may not have allowed for such. The letter sent to her at a hotel in Greenville in 1865 suggests that she may not have had ready access to a piano or an appropriate venue in which to sing. Her father's house had been confiscated, along with all he owned, after the war, and the piano that had been in the house was no longer there.[26] Moreover, letters exchanged between Harriet and her great-niece Marie Cottenet reveal that Harriet asked her to sell some jewelry in order to replace Henrietta's piano at the Aiken-Rhett House. She instructed Marie to have the jewelry valued in New York, with Marie knowing all the while that the money was for a new piano: "It pains me, dear Aunt Heart, to dispose of your ring, but of course you have thought it over well + made up your mind. I will take it down with me on Broadway [New York City], ascertain the value + write to you about it before taking the final steps. . . . I am glad however that there is a prospect of Etta's using her fine voice again + hope that next Winter you will invite me to some of the musical soirees you are contemplating."[27]

Marie added the postscript "Mrs Cottenet's experience + knowledge of pianos will be a very great advantage to me in selecting yours." This statement suggests two things. First, it was probably Marie Huger Cottenet, owner of SMB 32, a book of difficult piano music, who was referred to here as "Mrs Cottenet." Second, Marie—Mrs. Cottenet's daughter, the Marie Monck mentioned above— would be buying the piano in New York, not in Charleston. Why Harriet chose to have the piano brought to South Carolina from New York is unknown, but premium instruments may not have been available at local music warehouses such as Siegling's in 1867. Elizabeth Waties Allston Pringle commented in the early twentieth century that she had owned six Steinways.[28] Perhaps the cachet associated with instruments from New York prompted Harriet to have the new one for the Aiken-Rhett House purchased there. The Aiken-Rhetts did not, however, buy a Steinway but purchased a Chickering, which remains in the house today. Furthermore, the Aikens survived the war with more of their fortune intact than many of the neighbors because William had made substantial investments in Europe. These were able to support the family, to a degree, in the years following the war. Harriet's selling of her jewelry to buy a piano, rather than simply purchasing one outright, might have been part of an effort not to disclose the family's worth during the years of high taxation after the Civil War.[29]

Burnet Rhett died in 1879, at age forty-five, leaving Henrietta with five children between twenty-two months and ten years of age. Harriet lived with her daughter until her death in 1892, at which time Henrietta became sole owner of the Aiken-Rhett House.

CHAPTER 10

Other Music That Might Have Belonged to Henrietta

Of the four hundred or so individual pieces of sheet music from the Rhett bequest in the Charleston Museum, the largest percentage bearing names are those that belonged to Henrietta Aiken. Many of the others can be associated with other family members. Almost all of the music dates from between 1830 and 1865 and with a few exceptions is for voice and piano accompaniment or solo piano. Some of the music was purchased in Charleston or Philadelphia, but the bulk of it came from import dealers in New York City: Breusing or Scharfenberg & Luis; in Mainz: Weissenbruch; in London: various dealers; and in Paris: several publishers.

We can reasonably assume that Henrietta did not write her name on everything she sang or played; women rarely did so. Quite a few folders in the Charleston Museum contain pieces of music that for various reasons might have belonged to Henrietta, the most important reason being that they are part of the Frances Dill Rhett bequest. Table 10.1 shows music assigned to Henrietta based on the following criteria: 1) numerical sequence; 2) place of origination coupled with genre; and 3) manuscript music for a lower female voice. In several cases a combination of two of these criteria helps to attribute works to Henrietta's collection.

An excellent case can be made for segments of the collection. For example, SMS 351 through SMS 433 provide compelling evidence that more of the pieces here belonged to Henrietta than only those that bear her name.[1] Of the eighteen items between SMS 352 and SMS 397, thirteen have either "H. A. Aiken" or "H. A. Rhett" on them.[2] Given that almost all of these pieces were Henrietta's, it stands to reason that the few uninscribed pieces might also have been hers. Furthermore, the types of pieces are similar to others positively identified as hers, such as opera arias by Verdi and Meyerbeer.

Some of the repertory in the Frances Dill Rhett bequest is more obscure and points specifically to Harriet's interaction with her daughter's musical library.

The French romances almost certainly belong to the Aikens' music library, for it appears that Harriet's musical preferences influenced Henrietta's choices, particularly when she was young. Some of these are early enough to have been Harriet's, such as Masini's "Petite fleur des bois / Chansonnette" (SMS 571) and Panseron's "Le verras-tu jamais" (SMS 572), both of which were published circa 1820. It is not a stretch to imagine that Harriet, confident that she had learned the "correct" repertory as a young woman, encouraged Henrietta to sing the same genres. Four similarly styled French songs—SMS 373, SMS 430, SMS 519, and SMS 562—have Henrietta's name or initials on them. Harriet's influence would explain all of the other French romances, chansonettes, and similar pieces in the Charleston Museum collection.[3] Notably, these songs by composers active in Paris during the 1820s to 1840s—Puget, Panseron, among others—distinguished Harriet's accomplishments from those of her Charleston contemporaries. She would have been eager to have her daughter's collection similarly differentiated from those of other young women in Charleston in the 1850s. By the first decades of the nineteenth century, the romance had become a decidedly feminine genre, and many of its composers were women. It would have been suitable for Henrietta to learn such music for performance in their residences in both Charleston and Paris.

Henrietta's copy of Panseron's *Méthode de vocalization soprano et tenor*, published by the author in Paris in 1841, links these French songs to her collection. Henrietta's copy, SMB 189, came from Schott's in Brussels, per the seller's stamp. Unlike the single-sheet romances mentioned above, there is no doubt that this book belonged to Henrietta: the full leather binding has "H.A.A." stamped in gold on the front cover. A member of the family probably purchased Panseron's *Méthode* while in Paris during an antebellum journey. It distinguishes her collection from those of her acquaintances in Charleston.

Nonetheless, by the 1850s Italian opera in the style known as bel canto was the preferred music in American parlors, not French songs, as the letter from Elise Rhett (above) indicated. Furthermore, whereas they were heard in 1810s and 1820s concerts in Charleston, singers did not continue to program romances in the 1850s. Of course, it is possible that Elise never liked the French songs, as they seem to have been peculiar to Harriet's music collection and not representative of Charlestonians in general. These romances, then, keenly reflect the Aiken family's extended residences in Paris, where they remained in fashion well into the nineteenth century, and Harriet's influence on her daughter's musical library.

Some of the most intriguing music in the Frances Dill Rhett bequest is in manuscript form. Other than a few isolated examples, the bulk of these fall into two unusual groups: vocal exercises and opera arias.[4] Taken together, they seem to be the handiwork of a voice teacher, likely Henrietta's own. Figure 10.1 is an

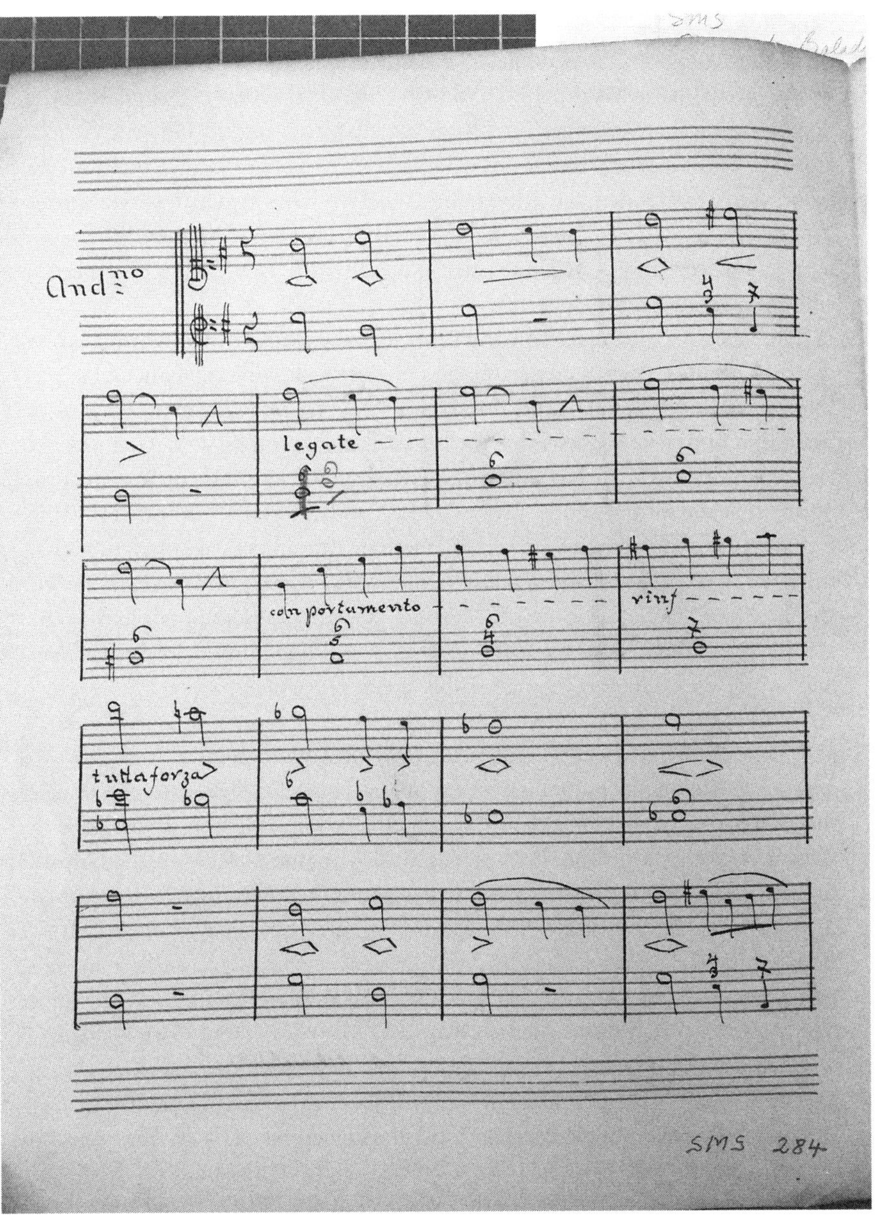

Figure 10.1. Folio of voice exercises, p. 1, SMS 284

example of the vocal exercises. It has a staff for the singer that is written in a C clef and an accompaniment part for a keyboard—possibly a guitar—written in figured bass. For the latter, the person playing that part would realize the chords based on the figures; for example, a "7" above a note means to play the seventh note above it, as well as the third and fifth. Figured bass was occasionally being taught to southern women and professional musicians during this period, although it is extremely rare to see it in such a score as this one.[5] Zimmerman's piano tutorial included something about it. No direct evidence survives confirming that any of the Charleston women of Henrietta's class could play from figures, but certainly a music teacher, especially one who might have been a composer as well, could do so.

The voice part in figure 10.1 indicates that the singer is working on subtle dynamic shading, such as crescendos and descrescendos on single pitches; legato singing; and other refined aspects of technique. The extended con portamento passage in mm. 9–11 suggests that the instructor was familiar with Manuel Garcia's use of this term.[6] Garcia differentiated between legato and con portamento, noting that the former simply meant smooth while the latter indicated slurring from one note to another. Garcia's explanation is apt in the case of Henrietta at least two times. First, she owned a copy of *École de Garcia, traite complet de l'art du chant par Manuel Garcia fils* (SMS 606; currently only the preface is in the archive). Second, there is a possibility that she studied music with Marie Siegling, who claimed to have studied with Garcia.[7]

Another connection between these uninscribed vocal exercises and Henrietta is that they are written in C clefs. Her copy of Zimmerman's *Encyclopédie du pianiste* (SMB 219) includes instruction in how to read C clefs. No other music that I have seen from a southern woman's collection includes music written with C clefs. Those used in the SMS exercises are "soprano clefs"—on the bottom line of the musical staff—and place the tessitura of a piece slightly lower than does the more familiar treble clef. Soprano clefs are atypical, even for C clefs.

All of these exercises were copied by one person, and two have the signature of Domenico Altrocchi, who left Lombardy as a political refugee in 1837 and began working as a music teacher in New York City. (See figure 10.2.) He taught voice and counterpoint at a school he founded in Manhattan, and these classes were reportedly so popular that one had to book them a year in advance. In 1845 Altrocchi was among the passengers headed to Liverpool via New York, and he was described in the *New Orleans Daily Picayune* as "of the Opera."[8] His passport of 1862 declared him to be an Italian-born citizen of the United States. On this journey he moved permanently to Italy.[9] How his manuscripts came to the Aiken-Rhett family is unknown, but the most probable venue would be that someone—probably Henrietta—had lessons with him while in Italy.[10]

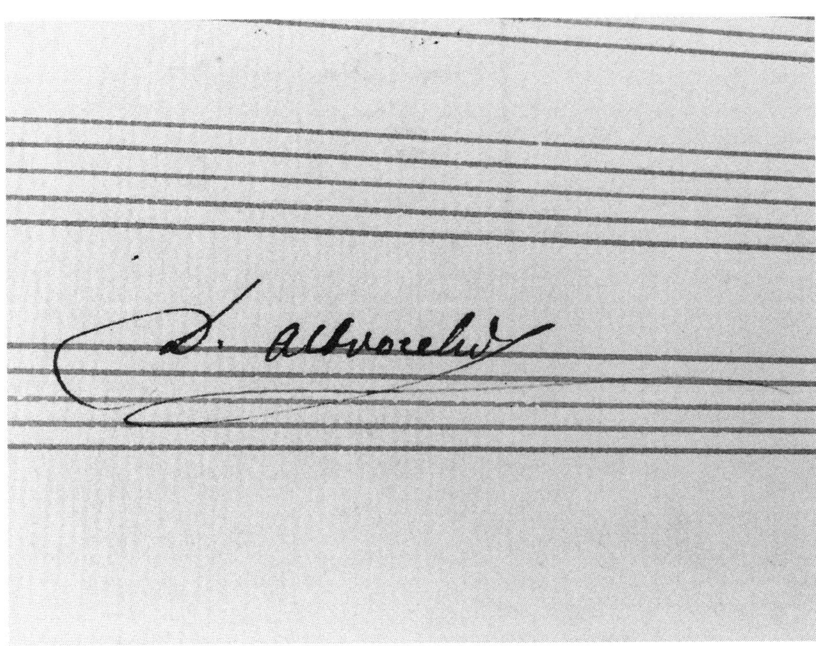

Figure 10.2. Altrocchi signature

Altrocchi copied a series of thirteen opera excerpts that were part of the Frances Dill Rhett gift in the Charleston Museum collection.[11] Each of these manuscripts begins with a title page declaring a work "nell'Opera" and usually includes the opera and composer. (See figures 10.3a and 10.3b.) The music begins on the second page of the folio (f. 1r), and all vocal parts are in C clefs. The text and music hand match those in the exercises.

The connection between the vocal exercises and these opera excerpts is undeniable, and the explanation is surely that the voice teacher copied the exercises as well as the arias for the pupil. The association with Henrietta is more tenuous, based primarily on the use of C clefs and the sheer number of these handwritten items in the collection. Her surviving music suggests that Henrietta had a lower voice, mezzo-soprano or even contralto, and she seems the likeliest candidate to have sung from these manuscripts.

While Henrietta Aiken's music collection outwardly represents the types of music a young southern woman might have performed in the late antebellum period, it also possesses distinctive characteristics that do not epitomize contemporary southern collections. Most immediately noticeable is that it remained unbound. Several possibilities could explain why hers is the only major southern collection from this period not to have been collected into bound volumes.

Figure 10.3a. Title page of "Cavatina nell'Opera L'Adelia [by] Donizetti," SMS 350

Figure 10.3b. First music page of "Cavatina nell'Opera L'Adelia [by] Donizetti," SMS 350

Perhaps there was not enough time between returning from the 1858–59 trip to Europe and the beginning of the Civil War, although others in this area, such as Louisa Rebecca McCord and Ann Beaufort Sims, had theirs bound in the early 1860s. During the war the family moved around; documentation shows that Henrietta married Burnet in Flat Rock, North Carolina, and late in the war lived in a hotel in Greenville. Boxes of sheet music would have been cumbersome and impractical to move. Another option, perhaps more likely, is that Henrietta continued to use her music through the war and afterward. If binding collections precluded pieces from practical use because this rendered them too tight or unwieldy on a piano desk and too heavy for singers to hold, assembling Henrietta's music into binder's volumes would have hindered her use of it. Thus, given what seems to have been her special talent for music, it might have been undesirable for her to have hers bound. We might also surmise that by not binding her music, the Aikens made a statement about not needing to keep all of her older music since they could easily afford to purchase newer items as styles changed.

It is possible to draw many conclusions concerning the broad repertory found in Henrietta's music collection. First and foremost is the influence of her mother's tastes on the daughter's collection, particularly early in her life. By the late 1840s music by composers such as Dalayrac and Grétry had disappeared from Charleston performances, but their music and that of their contemporaries still figure in Henrietta's repertory, and markings indicate that she did indeed perform from these scores. Harriet must have held dominant sway over her daughter, but except for a single letter from her soon-to-be fiancé that begged Henrietta to defy her parents, her music collection is all that remains as testimony to their relationship.[12] As she grew older, Henrietta followed musical styles more in line with those of her age, which ultimately revolved around vocal excerpts from and piano variations on popular Italian operas by Bellini, Donizetti, and Verdi.

Undoubtedly the family left these precious artifacts, foreign opera scores, rare pieces of sheet music, and fine books with French titles out for visitors to notice when they visited the Aiken-Rhett House, as they were silent testimonies to the European journeys these women undertook in order to extend their cultural knowledge beyond the limits of antebellum Charleston. The music scores functioned as a physical reminder to those who visited the Aikens that these women were accomplished and cosmopolitan.

More acutely, the acquisition of artifacts—music, paintings, sculpture, silver—by the Aikens fits comfortably into what Bushman has called the "spread of refinement" among Americans. He wrote that "the spread of gentility speaks for the enduring allure of royal palaces, great country estates, for the enticing mystery of nobility and gentry, for the enchantment of these seemingly charmed and exalted lives, for the enthrallment with their grace of movement, speech, and costume." That Americans were drawn to European culture and refinement as they negotiated between an aristocratic past and a democratic future seems particularly apt in describing the Aikens.[13] Harriet's disappointment with the new French Republic in 1848, the family's residency in Paris, and the addition of an art gallery to the house on Elizabeth Street all served to elevate the Aikens above South Carolina's elite families and to anoint them with a cultural preeminence that was primarily French.

As styles changed between 1820 and 1860, so too did Henrietta's music collection. Italian opera came to dominate the popular repertory of the 1840s and 1850s, and this is evident in her individual pieces. Her surviving sheet music testifies that she was a talented singer. The several vocal and piano tutorials that now exist in the Charleston Museum, either as single sheets (SMS) or bound sheets (SMB), tell us that her parents, probably Harriet, saw to it that Henrietta studied the preeminent tutorials in these areas, mostly of European origin. She eventually acquired arias from Italian operas, in addition to singular choices that might have served as souvenirs of her trips overseas. It is difficult to see some of the pieces, such as the simple Swiss songs, in any other light because Henrietta seems to have been an exceptionally accomplished singer.

The wide-ranging styles, languages, and difficulty of Henrietta's vocal music, when considered in conjunction with her method books, suggest that her interests in music were more than casual. That her relations considered her an exceptional musician further promotes the idea that music was important to her and not merely something to satisfy society's expectation of accomplishment. Her talent and frequent participation in music practice make a compelling case for why her sheet music remained unbound: Henrietta continued to use her music and did not intend to cease doing so, even after she married Burnet Rhett in 1862.

PART THREE

The McCord Family

Five binder's volumes in the Charleston Museum sheet music collection belonged to Louisa Rebecca McCord and her daughter, Louisa Cheves Smythe (1867–1939). Four are Louisa Rebecca's, and these vividly expose different aspects of a wealthy young southern woman's life between 1855 and 1865. Three, SMB volumes 30, 37, and 42, combine repertory from the halcyon days in Columbia and Charleston during the 1850s with her experiences while in Europe from the summer of 1858 until late fall in 1859. Her fourth binder's volume, SMB 29, elucidates cultural life during the Civil War and functions as a sort of microscope by which to observe how the war interrupted the lives of affluent young women in the South. It supplements other accounts of how the war impinged on young southern women and their music, such as Sarah Morgan Dawson's famous *A Confederate Girl's Diary*.[1] Her daughter's book, SMB 5, veers from antebellum music choices and manifests the new repertory expected of young women after the war.

The circumstances surrounding Louisa Rebecca's volumes are enhanced by an account of her life that she compiled around 1928: "Recollections of Louisa McCord Smythe." This typescript is held in the South Caroliniana Library at the University of South Carolina and is widely quoted by scholars whose research interest is Louisa Susannah Cheves McCord, Louisa Rebecca's famous mother.[2] "Recollections" primarily describes their lives between 1850 and 1877 and is rich in details of their day-to-day activities through this period. It is not entirely accurate, particularly concerning dates, but remains beneficial for examining her experiences as a young elite woman before and during the Civil War.[3] Taken together, the binder's volumes and memoirs provide a rich account of cultural life in mid-nineteenth-century South Carolina.

Like Henrietta Aiken, Louisa Rebecca belonged to a powerful political family in South Carolina.[4] Her maternal grandfather, Langdon Cheves (1776–1857), served as Speaker of the U.S. House of Representatives in 1814–15 and was made president of the Second Bank of the United States in 1819. He left his political career in Washington for that of a planter in South Carolina, a move that better positioned his children as candidates for prosperous marriages because planters occupied the top of the social ladder.[5] Consequently, Langdon purchased several plantations, including Lang Syne in what is now Calhoun County and Inverary and Smithfield in Jasper County.[6]

Severe dementia marked Langdon's final years, and during this period his daughter Louisa Susannah Cheves (1810–79), Louisa Rebecca's mother, was his primary caregiver. She was such a forceful personality that any interpretation of her daughter's musical education necessitates some context surrounding her life at home, which differed dramatically from that of Henrietta Aiken. In recent decades cultural historians have acknowledged Mother Louisa as a leading intellectual figure of the antebellum South. A complex woman who has been the subject of several studies, Mother Louisa grew up among the aristocracy of Charleston.[7] Her mother was Mary Dulles, the daughter of an influential planter in Orangeburg District, and she brought a new level of social respectability to the Cheves family. This can be seen in the family's social connections. Her granddaughter's memoirs tell the story of a dinner party given by Langdon where William Lowndes and Hugh Legare were in attendance, being "great friends" of Judge Cheves.[8] Such connections with elite Charlestonians continued throughout her life. Although her parents raised Mother Louisa in the traditional manner of young southern elite women of her generation, such as sending her to school in Philadelphia, several stories suggest that she longed for the more rigorous academic tutoring reserved for young men. She was a keen mathematician from a young age, and Langdon caught her eavesdropping on her brother's tutorials and thereafter allowed her to be educated in "branches of man's education."[9] One of her biographers, Jessie Melville Fraser, wrote in 1920 that she ranked among those of Charleston's literary school, which flourished during the 1840s and 1850s.[10]

A more recent biographer, Leigh Fought, has painted a more complex picture of Mother Louisa as a young woman with literary ambitions, noting that she did not follow in the footsteps of her older sister by marrying at the expected age but rather remained at home caring first for her ailing mother and then for her father. Fought has proposed that Mother Louisa initially avoided marriage for several reasons. A particularly compelling case can be made for her wanting to preserve a degree of freedom. Her grandmother willed thirty-eight slaves to her when she was the young age of twenty, and her father gave Mother Louisa her own plantation—Lang Syne, just outside of Columbia—when in 1840, at the rather late age of thirty, she married David James McCord, president of a

Columbia bank. This property remained in her name even after marriage, which testifies to her independence in an age when women rarely owned land and controlled it while married.[11] Fought also has suggested that Mother Louisa may have avoided tying herself to a husband out of her reverence for her father; because she placed Langdon on a lofty pedestal, no man would overcome her first allegiance to him. Indeed, when Langdon's library was fitted in 1852, Mother Louisa decked it out with matching desks on either side of the fireplace: one for him and one for her. As further proof of her adoration for her father, Mother Louisa lies buried beside her father and not her husband, and her tombstone lists the connection to her father first.

After their marriage, David and Mother Louisa built a home in Columbia on the northwest corner of Pendleton and Bull Streets. In modern studies, David's life story has often been eclipsed by that of his famous wife. Nonetheless, he contributed to Louisa Rebecca's development in numerous ways. She painted a picture of her father as a raconteur who loved fine wine and stylish dinner parties. David's career demonstrated that he valued educational reform, and he served as a trustee of South Carolina College. David also spent time with his children, Langdon, Hannah, and Louisa, in choosing, binding, and reading books.[12]

Nevertheless, in her "Recollections," Louisa Rebecca devoted much more space to her mother, perhaps because her father died relatively early in her life. It is possible, however, that in the early twentieth century she recognized the impact of her mother's contributions to southern literary culture. Mother Louisa achieved her place among southern intellectuals through her writings in several genres. She translated Frédéric Bastiat's *Sophismes économiques,* at the suggestion of her husband, in 1848. A secure knowledge of French was an accomplishment that elite southern belles were expected to have, but translating economic treatises was not. Nonetheless, editors impressed with her translation of Bastiat requested more translations, which she supplied. She wrote in several genres and penned numerous critiques, and her complete works contribute substantially to modern appreciations of legal issues and law in the antebellum South.[13] In addition to law and economic literary works, Mother Louisa wrote a book of poetry, *My Dreams,* in 1848 and published articles and essays in the *Southern Quarterly Review, DeBow's Review,* and the *Southern Literary Messenger* during the 1850s. She published a closet drama, *Caius Gracchus,* in 1851. Her writing style, consistent throughout her works, has been described as energetic with "hard-driving argument and invective."[14] Intellectually respectable though they may be, these terms hardly equate with attributes sought by most southern women.

Famously, Mother Louisa supported conservative values, upholding traditional southern codes of conduct while at the same time behaving in ways that were antithetical to those codes. Between 1848 and 1856 she published thirteen essays, a play, and several book reviews, all the while promoting slavery, women's subordination to men, and separate spheres because they were the basis of social order as she understood it. She believed that young women should be educated, but also that they should not participate in public life. Her actions challenge modern notions of the southern belle, although more recent evaluations by Fought; Richard Cecil Lounsbury, the editor of Mother Louisa's works; and Michael O'Brien have lent a more nuanced view to southern intellectuals in general and Mother Louisa in particular. She chafed against the tradition that bound her to home while simultaneously adamantly defending these values.[15] Thus, while Mother Louisa clearly falls under the "cult of real womanhood" as defined by Frances Cogan, she paradoxically enthusiastically supported the "cult of true [or ideal] womanhood" as coined by Barbara Welter.[16] This paradox is critical in considering how she raised her daughters.

Even as a married woman, Mother Louisa maintained much of her freedom, which strained her marriage because it challenged antebellum conventions. That she differed from other women is obvious in this regard alone. Her fellow South Carolinian Jane Caroline North described her in 1852 as "a masculine clever person, with the most mannish attitudes and gestures."[17] This nineteenth-century depiction of Mother Louisa confirms modern assessments of her literary work, but Jane North spoke of the woman herself, not her writing. Again, the picture is of a woman whose personality did not submit gently, as southern women were taught to behave. Nonetheless, she acquiesced in certain matters, including agreeing to David's choices of how long to remain in Columbia, where they made their home. Mother Louisa chafed at some of his decisions, and by 1852 she evidently desired to move away from Columbia and David's circle, presumably longing for the more cosmopolitan life available in Charleston. She wrote to Mary Dulles on 25 August 1852, "What would I not give for a walk on the beach . . . with my brats tumbling along before me. I am almost sick of this horrid little place Columbia. I hope that Mr. McC. will get his fill of it some day. For surely I cannot see where the society he dreams of is."[18] That she referred to her children as "brats" in a letter further highlights Mother Louisa's unconventional approach to her role in southern society. The conflict between Mother Louisa and David is manifested in Louisa Rebecca's music: she fulfilled society's expectations but only halfheartedly.

David died in 1855, when Louisa Rebecca was nine years old. He did not make any provision for his children by Mother Louisa in his will, dated 21 February 1854, presumably because she had her own plantation and its income. The fallout over the division of his estate further stressed any familial feelings between Mother Louisa and her stepchildren. Two of the children from his first marriage refused to see her after David's death because they suspected that she would challenge the will. One even called her insane.[19] Little information was recorded about the lives of her own children during this period, but they must have been aware of tensions in their mother's life.

Even without inheriting anything from her husband, Mother Louisa appears to have maintained the family in relative comfort. Nonetheless, Mother Louisa saw many struggles during her final decades. She began losing her eyesight in the 1850s, and in 1857 alone she pursued cures in White Sulphur Springs, Sweet Springs, and Old Sweet Springs in Virginia, with her children at each. Despairing of these treatments, she eventually sought the aid of oculists in Europe in 1858–59. When war came in 1861, she threw herself behind the Confederacy, using every means in her power to support it. In addition to giving her own money, Mother Louisa served as president of the Soldiers' Relief Association and the Ladies' Clothing Association, and she even worked in a military hospital at South Carolina College. Her only son, Langdon Cheves McCord, died at age twenty-one in January 1863 from wounds sustained in battle. Severely depressed after the Confederacy's defeat, she refused to take the oath of allegiance and immigrated to Canada, but only after coming to the realization that her first choice, Hawaii, was beyond her financial reach. Mother Louisa finally returned to South Carolina in 1871, the year in which she died.[20]

Without a doubt, Louisa Rebecca's mother differed significantly from the mothers of her peers; yet how Mother Louisa influenced her daughter is difficult to ascertain. Although Mother Louisa attended some of the best schools for girls in Philadelphia, including Mr. Grimshaw's and Monsieur Picot's, she did not send her daughter Louisa Rebecca, born 10 August 1845, to boarding school for an extended period. Louisa Rebecca explained that she did not go away to school because her mother did not believe it to be beneficial for young women. This reasoning, found in Louisa Rebecca's "Recollections," may be somewhat flawed, because Mother Louisa's older daughter, Hannah (1843–72), did go to school, as did Louisa Rebecca for a brief period. It is possible that Mother Louisa's own educational journey, living seven years in seclusion with a French family in Philadelphia, influenced her attitudes toward sending her daughters away.[21] Her approach to her own daughters' education can be described as lackadaisical, although Louisa Rebecca defended her by writing that "she was neither [negligent nor indifferent in the matter of their education], but she had her ideas, and one was that she saw no necessity especially for girls for so much school training. She believes in letting an education be absorbed unconsciously as much as possible."[22] Mother Louisa apparently allowed her children control of much of their time in Europe: perhaps this freedom reflects her desire that they "absorb" an education. Tellingly, Louisa Rebecca felt the need to defend her mother's actions concerning her own schooling.

Despite declaring that she did not go to school, Louisa Rebecca did, in fact, attend school for six months. Being a self-styled "mama's baby," however, she was allowed to come home. Unfortunately, she did not say where she matriculated.[23] That Mother Louisa's second daughter's schooling was so brief seems unusual, considering her own strong academic interests and learning, but it reflects the dual nature of many aspects of her actions and writings.

The McCord children, Langdon, Hannah, and Louisa Rebecca, unquestionably received instruction at home. Mother Louisa taught them French and read to them daily, including a heavy dose of Sir Walter Scott's fiction. She would read to them in the large hall in the center of the house, also called "the old dining room." David McCord bound some of their books himself, in calico and paste-board.[24] This particular memory of Louisa Rebecca's serves as a reminder that in this period most books were sold unbound, and consumers had them bound to match others in their libraries. This practice was already beginning to change by the 1850s, but the books of music examined in this study fall under the earlier practice.[25]

Other people took part in the education of the McCord children. According to Louisa Rebecca, she traveled from Lang Syne to Madame Davilliera's house in Columbia three times a week to practice French conversation so that she could speak it with her grandmother Hannah Turquand, David's mother, whom she described as "very frenchy."[26] Such instruction also reflects an emphasis on speaking French that many southern elite white children experienced as part of their regular education.

Less common was the McCords' instruction in German. Francis Lieber, a self-proclaimed professor of history and political economics at nearby South Carolina College from 1835 to 1856, came to Lang Syne during his time in Columbia to teach the McCord children German, or perhaps they went to him for lessons.[27] Lieber was not an obvious choice as a tutor for the McCords, and his views on slavery made him a controversial figure after 1860. However, Mother Louisa's selection of him reflects the eclectic education she provided for her children and provides a basis by which to view her influence on Louisa Rebecca's musical education. She chose the most prominent person available to teach German to her young progeny, but she also chose someone who worked as a professor in advanced studies and not an instructor with experiences as an elementary language teacher. Mother Louisa had good intentions in providing a well-rounded and thorough education for Langdon, Hannah, and Louisa Rebecca, but she rarely followed through with a consistent program of instruction. The same attitude resounds in Louisa Rebecca's music.

The McCord children had a number of other tutors during the antebellum period, including a Mr. Williams, who had been in the British army, and his wife. They remained at Lang Syne for one or two years. James Wood Davidson, from South Carolina College, arrived after the Williamses. The most memorable teacher Louisa Rebecca recalled was a Jewish tutor named Mr. Bendan, who Mother Louisa claimed came with a recommendation from Alexander von Humboldt, the famous Prussian philosopher and scientist. Bendan was let go for being too harsh and, more specifically, for directly accusing Hannah of lying.[28] Thus it seems that a string of instructors came to Lang Syne to work with the McCord children, and as far as can be determined from the "Recollections," the three children received their instruction together. In this Mother Louisa realized her own desire to receive the same instruction as her brother.[29]

The children also studied music at home, but there is little direct comment about what they practiced or with whom they studied, except for Miss Garnett, an Irishwoman; and Angelo Torriani—both after 1859.[30] Louisa Rebecca thought she recalled a piano at Pendleton in the hall, a space "extraordinarily long with eight little doors up and down."[31] Once their grandfather moved to Lang Syne, the children performed "theatricals" for him, and in return he taught them to drink good coffee and wine.[32] These types of "performances" were common during the antebellum period among wealthy southerners, and little shame seems to have been associated with such displays since they took place before private audiences at home.

Even though she rarely mentioned music studies in her "Recollections," Louisa Rebecca owned a substantial amount of music and must have studied with several teachers. Her four binder's volumes in the Charleston Museum—SMB 29, SMB 30, SMB 37, and SMB 42—are divided into two main parts. Three volumes—30, 37, and 42—are less clearly demarcated and belong to the antebellum period, mostly the 1850s. Almost all of her music is for solo voice, but there are a few exceptions. An examination of these three volumes considers their contents in light of the McCord family's sojourns of 1858–59. SMB 29 stands apart from the other three because most of it dates from the period of the Civil War.

CHAPTER 12

Louisa Rebecca's Antebellum Music Collection

Undoubtedly, SMB 30, SMB 37, and SMB 42 reflect the repertory that Louisa Rebecca owned before the Civil War, and each contains music purchased in the United States and abroad. Her maiden name is stamped on the outside of each in gold, signifying that they were bound before her marriage to Augustine Smythe in 1867. SMB 37 and SMB 42 look identical from the outside: both are covered in marbled paper, with spines of black leather and gold lettering and decoration on black nameplates. Both give her name as "Louisa R. McCord." These parallels imply that they were probably compiled and bound contemporaneously by the same binder. SMB 30 looks slightly different; for example, only "L R McCord" is stamped in gilt on the cover. However, more similarity in content marks SMB 30 and SMB 42 because of the haphazard organization of SMB 37. Moreover, both contain seventeen pieces, as opposed to the thirty-four in SMB 37. Indeed, the latter volume seems to reflect the McCords' European journey more closely than the others because of groupings by national type, but pieces purchased while overseas appear in the other volumes as well. As such, they divide less in chronological order, although most of SMB 30 and SMB 42 seems earlier than SMB 37. Louisa Rebecca was only sixteen when the war broke out, which means that she would have had less time than Henrietta did to accumulate music before the war. Thus, her three volumes confirm a decided interest in music as if it were not a mere passing fancy or something done only to please others.

The only one of these binder's volumes having an index is SMB 30, and unlike most other antebellum binder's volumes, this one lists the pieces by genres of sorts.[1] The groupings begin with the duets, follow with a "Selection of Scotch Songs," and end with the remaining songs. The entire repertory in SMB 30 may generally be described as Scotch songs and English ballads by popular composers such as Glover, Balfe, Stevenson, Bishop, Handel, and Mrs. Norton. Louisa

Rebecca included perennial favorites such as "Oft in the Stilly Night" and "Tis the Last Rose of Summer," and all of the texts are in English. She also had two Italian arias and two Handel works bound into this volume.

The songs in SMB 30 resemble more closely the types of pieces found in Harriet Lowndes's earliest binder's volume than in those from the 1850s, and indeed some of the music dates from the 1830s and 1840s. (See table 12.1.) They are uncharacteristic, though, of those found in the collections of wealthier women from the 1850s, and several of the compositions in SMB 30 were published in the 1850s. Bel canto arias, such as those from *Norma,* were more numerous in contemporary southern collections, such as that of M. P. (Marianne Porcher Smith?) Alston (SMB 27), which includes "Va crudele" ("Go Proud Maiden") from *Norma;* "Una voce poca fa," "as sung by Signorina Garcia," from *Il barbiere di Siviglia;* "I'll Pray for Thee" from Donizetti's *Lucia di Lammermoor;* and "Ah Where Flee So Rapidly" from Meyerbeer's *Il Crociato.*[2] This may be reading too much into the absence of bel canto arias in SMB 30, for Louisa Rebecca may have been too young to sing the arias of Verdi and Bellini at this time.

The index's division by genre in SMB 30 tells us something about how people interpreted music in mid-century Charleston, even if the person who organized it remains unidentified. The practical nature of isolating the duets would make them easier to find when the occasion warranted two singers, which suggests that the books could have been used in performance or that someone wanted the index to this binder's volume organized by genre.[3] The emphasis on "Scotch Songs" in particular is noteworthy, even if several others in that genre—for example, "Auld Lang Syne" and "Duncan Gray"—were not included in the index under this heading. But there was no such practical need to name the Scotch songs, which suggests that they were considered a standard genre and something Louisa Rebecca might have turned to more frequently than others. By 1860, however, the Scotch songs constituted a less significant part of the typical repertory performed by young southern women in their teens. Their presence here testifies to the continued popularity of this genre in the antebellum period, but we should also allow that they represent her mother's influence on Louisa Rebecca's music collection, much as Harriet exercised over Henrietta's. The McCords purchased more of the same styled music in Great Britain, and they visited Scotland and Ireland, whereas the Aikens do not appear to have done so. The McCords' preference seems to have been for England.

None of the sheet music in SMB 30 has a date, but searches of archives in the United States and Britain yield dates ranging from 1831 to 1859.[4] Five songs sold in the United States came from Ditson in Boston, Firth in New York, and Willig in Baltimore. "Home to Our Mountain," Dressler's arrangement of Verdi's "Si, La Stanchezza Moppri mi," does not include a publisher, but Firth, Pond & Co.

Table 12.1. Contents of SMB 30

No.	Title	Composer	Date	Notes
1	Spanish Ballad/Waneta or Juanita	Mrs. Norton		Baltimore: Willig. Lots of marks, duet.
2	What are the wild waves saying	S. Glover		London: Robert Cock. Lots of marks in both piano and voice parts.
3	A voice	S. Glover		London: Robert Cock
4	Vocal Beauties of Lucia di Lammermoor: Oh! Haste crimson morning	G. Donizetti; Edward L. White, arr.		Boston: Ditson. *Lucia di Lammermoor*
5	Home to our mountain ("Si, La Stanchezza Moppri me")	G. Verdi; arr. William Dressler		n.p.
6	List to thee	John Blockley		London: Addison
7	Selection of Popular Scotch Songs [series]	G. Macfarren	[1859–67]	Edinburgh: Wood; sold Liverpool: Hine & Son
8	Duncan Gray from the *Vocal Melodies of Scotland*	Finlay Dun	[1836]	
9	Angel's whisper	Samuel Lover	[1831–37]	London: Duff. "Louisa R. McCord / Paris Oct. 1858"
10	Tis the last rose of summer	John Stevenson	[185-]	NY: Firth & Pond
11	She is far from the land	Vincent Novello		London: Novello. "London June 8th 1859"
12	Go where glory waits thee	M. Balfe		London: Novello

13	Oft in the stilly night	John Stevenson	[old]	Boston: Ditson; sold Columbia: J. Rawl's
14	What tho' I trace?	G.F. Handel; arr. William Horsley	[ca. 1844]	London: Cramer, Addison & Beale; sold London: Charles Ollivier
15	Angels bright and fair	G.F. Handel		London: Charles Ollivier
16	God save the Queen	Vincent Novello, arr.	[ca. 1855]	London: Novello. "London June 8th 1859." Choral parts included
17	The mistletoe bough	Henry Bishop		Boston: Ditson

published this version of the aria in New York in 1856. None bears a Columbia or Charleston seller's stamp, and a member of the McCord family may have bought them while traveling in the North. The possibility also remains that a music dealer in Columbia or Charleston sold music but did not stamp it. Including familiar songs such as "Tis the Last Rose of Summer," the American imprints are old enough to have belonged previously to Mother Louisa or another member of the family before coming to Louisa Rebecca.

Louisa Rebecca bought eleven of the seventeen pieces in SMB 30 while abroad. Two—Macfarren's *Selection of Popular Scotch Songs* and Finlay Dun's "Duncan Gray" from the *Vocal Melodies of Scotland*—appear to have been picked up when the family traveled through Liverpool, possibly on their way home.[5] Of particular interest are two items purchased at Novello & Co. at 69 Dean Street, which she marked "London June 8th 1859." "Let Erin Remember," by Balfe, is similarly inscribed, and others bearing this date in SMB 37 show that she shopped at that establishment while in London in June 1859. Louisa Rebecca also acquired Vincent Novello's setting of "God Save the Queen," which may represent an attraction to English culture and customs.

SMB 30 also contains two songs by Stephen Glover that were purchased by the McCords; these occupy positions two and three in the volume. Consumers could buy Glover's music on both sides of the Atlantic, and Louisa Rebecca obtained both "What Are the Wild Waves Saying" and "A Voice" while in London. She used at least the former, as figure 12.1 illustrates. In this example someone has indicated that she should alter the text's setting on "Hath It Not" and finger the bass notes (left hand) in the following measure.[6] Glover's works also figure prominently in the beginning of SMB 37, but these came from American publishers.

Unlike the Scotch songs of SMB 30, the repertory in SMB 42 reflects both a fashionable fascination with traditional songs and a desire for newer music, qualities that can be gleaned from many southern binder's volumes of the 1850s. (See table 12.2.) Well-known songs associated with the "Old World" abound in SMB 42, including "The Blue Bells of Scotland," "Annie Lawrie [*sic*]," and "Kathleen Mavourneen." Louisa Rebecca's version of "The Blue Bells of Scotland" is for piano solo.[7] Most of the music in SMB 42 dates from the mid-1830s to the early 1850s, when both Hannah and Louisa Rebecca would have been younger than ten years old, and internal evidence indicates that Louisa Rebecca engaged with these songs when she was twelve to thirteen years old. Music from ten years earlier would not necessarily have been too old to be considered popular music during the antebellum period: many young women had music at least that old in their binder's volumes, especially those of less prosperous families. Indeed, it is rare and a sign of considerable wealth or opportunity that binder's volumes include music published only within a few years of their collection.[8]

Figure 12.1. "What Are the Wild Waves Saying," p. 7, with Louisa Rebecca's marking

One of the popular songs in SMB 42 is "Ben Bolt," a sentimental ballad that had at least twenty-seven printed editions by 1848. Composed by Nelson Kneass to words by Thomas Dunn English, "Ben Bolt" was the basis of a number of spin-offs, including several versions of "Ben Bolt Polka" and William Vincent Wallace's seventeen-page "Grand fantaisie de concert sur la ballade Americaine Ben Bolt," dedicated to Madame (Jeanne Roman) de la Villebeuvre of New Orleans (1853), daughter of the governor of Louisiana.[9] Its presence in SMB 42 testifies to Louisa Rebecca's familiarity with the popular repertory of the 1840s and 1850s.

She signed her name "Louisa Rebecca McCord" in pencil on "Annie Lawrie [*sic*]" on page 49 of SMB 42; however, several other names and places written or stamped into SMB 42 make its history less than straightforward. Most of the music in this binder's volume dates from before the family's trip to Europe in 1858–59, but Louisa Rebecca wrote "Louisa Rebecca McCord // Paris // January 18 [or 10—the number was cut off in the binding of the volume]" on the first page of "O! Would I Were a Boy Again!" (SMB 42, page 95). This notation might lead to the assumption that this piece came from the European tour, and

Table 12.2. Contents of SMB 42

No.	Title	Composer	Date	Notes
1	The last man	William Hutchins Callcott	[?1850; 1st published 1828]	NY: Firth & Hall; sold Philadelphia: Willig.
2	Farewell to the mountain	John Barnett	[1835]	Philadelphia: Fiot, Meignen & Co.; sold at Wm Fischer's, Washington. "Harry Drayton"
3	Of what is the old man thinking	Joseph Philip Knight	[1841]	London: Mori & Lavenu's New Musical Subscription Library, 28 New Bond Street
4	Live with a playful heart / Adapted to a celebrated Bohemian melody	A.F. Müllen	[?1845]	London: Joseph Williams
5	Agatha, or When the swallows homeward fly	F. Abt; arr. Max Zorer,	1849	NY: Firth, Hall & Co.
6	The blue bells of Scotland	[none]		London: W. Young
7	Ben Bolt Ballad	Nelson Kneass	[1848]	Cincinnati: W.C. Peters
8	Annie Lawrie [sic]			Boston: Ditson. "Louisa Rebecca McCord"
9	The watcher	Dr. William Lardner	[?1846]	Louisville: D.P. Faulds. Words by Sarah Josepha Hale
10	Favorite Songs and Ballads / Arranged as Duets ("Kathleen Mavourneen")	E.J. Loder, arr.	[ca. 1858]	Boston: Ditson. Duet
11	The seven sisters or The solitude of Binnore	John Rheyn		NY: Firth & Hall. "Henry Drayton from the Author's Brother."

12	Home! Sweet home!	Henry Bishop	[1858]	London: D'Almaine & Co. "Sung by Miss M. Tree in Clari, or The Maid of Milan at the Theatre Royal Covent Garden. Also by Miss Stephens at the Musical Festivals / Also by Madame Sontag and Mad'lle Jenny Lind"
13	Home again!	J.P. Ordway	1850	Boston: Wade. "Dedicated most affectionately to Lizzie C. Oakes, of Charleston, S.C."
14	I cannot smile dear mother	George Barker	[?1855]	London: Joseph Williams
15	Oh! Fly to the prairie	Joseph Philip Knight	1839	Philadelphia: George Hewitt
16	O! Would I were a boy again!	F. Romer	184[?]	NY: Hewitt & Jaques. sold in Philadelphia: Willig. "Louisa R. McCord // Paris January 18," "Henry Drayton" beside title.
17	Would I were with thee!	Carlo Bosetti	1850	Philadelphia: Lee & Walker. "Hannah McC[ord]" cut off

indeed Louisa Rebecca signed pieces she bought in Europe this way. She did not purchase this piece while in Paris, however, because this page has a Philadelphia bookseller's stamp. SMB 42 must have been bound after the family returned from Europe, because several of its songs were purchased in London. Most likely she took some music with her, which explains the notation of "Paris // January 18" on "O! Would I Were a Boy Again!" Such a habit perhaps explains why Samuel Lover's "Angel's Whisper" in SMB 30 has been marked "Louisa R. McCord / Paris Oct. 1858" even though it was published in London.[10] This inscription implies that Louisa Rebecca studied the song in Paris, perhaps with her music teacher.

"O! Would I Were a Boy Again!" also bears the name "Harry Drayton" written in ink. Henry Drayton (1823–62) was born in Charleston and later moved to Philadelphia, where he worked as a doctor. His name, as "Henry," also appears on "Annie Lawrie [*sic*]" on page 49. Moreover, "The Seven Sisters, or The Solitude of Binnore," on page 63, was given to Henry Drayton by the author's brother, according to an inscription on the first page. John Rheyn, the composer who set Wordsworth's poem, does not appear to have published any other titles.[11] In addition, "Harry Drayton" appears on "Ah! How I Love Thee" in SMB 37 (page 60)—the volume that represents the McCords' European journey. The most likely explanation for his name in SMB 42 is that one of the McCord sisters received the music from Henry Drayton while visiting family and friends in Philadelphia or (less likely) that Drayton sent them the music.

Several possibilities might explain why SMB 42 has connections to both "Paris" and "Philadelphia." Louisa Rebecca probably took the music with her on her journey overseas as a means of filling her time, expecting pianos to be available for her along the way. Such accommodations would have been expected by the McCords because they existed in South Carolina: when Micajah Adolphus Clark traveled to Columbia in the summer of 1857, he noted that his room at the Congaree Hotel included "a fine piano."[12] The McCords probably encountered instruments on which she could practice as they toured Europe, and she must have had access to a piano while in Paris as the music from her lessons includes markings for the piano part.

In SMB 42 "Hannah Mc" appears on "Would I Were with Thee!" on page 101, which suggests that Hannah Cheves, Louisa Rebecca's sister, used at least some of the music therein. Most likely the two young women played and/or sang from this sheet music. Evidence of music sharing among family members can be seen in numerous binder's volumes from this period, and that Louisa Rebecca and Hannah, the elder by two years, both used the same music is not unusual. This song has the number "101" written at the top, which suggests that the McCord girls owned quite a few pieces of sheet music.[13] Such numbers often appear at the top of initial pages in larger collections and seem to depict a cataloging system of sorts. They do not indicate binding order.

Several of the pieces in SMB 42 employ images of or associations with popular performers in order to sell them. For example, on "Farewell to the Mountain" (1835) the publisher included "as Sung by Mr. Sheppard in Barnett's Grand Romantic Opera of the Mountain Sylph." Another song in SMB 42, "Home Again," arranged by J. P. Ordway, advertises its performers as a selling point. The first page of this work proclaims that it was made popular by the Harmoneons, a blackface minstrel group whose members included Marshall Pike, the original composer of "Home Again." A simple song of limited vocal range, a sixth, its three verses tell of the singer's longing to return home from a "foreign shore." It must have been popular in this area of South Carolina, a proposition made all the more likely because the dedicatee, Charlotte "Lizzie" Oakes, lived in Charleston. The binder's volume of a student from the nearby South Carolina Female Institute at Barhamville, Sallie English Doby, contains this version of "Home Again" as well.[14]

In all likelihood, Louisa Rebecca acquired much of the music in SMB 42 before her trip to Europe in 1858. All of the dealers who can be detected in SMB 42 were from the United States, and all of the music is in English. Some of the London pieces remain an enigma: were they bought there or imported? The only German work in SMB 42 is Franz Abt's "Agatha or When the Swallows Homeward Fly," a popular song published in a number of versions in the United States, including this one from Firth, Pond & Co. in New York. Abt's music can be found in several antebellum collections and does not necessarily associate an owner with European travel. Abt was a German composer credited with over three thousand works published in six hundred opus numbers. His music was frequently sung by German singing societies, of which there were several in the antebellum South.[15] The musicologist Allen Lott found that in the years following the Civil War, Abt's works came to represent "German music" on American concert programs, much to the dismay of the well-known conductor Hans von Bülow.[16] Before the war, women sang his songs because they resembled many others in their collections.

Abt's music in SMB 42 should not be understood as exemplifying the emphasis on German in the McCord household. Rather, it corresponds to trends in other binder's volumes from across the South. Henrietta Aiken owned "When the Swallows Homeward Fly" (SMS 518), as did Margaret Sue Wingfield of Portsmouth, Virginia. Mary E. Capp Wilbur of Savannah included the same song from the 1848 *Gems from the German: A Collection of the Most Admired Songs of Beethoven, Spohr, Schubert, Weber, Kücken,* and she purchased her copy in Savannah at Zogbaum's store. In August 1853 John Sullivan Dwight reviewed the eighth series, noting that "When the Swallows Homeward Fly" was indeed Abt's claim to fame in America; he noted this again when he wrote in *Dwight's Journal of Music* of 1853 that "Franz Abt, author of 'When the swallows homeward fly,' is appointed second chapel-master in Brunswick."[17] Later publications of the song, including Confederate imprints by Schreiner, existed in several extant southern collections, proving its enduring popularity.[18] Missing from SMB 42 are the Italian and French operatic repertories. By the late 1850s many binder's volumes included at least simple versions of arias and duets by Rossini, Meyerbeer, and Bellini.[19] Louisa Rebecca may have been too young for these, although in her entire collection there are a few.

CHAPTER 13

Europe in 1858–1859

None of Louisa Rebecca's binder's volumes reflects the family's time overseas as well as SMB 37 does. In 1858 Mother Louisa determined that she would travel to Europe seeking remedy from renowned oculists for her failing eyesight, and this trip figures prominently in Louisa Rebecca's "Recollections." A substantial collection, SMB 37 confirms many of the points she made in the "Recollections," the sum of which demonstrates aspects of the music a twelve-year-old southern girl might experience abroad. (See table 13.1.) Her collection contrasts with that of Henrietta in many ways. It is important to remember that if the only music of Henrietta's that survived were from when she was the same age, around thirteen, her collection too would lack much of the bel canto repertory.

Somewhat surprisingly, Mother Louisa allowed her children to choose if they wanted to go to Europe. Since most southerners undertook such a journey in large part to introduce their children to European culture firsthand, Mother Louisa's option to travel or not seems irregular. Two of her own brothers traveled abroad at about this same time. One, Haynes Cheves, died in Florence, Italy, in 1856. Another, Langdon Jr., journeyed to Paris in 1858.[1] That she deliberately went for medical treatment, and not necessarily for a grand tour, might explain this lack of conviction to the cultural experience for her three children. Louisa Rebecca and her older brother Langdon Cheves (1841–63) opted to go. Hannah Cheves declined because she had recently settled in school with a close friend whom she did not want to abandon, and because she assumed that the family would be able to go again in the near future. Mother Louisa's personal physician, Dr. John W. Powell, accompanied them as both physician and male chaperone.[2]

Louisa Rebecca wrote that they left in the summer of 1857 and returned in late fall 1858, but their passport applications were dated 25 June 1858.[3] Furthermore, she related their return to the "eve" of Lincoln's nomination, which did not occur until May 1860. Finally, she wrote the dates of December 1858 and January

Table 13.1. Contents of SMB 37

No.	Title	Composer	Date	Notes
1	The Christian Graces (No. 1 "Faith")	S. Glover	[?1858]	NY: Hall & Son
2	Faith Hope & Charity / 3 Songs (No. 2 "Hope")	S. Glover	[?1849; 1859]	NY: Firth, Pond & Co. (inside Hall & Son
3	The Christian Graces (No. 2 "Charity")	S. Glover	[?1858]	NY: Hall & Son
4	When stars are in the quiet skies	Alexander Ball	1853	Boston: Reed
5	Let Erin remember	M. Balfe		London: Novello. "London June 8th 1859"
6	Willie we have missed you, or Welcome, welcome home / Song and Chorus	Stephen C. Foster	[1858]	London: Leader & Cock
7	The dream is past	S. Glover	[184-]	Philadelphia: Lee & Walker. [Fiot]
8	Ye sacred priests (recit and aria)	G.F. Handel; arr. William Horsley		London: Cramer, Addison & Beale. Sold London: Charles Ollivier
9	The bloodhound	Chevalier Sigismond Neukomm	[184-]	Boston: Ditson. "Harry Drayton" written sideways title.
10	I'll speak of thee, I'll love thee to	Maria B. Hawes	[1840]	London: W. Hawes. Dedicated to Countess of Essex
11	Ah! How I love thee	S.D.S.	1844	Philadelphia: F. Perring. "Harry Drayton"
12	Ave Maria	L. Puget	[?1839]	Paris: Meissonnier, and stamp. "Louisa R. McCord // Paris Dec. 1858." Dedicated to Princess Marie. Inside "Ave Maria Prière Par Melle Loïsa Puget."

13	À la grâce de Dieu	L. Puget	[?1836]	Paris: Meissonnier. Flaxland stamp?. "Louisa R. McCord // Paris Dec. 1858." Vocal line fingered for piano.
14	Huit ans / La prière sur le rivage	F. Masini	[1839–42]	Paris: Au Ménestrel, and stamp; and Meissonnier. Dedicated to Mme Iweins-d'Hennin
15	Près d'un berceau	Hippolyte Louel	[before 1846]	Paris: Au Ménestrel, and stamp; and Meissonnier. Chantée par Mme Iweins-d'Hennin
16	Se bouder	Etienne Arnaud	[1858]	Paris: Ikelmer, and stamp. Another stamp from Flaxland.
17	Daniel	A. de Latour	[1845]	Paris: A. Leduc, and stamp. Dedicated to Mme Iweins-d'Hennin
18	Le Retour de Daniel	A. de Latour	[184-]	Paris: A. Leduc, and stamp. Dedicated to Mme Iweins-d'Hennin
19	Le hautbois	A. de Latour	[1845]	Paris: A. Leduc, and stamp. Dedicated to Mme Cinti Damoreau
20	Norma / Tragedien Lirica Musica ("Me chiami o Norma" [recit] "Deh con te con te li prendi")	V. Bellini		Paris: Launer, and stamp
21	Farewell Leonora (Ah! Che la morte) / Air from the Opera Il Trovatore	G. Verdi	[1857 and 1858]	London: Young. Index: "Farewell Leonora"
22	Santa Lucia / Barcarola popolare	T. Cottrau	28 Oct. 1850	Naples: Stabilimento Musicale Partenopeo. Henrietta Aiken owned the same edition. Fingering in piano part.

Table 13.1. Contents of SMB 37 (*continued*)

No.	Title	Composer	Date	Notes
23	Lo Scoglio di Friso / *Nuove melodie poplar* [inside: Canzone popolare Napolitana] ("Lu vero Cardillo")	Pietro Labriola		Naples: Privilegiato Stabilimento Musicale Partenopeo di T. Cottrau
24	*Lieder Repertorium* / Songs of Germany, Scandinavia, etc. ("Am I not fondly thine own?," "Du, du liebst mir im herzen?")		[?1835]	London: C. Lonsdale. "Louisa R. McCord / Paris Dec. 1858
25	My son, the midnight hour is near / A Song ("Mein sohn, wo willst du hin so spät?")	F. Mendelssohn	1850	London: Addison & Hodson. "R" at top, more could have been cut off
26	No. 145 of Wessel & Co's Auswahl Deutscher Gesänge / Lebewohl / "Last greeting" / "Adieu" by Berganer / Voici l'instant supreme"	François Schubert		London: Wessel & Co. Importers and Publishers of Foreign Music. Sung by Miss Masson, Miss Wyndham, Miss Birch, &c.
27	No. 268 of Wessel & Co's Auswahl Deutscher Gesänge / Six Lieder ("'Tis thus decreed," "Es ist bestimmt in Gottes Rath")	Mendelssohn	[1845]	London: Wessel & Co. Importers and Publishers of Foreign Music. Publishers of ALL the works of Chopin, Kuhlau, Schubert, Henselt, Beethoven, Hummel, Mendelssohn, Reissiger, Thalberg, Rosenhain, Czerny, &c. University Library Cambridge
28	Stimmen der Völker / Sammlung Liedern aller Nationen ("Schweizer Lied: Steb nur auf")		[1844]	Berlin: Schlesinger. Sold in Philadelphia, chez Th. A. Schmidt. In German only.

29	Home Delights / A Sett of Beautiful Songs, composed by Glover, Cherry, Tully, Jarvis, &c.&c. ("Switzers Farewell"; inside "Abschied von der Sennerinn")	George Linley [cover has Mengis]	[ca. 1857]	Philadelphia: Beck & Lawton
30	Die schönsten Augen von Heine / The brightest eyes	G. Stigelli	[1857]	Paris: Offenbach. London stamp: J.J. Ewer & Co., 390 Oxford St. "Louisa R. McCord // Paris Oct. 1858. Has English translation
31	Airs suisses / Schweizerlieder (No. 19 "Schweizer Heimweh")			Basel: A. Hegar. Stamp Zurich: Fries & Holzmann
32	Airs suisses / Schweizerlieder (No. 16 "Des Alpenrösle")			Basel: A. Hegar. Stamp Zurich: Fries & Holzmann
33	Frühlingsgness des Schweizers an die Heim[?]			
34	Betrogne Liebe			

1859 on music purchased in Paris.[4] The sum of these facts clearly places the trip in summer 1858, with a return in late fall 1859.

The McCords began their itinerary in Ireland, Scotland, and England. Toward the end of her life, Mother Louisa wrote that the family spent a day in Aberdeen, took a "hurried tour through Scotland," and then went to the Orkney Islands. Louisa Rebecca recalled in her "Recollections" that while there, she happened upon a copy of *Uncle Tom's Cabin* for the first time; not surprisingly, given that her mother had been one of the first southerners to review the volume, Louisa Rebecca's encounter with the influential novel was not a positive one.[5] The family then traveled to Aberdeen once again before moving south into England.

The McCords moved on to Paris, where they initially lived in a hotel but later moved to an apartment on the Champs Élysées. There Mother Louisa engaged two servants along with a coach and pair of horses and a coachman, and the McCords "entered society." In Paris, M. Bretonnière, "some old white-haired Frenchman formally one of the orchestra of the Italian opera," taught Langdon flute and Louisa Rebecca "music."[6] The person with whom the McCord children studied music in Paris was Victor Joseph Barthélémy Bretonnière (1811–65), a French flutist who published several books of arrangements of popular melodies by Gounod, Verdi, and others.[7] Since Louisa Rebecca wrote that this teacher noted "signs of a very fine voice in me, so young as I was, I had singing lessons from him two [*sic*] of which I doubt the wisdom now," he must have instructed her in voice; the "too" probably meant that she also had piano lessons. Further confirmation of this exists in fingerings in music acquired during this journey, which suggests that she was playing the piano as well as singing.

Louisa Rebecca's music lessons continued the tradition for southern girls. In this case, however, Mother Louisa's motives were a bit unclear. According to her, the children received music lessons to abate their boredom while in Paris. She wrote to her brother on 30 October 1858, "My children are taking some lessons which serve to keep them amused and prevent too much homesickness." She did not mention any another purpose for her children's music lessons, which is strange considering that most other writers of her day described music as the most important accomplishment for young women. This is but one hint that Mother Louisa's approach to raising a southern lady differed from that of her contemporaries, including Harriet Lowndes. That Bretonnière also taught Langdon implies that Mother Louisa saw music lessons as one way to fill her children's days while she participated in more adult activities, including attending salons and visiting with oculists.

Whatever her mother's reasoning, Louisa Rebecca profited not only from the applied instruction with Bretonnière but also from broader issues of music aesthetics. She noted that "at the time I enjoyed it immensely and our intercourse with a good musician certainly enabled us to enjoy much more the music we were hearing."[8] Spending time with the French musician helped the young southerners better appreciate their experiences at the opera. Louisa Rebecca noted that it was a "splendid opera season," and her first visit to the opera was to see Bellini's *Norma,* a memorable evening in which "I could hardly be kept from standing up with excitement—I was wild!"[9] What precisely Louisa Rebecca understood as "wild" remains unknown, but southern women rarely described themselves as such. In the context of the standards decreed for demure southern belles, she obviously did not contain herself at the *Norma* performance. Indeed, when Catherine Boykin Jones of Georgia wrote about her two visits to operas in Paris in the summer of 1851, she expressed a distinctively different reaction. While she "was much interested in the set and scenery of 'La Prophet'" (Meyer-beer's *Le prophète*), she complained that everything was in French. Her final remarks evinced the genteel cultural education of young southern women: "I do not think, however, that I shall ever grow Opera mad. There is too much unnecessary & disgusting exposure, too much to tint the cheek of the modest & refined woman with the blush of shame. I find singing is not a sufficient pallia-tive for all this, and the result most to be dreaded is the feeling of indifference to these shocks of delicacy."[10] Catherine's response was in contrast to Louisa Rebecca's attraction to opera in Europe and serves as another reminder of the individual variation in southern women's culture.

What exactly did Louisa Rebecca hear? What prompted her to be so "wild"? In October 1858 Rosina Penco (as Norma), Francesco Graziani (as Pollione), and Mathilde Jeanne Cambardi (Chambard, as Adalgisa), sang in *Norma* at the Théâtre Italien. The performance on the 21st caused some notoriety because a famous chess match between Duke Karl of Brunswick, Count Isouard, and the American chess master Paul Charles Morphy also took place in the theater.[11] If Louisa Rebecca had been in attendance, she did not mention chess—a fact sug-gesting that she probably heard it on a different date.

Even without such a highly public diversion, the performance would have been memorable: Penco was at the height of her fame during the later 1850s, hav-ing debuted Verdi's Leonore in *Il trovatore* in 1853. She sang other performances of *Norma* at the Théâtre Italien besides the famous one on 21 October, and Louisa Rebecca most likely heard her in the title role. At such a performance, the girl from antebellum South Carolina might well have acted in a manner unbefitting a young lady. Although Charleston was the second-largest city in the South at this time, its theaters could not compare to the major opera houses of Europe. The sheer size of the opera house, orchestra, and chorus and the grand scenery contrasted dramatically with any performances that would have played in Charleston or Columbia, where traveling troupes often staged abbreviated versions of popular works. Another distinction Louisa Rebecca must have noticed is how the audience behaved during the performance. As Jennifer Hall-Witt has demonstrated in *Fashionable Acts: Opera and Elite Culture in London, 1780–1880,* European audiences by this time were quiet during performances, as compared to those in America, who were not.[12] Southern women noticed this difference too. When Octavia Walton Le Vert, the "Belle of the Union" from Alabama, heard Daniel Auber's *L'ambassadrice* on 26 July 1853 at the Opéra Comique, she observed that the audience seemed "perfectly absorbed" in the performance and no one whispered during it.[13] This circumstance stood in contrast to her experiences in American theaters, which were numerous.

While in Paris, Americans figured prominently in the McCords' association, and this may have influenced their choices in entertainment. For example, they kept company with Princess Murat, formerly Miss Caroline Georgina Fraser (1810–79) of Charleston and a school friend of Mother Louisa.[14] Other Americans with whom they socialized included "an American woman now a Marchioness"; John Young Mason, the American minister plenipotentiary, and his wife Mary Ann Fort, both of Virginia; the Prestons, John Smith and Caroline Martha Hampton; and Dr. Alfred Stillés and his wife, cousins from Philadelphia.[15] Other Americans interacted with them in various ways. The American minister arranged for Mother Louisa to meet Louis Napoleon; they inquired if Louisa Rebecca might also be present, but the American minister's wife (Mrs. John Mason) decreed this impossible.[16] Mother Louisa also attended a salon given by the Doer family of Boston in which her own literary works were featured. No mention was made of musical performances in Parisian salons.

After a few months in the apartment, the McCords moved to rooms overlooking the Jardin de Tuileries at the Hôtel Meurice on rue Rivoli, the most fashionable hotel for Americans in Paris and near where the Aikens and other Charlestonians sometimes stayed.[17] Here the staff spoke English, served meals that were similar to those in the United States, and handled many of the difficulties of living abroad. In 1853 Octavia Le Vert too had established a temporary home at the expensive and tourist-laden Hôtel Meurice.[18] This choice is indicative, for in 1854 the Virginian John R. Thompson described the hotel as "the head-quarters of Americans in Paris" and wrote that he was somewhat surprised at all the southern food, such as Virginia ham, in French restaurants.[19] In light of this, Louisa Rebecca's time with a French music instructor might have constituted the most extended conversations she had with people whose demographics differed substantially from her own.

While in Paris, Louisa Rebecca not only had voice lessons and attended the opera but also purchased music. Beginning on page 63 of Charleston Museum SMB 37, there is a string of pieces she purchased in Paris in December 1858.

Unlike the single piece in SMB 42 marked "Paris // Jan. 18," those in SMB 37 bear stamps from Parisian publishers and sellers. She bought music from the Flaxland store at 4, place de la Madeleine, where Henrietta Aiken had purchased her *Échos de France* in 1854.[20] Flaxland's was a well-respected music-publishing house that specialized in vocal anthologies; it was located in the first arrondissement. Indeed, the other stores from which the women discussed here purchased music were in the first arrondissement or on the edges of it.[21] Whether Louisa went to this shop or her teacher bought the music for her is unknown, but given its proximity to her lodgings, she may have gone with her mother or Langdon to purchase it.

As in the case of Henrietta Aiken, Louisa Rebecca's European music includes women composers. One is the Parisian Loïsa Puget.[22] Puget held musical salons in Paris beginning in the early 1830s; there she sang her own romances. It is unlikely that Louisa Rebecca attended these salons, being only twelve years old, and her mother left no record of her daughter doing so. Nevertheless, Puget's music sounds much like that of other composers whose music figures in SMB 37, such as Stephen Glover and Maria B. Hawes. The style of Puget's compositions is simple conjunct melody in the vocal part accompanied by an arpeggiated left hand with a right-hand part that punctuates the singer. These mimic, to a degree, those found in the romances in Harriet Lowndes's music, but their presence in Louisa Rebecca's binder's volume places them significantly later. Louisa Rebecca had two of Puget's pieces bound in SMB 37: "À la grâce de Dieu" and an "Ave Maria" dedicated to Princess Marie.[23] Her copy of the first of these has piano fingerings—fingers numbered 1–5—on the vocal part, which points to her having learned the melody by playing it on a piano. This, in turn, implies a piano in the place where the McCords lived. Louisa Rebecca dated both pieces December 1858 and noted "Paris" on them. Both have Parisian music sellers' stamps.

In early 1859 the McCords left Paris and traveled by rail to Rome, or at least that is what Louisa Rebecca remembered. She later mentioned Florence, which the family probably visited on their way south to Rome. At the beginning of Lent in March they left Rome and went to Naples, where they stayed in a pension run by Madame Schiassi that was frequented by American and English visitors.[24] Louisa Rebecca did not mention whether she had lessons, but John Murray's *Handbook for Travellers in Southern Italy: Being a Guide for the Continental Portion of the Kingdom of the Two Sicilies* noted that there were so many good music teachers in Naples that only the best could be listed. These included eight instructors for voice, five for piano, and one for harp. Murray listed only men, mostly Italian but a few with English or American surnames.[25]

In Naples the McCords "did everything to do all around Naples"; and in 1928 she compared their expansive time there to more modern trips where people did not get to do as much "in these days of hurried traveling."[26] This attitude reveals the pace with which the McCords and others in the 1850s took in the places they visited. Because they had letters of introduction, the McCords had the advantage of being invited to the opera, including the Teatro Reale di San Carlo, which the *Penny Magazine* described as "the most extensive and, on the whole, most splendid opera-house in Europe."[27] The theater had a distinguished history: Rossini and Bellini were house composers during their early years, and Verdi had links to it as well. The famous singer Anna Bishop sang at the Teatro Reale di San Carlo 327 times in twenty-four different roles. She had also sung in Charleston. While these associations existed more than a decade before the McCords arrived, the theater's aura of being the most important opera house in Naples remained until the unification of Italy in 1861. In 1862 the travel writer John Murray described it: "On entering it for the first time, when it is lit up at night, the stranger cannot fail to be struck with its great size and the splendor of its general effect."[28]

Nonetheless, Louisa Rebecca preferred the nearby opera house San Carlino, which had a considerably less stellar reputation. She called it "a funny little bit of an opera house where all sorts of absurd burlesques were acted."[29] The same article that described the Teatro Reale di San Carlo in the *Penny Magazine* of 1845 provided a somewhat humorous description of San Carlino that helps bring its reputation into context here. At this unusual theater, plays and farces were performed in the Neapolitan dialect and included stock characters who acted out plots that spoofed those of antiquity or were entirely new. The author of the *Penny Magazine* article considered San Carlino a "truly national theatre" because it represented the people of Naples. Louisa Rebecca's description did not fall short of the mark: the theater was small; the boxes were on the street level; and to get into the pit one had to descend almost thirty feet beneath ground level. Admission was inexpensive: a shilling for a box seat or a penny to sit in the pit. According to the *Penny Magazine,* "Everywhere there is a 'fashionable world,' and a set of superfine people who deprive themselves of much racy and innocent amusement from a notion that it is not *genteel.*" The San Carlino, apparently, appealed to those unafraid to witness such performances. Native "fashionables" did not attend because it was "low," and "very few foreigners ever acquired a sufficient knowledge of the patois or dialect to enjoy and fully understand these rich Neapolitan farces"[30]

In 1858 a writer described San Carlino in similar terms in the *Athenaeum.*[31] He noted that the tunes there were "mostly incomplete, and rising little above the level of such things as amateurs fling off," although music shops in Naples sold "a more tastefully produced and aristocratic collection" of these melodies attributed to Signor Cafferecci. This was not, however, the "wall-music" that was "more real," and the writer sarcastically observed that perhaps one day it too might "find itself touched, polished, and refined—in every one's mouth—on every one's guitar—and be sung, played, chorused, and taken as a theme for variations by way of a genuine Neapolitan melody!"[32] Undoubtedly, most of the music that made it into American collections of "Old World" music had been subjected to such treatment. The political and cultural implications of these changes appear to have been lost on Louisa Rebecca, and probably most other American consumers, who took them for the real thing.

Evidence of this type of consumerism can be seen in a song in SMB 37. Someone in Naples introduced Louisa Rebecca to local culture, if only in isolated bits. Her binder's volume SMB 37 includes the well-known "Santa Lucia," a traditional Neapolitan song, on pages 116–17. Its printed history does not extend much further back than when Louisa Rebecca visited Naples, and its translation into Italian in 1848 marks it as the first Neapolitan song to have been published in Italian.[33] Without a doubt, Louisa Rebecca used her copy: there are fingerings entered over a brief passage of running thirds in the right-hand accompaniment. She may have added these herself either in Italy or once back home, since she did not mention a music teacher while in Italy.

It is difficult to imagine that Louisa Rebecca's familiarity with the dialect spoken in Naples proved adequate for her to appreciate all the subtleties and wit presented at San Carlino, but the obvious slapstick humor probably did not escape her. Such comedy likely appealed to a girl of twelve or thirteen, which could explain why she preferred this opera house to the stately Teatro Reale di San Carlo. Joseph Forsyth commented in 1803, "This is a theatre where any stranger may study for nothing the manners of the people. At the theatre of San Carlo the mind, as well as the man, seems parted off from its fellows in an elbow-chair. There all is regulation and silence: no applause, no censure, no object worthy of attention except the court and the fiddle. There the drama—but what is a drama in Naples without Punch? . . . Here, in his native tongue, and among his own countrymen, Punch is a person of real power: he dresses up and retails all the drolleries of the day; he is the channel and sometime the source of the passing opinions."[34] Forsyth's comments were frequently repeated in nineteenth-century magazines and newspapers until at least the 1880s; enough people used them that most English-speaking people preparing to visit southern Italy would have encountered them. The display in his account is in contrast to any described by Henrietta or Harriet, although their papers were unusually silent on the details of their trips abroad. It hardly fits the types of entertainments young women were instructed to attend by etiquette manuals and articles from sources such as *Graham's* or *Godey's Lady's Book,* and it is difficult to imagine Mother Louisa in attendance. Nonetheless, going to the San Carlino theater proved to be Louisa Rebecca's favorite and most memorable adventure in southern Italy.

The McCords spent the entirety of Lent away from Rome but returned for Holy Week—Easter was on 17 April in 1859. Louisa Rebecca erred in "Recollections" concerning some details of the Italian trip: one does not leave Rome and head south to Florence. They probably journeyed through Florence on the way to Rome and then Naples, because she discussed Naples in such detail. She admitted that she could not recall precisely the order they visited cities in Italy. Their passage included Pisa, Genoa, Leghorn (now Livorno), but not Venice because of an ongoing war between France and northern Italy. Once back in Rome, Louisa Rebecca rode in the pope's carriage and accidentally encountered the Prince of Wales going up the steps of the Dome of St. Peters. She also ran into John Taylor Rhett, her future brother-in-law, while being "crushed" in the crowd at the Sistine Chapel. She had not seen him since meeting him by chance on her way for a lesson with Dr. Lieber at South Carolina College.[35] Presumably Langdon accompanied her on these excursions, as traveling without a chaperone was not an option for southern women.

From small hints about her lifestyle while in Italy and Paris, it seems that Mother Louisa did not keep a tight rein on her children while abroad. Louisa Rebecca mentioned that she wore her hair loose most of the time, not pulled up as was the style for a young lady.[36] That she attended the farces at San Carlino is remarkable, as both the place and the entertainment were inappropriate for the sheltered life of a young southern women.

After eleven English and then eight French songs, the repertory in SMB 37 turns to Italian opera with "Me chiami, o Norma"—a rather dramatic duet for two women that includes sustained high C's. Remembering that *Norma* was Louisa's first opera, this makes for a logical first aria, but the technical demands on the singer surpass those typical of a thirteen-year-old. Moreover, no evidence other than these Italian arias suggests that Louisa Rebecca was a particularly talented singer, in contrast to the comments made about Henrietta's singing. Another aria in the Italian section of SMB 37 is Leonore's "Farewell" from *Il trovatore*—in Italian in spite of the English subtitle on page 117. When in retrospect Louisa Rebecca voiced her concerns as to Bretonnière's literature choices— "so young as I was"—she might have been referring to these arias. She may have acquired these because she wanted to sing something from her favorite operas, but they seem inappropriate for someone her age. In the excerpt from *Il trovatore,* Bretonnière modified one of the cadenzas, sparing Louisa Rebecca the necessity of having to sing a high D (D6). He did not merely simplify the part, however; he wrote a new cadential passage for her to negotiate without the high note. (See figure 13.1.)

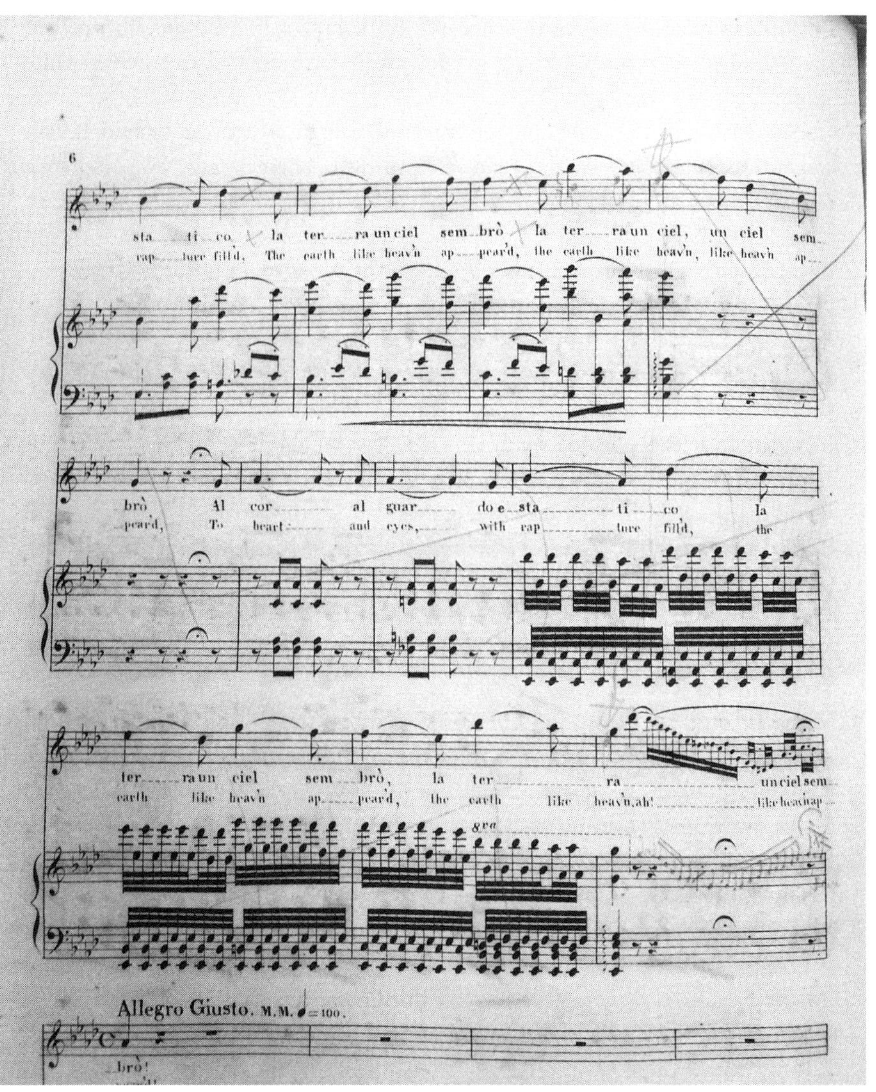

Figure 13.1. Bretonnière's modification of Louisa Rebecca's copy of Leonore's "Farewell," SMB 37

The final piece in this section is "Santa Lucia," with fingering added to the piano part (pages 126–27), as if Louisa were trying to learn her part on the piano. Louisa Rebecca referred to singing whenever she mentioned music, and vocal music dominates the contents of her binder's volumes, but she probably played the piano as well because young women often accompanied themselves while singing.

The McCords left Italy and returned to Paris to escape the second Italian war of independence, which began in April 1859. Their passage from Florence to Marseilles was crowded, and Louisa Rebecca noted that the talk centered on "Signor Garibaldi" and Victor Emmanuel. Apparently their arrival in Paris lacked the preplanning of the first visit, because they lodged in a "French pension where old women smoked cigarettes and drank coffee"—certainly not the Hôtel Meurice.[37]

They did not remain in Paris long it seems, for the next entries in the "Recollections" refer to events in London. Here they took rooms over a Mr. (Thomas) Day's chemist shop on Sloane Street, near fashionable Hyde Park.[38] While in London the second time she purchased a number of pieces of sheet music, including the first three pieces now in SMB 37: "Faith," "Hope," "Charity"—all by the London-born composer Stephen Glover. (See table 13.2.) Other early pages in this volume closely identify with London, and Louisa wrote "London June 8th 1859" on three pieces: Vincent Novello's "She Is Far from the Land"; Novello's arrangement of "God Save the Queen"; and Balfe's setting of Moore's "Let Erin Remember." Glover and especially Balfe were popular on both sides of the Atlantic, so there is nothing striking in her owning their works, but the two Novello publications prove a connection with London. Similarly, SMB 37 contains Handel's "Ye Sacred Priests," recitative and aria—"Farewell Ye Limpid Springs"—from *Jephtha* (1751). This is another sign that the musical repertory in SMB 37 stands in contrast to those of binder's volumes owned by other southern women. A quick perusal of the Library of Congress's *Music of the Nation* site reveals that the only Handel vocal work deposited there in the antebellum period is "I Know That My Redeemer Liveth" from *The Messiah.* A couple of other works from *Jephtha* were popular during the nineteenth century, particularly "Waft Her, Angels," but "Ye Sacred Priests / Farewell Ye Limpid Springs" was not one of them.

Louisa Rebecca also owned "I'll Speak of Thee, I'll Love Thee Too," composed by the well-known English contralto Maria (Dowding) B (Billington) Hawes (1816–86) and dedicated to the Countess of Essex. Hawes's reputation as a singer in England at this time was notable: Mendelssohn wrote "O Rest in the Lord," from *Elijah,* for her, and she debuted his *Lobegesang* in 1840.[39] The countess to whom Hawes dedicated "I'll Speak of Thee, I'll Love Thee Too" was Catherine

Table 13.2. Pieces purchased by Louisa Rebecca McCord in London

Title	Composer	Publication and other information
Angel's Whisper	Samuel Lover	London: Duff. "Louisa R. McCord / Paris Oct. 1858"
She is far from the land	Vincent Novello	London: Novello. "London June 8th 1859"
Go where glory waits thee	M. Balfe	London: Novello
What tho' I trace?	G.F. Handel; arr. William Horsley	London: Cramer, Addison & Beale; sold London: Charles Ollivier
Angels Bright and Fair	G.F. Handel	London: Charles Ollivier
God save the Queen	Vincent Novello, arr.	London: Novello. "London June 8th 1859"
What are the wild	S. Glover	London: Robert Cock. Lots of marks in both piano and voice parts
A voice	S. Glover	London: Robert Cock
Selection of Popular Scotch Songs [collection]	G. Macfarren	Edinburgh: Wood; sold Liverpool: Hine & Son
Duncan Gray from the Vocal Melodies of Scotland	Finlay Dun	Edinburgh: Paterson; sold Liverpool: Hine & Son
Let Erin remember	M. Balfe	London: Novello. "London June 8th 1859"
Willie we have missed you, or Welcome, welcome home / Song and Chorus		London: Leader & Cock
Ye sacred priests (recit and aria)	William Horsley, arr.; G.F. Handel	London: Cramer, Addison & Beale. Sold London: Charles Ollivier
Farewell Leonora (Ah! Che la morte) / Air from the Opera Il Trovatore	G. Verdi	London: Young. Index: "Farewell Leonora," *Il trovatore*

Table 13.2. Pieces purchased by Louisa Rebecca McCord in London (*continued*)

Title	Composer	Publication and other information
My son, the midnight hour is near / A Song ("Mein sohn, wo willst du hin so spät?")	F. Mendelssohn	London: Addison & Hodson. "R" at top, more could have been cut off. Dated 1850 on publication.
No. 145 of Wessel & Co's Auswahl Deutscher Gesänge / Lebewohl / "Last greeting" / "Adieu" by Berganer / "Voici l'instant supreme"	François Schubert	London: Wessel & Co. Importers and Publishers of Foreign Music. Sung by Miss Masson, Miss Wyndham, Miss Birch, &c.
No. 268 of Wessel & Co's Auswahl Deutscher Gesänge / Six Lieder ("'Tis thus decreed," "Es ist bestimmt in Gottes Rath")	F. Mendelssohn	London: Wessel & Co. Importers and Publishers of Foreign Music. Publishers of ALL the works of Chopin, Kuhlau, Schubert, Henselt, Beethoven, Hummel, Mendelssohn, Reissiger, Thalberg, Rosenhain, Czerny, &c.
Of what is the old an thinking	Joseph Philip Knight	London: Mori & Lavenu's New Musical Subscription Library
Live with a playful heart / Adapted to a celebrated Bohemian melody	A.F. Müllen	London: B. Williams
The blue bells of Scotland	[none]	London: W. Young
Home! Sweet home!	Henry Bishop	London: D'Almaine & Co. "Sung by Miss M. Tree in Clari, or The Maid of Milan at the Theatre Royal Covent Garden. Also by Miss Stephens at the Musical Festivals / Also by Madame Sontag and Mad'lle Jenny Lind"
I cannot smile dear mother	George Barker	London: Joseph Williams

"Kitty" Stephens (1794–1882), a veteran of the English stage who appeared frequently at Covent Garden and even more often in concerts and festivals. She married the octogenarian fifth Earl of Essex in 1838; he died the following year. Both English women were associated with musical performance.[40] No record establishes whether Louisa met either woman or heard them perform, but if she did, both were unlike the women in her acquaintance in Charleston. The wives of planters rarely moved from a life on the stage to life on the plantation—Fanny Kemble being the most famous exception. Furthermore, Americans viewed public recognition of upper-class women in a different light from that of their European counterparts. In both France and England, newspapers would print the names of upper-class women who performed in semiprivate house concerts or salons, but in the South, at least, the press did not print "amateur"—as in not wage-earning—women's names.[41] A few southern elite women, such as Octavia Le Vert in Mobile, socialized with women artists from the stage, concert, or gallery while in England, so it is possible that the McCords did likewise. However, that no one mentioned such events renders this possibility a small one.

From London, the McCords traveled east again, this time to the Netherlands and Germany. Near Wiesbaden, Mother Louisa sprained her ankle, and this part of their journey was cut short. They moved on to see Switzerland and the Alps, and their itinerary included Lucerne, the Rigi, Grimsel Pass, Interlaken, Geneva, Chamonix, and Bern.[42] Louisa Rebecca's music collection contains several pieces purchased during this leg of their trip. All of this music appears at the end of SMB 37. Louisa knew lieder by both Mendelssohn: "My Son, Thou Knowest the Hour Is Near" ("Mein sohn, wo willst du hin so spät") of 1850; and Schubert: as François Schubert, "Lebewohl" ("Last Greeting"), which was a London purchase; as well as folksongs, Swiss airs, and settings of Heine's poetry. Mendelssohn's music is rare, and Schubert's is not common in southern binder's volumes of this period. Louisa Rebecca's copy of Mendelssohn's *Six Lieder for Voice and Piano* was published by Wessel & Co., 229 Regent Square, London, and she probably purchased it while there. Interestingly, several of the German pieces came from Oxford Street in London, while others originated with Swiss dealers, and at least one—the *Stimmen der Völker*, in German—came from Philadelphia, having been imported from Berlin.

A striking aspect of SMB 37 is that the organization of the music closely resembles the course of the McCords' European journey of 1858–59. The pieces in this binder's volume can almost be read as a travel diary, beginning with England, moving to France, then to Italy, and finally through Switzerland— even if some of the German-language music came from London. SMB 37 also reveals that Louisa Rebecca obtained most of her foreign music in London, and her other two volumes, SMB 29 and SMB 42, demonstrate the same pattern. In this her collection differs from those of Harriet and Henrietta, who tended to prefer French music publications.

This piecemeal collection also reflects Mother Louisa's haphazard approach to Louisa Rebecca's musical education, and her education in general. It mirrors Mother Louisa's complicated attitude about what it meant to be a woman in southern society and the freedom that was possible outside of southern society.

CHAPTER 14

The Civil War and Beyond

The McCord family sailed back to New York City in October 1859 on the *Persia,* the same ship that had taken them to Europe more than a year earlier, and arrived back on the 26th of that month. While they were in Europe, Mother Louisa had a large music room added to the house in Columbia, and Louisa Rebecca remembered that there "we took all our lessons and did what we pleased" after they arrived back in South Carolina. During the months before the war, the McCord family hired a "variety of German music teachers" before committing to a Miss Garnett.[1] These German teachers manifest Mother Louisa's preference for German-language instruction and distinguish the McCord children's experiences from those of their contemporaries. Music, as entertainment and lessons, again formed part of the regular activities. Christmas at their Lang Syne plantation included dancing in the library.

Louisa Rebecca noted, perhaps with more than a hint of hindsight, that through all of this "quiet life ran a succession of intensely exciting events" as southern states began to secede from the Union. Mother Louisa penned new secessionist lyrics to the tune *Gaudeamus* and Robert Scott Burns's "Scots Wha Hae Wi Wallace Bled," and these were sung by students at South Carolina College. Music lessons appear to have ceased once the war began, and the McCords left Lang Syne and established themselves in the Charleston Hotel during the winter of 1861–62. The war years were spent moving among various lodgings in Charleston—the fire of 1861 causing the first move—and intermittent trips to the house in Columbia. They eventually evacuated Charleston and moved back to Lang Syne.[2]

The Civil War affected Louisa Rebecca's musical education in ways that have not been investigated by modern scholars: musicologists have focused on the publication of patriotic songs; and historians have concentrated on other aspects of women's lives during the war.[3] SMB 29, however, provides an intimate view into what a young woman of means might have experienced, and it further elucidates the depravities she suffered as a result of the war. With its cheap paper, old-fashioned music and text type, slipshod binding and impermanent name stamp, and even its manuscript music section, this binder's volume vividly illustrates the ineluctable effects of the conflict on Louisa Rebecca's day-to-day existence. In marked contrast to the exotic foreign stamps on music in SMB 37, SMB 29 consists predominantly of southern imprints, gathered together while she was in Columbia. (See table 14.1.) Louisa Rebecca signed the book on the flyleaf, including "Columbia, S.C." (See figure 14.1.) That she wrote in it after it was bound but while she was still in Columbia is intriguing. The publication dates do not continue later than 1864, which means it is possible that the McCords had SMB 29 bound before the war reached their doorstep, as it eventually did.

Even though the frontispiece bears the binder's name—Welch, Harris & Co. in Charleston—and the date 1862, several of the prints date from 1864.[4] Most likely the binder simply used a leftover colorful page as the first in the volume, which would render it more aesthetically pleasing. It stands in contrast to both the outer binding and the contents. Residual songs from her time in Europe appear here too, as do a few pieces from northern publishers, suggesting that she began collecting this repertory before the war and continued to add to it until at

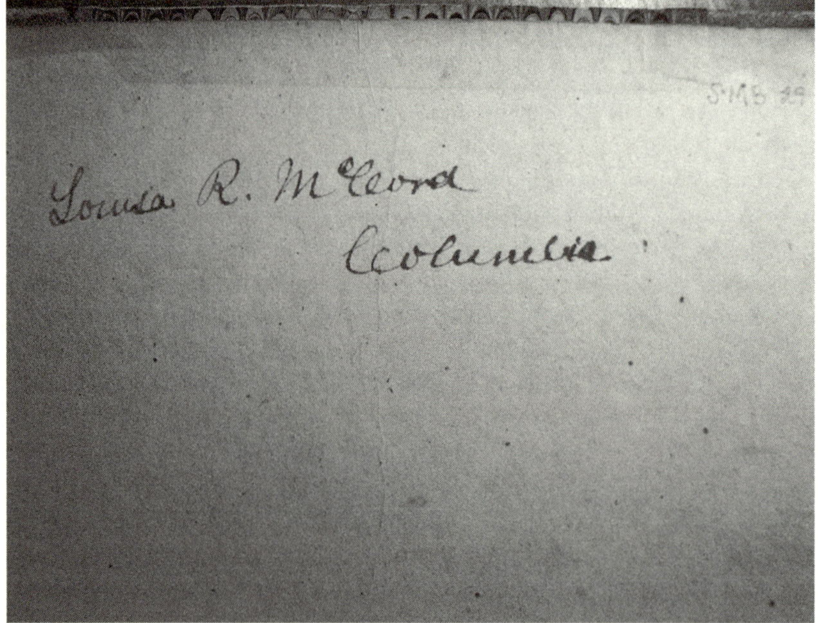

Figure 14.1. Louisa Rebecca's signature in SMB 29, with "Columbia, S.C."

Table 14.1. Contents of SMB 29

No.	Title	Composer	Date	Notes
1	The Southern Musical Boquet [sic] (No. 12 "Parthenia to Ingomar")	S. Foster		Macon: Schreiner. Several other places listed. Duncan, Lith., Columbia. Sold Siegling
2	The Exotics / Flowers of Song / Transplanted to Southern Soil ("I see her still in my dreams")	S. Foster		Augusta: Blackmar; Duncan, Lith., Columbia
3	Gems of Southern Song ("Gentle Nettie Moore")	J. Pierpoint		Macon: Burke; Duncan, Lith., Columbia
4	Parlor Gems ("Officer's Funeral")	Mrs. Norton		Macon: Schreiner
5	Bingen on the Rhine, or A soldier of the Legion	Judson I. Hutchinson		Macon and Savannah: Schreiner; Jas. F. Weeks, printer. "As sung in the concerts of the Hutchinson family"
6	The Goodbye at the Door	S. Glover		Augusta: Blackmar
7	No One to Love	W.B. Harvey		Columbia: Julian A. Selby
8	Her bright smile haunts me still	W.T. Wrighton		Macon and Savannah: Schreiner
9	La Zingara	[G. Donizetti]		MS. *La zingara.* Breath marks
10	Romanza ("O fatidica")	Verdi		MS. *Giovanna d'Arco*
11	The Tear	[F. Kücken]		MS. English in ink, more English faint in pencil, breath marks, corrections
12	Thou who know'st each human feeling	G. Verdi		MS. Only Italian words in music. *I due Foscari.* Seems to be from Fiot's 1851 edition
13	Love's young dream			MS
14	The Wanderer	A. Fresca		MS

Table 14.1. Contents of SMB 29 (*continued*)

No.	Title	Composer	Date	Notes
15	Kathleen O'Moore			MS
16	*Exercises for the Voice with Piano Forte Accompaniment*	J. Concone		MS. Markings in score
17	Each hour of life, or the Maiden's prayer	Thekla Badarewska		Augusta: Blackmar. Sold Siegling
18	Deem not the maiden heartless / "Quel guard oil Cavaliere" / Cavatina from the Opera Don Pasquale	G. Donizetti	1852	Philadelphia: Fiot. Sold Schreiner (stamp has both Macon and Augusta)
19	Pray, maiden, pray / A Ballad for the Times Respectfully Dedicated to the Patriotic Women of the South	A.J. Turner	1864	Richmond: Dunn. Sold Siegling
20	Mary of Argyle	S. Nelson	[1848–62]	London: Harry May
21	Remember the hour we sadly parted / Companion to When this cruel war is over / Song and Chorus		1864	Mobile: H.C. Clarke. Stamps from Siegling and Willig in Philadelphia
22	*Gems of German Song* / from the most admired compostions of Schubert, Thalberg, Kalliwoda, Weber and others, Second Series (No. 7 "La Serenade")	F. Schubert		Boston: Reed. Sold Philadelphia: Willig. Schubert's "Ständchen"
23	Musical Album / When I saw sweet Nellie home	John Fletcher		Macon and Savannah: Schreiner. Sold Siegling
24	Improvisation on the Favorite Melody / Her bright smile haunts me still	Theodore von La Hache		Augusta: Blackmar; litho. Duncan, Columbia. To his pupil Miss Belle Otman

25	Where roses fair	George Linley		NY: Firth, Pond & Co. "L.R. McCord" Markings, photo
26	Drift my bark / Duett for Soprano & Contralto	F. Kücken	1853	Brooklyn: Carl Prox
27	Southern Edition. Silvery shower tremolo etude on a Melody of Balfe	Balfe; arr. Adolph Baumbach		Augusta: Blackmar; litho. Duncan, Columbia
28	Nocturne	Théodore Döhler		Augusta: Blackmar; litho. Duncan, Columbia. $2.50. photo of complete work
29	6 Two-Part Songs, op. 63 (No. 3 "Greeting")	F. Mendelssohn		NY: Hall & Son
30	Un hiver à Paris 1838–1839 / nouvel album lyrique par G. Donizetti (Duettino "L'Addio / Dunque addio mio caro amore")	G. Donizetti		Naples: Successeurs de Girard. À Madame Fanny Persiani, 30 Gr. Breath marks in both parts on p. 9
31	Something to love me	E.L. Hime		Richmond: Dunn. Selby sold in Columbia
32	Beauties of the Opera of Il Trovatore (No. 3 "Tacea la notte placida," "The night, calmly and peacefully)	G. Verdi	1857	Boston: Ditson. "LR. McCord"
33	Bird of beauty	Miss M.B. Scott	1864	Augusta: Blackmar; Litho. Paterson in Augusta
34	*Beauties of Italy* / A Collection of favorite cavatinas, songs, duetts & trios / with Italian and English words / Selected from the original MSS. Of Mozart, Rossini, Donizetti, Bellini, Meyerbeer, Mercadante and other celebrated composers (No. 16 Preghiera, "Se ti son cara," "Ah if in truth you love me now")	G. De Begnis		NY: Hall & Son. "Louisa R. McCord"

Table 14.1. Contents of SMB 29 (*continued*)

No.	Title	Composer	Date	Notes
35	*Gems of Southern Song* ("Brightest Eyes")	G. Stigelli	[1861–65]	Macon: Burke
36	*Jenny Lind's Operatic Songs* (No. 6 "With what rapture")	G. Verdi		NY: Hall & Son. L.R. McCord. Italian words are penciled in. From *I Masnadieri*
37	*Southern Musical Bouquet of Favorite Songs and Ballads,* no. 9 "Parthenia to Ingomar"	S. Foster		Macon: Schreiner. "To Miss L M and something else in pencil"
38	Recitative / Without friends and without a home / Aria tis sad to leave our father land	M. Balfe		NY: Hall & Son. "As sung by Mr. Frazer in the Opera of The Bohemian Girl"
39	Blackmar & Bros. Collection of Standard Music, "How can I leave thee:	H. Cramer		Augusta: Blackmar; litho. Duncan, Columbia
40	Gems of Southern Song, "Chimes of the Monastery"	Hawthorne		Macon: Burke; litho. Duncan, Columbia
41	*Donizetti's Grand Opera Linda di Chamonix,* Rondo Finale "Ah! With Rapture My Hear is Beating" ("Senti il core amato bene")	Donizetti; arr., Clare W. Beames	1847	NY: Firth, Pond & Co. *Linda di Chamounix.* Louisa R. McCord. Ornamented, in Italian

least 1864. Nevertheless, much of the published music in SMB 29 came from southern publishers and sellers: Burke and Schreiner in Macon; Selby in Columbia; Dunn in Richmond. The lithographers too were in the South: Duncan in Columbia and Paterson in Augusta. As a text, this binder's volume documents the rise of southern publishers during the short-lived Confederacy.

The repertory resembles those found in sources from the 1850s, such as "Jenny Lind's Operatic Songs: With What Rapture" from Verdi's *I Masnadieri* or Stephen Foster's "Parthenia to Ingomar," originally published in 1859 but here under the *Southern Musical Boquet [sic] of Favorite Songs and Ballads*. Such published "southern" collections were popular during the war and often included songs previously published in the North. An advertisement on the back of "Each Hour of Life, or the Maiden's Prayer" lists the music available from Blackmar & Bro.'s [*sic*] in Augusta, Georgia. Others in SMB 29 include Stigelli's "Brightest Eyes" from *Gems of Southern Song,* Foster's "I See Her Still in My Dreams" from *The Exotics / Flowers of Song / Transplanted to Southern Soil,* and the "Southern Edition" of Adolph Baumbach's "Silvery Shower Tremolo // Etude on a Melody by Balfe."[5] The printed songs are simple, typical pieces, including perennial favorites such as Bishop's "Home! Sweet Home!"

Louisa Rebecca's copy of "Parthenia to Ingomar" is marked in pencil "To Miss L M" followed by something now illegible. The front page of Foster's song names dealers in southern cities and towns who sold it and lists James Weeks in Macon as the printer. It illustrates a growing music industry in the Confederate states. Many of these music sellers existed before the Civil War but were not recorded by name on the fronts of pieces. Compositions by authors such as Verdi and Norton appeared throughout the United States, but since the Confederacy had declared itself a separate country, new copyright standards applied. Since copyright law at this time was in a state of flux, to say the least, southern publishers put out new editions of popular works, as can be seen in the contents of the *Southern Musical Boquet* in figure 14.2. Louisa Rebecca's "Pray, Maiden, Pray," also bears Siegling's stamp from Charleston, thus proving its availability outside of those given here, in addition to confirming where music was sold in towns such as Selma, Alabama, and Athens, Georgia.

Similarly, an advertisement for Blackmar & Bro.'s in Augusta, Georgia—after Armand Blackmar was forced to leave New Orleans for, among other issues, printing "The Bonnie Blue Flag"—indicates what music one might buy in Augusta. Blackmar's ad names several piano instruction books, which include those by Bertini, Beyer, Hünten, Cramer, and others; as well as method books for guitar, voice, flute, violin, organ, melodeon, and voice. The company offered "Orchestral Music" and "Collections of Piano Music" as well. The vocal collections included *100 Songs of Scotland* and *100 Songs of Ireland* as well as *Ordway's*

Figure 14.2. Front page of the *Southern Musical Boquet* [sic], Foster's "Parthenia to Ingomar," SMB 29

Parlor Glees and *The Sacred Harp*. Consumers could acquire "Old Magazines"—presumably antebellum issues—comprising *Harper's, Graham's, Peterson's,* and *Godey's*. Large choral works were available, and the ad lists Handel and Haydn oratorios as well as lesser-known works, such as "Farmer's Mass in B Flat." Under the category "Oratorios, Masses, &c.," Blackmar offered a *Piano Primer,* a *Catechism of Music,* a *Musical Spelling Book,* a *Guide to Musical Composition,* a *Thorough Bass Primer,* and a *Dictionary of Musical Terms*. Clearly these are not oratorios or masses, but Blackmar needed to advertise their availability. The final two items on the list of "Books, Sheet Music, &c." are the *Bonnie Blue Flag Song Book,* 2nd edition; and *The Dixie Land Songster*. Patriotic songs praising the South appeared in these: "The Dixie War Song" was included in both.

"Pray, Maiden, Pray! / A Ballad for the Times to the Patriotic Women of the South" from 1864 provides an image of how the dedicated, devout young southern woman should look during the dire years of the war. (See figure 14.3.) George Dunn in Richmond published this song, but it includes advertisements for music sellers in London (Harry May in Holborn), Edinburgh (Wood & Co. at Waterloo Place), and Glasgow (J. Muir Wood & Co.) as well. Despite these European connections, Louisa Rebecca obtained her copy from Siegling's in Charleston, whose stamp appears at the bottom of the page. Siegling must have maintained a large inventory even during the last years of the war, for he also sold pieces published as far away as Mobile—for example "I Remember the Hour When Sadly We Parted," a companion piece to "When This Cruel War Is Over"—to the McCords.

Angelo Torriani

In 1863 the Irish music teacher Miss Garnett was still with the family, for Louisa Rebecca recalled having a music lesson with her. Indeed, Louisa Rebecca remembered music as a "great resource" during those days on their plantation, and after Miss Garnett left there was another teacher.[6] Mother Louisa would send a carriage out twice a week over the course of several months to bring Angelo Torriani from the "fashionable boarding school" known as the South Carolina Female Institute at Barhamville to give singing lessons to Louisa Rebecca and some others who lived near the McCords.[7]

Torriani had extensive experience with opera in the United States, and in 1860 he conducted some performances of the Italian Opera Company when it was in Columbus, Georgia.[8] Born in Milan in 1829, he toured the United States in 1848 with Adelina Patti's parents, working primarily as a conductor. Some reported that he taught the famous opera star. Among his accomplishments, Torriani had conducted the American premiere of Verdi's *Aida* in November 1873, and his obituary in the *Chicago Tribune* described him as the "father of

Figure 14.3. "Pray, Maiden, Pray!," A. J. Turner, SMB 29

Italian opera in this country."[9] He partnered for a time with the conductor and impresario Max Maretzek, and he spent his final years in New York. He performed in Charleston and other cities in the South in 1861 with an opera company, giving the proceeds of the concert to the Ladies' Relief Association and similar organizations.[10]

Torriani's contributions to Louisa Rebecca's voice instruction typify those found in binder's volumes that belonged to young women who had been at the South Carolina Female Institute at Barhamville, such as Ann Beaufort Simms.[11] More significantly, they betray how problematic it was for southerners to maintain normalcy by 1864. Over the course of that year, southerners found it increasingly challenging to find paper goods, and printed sheet music was no exception. Louisa Rebecca's binder's volume SMB 29 reflects these struggles. Bound into SMB 29 are a number of manuscript copies of songs, even a vocal tutorial. Granted, earlier binder's volumes such as those of Harriet Lowndes included manuscript music from time to time. Each situation must be considered individually, though, and Louisa's manuscript music indeed reflects the times. She confirmed as much when she wrote, "It was impossible to buy music in those days except a few popular songs composed at the time, so with few exceptions we used manuscript music."[12] The music and the diary correlate best at this point because seven pieces in the volume, plus Concone's method, are here only as handwritten music, probably in the hand of Torriani.

Torriani's handiwork is exhibited in other places in Louisa Rebecca's collection. On her copy of "With What Rapture" from Verdi's *I masnadieri* someone, most likely Torriani, added the Italian words in pencil above the printed Italian text. (See figure 14.4) This signals an awareness that English is not the original and a desire to sing it properly, especially under the tutelage of an Italian opera conductor. After all, Louisa Rebecca had heard Italian operas in Italian while in Europe only a few years earlier; she knew what it was supposed to sound like.

Torriani also added ornamentation to several of her pieces, as Bretonnière had done to her aria from *Il trovatore* a few years earlier. On her copy of Donizetti's "Ah! With Rapture My Heart Is Beating" ("Senti il core" from *Linda di Chamounix*), Louisa wrote her name in pencil on the title page. Her teacher added ornamentation on this aria, such as a turn and appoggiatura on the final word ("guibilar"). These types of additions to arias reveal how southern women sang their music in their parlors and at school recitals and further confirm that they performed their music—it did not simply lie on the piano for display.

Toward the end of SMB 29 Louisa Rebecca added "L'Addio-Duettino Poesia di F. Romani" from the collection "Un hiver à Paris // 1838–1839 // novel album lyrique par G. Donizetti // faisant suite aux Nuits d'été á Pausilipe et aux Soirées d'automne á l'Infrascata." In spite of its French title, this particular edition was

Figure 14.4. "With What Rapture My Heart Is Bounding," by Verdi, in SMB 29, showing Italian words added, probably by Torriani

published by B. Girard in Naples in the 1840s. This may be a piece of sheet music that she purchased while in Naples, given the difficulty of procuring foreign music during the Civil War.[13] Louisa Rebecca sang it with a partner, and breath marks have been inserted in both parts of the duet. Her partner may have been her sister or one of the other young women who benefited from Torriani's visits to the countryside.

The manuscript pieces begin with the ninth work bound into the volume, labeled "La Zingara." This is an aria, "Fra l'erbe cosparse di rorido gelo," from Donizetti's early (1822) opera *La zingara*. Louisa Rebecca sang this aria, as indicated by numerous breath marks throughout the score, probably under the tutelage of Torriani. She also studied Verdi's "O fatidica foresta" from *Giovanna d'Arco* (1845). Another aria by Verdi, "Tu al cui sguardo omniposente," a cavatina from the 1844 *I due Foscari,* follows. Except for the fact that only the Italian words are in Louisa's binder's volume version, this matches perfectly—even the same accompaniment—one published by Fiot in Philadelphia in 1851.[14]

The vocal works in the manuscript portion of SMB 29 include a complete copy of *J. Concone's Exercises for the Voice with Piano Forte Accompaniment* at the end, and it was copied verbatim from the published version by the same person who copied most of the other manuscript music in SMB 29. Similarly, Louisa Rebecca's manuscript copy of Alexander Fesca's (1820–49) "The Wanderer" reproduces the printed sheet version published in London.[15] The hand that wrote this song differs from that of the other manuscript pieces in SMB 29.

As with her other binder's volumes, vocal music forms the bulk of SMB 29. However, a few piano pieces in this book reveal that Louisa Rebecca was also an accomplished pianist, which further suggests that she had other music, for solo piano, that did not survive. Among those extant are Théodore Döhler's "Nocturne" and La Hache's "Improvisation on the Favorite Melody Her Bright Smile Haunts Me Still." The Döhler work cost $2.50, an exorbitant price for a single piece of music, which before 1861 would have cost $1.00 or less. By comparison, most songs of the 1850s could be had for $0.25 or $0.35. Döhler's Chopinesque "Nocturne," his op. 24, was first published in 1838 by Mechetti in Vienna, but Louisa's version was published by Blackmar at his Augusta office. It must have been a popular work, because it was sold in Richmond, Macon, Mobile, Savannah, Columbia, Montgomery, and Charleston.[16] Louisa Rebecca's Augusta edition appears in the binder's volumes of at least two other southerners, Eva Thornton and Mary Glenn, the latter of whom dated her copy April 1864.[17]

An extended work of seven pages long, La Hache's "Improvisation" requires a degree of physicality with fortissimo full chords, octaves, and other aspects that demand exertion on the part of the performer. If Louisa Rebecca played such works on the piano, she must have been a decent pianist. It is reasonable to assume that she did play these compositions as it seems unlikely that, at a time when prices for basic necessities were continually rising, the McCords would purchase expensive music if they did not intend to use it.[18]

Louisa Rebecca's last volume of music reflects distinctively southern connections. The fact that SMB 29 contains mostly Confederate imprints purchased during the war, and others probably acquired before it began in 1861, reflects several aspects of her life during those years. This may have been the only music available. Several manuscript pieces in this binder's volume, including an entire vocal manual written by hand, lend credence to this possibility. The daughter of a staunch Confederate, she may have felt it her patriotic duty to support only southern businesses. SMB 29 includes a newspaper clipping of alternative words to "Annie Laurie" (which music is in the volume) that celebrates the Twenty-Fourth Georgia Regiment. Only 60 of this group's 660 men survived the war. This is yet another marker of use for this volume. The significance of SMB 29 in documenting how the Civil War impacted the pursuit of culture by young southern women cannot be ignored. Until 1861 southern women in the social position occupied by Louisa Rebecca knew how to negotiate their world, how to meet expectations, and what they needed to do to succeed in making a suitable marriage match. Music was one of the most important accomplishments in this regard. The disruption of this predictability must have shattered many other expectations. Its clear effect can be interpreted from this binder's volume.

SMB 29 differs substantially from Louisa Rebecca's three other binder's volumes in that most of the music therein came from southern publishers or from the hand of Torriani, in manuscript form. But SMB 29 carries similarities with the others. The European music in SMB 30, SMB 37, and SMB 42 closely adheres to what girls Louisa Rebecca's age were singing in the American South. The repertory naturally includes regional music as well as European composers whose music was popular in the United States—for example Glover and Puget. Overall her collection documents her music studies as she progressed from simple songs to ornate Italian arias. It also reflects a willingness to sing music outside the "normal" literature for southern girls, such as songs in German.

The influence of Mother Louisa on Louisa Rebecca's music collection is difficult to ascertain and yet easy to see: it is conspicuous by its absence. On one hand, Mother Louisa espoused ideas about southern womanhood that closely bound it to all the restrictions and rules established for young elite women. Louisa Rebecca followed those rules by studying voice while in Europe and attending the opera. Both of these she would have done in Charleston or Columbia. On the other hand, Mother Louisa translated and published essays, wrote a play, and earned a reputation as a writer, a literary woman. These actions did not follow her own guidelines for the ideal woman. By her own account,

Louisa Rebecca indecorously ran around Paris and elsewhere, and attended all sorts of musical entertainments with surprising freedom. Mother Louisa seems to have broken the rules when she wanted or needed to, and she did not adhere to them closely in her own daughter's upbringing. She accepted the expectation to expose her daughter to music as an accomplishment, but she did not bother with the details.

Unlike most southern women writers, Mother Louisa did not write about motherhood directly, even if she mentioned it often. None of her private writing described her feelings for her own son and daughters, except the singular use of "brats" mentioned above. As J. William Harris has noted, "her dedication of *Caius Gracchus* contains the most direct expression of her feelings as a mother: 'To My Son.'"[19] Mother Louisa's sentiments toward her son overshadowed those for her daughters.

As artifacts, binder's volumes provide a general observation of southern society during the antebellum period, but each collection bears the stamp of its owner. Louisa Rebecca's four books reveal both and embellish our knowledge of her famous mother. The conservative, obedient southern matron and the rebellious intellectual, champion of ideal womanhood through the reality of real womanhood: these dual sides of Mother Louisa are borne out in her daughter's four binder's volumes. As to Louisa Rebecca, we can trace her maturation as a singer, especially, from simple ballads to Verdi arias. Her music invites us to consider what music might have been assigned by a Parisian instructor and by an Italian opera director. It also provides a tangible example of how the Civil War affected the day-to-day life of a wealthy southern woman, with samples that diverge from the more familiar diary.

After their marriage in 1867, Louisa Rebecca and Augustine "Gus" Smythe lived first at Lang Syne and then in Charleston, where their daughter Louisa Cheves Smythe was born in 1868. He worked as a lawyer and served in the state senate from 1880 to 1894. Conspicuously, when Louisa Rebecca married, Mother Louisa signed the title of Lang Syne over to Augustine. She did not bestow it upon her daughter, as her father had given it to her. Augustine could not meet the costs of sustaining the property and sold it in 1870.[20]

Louisa Cheves Smythe: SMB 5

Louisa Rebecca and Augustine Smythe had six children, the eldest of whom was Louisa Cheves Smythe (1868–1939). A bound volume of music that belonged to her survives as SMB 5 in the Charleston Museum, and this collection represents a significant change in the piano music played by young southern women after the Civil War. Its cover has "Louisa Cheves Smythe" stamped in gold, and the spine reads "Clementi & Kuhlau." That complete books of music by these two composers appear together—and only these two—was the first item that suggested the importance of the Charleston Museum collection when I visited in 2005.

This single volume consists of three different publications of sonatinas and rondos by Muzio Clementi and Friedrich Kuhlau. These piano pieces have formed a regular part of students' repertoires from the late nineteenth century to the present day, and the particular editions that Louisa Cheves Smythe owned were reprinted well into the twentieth century. Louis Köhler (1820–86) edited the works, but there are, unfortunately, no publication dates on her music. Perhaps the most indicative clue for their dates is her maiden name on the cover, placing the publications before her marriage to Samuel Gaillard Stoney in 1890, when she was in her early twenties. Existing prints in several southern collections do not help pinpoint the date of Louisa's copies, although some clues can be mined from other binder's volumes. For example, the University of North Carolina at Chapel Hill Music Library collection includes Clementi's sonatinas, op. 38, in a book bound for Helen E. McKee of Pennsylvania (new series, 6, 006), and McKee's name and the date 1878 have been written on other works in this volume. The Historic Sheet Music Collection at Duke University has a copy of op. 36, edited by Köhler, from 1884, and the Center for Popular Music at Middle Tennessee State University owns a copy of a significantly earlier edition from the first decade of the nineteenth century.[21] These binder's volumes represent two periods of popularity for Clementi's piano music: many young women played his sonatinas around the time he composed them, although they disappeared from the popular repertoire during the mid-century; and students once again met with them after Reconstruction.

In this one volume Louisa Smythe included a complete set of Clementi sonatinas, seven rondos by Kuhlau, and a volume of "Beliebte Rondos" that Kuhlau based on popular melodies by other composers. Of the two, Kuhlau's music is rarer among southern collections, but a few rondos can be found in the larger collections. A comparison with the contents of volumes owned by Harriet, Henrietta, and Louisa Smythe's mother illustrates a strikingly different approach to music collecting. It further documents changes in music publication habits at the end of the nineteenth century, because these groups of pieces were sold together, not as the single pieces typically found in earlier binder's volumes. Granted, Henrietta owned a few complete books of music that had been bound, but almost all were methods for piano or voice. Her *Échos de France* stands alone in this regard, and it appeared in the late 1850s, at precisely the time European publishers regularly began to sell their music as collections.

Another new aspect of SMB 5 is that it is retrospective. Both composers represented in SMB 5 were older than those whose music features in Louisa

Rebecca's and Henrietta Aiken's binder's volumes. Some of the music even pre-dates that owned by Harriet Lowndes. That Louisa owned music composed approximately a hundred years before she played it speaks to a significant shift in taste. The music owned by her mother, for example, stretched back only a few decades. At least one item had belonged to her older sister, and some of the others could have been used by older female relatives. Harriet's music was usually the most modern available, an aspect that distinguishes it from that of her contemporaries. Henrietta's music includes some older pieces, but these so closely resemble those of her mother that they point to a direct influence from Harriet, rather than a trend toward antique music.[22]

Muzio Clementi (1752–1832) was an Italian keyboard performer and teacher who achieved great fame in London. He taught Johann Baptist Cramer, whose piano studies would become popular in the United States. Around the turn of the nineteenth century, Clementi performed in numerous "benefit" concerts, performances that benefited the principal person named in the program, and played concertos between the acts of oratorios at Covent Garden. Clementi composed and published the twelve sonatinas collected in SMB 5 under separate opus numbers in the late eighteenth century, but Köhler edited the three sets in a single volume for C. F. Peters in Leipzig and Berlin: *Sonatines par M. Clementi Op. 36, 37, 38. Revues et doigtées par Louis Köhler.*[23]

The second Kuhlau collection is particularly intriguing because it includes settings of songs by Beethoven, among others. This volume, published as *Beliebte Rondos für Pianoforte von F. Kuhlau mit Fingersatz versehen con Louis Köhler u. F. A. Roitzsch,* appeared through C. F. Peters in Leipzig and Berlin. Kuhlau's "rondos" include famous arias from Mozart's *Don Giovanni*—called *Don Juan* in the edition—which is Kuhlau's op. 31, no. 1. The next two, op. 31, no. 2, and op. 56, no. 1, are from *The Marriage of Figaro,* including "Non piu andrai." The fourth rondo, "Non so piu cosa son, cosa faccio," is from *Don Giovanni* as well. The fifth, op. 73, no. 2, is an arrangement of an aria from Rossini's *Barbier von Sevilla.*

Each of these "rondos" plays on the main theme of the aria and treats it somewhat like a set of variations. Themes and variations were extremely popular in the antebellum period, and several series based on favorite opera melodies, by composers such as Beyer and Rosellen, exist in binder's volumes. These compositions, however, were not entitled "rondos." The attractiveness of the rondo appears to have peaked in the first two decades of the century, although rondos continued to be published through the mid-century.[24] The music is not difficult and exemplifies the type of music one might hear at a piano studio recital today.

Louisa Cheves Smythe owned music in publications by single composers, especially Clementi, and Kuhlau's arrangements of popular tunes. The inclusion of melodies by Beethoven and Schubert in SMB 5 confirms a move to German romantics after the Civil War. Was it a welcome change to her mother, Louisa Rebecca, who knew German music and had owned some by Schubert and Mendelssohn before it was commonplace to do so in South Carolina? Little of Louisa Smythe's biography has been identified; thus, to attribute Kuhlau's music to her mother's experiences is risky. Publishers began to issue music in sets such as these during the second half of the nineteenth century, and Louisa Smythe's SMB 5 shows that she fell in line with other pianists who played these relatively simple but well-crafted pieces heard throughout parlors and school recitals in the United States. SMB 5 also documents the rising popularity of German music and signals the end of the style of music preferred by Henrietta Aiken and Louisa Rebecca.[25]

Conclusion

Women from all over the South traveled to Europe in the decades before the Civil War, and the impact of these journeys varied considerably—there was no one-size-fits-all transformation simply because women went overseas. The three women who form the basis of this study all spent time in Europe, but their narratives diverge widely. This is all the more apparent when comparing the Aikens with the McCords. Their cases illustrate the need for more comprehensive studies of this aspect of individual southern women's lives so that we may better understand how music functioned in their cultural circles. That Harriet Lowndes, Henrietta Aiken, and Louisa Rebecca McCord participated in roughly the same social world and yet left such different music collections illustrates the need to investigate individual variations on the common generalization of women's music in the parlor. Narrative by synecdoche will not suffice.[1]

Harriet's Cultivation of French Culture

For Harriet Lowndes, outward signs of "culture"—some of which she acquired before she made the journey overseas—were essential to her self-definition. From the time she first traveled to Paris in the 1830s, she used European culture, as she experienced it, to reinvent herself as someone who lived in both worlds: Charleston and Paris. Her fascination with the cultural feast that was Paris began early and is manifested in the binder's volumes she collected before her marriage in 1831.[2] She had been inculcated with the idea that European culture was something she should desire and emulate, and her volumes of a predominantly French repertory purchased in Paris and Brussels began a lifelong attraction to French and Italian fine arts.[3] She decorated her art gallery with foreign paintings, sculpture, and other items, and her parlor with luxuriously bound volumes of complete operas purchased from Weissenbruch in Brussels. The people she entertained at her home on Elizabeth Street would have seen these and other precious artifacts, and they would have understood that she epitomized taste, culture, and refinement. She and William even had a French stove, a *potager*, installed in their home in Charleston in the 1850s, and if her guests did not see this because it was in the private area of the house, they must have heard about it.[4]

The Aikens not only reigned over most other South Carolinians but also rose above many in their own social class through their adoption of European cultural models. Harriet's comments during the 1848 revolution in Paris about having "had enough" of a republic at home provide a telling anecdote of her attitude toward egalitarianism. She saw herself and her family as in a different social realm and used the acquisition of foreign music as one means of maintaining her distinction among her peers in Charleston while sharing the same elite southern culture. As Elizabeth Garrett has shown, while other Charlestonians imported or went to Europe to purchase art and other furnishings for their homes, the Aikens went a step further and built an art gallery. This gallery functioned as a physical reminder of their refinement, tastes, and overall quality of life. They had the family crest inscribed on the silver service. All of their displayed items visually confirmed their wealth, status, and culture.[5] So too did the music, which has not been seen in this context until now.

Harriet carefully guided Henrietta in acquiring superior cultural ideals, and she accomplished this in a number of ways. Most obviously, Henrietta spent several years living in Paris, and her parents made certain that she learned to communicate in French, written and spoken. Her French textbooks required fluency in the language and complemented her parents' investment in her education. We can safely assume that she dressed according to Parisian fashion and that her parents exposed her to a variety of foreign social situations, as deemed appropriate to her age and station. Initially her mother provided Henrietta with the same type of music that she had sung as a young woman: French romances and other pieces that hearkened back to the repertory young women in Paris sang in the 1820s. This direct influence on her musical education distinguishes the Aikens' oversight of their daughter's cultural development. Even when Henrietta's taste and musical maturity reached the point where she could sing difficult Italian arias, Harriet continued to buy Parisian romances and other French repertory—as in *Échos de France*—that reflected a style more aligned with what she had sung as a teenager.

From the few mentions of the Aiken women in contemporary diaries and letters to the emphasis on Parisian music, Henrietta's personality is overshadowed by that of her mother. Certainly, the Civil War interrupted her life at a time when she reached adulthood, which makes comparisons more difficult. But the fact that Henrietta and her family lived in the house on Elizabeth Street with her mother until the latter died in 1892 made it possible for Harriet to continue to exert influence over her daughter. Moreover, Henrietta's preservation of Harriet's things throws further light on their relationship, though whether positive or negative is less obvious.

Harriet's desire that the Aikens be seen as cosmopolitan in their everyday existence—not simply that everyone knew they traveled extensively—resulted in Henrietta being brought up outside the close social circles that other young women who spent more time in Charleston experienced. Her closest friends appear to have been her cousins. Her reputation as a musician, as in her fondness for French songs or standards of performance, was known among them. That Basvecchi composed a challenging Italian *romanza* for her further represents acknowledgment of her musical training and probably talent.

Henrietta's Musical Connections

Henrietta's music collections can be contrasted with those owned by some of the women closely connected to her. Binder's volumes that belonged to Mary Lowndes, her first cousin, and Mary Rhett, her eventual sister-in-law, survive in the Charleston Museum collection, and other single-sheet music publications have the names of other relations inscribed on them. These supply more background information on the music of women connected in some way to Harriet Lowndes. Through them we can understand better how Henrietta's unbound collection stands alone in its range of styles, composers, and genres.

Mary Huger Lowndes (1832–1905) was the daughter of Charles Tidyman Lowndes and Sabina Elliott Huger. That she accompanied Henrietta and her parents to Europe in 1851 is confirmed by her name on the passenger list. Her binder's volume, SMB 32, evinces an accomplished pianist, for the music therein surpasses the difficulty seen in the music of most of her contemporaries. Markings that appear throughout the volume testify to its use. SMB 32 is a sizable binder's volume of almost four hundred pages. Piano arrangements of melodies from popular operas fill its pages, and some of these constitute the most difficult music available in the United States before the Civil War.[6] These include three such settings by Beyer and eight by Rosellen, in addition to Leopold de Meyer's "Carnival de Venise," Thalberg's "Fantaisie pour le piano zur des themes de l'Opera Moise de G. Rossini" (op. 33, twenty-three pages long), and four grandiose transcriptions by Charles Voss. These men were some of the most famous touring pianists of the period. Similarly, the opera composers and the tunes were the most popular: Verdi, Bellini, Donizetti, and Rossini; and only one by the latter further confirms a growing preference for the later Italian works. Mary's music confirms standard tastes of the late 1840s and 1850s, as can also be seen in Henrietta's music choices. Nonetheless, she did not own anything out of the ordinary, certainly nothing like Henrietta's *Échos de France.*

Five of Mary's piano compositions were published abroad: one in Berlin (or London); one in Mainz; and the remainder in Paris. Unlike Henrietta's music, however, all of Mary's foreign pieces were imported to the United States through New York City. The firm of Scharfenberg & Luis was responsible for most of them, and Zogbaum's brought one of them to Charleston via this importer.[7] Mary wrote "Mary H. Lowndes / 1848" on some of the Boston publications, and others appear to have been purchased in New York. Thus, Harriet's niece, who traveled with the family in 1850–51, did not acquire her piano music while abroad.[8]

Another of Harriet's nieces, Caroline Lowndes (1845–1919), owned three pieces now in the Charleston Museum. Caroline was born the same year as Louisa Rebecca, and her music includes the same nocturne by Döhler—SMS 331, his op. 24—as does Louisa Rebecca's SMB 29. Caroline owned the Viennese edition, but it had been sold by Scharfenberg & Luis in New York. Her other two compositions are for the piano as well. "Ah che la morte / Miserere" from Verdi's *Il trovatore,* in an arrangement by G. A. Osborne, bears the inscription "Miss Caroline Lowndes" and was published in Mainz by Schott. Its fanfares and tumultuous passages require an appreciable piano technique. Her copy of Richard Hoffman's "Crispino e la Comare / Caprice de concert" (SMS 327) was a gift from Harriet in 1866. That Harriet was in the financial position to gift sheet music in 1866 reinforces that the Aikens survived the Civil War with more of their fortune intact than their neighbors did, thanks to William's investments in Europe during his extended stays there.

Two binder's volumes associated with the Aiken-Rhetts belonged to Mary Rhett: SMB 24 and SMB 53. Mary Burnet Rhett (1836–72) was the daughter of Robert Barnwell Rhett, an ardent secessionist and editor of the *Charleston Mercury,* and Elizabeth Washington Burnet (1809–52). When Henrietta married A. B. Rhett, Mary became her sister-in-law. Mary's mother was a graduate of the Columbia Female Institute in Tennessee, which employed an unusual and serious music instructor named Sarah Smith.[9] Whether Elizabeth took advantage of such is unknown. Her daughter's volume contains a variety of types of music, mostly light songs and ballads from the antebellum period.[10] Like Henrietta and Louisa Rebecca, she sang some difficult repertory. For example, Giulio Alary's "My Love with Joy Is Bounding Light" (a "Polka Song with variations") includes the variations supposedly sung by Henriette Sontag, some of which are florid and ascend to a high B (B6). Others, though, typify the types of pieces found in the binder's volumes of less affluent women, including works by Bishop, Balfe, Alexander Lee, Foster, and Horn. Some of these were rather old-fashioned by the 1850s. She also knew pieces by southern-based composers, such as John Whitaker (eastern North Carolina) and A. S. Pfister (Alabama). An entire popular collection, *English and American Ballads by Celebrated Composers,* constitutes the final part of her binder's volume. With two exceptions, all of those with dates fall between 1852 and 1855.

Mary Rhett's two volumes are divided into one for piano and one for voice. Bound by Welch & Harris, Premium Book Binders on 59 Broad Street in 1856, SMB 24 consists of vocal music only, even though the index page is entitled "piano music." Mary Rhett's binder's volume hardly approaches the seriousness of the pieces associated with Henrietta or even Mary Lowndes. The Rhett family traveled to Paris; Gabriel Manigault mentioned seeing the "Rhetts" in 1848, but whether Mary was with them is unknown. SMB 24 does not evince a keen interest in music, even if she could manage the Sontag variations. It also lacks the cosmopolitan contents of her sister-in-law's collection. It serves to illustrate how remarkable Henrietta's music collection is as well as Harriet's influence on the cultural education of her daughter.[11]

Mary Rhett's other binder's volume, SMB 53, dates from about 1850 and consists only of solo piano music. Waltzes dominate this collection, along with a few variation sets, popular melodies, and a few character pieces.[12] Some of the arrangements challenge the pianist, such as Grobe's "Les ideales variations amusants sur la polka favorite de Jenny Lind" (op. 114, 1848) and his "Amusement des amateurs variations brillants sur un theme favori de M. Keller 'The Ravel Polka'" (op. 111, 1847). Others, however, do not. These include simple character pieces, such as "The Bridal Bell" by T. Bricker (1847) and "La Carolina" by J. Dodsley Humphreys (1843). The most significant contribution that SMB 53 makes is in documenting the popularity of the waltz in the United States: twenty-six of its thirty-eight pieces have "waltz" or "valse" in the title. Some of these display a proclivity for a "Spanish" sound, while others bear more humorous titles—for example "The Giraffe Waltz." The six variation sets hold pride of place in SMB 53, being bound at the beginning. Only six pieces do not fall into one of these two genres.[13] None of the music was published abroad.

Two other women connected to Harriet Lowndes Aiken help paint an accurate picture of music among the women in this extended family. A few compositions owned by Elise Rhett (1841–1924), Mary's sister, exist among Frances Dill Rhett's bequest. These include advanced pieces for solo voice and solo piano. Her vocal method book *Vocalises pour voix de soprano* by Marco Bordogni (SMB 194) has breath marks that imply use in voice lessons. This suggests that Elise studied voice, but her extant music in the Charleston Museum is all for solo piano, and its technical demands are considerable. This music includes two Rosellen arrangements: op. 154 of Verdi's *La traviata* and his arrangement of Puget's "Le rêve de Marie"; and Mennechet de Barival's "L'Aveu / Nocturne." She also owned "Douce pensée" by Henri Ravina (his op. 41), and this is inscribed "Mlle Marmiez //

Elise." Mlle. Marmiez's name also appears on pieces of Henrietta's, but her connection to these young women is unknown. Sally Rhett (1844–1921), sister of Mary and Elise, owned an "Allegrezza Caprice / Etude de concert, op. 66" by Goria that is inscribed "Mlle Marmiez / Sally Rhett / Christmas / 1859 December 25th." Henrietta too had some music from Mlle. Mariez. It is possible that Mlle. Marmiez was a local music teacher in Charleston just before the Civil War, but her name does not appear in census records or city directories.

Louisa Rebecca McCord's Musical Connections

Even though Louisa Rebecca spent more of her prewar life in Columbia than in Charleston, links to the port city can been seen through Charleston Museum binder's volumes that belonged to young women who attended the South Carolina Female Institute at Barhamville. The strength of the music faculty at that school is shown in the impressive six-volume collection of Ann Beaufort Sims (1839–1920) in the Charleston Museum. Hannah (1843–72), Louisa Rebecca's sister, matriculated there, and one of the pieces in Louisa Rebecca's SMB 42 has Hannah's name on it. Other pieces in Louisa Rebecca's music collection may have originally been Hannah's as well, but not the foreign music, since Hannah did not travel to Europe.

The most conspicuous binder's volume in the Charleston Museum that probably originated at the South Carolina Female Institute belonged to Elizabeth Waties Allston Pringle (1845–1921), who struggled to maintain the family's plantation in the late nineteenth and early twentieth centuries. She documented her endeavors in *A Woman Rice Planter* (1913) and *Chronicles of Chicora Wood* (1922), writing under the pseudonym Patience Pennington. The daughter of Robert F. W. Allston and Adèle Petigru, she was known as "Bessie" as a child.[14] Her binder's volume in Charleston is SMB 15, bound by Welch & Harris, which seems to have been the bindery of choice in mid-century Charleston.[15] Piano music fills SMB 15, much of it consisting of long and demanding pieces, similar to those in Mary Lowndes's binder's volume SMB 32. She too owned difficult arrangements of popular operas, such as Beyer's op. 42 settings of *La traviata* and *Il trovatore*. Other famous pianists whose works populate SMB 15 are Hünten, Herz, and Cramer. Bessie included some non-opera-based compositions in her book, including several based on "popular airs." Representing this sort of work are "Morceaux faciles sur des air populaires les plus favoris, H. Cramer, Op. 89, #14 Les yeux bleus de Arnaud" and "Trois sentimentales melodies allemandes, F. Hünten, Op. 179, 'L'Éloge des Larmes,' Schubert." The latter seems to have been a favorite because there are many markings and even smudges from its pages being turned.

In her *Chronicles of Chicora Wood,* Bessie described music at Barhamville on different occasions. She wrote of her voice lessons with Angelo Torriani with a sentimentality that borders on the saccharine, remembering that she broke down in tears over her lack of singing skill and remarked, "Oh, Mr. Toiriani [*sic*], there is no use for me to go on: I have no voice," at which he "turned fiercely" and said, "Voice—what does that matter? You must go on. Vous avez le feu sacré."[16] This is the same Torriani that Mother Louisa had brought to Lang Syne to teach Louisa Rebecca: the same man who assigned Concone's vocal method to Louisa Rebecca, wrote florid cadenzas for her, and probably copied the manuscript music in SMB 29.[17] Louisa Rebecca and Bessie were the same age, and Bessie arrived at school in November 1862, about the same time Louisa Rebecca received lessons from Torriani. Presumably, Torriani treated Louisa Rebecca similarly.

Bessie seems to have been a better pianist than vocalist; she recalled three pianos at the school and not being allowed to practice more than two hours a day on them. No vocal music of hers survives, so we cannot compare her repertory to that of Louisa Rebecca. She did sing, however, because Torriani assigned her the final music from *Martha,* act 2, scene 3, but whether or not she actually managed to sing it well remains unknown.

Not unexpectedly, Torriani assigned both young women music primarily in Italian. That Bessie had to sing Flotow's *Martha* in Italian was unusual because the original is in German and young southern women of her class were more familiar with French. That students at Barhamville were not as fluent in French as Bessie came as a surprise to her. She knew Mme. Togno, the French principal at the South Carolina Female Institute at this time, from her previous school in Charleston, where everyone was required to speak French. Apparently, Mme. Togno attempted to instill this rule at Barhamville, to little effect. Many of the older students (eighteen and nineteen) had never learned French conversation, so Mme. Togno soon abandoned the project.[18]

Did this lack of French characterize the milieu in which Louisa Rebecca grew up? In 1860 Columbia had at least seven music teachers, five of whom were German men.[19] The other two were women, including Mary A. Garnett, who was probably the "Miss Garnett" whom Louisa Rebecca remembered as a temporary music teacher. There were several German teachers at the nearby South Carolina College too. Mother Louisa socialized with those who taught at the college, so her interest in having the children speak German might have stemmed from these associations. Louisa Rebecca purchased songs in German while the family visited Switzerland, but these typified what tourists bought, as can be seen from the fact that Henrietta owned the same editions.

The music collection from the Aiken-Rhett House constitutes one of the most significant resources of music owned by elite women of antebellum Charleston. Undoubtedly it shows what music these women performed in their parlors. The extent to which it represents what other young women in the South or even the

United States performed has not been considered, but the fact that it confirms both continuity and diversity serves to underline the importance of considering data from across the country before making generalizations.

Harriet's music is the most unusual for the three women who form the basis of this book. After her first volume, SMB 49, her collection looks like it could have been that of a young woman from Brussels or Paris but certainly not Charleston. That the closest comparison can be made with a binder's volume that belonged to a well-known French salon amateur singer places Harriet's music in a unique place among American collections. The repertory of the French salon and the social world of its aristocracy constituted an entirely different culture from that of the American parlor and elite society in the United States. In light of this, Harriet's collection is all the more worthy of consideration because she collected these pieces before traveling to Europe. Nevertheless, French culture had already left an indelible mark on the young Harriet Lowndes.

When she married William Aiken Jr. in 1831, she aligned herself with a man with whom she shared many cultural and social interests. He was born and had been abroad and went on the grand tour in the 1820s. William Aiken Sr. had been successful in his North American endeavors while maintaining a number of European business interests. In marrying Harriet, William Jr. tied his father's financial success to the respectability of Charleston's aristocrats of Huguenot descent. The union produced a couple fascinated with European culture and the economic means to explore the cultural delights of Paris and the rest of Europe, to travel there several times, and even to live there. Several aspects of their acquisition of European goods have been studied; yet there has been little attention paid to the music in the house and how it confirms the Aikens' aspirations.[20] It too formed a part of the family's display of taste, wealth, and rank among their social circle. Harriet raised the cultural bar ever higher among Charlestonians, and through this she was able to maintain their distinction above their contemporaries.

Henrietta was brought up in this household, and not surprisingly, her music collection is at odds with others from Charleston and throughout an even broader area. Indeed, the amount of material purchased abroad exceeds that in other southern binder's volumes: French method books for voice and piano; romances even in the 1840s. Even her cousin Mary, who accompanied her to France in 1850, purchased her music in New York, and no evidence suggests that she followed Henrietta's habit of buying it abroad. Henrietta was special, and her parents ensured this by educating her in Paris, providing her with multiple experiences abroad, and seeing that her curricular materials, including music, were French.

Her music remained unbound, which could be because the war interrupted her collecting. However, that Louisa Rebecca managed to have hers bound in

1864 or 1865 suggests that this is not probable. She may have left it as is because she continued to use it, and in the 1850s most binder's volumes were heavy and sewn tightly together, hindering their use. As another explanation, leaving her music unbound may have been a sign of wealth. It could be replaced easily, so for Henrietta—a woman whose family figured among the wealthiest in the state—it may not have been necessary to preserve her music as others did. Moreover, music was a more transient commodity than sculpture or paintings, and musical styles changed rapidly.

Louisa Rebecca traveled to Europe only once, but she too bought music there. Her purchases were connected with London, not Paris or Brussels, and in this she differed from her near contemporary Henrietta. Louisa Rebecca was younger, and perhaps the operatic arias that Henrietta owned were out of her capabilities at age twelve. Songs by Glover and even romances by Puget were popular on both sides of the Atlantic. M. Bretonnière apparently assigned her difficult pieces, but she questioned the appropriateness of these in her "Recollections." She also seems to have had more freedom to explore places such as Naples, attending burlesques at the San Carlino. Nevertheless, her collection does not have the transatlantic implications that Henrietta's does. She purchased a few pieces while abroad but did not actively work to live that culture once she returned to South Carolina.

Louisa Rebecca owned four binder's volumes, a fact that speaks to her family's wealth and position. In the 1860 census Louisa M. McCord was given the occupation of "Farmer," and her worth exceeded one hundred thousand dollars. This alone marked the McCord family as distinct in Columbia. It is difficult to imagine Harriet calling herself a farmer. Such differences must have weighed in on the two mothers' views of how to raise their daughters. And yet each daughter trained with an Italian music teacher in South Carolina (Basvecchi for Henrietta, Torriani for Louisa Rebecca), probably studied music in France (of Louisa Rebecca we are certain, and Henrietta almost surely would have done so as well), owned a significant amount of music, eventually sang expansive Verdi arias, and spent part of their lives in Charleston. These commonalities justify interrogation of their musical practices in order to establish what young elite women could have experienced in urban antebellum South Carolina.

More importantly, within a small community of wealthy white women existed substantial variation in music collecting. All had music, but some, such as Mary Rhett and possibly Hannah McCord, appear to have been less invested in it. Most of the young women in Charleston's aristocracy gained considerable technique and performed difficult music. Few binder's volumes in this group adhere to today's expectations of an "ordinary" or "typical" collection. A comparison of Henrietta's music with that of Emily McKissick of Albany, New York, proves how distinctive the music in the Charleston Museum truly is. Emily and Henrietta were born in the same year. One binder's volume of Emily's survives, and it includes two arias by Donizetti but no Verdi or Meyerbeer.[21] The music in Emily's collection manifests the description given in standard texts about American parlor music, particularly those who focus on the middle class. For example, in Richard Crawford's influential *America's Musical Life,* Verdi's name hardly appears except with opera performances or band music. Yet his music was exceptionally popular among these women from Charleston and figured prominently in their musical lives—enough so that Harriet wrote to a friend asking him to send something from *Il trovatore* to Henrietta. A comparison of the collections of Henrietta and Emily illustrates how important it is to evaluate women's music in specific times and places in order to understand music circulation and performance in the nineteenth century better.

Not only do mid-century collections include a broad variety of composers, but the music in them can be challenging to perform as well. Leading music history textbooks do not acknowledge either the diversity or technical difficulty found in many binder's volumes but focus instead on parlor songs by Stephen Foster. Foster's contributions are undeniably important, particularly in later years, but much more variety exists in mid-century collections. Nevertheless, textbook authors have tended to paint all home music-making in the nineteenth century with a single brush, which clearly does not suffice.[22] The frequent appearance of music by Verdi and Meyerbeer in southern collections of the 1850s might yield a different view of the music history of this period, especially when compared to the slight presence of Beethoven's music at the same time.

Does this mean that the standards were higher in Charleston or for elite women? Perhaps. To many people, Charleston represented the epitome of taste and refinement. Wealthy residents of the city traveled to New York and to Europe, and some took their extended families on lengthy trips abroad. The experiences of Harriet, Henrietta, and Louisa Rebecca reveal that we still have much to learn about music and how it defined culture in the United States. Charleston's elite women employed music as a form of cultural capital to maintain their position above an increasingly prosperous and growing middle class.[23] When women who had visited Europe returned to the United States, they must have triggered anxieties among those who considered themselves of equal social status but lacked this cultural capital.

Nonetheless, everyone did not take away the same musical experiences after traveling to Europe. This point might seem obvious, but until now no author has focused on such a limited set of collections for comparison. Harriet's collection of Parisian romances, all published in Paris or Brussels, dramatically expands our knowledge of what Americans performed in the 1820s. Henrietta's stands alone for not being bound and for including such a variety of genres—romances to arias to Swiss songs—and foreign-language method books. Louisa Rebecca's binder's volumes reveal much about life in the late 1850s and 1860s: SMB 37 matches her family's journey through Europe; SMB 29 manifests the consequences of the Civil War on a young woman's pursuit of accomplishment; and pieces within the collection tell us where she shopped in London. Taken together, these three provide a significantly more complete record of what was happening in a relatively small region of the United States. Similarly unique stories can be found from antebellum Mobile, Richmond, Savannah, Nashville, and most of all New Orleans. Women's collections from these cities, as well as others, reveal that we have much to learn about music in southern areas. Data from less urban/cosmopolitan binder's volumes contribute another side to music circulation patterns. Examining these in detail reveals a rich imbrication of divergent musical experiences that southern women negotiated in the antebellum period, which in turn enables musicologists to begin new dialogues with historians who research this period with differing methodologies. Thus it may be possible to reconfigure the rich body of scholarship of American music to 1865 as we seek to include a more nuanced approach to women's participation in the larger narrative. By looking at a small sample of the population in a limited geographic area, this book provides a foundation for additional research into women's music practice in the United States and Europe during the nineteenth century.

Appendix A

Contents of Related Binder's Volume

SMB 24. Mary Rhett, Vocal Volume

No.	Title	Composer	Date	Notes
1	Selections from the Opera of Il Trovatore ("Ah'si! ben mis")	G. Verdi; arr. Signor Augusto Bandalari	1854	Boston: Reed. "Mary Rhett"
2	Selections from the Opera of Il Trovatore ("D'amor su l'altri pesce")	G. Verdi; arr. Signor Augusto Bandalari	1854	Boston: Reed
3	A dream of bygone days	J. H. Tully		Boston: Ditson
4	My love with joy is bounding light—Polka Song with variations	Giulio Alary	1852	New York: Hall & Son. "Sung by Miss Henriette Sontag." Difficult—very florid variations to be sung on "Ah" and high B
5	Darkeyed one, darkeyed one	[W. A. Mozart]; arr. Charles Horn		Charleston, S.C.: Siegling (Musical Warehouse, Bend of King Street). "Sung by Mr. Horn as Sarastro in the Opera of the Magic Flute"
6	Bright star of hope			
7	The long, long weary day ("Den lichten langen Tag")—A German Melody		1853	Baltimore: Miller & Beacham
8	Reject me not	M. Balfe; arr. Alfred Bunn	1853	Boston: Ditson. "Sung by Mrs. Thillon in Balfe's Opera The Devil is in it."
9	Five Favorite Songs in the Operatic Drama Paul Clifford—No. 5 ("Maiden I'll ne'er deceive thee")		1852	New York: Vandebeek

SMB 24. Mary Rhett, Vocal Volume (*continued*)

No.	Title	Composer	Date	Notes
10	Boquet de Florence—No. 4 ("Il desio")	Harrison Millard		Boston: Ditson
11	They say thou has forsaken me—Arranged to the Celebrated Waltz Le Desire	Charles E. Horn	1837	New York: Dubois & Bacon
12	Flowers & stars ("Blumen und Sterne")	F. Kücken	1855	Baltimore: Miller & Beacham. "Translated from the German by Mrs. E. W. Long"
13	Beauties of German Song ("May Breeze")	J. Kreipl	1855	Baltimore: McCaffrey. Julius E. Müller responsible for the series.
14	Beauties of German Song ("Brightest eyes")	G. Stigelli	1855	Baltimore: McCaffrey. Julius E. Müller responsible for the series.
15	My little valley home		1854	Philadelphia: Lee & Walker; sold Charleston, S.C.: Siegling (233 King St.). "Sung by Henry Devere in the Philadelphia Opera Troupe."
16	Do they miss me at home?	S. M. Granis	1852	Boston: Ditson (Music dated 1853, copyright listed as 1852)
17	Yes, we miss thee (Reply to "Do they miss me at home?")	F. Buckley	1853	New York: Firth, Pond & Co.
18	Annie Lowe	G. Friedrich Wurzel	1853	New York: Hall & Son
19	Sad news from home	P. S. Gilmore		
20	The banks of Allen Water	Charles E. Horn		New York: Firth, Pond & Co.
21	Wert thou to speak farewell (Reply to "I'd offer thee his hand of mine")	A. Sedgwick	1853	New York: Firth, Pond & Co.

22	Cradle song	W. V. Wallace	1851	New York: Hall & Son
23	Twas but a fleeting dream (Ballad)	George Linley		Baltimore: Miller & Beacham
24	I have no joy but in thy smile	J. M. Stewart		Boston: Ditson. "Written expressively for Godey's Lady's Book"
25	At eve I miss thee when alone	L. V. H. Crosby	1847	Boston: Ditson
26	One careless word	A. Lee		New York: Firth, Pond & Co.; New Orleans: Mayo; sold Charleston, S.C.: Siegling
27	The forsaken one (to an Air of Mercadante's)	G. F. Cole		Baltimore: Willig
28	Those evening bells—Air "Bells of Saint Petersburg"	John Stevenson		Philadelphia: Blake. Moore's Popular National Melody
29	Then, fare thee well—(Popular Old English Melody)	H. Bishop		
30	Time, am I faithful fair	John Whitaker		New York: Dubois
31	Oh! Henry! Don't ask me to go	F. Dorigo	1850	Philadelphia: Fiot
32	Maggie by my side	S. Foster	1852	New York: Firth, Pond & Co. Sold at Zogbaum
33	Ella Dee	A. S. Pfister	1852	New York: Firth, Pond & Co.
34	The violets—Duetts for two sopranos	William Dressler	1852	New York: Hall & Son
35	Wilt thou be gone love-Duett	S. Foster	1851	New York: Firth, Pond & Co.
36	Wilt thou tempt the waves with me?-Duett		1829	Baltimore: Willig
37	I've wandered in dreams	J. A. Wade		New York: S. C. Jollie
pp. 215–52	*English and American Ballads by Celebrated Composers*			

SMB 32. Mary H. Lowndes, Index

No./ Page*	Title	Composer	Date	Notes
1/1	Fantasia on motives from Verdi's opera of Attila, op. 162	G. Verdi; arr. J. B. Duvernoy	[1840–55]	Philadelphia: Fiot. Zogbaum stamp
2/15	Le Carnival de Venise	Leopold de Meyer	[1848–55]	Philadelphia: Fiot. Geo. Oates Book & Music Store, 218 Regent St., Charleston stamp. "Mary H Lowndes"
3/27	Fantaisie Pour le Piano Sur des Themes de l'Opera Moise de G. Rossini, op. 33	G. Rossini; arr. S. Thalberg		Louisville: W. C. Peters. Siegling stamp. Pedal markings photo. $1.25. Pedal markings p. 39 + fingering; p. 44 lining up notes; p. 46 fingering; p. 48 leave out 10ths. Difficult. Fingered. "Mary H Lowndes"
4/49	Quadrille sur l'Opera de Giacomo Meyerbeer Le Prophète	G. Meyerbeer; arr. J. Strauss		Philadelphia: Fiot. Hoyer, NY stamp. Originally published in Brussels in Antwerp: A. P. Hogeschool
5/57	Les Quatres Airs de Ballet et la Marche, de Sacre de l'Opera Le Prophète de Giacomo Meyerbeer	G. Meyerbeer; arr. Garaudé	[1844–49]	Paris: Brandus et Cie. Scharfenberg & Luis, NY stamp.
6/67	Reminiscences de l'Opera Le Prophète de Giacomo Meyerbeer, Duo brillante, op. 158	G. Meyerbeer; arr. Edouard Wolff		Paris: Brandus et Cie. Scharfenberg & Luis, NY stamp. Piano duet
7/105	Les Nationalités Musicales—Six Esquisses (L'Écosses [schottische], la Russe [nocturne], Naples [tarantella], l'Angleterre [military march], l'Allemande [waltz], et l'Irlande [Irish tune]), op. 185p	F. Kalkbrenner	[1849?]	Leipzig: Breitkopf & Härtel. Scharfenberg & Luis, NY stamp

No.	Title	Composer / Arranger	Date	Notes
8/129	The celebrated duet in the opera of Linda di Chamounix	G. Donizetti; arr. Steyermarkische	1848	Boston: Reed. "The only correct copy / As played by the Steyermarkische Musical Company." "Marie H Lowndes / 1848"
9/137	Variations brillantes avec introduction & finale pour le piano sur l'air favori de célèbre Balfe "The light of other days" de l'Opera The Maid of Artois, op. 16	M. Balfe; arr. G. P. Manouvrier of New Orleans	[1838]	Philadelphia: Willig; New Orleans: E. Johns. "Mary H. Lowndes"
10/149	Choeur de Norma—Improvisation pour piano, op. 41	V. Bellini; arr. C. Voss	[1852] and 1854]	Berlin: Bote & Bock Scharfenberg & Luis, NY stamp. "Mary H. Lowndes" [also published in London]
11/159	Les Huguenots, Fantaisie brillante, op. 66	G. Meyerbeer; arr. C. Voss		Paris: Offenbach. Scharfenberg & Luis, NY stamp. "Mary H. Lowndes"
12/177	Lucrezia Borgia, Fantaisie brillante, op. 86	G. Donizetti; arr. C. Voss		Paris: Offenbach. Scharfenberg & Luis, NY stamp. "Mary H. Lowndes"
13/191	Les Huguenots, Fantaisie brillante, op. 66	G. Meyerbeer; arr. C. Voss	1841	Philadelphia: Hupfield & Son. Same piece as p. 159. "Mary H Lowndes 184[?]"
14/209	Pensées Italiennes—3 Cavatinas Variées (No. 2, Anna Bolena), op. 16	G. Donizetti; arr. H. Rosellen		Boston: Reid. "Mary H Lowndes / 184[?]"
15/221	Fantaisie brillante pour le piano sur La Muette de Portici, op. 75	D. Auber; arr. H. Rosellen		Boston: Reid. "Mary H Lowndes / 184[?]"
16/241	Fantaisie Lucia di Lammermoor, op. 80	G. Donizetti; arr. H. Rosellen	[ca. 1850]	Missing title page. Pedal markings
17/261	Decameron des jeunes Pianistes. Collection progressive de Fantaisies, Variations etc. (No. 9 "Souvenir d'Otello et de Bianca et Faliero"), op. 55	Arr. H. Rosellen	[1843]	Mainz: Schott. Sold New York: Millet's Music Saloon. Marks on p. 249

SMB 32. Mary H. Lowndes, Index (*continued*)

No./ Page*	Title	Composer	Date	Notes
18/269	Fantaisie brillane sur la Rose de Péronne	Adolphe Adam; arr. Henri Rosellen	[1850?]	New York: Hall & Son. "Mary H. Lowndes"
19/283	Variations on a favorite cavatina in Donizetti's Opera Parisina, op. 18	G. Donizetti; arr. H.Rosellen	[184?]	Philadelphia: Fiot. "Mary H. Lowndes"
20/293	Les Charmes de Naples—3 Fantaisies pour le piano sur les Opéras de Donizetti, op. 25 (No. 2 Roberto Devereux)	G. Donizetti; arr. H. Rosellen	[1840]	Paris: Brandus et Cie. Scharfenberg & Luis, NY stamp; Zogbaum stamp [date from Mainz: Schott].
21/307	Fantaisie et variations sur l'Opèra Il Templario, op. 65	N. Isouard; arr. H. Rosellen	[1844]	Philadelphia: Willig. "Mary H. Lowndes" [Paris: Schlesinger]
22/323	Fantaisies, Variations, & Rondeaux pour le Piano Forte sur des motids favoris de l'Opèra La Somnambula, op. 53/no. 2	V. Bellini; arr., F. Beyer	[185?]	Boston: Reed. "Mary H. Lowndes / 1848"
23/339	Fantaisies, Variations, & Rondeaux pour le Piano Forte sur des motids favoris de l'Opèra La Somnambula, op. 53/no. 3	V. Bellini; arr. F. Beyer	[185?]	Boston: Reed. "Mary H. Lowndes / 1848"
24/355	Bouquet de Melodies—Ernani de Verdi, op. 42/no. 9	G. Verdi; arr. F. Beyer		New York: Hall & Son. "Mary H. Lowndes"

SMB 53. Mary B. Rhett, Piano Volume

No.	Title	Composer	Date	Notes
1	[pages missing, details unknown]			
2	Italy / 3 Favorite Airs Duetts	C. T. Brunner		Philadelphia: Fiot. Sold by Zogbaum
3	Salut à la France / La fille du Regiment	G. Donizetti; arr. C. T. Brunner		Philadelphia: Fiot
4	The last rose of summer [op. 159]	H. Herz	1848	New York: Firth & Pond
5	Favorite Irish Melodies arranged in brilliant style with Introduction and Variations / #2 "The soldier's greeting"	W. V. Wallace		New York: Hall. Sold by Oates. "Mary B. Rhett / Charleston / So. Caro."
6	Heures de Loisir / Variations on "Flow gently sweet Afton" [op. 73]	C. Grobe	1846	Philadelphia: Willig
7	Les ideales variations amusants sur la polka favorite de Jenny Lind [op. 114]	C. Grobe	1848	Philadelphia: Lee & Walker
8	Amusement des amateurs variations brillantes sur un theme favori de M. Keller / "The Ravel Polka" [op. 111]	C. Grobe	1847	Philadelphia: Lee & Walker
9	Miss Lucy Neale	W. R. Coppock	1845	New York: Firth & Pond. Sold Fischer's, Washington, D.C.
10	Poland is not yet lost Variations [op. 105]	C. Grobe	1847	Baltimore: Benteen
11	The Swiss Herdsman Variations	A. Nebauer		Philadelphia: Fiot
12	Welcome to Jenny Lind Valse	M. Strakosch	1850	New York: Hall & Son
13	Sunnyside Waltz	Henry Oates	1850	Charleston: George Oates. Dedicated to Miss Ella Ford of Augusta, Ga.

SMB 53. Mary B. Rhett, Piano Volume (*continued*)

No.	Title	Composer	Date	Notes
14	Spanish Waltz / La Lincania	W. V. Wallace	1844	New York: Firth & Pond. Sold George Oates
15	Rosita / Grande Valse Espagnole	L.-A. Julien; arr. Gomion		Philadelphia: Fiot
16	Midnight Waltz	W. V. Wallace		New York: Firth, Hall & Pond
17	La douce Mélancholie / Rondo Valse	F. Hünten		Philadelphia: Fiot
18	La feu	C. Marcailhou		New York: Hall & Son
19	Firth, Pond & Co.'s Collection of Celebrated Waltzes / #5 "The Elfin Waltz"	Joseph Labitsky		New York: Firth, Pond & Co.
20	Triumph of the Waltzes / #1 Strauss	Arr. N. Bochsa		Baltimore: Willig. Sold Charleston: Oates
21	Tres Favorites Valses Españoles / #3 Le Grande Antilla	Antonio Raffelin	1847	Baltimore: Willig
22	The Flowers of Virginia / Two Favorite Waltzes / #2 "The Laurel Waltz	Signor G. George	1847	Philadelphia: Willig
23	Three Favorite Waltzes	F. Egan		London: Balls & Son. Also mentions Kingston, Jamaica
24	Les Rayons Valse	Edward Wolfe		Boston: W. H. Oakes
25	Valse à cinq temps	A. J. R. Conner	1847	Philadelphia: Fiot. Performed by Conner's Band
26	The Dream Waltz	Beethoven		Philadelphia: J[ohn] F. Nunns
27	Two Waltzes: The Question and The Answer	J. C. Viereck; Czerny		
28	The Paredisi Waltz	Louis Reimer	1847	Philadelphia: Lee & Walker

29	The Fairy Lake Waltz	Emanuel Brandeis	1850	New York: Hall & Son
30	La Rose-Valse Sentimentale	J. C. Viereck		Philadelphia: Fiot
31	The Giraffe Waltz	Zaleucus		New York: Firth & Hall
32	Lattice Waltz	Thomas Carr		Boston: Ditson. "Miss Mary B. Rhett." Easy piece, fingerings added
33	La Carolina	J. Dodsley Humphreys	1843	New York: John F. Nunns. Pedagogical markings
34	Empress Henrietta's Waltz	H. Herz		Philadelphia: Fiot
35	El Caballero (The Gentleman) A Spanish Waltz	C. Grobe	1843	Philadelphia: Willig
36	The Bridal Bell	T. Bricker	1847	Boston: Ditson. Sold by Oates in Charleston
37	The Fountain of Pearls / Valse Brillante sur un Romance D'Etienne Arnaud	F. Burgmuller		Baltimore: Benteen
38	The Saratoga Lake Waltz	Frederick C. Crambs		Baltimore: Benteen
39	Recreation No. 12—Cromatic [sic] Waltz		1845	Baltimore: Samuel Carusi
40	Recreation No 7—Promenade Waltz		1845	Baltimore: Samuel Carusi

SMB 218. MS without Attribution

Page	Hand	Titles from MS	Composer	[Date[1]]	Comments
2	A	La procedure des Yeux noirs & des Yeux bleus	Joseph-Léon Gatayes	1820–25	Guitar. Same text hand as SMB 48 #2
4	B	Le diable, couleur et Rose	Pierre Gaveaux		Opèra comique. Guitar
5	B	My Henry is Gone	E. E. Ulmo		Guitar
6	C	Le Petit Chaperon rouge—Romance ("Le noble eclat")	A. Boieldieu		
8	C	La Suissesse au Bord du lac	Jacques Nicholas Goulé	1810–11[2]	Lyre ou guitarre
10	C	Benedetta	Signor Verini		For one or two voices
11	Unk.				Pencil worksheet "Intervals proved by Semitones"
12	C	Adèle	A. Romagnesi	183?	
14	Unk.	Walse [*sic*]			Possibly a single treble part; staves joined in pairs before music was determined
15	Unk.				More intervals
16	Unk.				Intervals continue
		REVERSE			
1	D	Air De Montano et Stephanie	Henri-Mouton Berton fils	ca. 1820	In SMB 50, #1
14	E	Je Pense à Toi	[Algaé Quenedey]		Published by the author in Paris, ca. 1820?
16	E	Au Rossignol	F. Blangini		

18	E	Colas, Colas sois moi fidèle	[Louis-Emmanuel Jadin]		Also in *Échos de France*, 2
20	E	Rondeau—de Gulnare ou l'Esclave Persanne	N. Dalayrac	1798	
28	E	Croyez			
30	E	L'Orage	A. Romagnesi	1819	In *Collection des romances, chansonnettes et nocturnes* . . . [2e] volume
32	E	On est si méchant au Village!	A. Romagnesi	1819	In *Collection des romances, chansonnettes et nocturnes* . . . [2e] volume, 1819. Exactly like published version[3]
34	E	La Bergère inquiète	Henry Jacqmin		
35	E	L'Heure de Rendezvous	[A. Romagnesi]	1819	In *Collection des romances, chansonnettes et nocturnes* . . . [2e] volume
36	E	Le Retour au Village	Marese		
38	E	L'Amant et L'Hirondelle	[A. Romagnesi]		
40	A	Ma Zetulle Rondo			
48	C	Le Sentiment a la Mode	A. Romagnesi		In *Collection des romances, chansonnettes et nocturnes* . . . [1e] volume, 1807
50	C	La Consigne	A. Romagnesi		[Bibliothèque Nationale de France, Paris, has one of similar name by Antoine-Louis Clapisson (1808–66); Paris: Delahaute]
52	C	Le Jeune Grec	A. Romagnesi	1819	In *Collection des romances, chansonnettes et nocturnes* . . . [2e] volume
54	C	Fi Que C'est Said D'Etre Jaloux	A. Romagnesi		In *Collection des romances, chansonnettes et nocturnes* . . . [3e] volume[4]

SMB 218. MS without Attribution (*continued*)

Page	Hand	Titles from MS	Composer	[Date[1]]	Comments
55	C	Un Mot de Toi	A. Romagnesi		In *Collection des romances, chansonnettes et nocturnes* . . . [3e] volume
56	C	Le Vieux Clocher de Mon Village // Romance d'un Esclave à Alger	A. Romagnesi		In *Etrennes lyriques ou Recueil de romances et nocturnes, avec accomp.nt de piano ou harpe, publiées par A. Romagnesi et ornées de dessins lithographiés,* 1829
58	C	Reviens a Moi	A. Romagnesi	1819	In *Collection des romances, chansonnettes et nocturnes* . . . [2e] volume
60	C	La Petite Bergére	A. Romagnesi		In *Collection des romances, chansonnettes et nocturnes* . . . [3e] volume
61	C	Qu'est-ce que la Vie	A. Romagnesi	1819	In *Collection des romances, chansonnettes et nocturnes* . . . [2e] volume
62	C	Le Premier Amour du Troubadour	[A. Romagnesi]		Paris, Lemoine

Appendix B

Manuscript Materials in the Hand of Domenico Altrocchi

SMS 350. Cavatina nell'Opera L'Adelia (Me perduta!), Donizetti, 1841
SMS 353. Romanza nell'Opera Il templario, Nicolai, 1840
SMS 396. Miserere nell'Opera Il trovatore di G. Verdi, 1853
SMS 402. Cavatina nell'Opera Maria Padilla, Donizetti, 1841
SMS 406. Barcarole del Maestro Mercadante
SMS 407. Barcarole del Maestro Donizetti
SMS 412. Romanza nell'Opera la Regina di Cipro, Halèvy
SMS 413. Aria nell'Opera i due Figaro, Mercadante, 1835
SMS 448. Cavatina nell'Opera i Capaleti, e Montecchi, Bellini
SMS 449. Scena e Romanza nell'Opera i Capaleti, e Montecchi, Bellini
SMS 502. Aria nell'Opera Saffo, Pacini
SMS 506. Cavatina nell'Opera Gemma di Vergey, Donizetti
SMS 567. Barcarola nell'Opera Marino Falliero, Donizetti

The titles given here are exactly as they appear on the sheet music itself, with no added formatting or standardization

Appendix C

List of Composers and Performers

Abt, Franz (1819–85)—German composer of over three thousand items, including lieder that were popular in the United States during the mid–nineteenth century; toured there in 1872.

Adam, Adolphe (1803–1856)—French composer of at least eighty stage works.

Alkan, Valentin (1813–88)—French pianist and composer.

Auber, Daniel (1782–1871)—French composer of opéras comiques.

Balfe, Michael (1808–70)—Successful Irish opera composer; author of *The Bohemian Girl,* from whence comes "I Dreamt That I Dwelt in Marble Halls."

Basvecchi, Pietro O. (fl. 1840s–50s)—Italian composer based in Charleston in early 1850s.

Beauplan, Amédée Rousseau de (1790–1853)—Composer of romances.

Beethoven, Ludwig van (1770–1827)—Highly influential German composer of symphonies, piano sonatas, and *Fidelio,* among others.

Bégrez, Pierre-Ignace (née Namur, 1787–1863?)—Belgian composer who worked in Paris and London.

Bellini, Vincenzo (1801–35)—Italian opera composer, bel canto style, from Sicily; eventually lived in Paris; operas include *Norma* and *La sonnambula.*

Bertini, Henri (1798–1876)—French pianist and composer; author of a popular piano method.

Berton, Henri-Mouton fils (1767–1844)—French-born composer and guitarist.

Besanzoni, Ferdinando (1820–68)—Composer of romances.

Beyer, Ferdinand (1803–1863)—German composer and pianist. His arrangements of operas, ranging from simple settings of a single tune to medleys of many of the melodies, circulated widely in the antebellum South.

Bishop (née Riviere), Anna (1810–84)—English soprano; several international tours, including with harpist Nicholas Bochsa; estranged wife of Henry Bishop.

Bishop, Henry (1786–1855)—English composer of operas and songs, such as "Home! Sweet Home!"; estranged husband of Anna Bishop.

Blanchet [Couperin], Élisabeth-Antoinette (1729–1815)—French keyboard player and composer.

Blangini, (Guiseppe Marco Maria) Felice (1781–1841)—Italian tenor, French composer and voice instructor. Specialized in opéras comiques, romances, and nocturnes (usually romances for two voices).

Bochsa, Nicolas-Charles (1789–1856)—French-born harpist, composer, and accompanist of Anna Bishop; from Bohemia.

Boieldieu, François-Adrien (1775–1834)—Opera composer known as "the French Mozart"; composed *La dame blanche.*

Bruguiere, Edouard (1793–1863)—A native of Lyon, France. Active in Paris in 1820s and 1830s; composer of romances.

Carulli, Ferdinando (1770–1841)—Guitarist and author of a popular method of playing the guitar.

Chopin, Frédéric (1810–49)—Polish composer of piano music; lived in France most of his adult life.

Clementi, Muzio (1752–1832)—Italian pianist and composer who spent much of his life in England; works enjoyed popularity around 1800 and then later in the nineteenth century; Louisa Cheves Smythe owned some of his works.

Concone, J. (Paolo Giuseppe Gioacchono, 1801–61)—Singing teacher from Turin; published *50 leçons de chant,* op. 9 (*Fifty Lessons for Medium Voice,* Boston: Ditson); Henrietta Aiken and Louisa Rebecca McCord both owned this manual.

Cramer, Johann Baptist (1771–1858)—Performer, composer, pedagogue from Mannheim, spent most of his life abroad, from 1800 almost exclusively in England.

Crescentini, Girolamo (1762–1846)—Italian castrato and composer; favorite of Napoleon.

Czerny, Carl (1791–1857)—Austrian pianist, composer, and instructor; pupil of Beethoven; his pedagogical materials were used by young women throughout the South, including Ann Beaufort Sims.

Dalayrac, Nicolas-Marie (1753–1809)—French composer, mostly of opéras comique; overture to *Nina* was popular and performed in Charleston.

Döhler, Théodore (Theodor) von (1814–56)—Austrian composer and pianist; lived in Italy.

Donizetti, Gaetano (1797–1848)—Composer of Italian opera, bel canto style; many melodies from his operas are in the Aiken-Rhett Collection, including *Lucia di Lammermoor, Adelia,* and *Gemma di Vergy.*

Duchambge, Pauline Montet (1778–1858)—French composer born in the West Indies; published almost four hundred romances.

Dussek, Jan Ladislav (1760–1812)—Czech pianist and composer who worked in France and England.

Fétis, François-Joseph (1784–1871)—Belgian composer and musicologist.

Field, John (1782–1837)—Irish pianist and composer; credited with inventing the "nocturne," the type made more famous by Chopin, for solo piano.

Gail, Sophie Garre (1775–1819)—French composer, singer, accompanist, and *salonnière.*

Gambati, Alessandro (fl. 1830s–1840s)—Trumpeter and voice teacher. Arrived in the United States in 1833 to perform with Italian Opera Company in NY, famously performed in a trumpet "battle" at Niblo's Garden in 1834. Performed and taught in Charleston in the 1840s, his students included Marie Siegling.

Garat, Pierre (1762–1823)—French singer and instructor; also composed romances.

Garcia, Manuel, II (1805–1906)—Italian voice pedagogue, inventor of laryngoscope.

Gaveaux, Pierre (1760–1825)—French singer and composer; wrote songs and some opéras comique.

George, Signor G. (fl. 1830s–1840s)—Music teacher and performer in Norfolk and Richmond.

Gilmore, Patrick S. (1829–1892)—Composer and bandmaster from Ireland who settled in the United States in 1849. Known for his role in the National Peace Jubilee (1869) and the World Peace Jubilee (1872).

Gilfert, Charles (1787–1829)—Composer who dominated music in Charleston in the 1810s.

Glover, Stephen (1813–70)—English composer of songs, several of which were popular in the United States.

Gluck, Christoph von (1714–87)—Bohemian composer of opera; credited with opera reform in the mid–eighteenth century.

Grétry, André-Ernest-Modeste (1741–1813)—French composer of Walloon descent; wrote opéras comique as well as comedies with sung recitatives for the Paris Opéra.

Große, Charles (ca. 1817–1879)—Pianist and composer, born in Germany but immigrated to the United States early. Spent most of his time in the North. Published almost 2000 works.

Guédron, Pierre (ca. 1570–1620)—French composer, singer, and teacher; wrote *airs de cour.*

Handel, George Frideric (1685–1759)—German composer of Italian opera and English oratorios; lived most of his life in London; works include *Giulio Cesare* and *Messiah.*

Haydn, Franz Joseph (1732–1809)—Austrian composer in all genres; one of Beethoven's teachers; found success in London and Paris later in life.

Henry, Bénigne (fl. 1810–40)—Composer, lyre and guitar teacher in Paris, 1820s and 1830s; publications beginning in 1807.

Herz, Henri (1803–1888)—Pianist, composer, and teacher from Austria who toured widely. Gave several concerts in the United States between the years 1845 and 1851. Arranged many popular melodies, and some attributed to him circulated with doubtful attributions.

Hoffman, Richard (1831–1909)—Student of Hummel and Kalkbrenner, born in England but moved early to the United States. His publications of the 1850s and 1860s circulated widely.

Hummel, Johann Nepomuk (1778–1837)—Pianist, teacher, composer, and conductor from Austria. Child prodigy whose compositions were particularly popular in the early nineteenth century.

Hünter, Franz (1793–1878)—German composer and teacher. Specialized in piano music.

Isouard, Nicolas (1773–1818)—Maltese opera composer of French origin who moved to Paris in 1800. Composer of opéras comiques.

Iweins-d'Hénnin, Mme. (fl. 1840s–50s)—Salon singer.

Jadin, Louis-Emmanuel (1768–1853)—French keyboard performer and opera composer.

Kalkbrenner, Frédéric (1785–1849)—French composer, pianist, and teacher, born to German parents.

Kücken, Friedrich (1810–82)—German composer and conductor; his songs were popular in the United States.

Kuhlau, Friedrich (1786–1832)—Born in Germany, worked primarily in Denmark. Composer in many genres.

La Hache, Theodore Felix von (1822–1869)—Dutch composer, pianist, and director who settled in New Orleans in 1842. Remained there through the Civil War.

Lee, (George) Alexander (1802–1851)—English composer who arranged popular melodies that figured prominently in American collections.

Liszt, Franz (1811–86)—Hungarian pianist and composer.

Lully, Jean-Baptiste (1632–87)—Italian composer credited with defining the genre of French opera under Louis XIV.

Martini, Giovanni Battista (1706–84)—Italian composer and teacher; also wrote about music.

Masini, Francesco (François; 1804–1863)—Italian composer.

Méhul, Étienne-Nicolas (1763–1817)—French composer, of mostly opera, from the revolution to Napoleonic era.

Mendelssohn, Felix (1809–47)—German composer and pianist; wrote numerous short piano works, lieder, and two oratorios.

Mercadante, Saverio (1795–1870)—Italian opera composer and teacher.

Merlin, Comtesse de (María de las Mercedes Santa Cruz y Montalvo; 1789–1852)—Amateur singer in Parisian salons; frequently lauded in newspapers.

Meyer, Leopold de (1816–1883)—Austrian composer and pianist. Toured the United States in the second half of the 1840s.

Meyerbeer, Giacomo (1791–1864)—German composer of French opera, including *Il crociato, L'étoile du Nord,* and *Le prophète;* one of the most frequently performed opera composers during the nineteenth century.

Monsigny, Pierre-Alexandre (1729–1817)—French opera composer.

Moore, Thomas (1779–1852)—Irish poet and musician; had several successful publications of folk or folklike songs.

Mozart, Wolfgang Amadeus (1756–91)—German opera composer as well as performer and composer in most other genres; wrote the popular operas *Le nozze di Figaro* and *Don Giovanni.*

Naderman, François-Joseph (1781–1835)—French harpist and teacher.

Paër, Ferdinando (1771–1839)—Italian composer of semi-serious opera; worked in Paris beginning in 1807; wrote *Agnese.*

Panseron, Auguste (Mathieu; 1795–1859)—French composer and teacher. Published a popular singing tutor.

Parodi, Teresa (1827–after 1878)—Italian soprano.

Patti, Adelina (1843–1919)—Italian soprano.

Piccini, Niccolò (1728–1800)—Italian and French opera composer.

Plantade, Charles-Henri (1764–1839)—French composer and teacher, professional cellist.

Potharst, Jacques (fl. 1850s)—composer of romances

Prudent, Émile (1817–63)—French composer, pianist, and teacher.

Puget, Loïsa (1810–89)—French singer and composer of romances.

Rameau, Jean-Philippe (1683–1764)—Major composer of French opera after Lully.

Romagnesi, Antoine Joseph Michael (1781–1850)—French composer of romances.

Rosellen, Henri (1811–1876)—Parisian composer and pianist. His arrangements of operatic melodies circulated among southern pianists

Rossini, Gioacchino (1792–1868—Successful composer of Italian operas; lived in Paris part of his life; works include *Il barbiere de Siviglia, Otello,* and *Guillaume Tell.*

Roucourt, Jean-Baptiste (1780–1849)—Belgian composer and vocal pedagogue.

Sacchini, Antonio (1730–86)—Italian composer of serious opera who moved to Paris in 1781; his *Œdipe à Colone* was his most famous and successful work.

Scarlatti, Domenico (1685–1757)—Italian composer and harpsichordist, primarily known for his *Essercizi* (sonatas, today).

Schubert, Franz (1797–1828)—Prolific German composer of lieder; over nine hundred works survive.

Schumann, Clara (née Wieck; 1819–96)—German composer, pianist, and teacher; wife of Robert Schumann.

Schumann, Robert (1810–56)—German composer, pianist, and critic; married to Clara Wieck Schumann.

Siegling, Marie (Mary) Regina (1824–1920)—Composer and performer from Charleston, SC. After her marriage in 1850 she seems to have stopped composing. Lived the remainder of her life in Europe.

Sloman, Ann (1827–1915)—English musician, pianist, and teacher in mid-century Charleston; sister of Elizabeth and Jane, daughter of John.

Sloman, Elizabeth (1826—after 1910)—English musician, harpist, singer, and teacher in mid-century Charleston and later New York; sister of Ann and Jane, daughter of John; studied harp with Bochsa.

Sontag, Henriette (1806–54)—German soprano.

Stevenson [Stephenson], John (1761–1833)—Irish composer; known for his settings and arrangements of Thomas Moore's melodies.

Stigelli, Giorgio (1819?–68)—German singer and composer.

Strakosch, Maurice (1825–1887)—Czech composer and impresario who moved to New York in 1848.

Strawinski, Felix (fl. 1860s)—Polish guitarist and teacher who taught at the South Carolina Female Institute at Barhamville in 1860s; Ann Beaufort Sims had his method book.

Thalberg, Sigismond (1812–71)—German pianist and composer; toured the United States, including Charleston.

Torriani, Angelo (1829–93)—Director of the Italian opera in New York; credited with teaching Adelina Patti; taught at the South Carolina Female Institute at Barhamville during the Civil War; taught Louisa Rebecca McCord.

Ulmo, Edme E. (fl. 1840s)—Organist, pianist, and composer. Worked in southern cities.

Verdi, Giuseppe (1813–1901)—Most popular composer of Italian opera after Rossini; wrote *Ernani, Il trovatore,* and *La traviata,* still the most frequently performed opera in the world.

Wagner, Richard (1813–83)—Composer of German opera.

Wallace, William Vincent (1812–65)—Irish composer, violinist, and pianist who began touring the United States in 1842.

Weber, Carl Maria von (1786–1826)—Composer, pianist, conductor, and critic; composed *Der Freischütz.*

Whitaker, John (fl. 1820s)—Possibly husband on Harriet Whitaker, a woman involved in music business and education in Wilmington and Raleigh, NC. Her father built pianos in the 1810s and 1820s. Several male members of the family were music teachers and composers.

Zimmerman, Pierre-Joseph-Guillaume (1785–1853)—French pianist and teacher; hosted popular salon in Paris.

Notes

Introduction

1. Of course the statement that scholars of nineteenth-century music do not do archival work is a gross oversimplification and in many cases utterly incorrect. At the same moment I began working in seventeenth-century music, musicologists investigating music in the romantic period renewed interest in such research as sketch studies, women's music, and music in social contexts—all of which required more work with the primary sources. Nonetheless, criticism of objective musicology blossomed at the same time.

2. This is not to declare a distinctive tradition in the South, but to date so little attention has been paid to it that we cannot say one way or the other.

3. O'Brien, *Placing the South,* 97. This essay was a reprint of his "Biography and the Old South: A Review Essay," *Virginia Magazine of History and Biography* 93 (October 1985): 375–88.

4. Women went to the opera in Europe, in New York, and elsewhere, so we might reasonably assume they also did so in the South. Lizzie Randall wrote from New Orleans in 1851 that her uncle had intended to get tickets for her to see Verdi's "The Two Foscari" (*Il due Foscari*), but since they had already seen it, they declined. Later Lizzie commented, "Here we have heard the Opera constantly," mentioning Meyerbeer's "Prophet" (*Le prophète*) and *Robert le diable,* Verdi's "Jerusalem" (*I Lombardi*), and Bellini's *Norma.* She wrote in the same letter that they had also heard Jenny Lind. See Lizzie Randall to Mary, 11 March 1851, Hill Memorial Library, Louisiana State University, New Orleans. The opportunities in New Orleans exceeded those of most southern cities and towns because of the thriving opera scene there.

5. For example, Gertrude Clanton Thomas, daughter of a Georgia planter, declined an invitation to hear the operatic star Teresa Parodi in concert in 1852 because it was raining. This suggests that she might ordinarily have done so, but it also implies that such an event was not important. See Thomas, *Secret Eye,* 99.

6. And even these have suffered through the years as many libraries and archives unbound their volumes in order to preserve the names of composers and titles but not those of the owners who collected them. Thankfully this practice is becoming obsolete

in institutions, but unscrupulous sellers still take them apart to peddle individual sheets.

7. The present author discussed the repertory of free women of color in Bailey, "Binder's Volumes and Women of Color in the Antebellum South"; and Bailey, "Binder's Volumes as Musical Commonplace Books."

8. Bremer and Howitt, *The Homes of the New World,* 1:263. See also Pearson, "When Fredrika Bremer Came to Charleston."

9. Any study of Charleston's music must begin with Butler's *Votaries of Apollo.* Hindman, "Concert Life in Ante-Bellum Charleston," includes catalog references to music performances in Charleston in antebellum newspapers, and these greatly assisted me in my initial research.

10. Pringle, *A Woman Rice Planter,* 85.

11. Gross et al., *Old Houses,* 92.

12. Smythe, "Recollections of Louisa McCord Smythe," 59.

13. The house is known as the Aiken-Rhett House, but the majority of the music belonged to Harriet and her relatives, as well as Mary and Elise Rhett.

14. In some cases family members and friends brought back music from Europe for acquaintances in the South, but this does not appear to have been the case with the collections in this study.

15. Not to be confused with the literary form, as this term derives from the Spanish *romance,* which itself can be loosely translated as "ballad."

16. Butler's *Votaries of Apollo* remains the quintessential book on Charleston's early musical history and provides the reader with a full sense of the opportunities people in the city would have had to participate in and listen to music.

17. Kilbride, *Being American in Europe,* 82. See also Bushman, *The Refinement of America;* McInnis, *The Politics of Taste,* 8–11. McInnis described this class: "Charleston's aristocracy, according to its members, drew from those families who were prominent during the Revolutionary period" (*The Politics of Taste,* 9). They fall in three groups: seventeenth-century English immigrants who were granted large tracts of land; late seventeenth-century Huguenots; and eighteenth-century families who came to Charleston in trade or a profession but then established plantations.

18. O'Brien, *Conjectures of Order,* 16.

19. Kilbride, *Being American in Europe,* 83–84. O'Brien, *Conjectures of Order,* 91, has detailed the types of southerners who went to Paris and includes a list of names.

20. George Palmer Putnam's popular *The Tourist in Europe* of 1838 began a trend for the publication of such materials throughout the remainder of the century and beyond. On other travel books used by Americans, see Levenstein, *Seductive Journey,* 32–33.

21. Quoted in Kilbride, *Being American in Europe,* 85. O'Brien, *Conjectures of Order,* 366, has found the use of the word "class" throughout southern writings of the 1830s–50s.

22. Bushman, *The Refinement of America,* xix.

23. An investigation of transnational exchanges is not the purpose of the present work. Little, if any, evidence exists to suggest that antebellum southerners wielded much influence on their European counterparts. Transnational studies of relevant topics

within Europe are presented in Borsay and Furnée, *Leisure Cultures in Urban Europe.* The essays in this volume investigate many of the same experiences that Harriet, Henrietta, and Louisa Rebecca participated in, but the book does not extend to the United States.

24. Garrett, "Entertainment of the Most Beautiful Kind," 54; Angela D. Mack and J. Thomas Savage in McInnes et al., *In Pursuit of Refinement,* 35.

25. Such is the case with other diaries examined in this book. Lucy Pickens's life has been recently explored in Lewis, *Queen of the Confederacy.* Hortensia Mordecai's travel diary has been digitized and is available online at http://lcdl.library.cofc.edu/lcdl/cata log/lcdl:31741#!prettyPhoto (accessed 3 May 2014).

26. McInnis et al., *In Pursuit of Refinement,* 11–12.

27. Buckingham, *The Slave States of America,* 1:564; quoted in McInnis, *The Politics of Taste,* 24.

28. Grier, *Culture and Comfort,* 76. See also Ruth, *Social Culture;* and Levenstein, *Seductive Journey,* 53, 117. On the differences between London and Paris, see Olsen, *The City as a Work of Art,* 204–5; Hancock, "Your City Does Not Speak My Language"; and Hancock, *Paris et Londres au XIXe siècle.*

29. Mrs. Samuel Jaudon to Harriet Colles, 14 July 1844, quoted in Kilbride, *Being American in Europe,* 110.

30. Mary Fenwick Lewis to younger sister, 11 August 1844, cited in Rohr, *An Alabama School Girl in Paris,* 198.

31. Pringle, *Chronicles of Chicora Wood,* 144; Grier, *Culture and Comfort.* On Della's musical education, see Bailey, *Music and the Southern Belle,* 53–54. Della was the sister of Elizabeth Waties Allston Pringle, the Bessie mentioned above whose binder's volume is in the Charleston Museum.

32. P. G. T. Beauregard to Octavia Walton Le Vert, 21 June 1863, section A, box 81, Octavia Walton Le Vert Papers, Rubenstein Special Collections, Duke University Library, Durham, N.C.

33. A list of composers with dates and a brief summation of their noted contributions can be found in appendix C at the end of this book.

34. Bremer and Howitt, *The Homes of the New World,* 273; Gabriel Manigault diary, Southern Historical Collection, University of North Carolina, Chapel Hill, p. 58. In her two books entitled *Souvenirs of Travel* (to Europe in 1853 and 1857), the Alabamian "Belle of the Union" Octavia Walton Le Vert also listed southerners as her acquaintances, almost to the point of excluding everyone else. See http://www2.lib.unc.edu/ mss/inv/m/Manigault_Family.html#folder_10#1; Gabriel Manigault diary, Southern Historical Collection, University of North Carolina, Chapel Hill, pp. 65, 67; letter to his father, Charles Izard Manigault, 13 September 1854, John R. Thompson Papers, University of Virginia, quoted in O'Brien, *Conjectures of Order,* 122; Mordecai Family Papers, 5A/14, College of Charleston, Charleston, S.C. Mordecai died of tuberculosis in Germany in 1859 (Jacob Mordecai Papers, 1858–59, vol. M-3002; 1859–61, vol. M-3003, Charleston, S.C.).

35. Yorke's guardians in Paris were M. and Mme. Achille Jubinal. See Gacs, *Women Anthropologists,* 344; Rohr, *An Alabama School Girl in Paris.*

36. Charles Izard Manigault to R. Habersham & Sons, 1 November 1846, Charles Izard Manigault Papers, South Caroliniana Library, University of South Carolina, Columbia, quoted in O'Brien, *Conjectures of Order,* 112.

37. Charles Izard Manigault to Charles and Louis Manigault, 1 June 1847, Charles Izard Manigault Papers, South Caroliniana Library, University of South Carolina, Columbia, quoted in O'Brien, *Conjectures of Order,* 113.

38. Mordecai Family Papers, 5A/10, College of Charleston, Charleston, S.C. Hortensia Mordecai (1830–99) was the daughter of Moses Cohen Mordecai, whom Robert Rosen has described as "the most prominent Jewish Charlestonian of the 1840s and 1850s" (Rosen, T*he Jewish Confederates,* 40).

39. Bellaigue, *Educating Women,* 34–35, 183. Bellaigue's study elucidates the differences between schools for young women in France and in England, which in turn complements our understanding of those in the United States.

40. Isabel included the names of the hotels where she lodged as well (Isabel Mordecai Journal, Jacob Mordecai Papers, 1784–1936, David M. Rubenstein Rare Book and Manuscript Library, Duke University, Durham, N.C.).

41. This situation differed from that of the 1860s and 1870s, when some southerners, including women, such as Eliza Smedes of Raleigh, N.C., deliberately sought out Leipzig for music study.

42. Mary Fenwick Lewis to her mother, 25 February 1844, cited in Rohr, *An Alabama School Girl in Paris,* 167–68. Pettigrew's opera list is in his travel book, Pettigrew Papers, Southern Historical Collection, University of North Carolina, Chapel Hill. For the 1850–51 season, they include Weber's *Der Freischütz,* Flotow's *Martha,* Mozart's *Die Zauberflöte* and *Don Giovanni,* Rossini's *Il barbiere di Siviglia,* Bellini's *La sonnambula,* Beethoven's *Fidelio,* and Donizetti's *La fille du regiment.*

43. See Butler, *Votaries of Apollo,* 113–49.

44. The history of such performances extended back a century in Charleston. The first ballad opera performed in the United States was in Charleston in 1735, and the first English comic opera, Thomas Arne's *Love in a Village,* was staged in both Charleston and Philadelphia in 1766. See Abel, *Singing the New Nation,* 242; Crawford, *America's Musical Life,* 97.

45. This practice mirrors the spoken dialogue operagoers would have heard at the Opéra Comique but not the Opéra or the Théâtre-Italien.

46. Occasionally a binder's volume bears the name of a man, such as Grundy McGavock of Nashville, whose binder's volumes CPM 76 and 77 are at the Center for Popular Music at Middle Tennessee State University; or Robert S. Phifer, University of North Carolina at Chapel Hill, New Series 001.

47. By "complete books" I mean anthologies or collections of music, not method books.

48. "SMB" for "sheet music bound."

49. Tatham, *The Lure of the Striped Pig,* 23.

50. This might have been because states had to register copyrights in a district office, and the publication dates documented when they had done so.

51. These are discussed in detail in Bailey, "Women, Music, and the Performance of Gentility in the Mid-Nineteenth Century South," forthcoming, ms. in possession of the author.

52. On Érard, see Gillespie, *Five Centuries of Keyboard Music,* 12. Curiously, the commemorative centennial booklet and recital program (published in 1919) makes no mention of John's daughter, Marie, a composer, performer, and teacher of note who figures later in this book. See Siegling Music House, *The Test of Time,* 1–4.

53. Hagy, *Directories for the City of Charleston.*

54. I have not seen evidence that Charlestonians acquired music from New Orleans, which was in a direction that most upper-class women did not travel.

55. Mid-century works could be twenty pages or longer, especially if they were piano versions of operatic material. On sheet music in general, see also Rickards et al., *The Encyclopedia of Ephemera,* 291–95.

56. This practice began in the eighteenth century. Perhaps the first of these was George Bickham's *Musical Entertainer,* published in London between 1736 and 1739. In this beautifully made volume, the first one hundred plates were compiled into a single volume, each one of the eighty-nine songs having its small picture at the top, called a vignette. The *Musical Entertainer* had several printings, and some of these reached the American colonies. Part of a copy of this book survives in the Charleston Museum (SMB 79).

57. Siegling's music advertisements can be seen faintly in a daguerreotype of 1853 currently held in the South Carolina Historical Society, Charleston, 1194 SC Hist Soc MS, Siegling Records.

Chapter 1: The Lowndes Family and Harriet's Music Collection

1. This painting is now in the Gibbes Museum, Charleston, S.C.

2. On the family's extended history, see Chase, "The Lowndes Family of South Carolina," 156–57.

3. Rawlins was the second male child named Rawlins Lowndes. His second marriage was to Gertrude Julia Livingstone of Hudson River Valley, which brought him to New York. He remained there during the Civil War. See Davidson, *The Last Foray,* 14. See also Chase, *Lowndes of South Carolina;* William and Thomas Lowndes Letters, 1795–1846, Rubinstein Rare Book and Manuscript Library, Duke University, Durham, N.C.

4. Fant, *The Travelers' Charleston;* Thomas Lowndes Papers, South Caroliniana Library, University of South Carolina, Columbia. More letters from Sarah Bond I'on Lowndes exist in the Bayard Family Papers, Princeton University Libraries, Durham, N.C. Hall qualified her praise, however, by saying that they dressed so "ill" that it marred their beauty. She did appreciate the hospitality offered to her by South Carolinians, but she demurred when asked to compare American and British women. See Hall and Pope-Hennessy, *The Aristocratic Journey,* 214. See also Fant, *The Travelers' Charleston.*

5. Chase, *Lowndes of South Carolina,* 22.

6. Russell, *Legacy of a Southern Lady,* 95.

7. The scores are essentially complete: as was common during this period, some of the music (especially recitatives) may have been left out, but the intent of the collection is to present the entire opera.

8. She remained in France while her father worked in Spain (Ravenel and Ravenel, *Life and Times of William Lowndes,* 60). On music at Mme. Campan's, see Geoffroy-Schwinden, "L'école des jeunes filles de Madame Campan" and "Madame Campan's Music Curriculum for Girls." Elizabeth married William Jones Lowndes (1782–1822).

9. Chase, *The Lowndes Family of South Carolina*, 32.

10. Ravenel and Ravenel, *Life and Times of William Lowndes*, 233–34. The option of returning to South Carolina after William Pinckney died would have presented several obstacles involving timing, planning, cost, and so forth. Continuing on with their journey was a logical choice.

11. Elizabeth's volumes included literary works by Racine and de La Fontaine (Ravenel, *Charleston*, 391.

12. Kilbride, *Being American in Europe*, esp. 135–41; O'Brien, *Placing the South*, 26–37.

13. A few isolated examples exist in the cases of those who shared music with relatives. Multiple binder's volumes have survived intact, including those that belonged to Eliza Fisk Harwood of Williamsburg (1830s), Amelia Gayle Gorgas of Tuscaloosa (1840s), Kate Berry of Nashville (1850s), and a few others. The six binder's volumes of Ann Beaufort Sims, from the Civil War period, are particularly noteworthy. See Bailey, *Women, Music, and the Performance of Gentility in the Mid-Nineteenth Century South*, forthcoming.

14. From the time of its invention in the late seventeenth century until the mid-nineteenth century—when steel frames were used—the size and strength of pianos grew steadily. It is not known what type of keyboard instrument Harriet played.

15. Michael Broyles has noted that Beethoven "first landed in America" in Charleston in 1817, with a publication by none other than Charles Gilfert in Charleston (Broyles, *Beethoven in America*, 25). Several Beethoven performances in Charleston occurred as early as 2 April 1806, when a "Grand Ouverture" and "Finale" were part of an oratorio concert conducted by Mr. Eckhart (Hindman, "Concert Life in Ante-Bellum Charleston," 333). Nonetheless, the composer's instrumental music did not have immediate popularity except for an unnamed overture and waltzes that are almost certainly spuriously attributed.

16. Butler, *Votaries of Apollo*, 189, 240.

Chapter 2: Vocal Music in English

1. The Charleston City Directory for 1828 listed his establishment at 75 Queen Street.

2. The signature looks mature for such a young woman, and someone else may have written it in the book. It does compare favorably, however, with other examples of her signature from the 1830s and 1840s.

3. On the origins of this popular opera, see Kirk, *American Opera*, 74–77.

4. The first ballad opera performed in the United States was shown in Charleston, in a courtroom, on 17 February 1735: Colley Cibber and John Hippesley's *Flora; or, Hob in the Well* (Kirk, *American Opera*, 12–13). Butler, *Votaries of Apollo*, 176–78, has described the Charleston Theatre's English-language dramas between 1793 and 1820.

5. Preston, *Opera on the Road*, 100, has asserted that Italian opera troupes traveled around the United States as early as 1825 but that until 1847 their activity was "sparse and intermittent." The music from Italian operas, however, occurred with much more regularity, usually as printed sheet music.

6. Several of the pieces bear the extra directions for Siegling's establishment as "Opposite the Circular Church," as if potential customers might not know where to find him.

7. Watson, *The History of Southern Drama*, 28–29, has painted a colorful picture of Gilfert.

8. The advertisement of this concert appeared on 16 January, according to Butler, *Votaries of Apollo*, 196, 324n99.

9. Gilfert returned to New York later in life (Finson, *The Voices That Are Gone*, 14).

10. Siegling opened his publishing house in 1819 at 69 Broad Street (Krummel and Sadie, *Music Printing and Publishing*, 428). But see also Kearns and Reeves, *Report of Proceedings*, 57; and Crew, *Presidential Sheet Music*, 233.

11. Signorina Garcia, Maria Garcia Malibran was considered "one of the finest possible Sopranos" in 1825, according to Sands and Bryant, *New-York Review*, 81. Boudet advertised in the *Savannah Republican* on 14 October 1820.

12. The work is available online at Johns Hopkins University, Levy Sheet Music Collection, box 121, item 073, http://jhir.library.jhu.edu/handle/1774.2/29710 (accessed 13 January 2016). Clifton (1784–1832) was born "Philip Antony Corri," the son of the Italian composer Domenico Corri. He lived and worked in London before 1814, when he arrived in Baltimore. Debra Brubaker suspected that Corri left England because of a marital problem. He was christened Arthur Clifton on 31 December 1817 and (re)married on New Year's Day 1818. His works (solo piano and voice) saw publication in Baltimore beginning in 1820. See Brubaker, "A History and Critical Analysis of Piano Methods," 1:58. More information on Corri is available in Mullaney-Dignam, *Music and Dancing at Castletown*, 33–34.

13. Tawa, *Sweet Songs for Gentle Americans*, 199.

14. Other settings by Gilbert from *Rokeby* date from 1813 (Todd and Bowden, *Sir Walter Scott*, 279–80).

15. Duets were popular throughout the nineteenth century, as shown on many commencement recital programs.

16. Rose married Frederick A. Ford in 1827.

17. Quoted in Butler, *Votaries of Apollo*, 171.

18. Some newspaper shows through the marbling of this binder's volume, but it is illegible.

19. Most of the pieces attributed to Thomas Moore have lyrics and tunes collected by him and the music arranged for publication by John Stevenson. Beginning in 1808 these two collaborated on an extremely popular series called *Irish Melodies*. Among the popular songs included were "Oft in the Stilly Night," "The Minstrel Boy," "Believe Me if All Those Endearing Young Charms," and "The Last Rose of Summer."

20. In *Votaries of Apollo* (231–36), Butler has provided the titles of many popular pieces in Charleston during the first two decades of the nineteenth century. In these pages are listed essentially the same composers noted in the binder's volumes of Emma and Harriet, even if the titles differ.

21. Fisher et al., *Best Companions*, 48.

22. The cover has only the name "Emma" on it, but "E M Huger" and related names occur throughout the volume.

23. Paisiello's "Nel cor piu non mi sento" remains a staple of the young singer's repertory, even in the twenty-first century, having been included first in Alessandro Parisotti's *Arie Antiche* of 1885 and then in Schirmer's popular *Twenty-Four Italian Songs and Arias.*

24. "Madamina!" is sung by Don Giovanni's servant Leporello, a bass; "O statua gentilissima" is a duet for two basses; and "La ci darem la mano" is a duet for soprano and baritone. Performances of Italian vocal music, including pieces by Paisiello as early as 1801 and Mozart in 1802, have been documented in Butler, *Votaries of Apollo,* 234–35, 337n58.

25. This is from a personal conversation with Professor Charles McGuire, who is compiling a database of English music festivals. One review describes Signorina Garcia's performance of "Una voce poca fa" in 1825, counting among "the innumerable fine points" the "beautiful divisions [fast notes]" on the words "Lindoro" and "cento trappole faro giocar," as well as expression and changes of "tone and manner" (Sands and Bryant, *New-York Review,* 22).

26. Butler, *Votaries of Apollo,* 191–92, 220, 230.

27. Sola moved to England in 1817 to further his career, and his music had some popularity in the United States. A few of Sola's pieces—ones he composed or arranged—can be found in American collections, either imported from Europe or published by such firms as E. Riley in New York or G. Willig in Philadelphia.

28. Two New York firms that later specialized in imported music were Scharfenburg & Luis and Breusing. Their stamps can be found on several pieces of sheet music in the Charleston Museum. Scharfenburg, a student of the composer Louis Spohr, immigrated to the United States in 1838. He was a strong supporter of foreign musicians in the city and was known for assisting them in finding work. See Newman, *Good Music for a Free People,* 44. Several music sellers in New Orleans imported music too, but it does not appear that Harriet visited the Crescent City or that any of her music was purchased there.

Chapter 3: Vocal Music in French

1. Kmen, *Music in New Orleans,* 97. On Garcia, see chapter 7.

2. A few other versions of these arias have bass clefs, mostly from collections that have music purchased in New Orleans.

3. Emma's versions came from Robert Birchall in London, while Harriet's were from Weissenbruch in Brussels.

4. *Guillaume Tell* appeared for the first time on the English stage (in English) in 1830 but not in French until an 1845 performance at Covent Garden. Its American debut was on 19 September 1831 in New York. See Holden, *The New Penguin Opera Guide,* 794; Kobbé, *Kobbé's Complete Opera Book,* 370–73.

5. Eventually Auber and then Meyerbeer and Halevy overtook Boieldieu in sales. The Philadelphia publisher Benjamin Carr popularized the composer's works in keyboard arrangements in his series *Le Clavecin: A Collection of Sonatos, Rondos, Marches, Waltzes, Airs with Variations &c.* Carr's version of the overture from *La dame blanche* was no. 5 in this series, issued in 1825.

6. Favre and Betzwieser, "Boieldieu, Adrien." *Grove Music Online.*

7. Loewenberg, *Annals of Opera,* cols. 698–700. On Boieldieu in New Orleans, see Baron, *Concert Life in Nineteenth-Century New Orleans,* 147.

8. Robinson and Hibberd, "Gail, Sophie." *Grove Music Online.*

9. See below, p. xxx.

10. The Bohemian hornplayer Ludwig Wenzel Lachnith (1746–1820) arranged the pieces from *Œdipe* in both of Harriet's volumes.

11. She sang these on 28 February and 11 April (Hindman, "Concert Life in Ante-Bellum Charleston," 314).

12. Romagnesi is not listed in *Oxford Music Online.* Several of his extant works can be found in the Bibliothéque Nationale in Paris. The Rubenstein Library at Duke University owns one of his pieces: "Adieu to War! Adieu to Glory!" (Rare Books, folio, music A-4743).

13. On Romagnesi's advice for singing romances, see Macfarlane, "Il faut savoir l'italien pour déchiffrer une romance française," 31–33.

14. This is according to a score published in Paris and now archived in the Harvard University Theatre Collection.

15. A little of Romagnesi's music was apparently known to a few southern women. His "Je l'aime ancor" exists in a binder's volume in which someone wrote "29 January 1829" and "Petersburg, Va." This volume is associated with Mrs. Selia Robertson, Earl Gregg Swem Library, College of William and Mary, Williamsburg, Va., Music Volume 35. It also has an unusual repertory, including music by Plantade, Boieldieu (from *La dame blanche*), and Madame Gail.

16. Borsay and Furnée, *Leisure Cultures in Urban Europe,* 126. See also Lemmers, "Fétis et l'enseignement du chant en belgique," 147–61.

17. Nos. 32 and 41 have a different textual style.

18. In Paris, Roucourt's works are located in the Bibliothèque Nationale de France; in Amsterdam at the Amsterdam Public Library (Openbare Bibliotheek Amsterdam). Worldcat.org lists three nocturnes in the Bibliothèque Municipale de Lyon.

19. There is no indication who might have sung the duets with Harriet or which part she may have taken in them.

20. From this set SMB 50 contains nos. 8, 6, 12, 9, 11, 5, 4, 1 (in that order, pp. 148–77). The manuscript is available online at http://conquest.imslp.info/files/imglnks/usimg/d/d1/IMSLP298461-PMLP483547-Crescentini_-_Dodici_canzoni.pdf Accessed 19 Sept. 2017.

21. Nozari was known as a singer; I have not been able to confirm his authorship of this music.

22. Several versions of this song—alternately called a "ballad" and a "canzonet"—exist in archives throughout the United States.

23. Chopin played there in 1841, 1842, and 1848, later than the period that produced the music in Harriet's binder's volume (Eigeldinger, "Chopin and Pleyel," 389).

24. The most extensive description of Bruguière can be found in Jean-Paul Bouyer, *Musée virtuel de la musique maçonnique,* http://mvmm.org/m/docs/brug.html (accessed 6 June 2016).

25. Tsou and Cheng, "Duchambge, Pauline." *Grove Music Online.*

26. See Launay, *Les compositrices en France,* 29, 32, 86–87, 90, 99, 119, 143, 172–73, 184, 330.

27. The writers who complimented Blanchet include Choron, François-Joseph Fayolle, and Fétis, among others. See ibid., 240–41.

28. Fauveau, "Une dynastie de maîtres d'armes." "Dormez donc, mes cher Amours" also appears in Earl Gregg Swem Library, College of William and Mary, Williamsburg, Va., Music Volume 35, also in manuscript form. This binder's volume includes dates of 1829 and pieces by Gail and Romagnesi, as well as "Il est vrai que Thibaut" and selections from *La dame blanche.*

29. *Athenaeum* 1367 (1854): 25. Ferdinand Hérold's *La somnambule* (1827 production) was a precursor to Bellini's *Somnambula.* See Hibberd, "Dormez donc, mes chers amours," 124.

30. Available at http://petrucci.mus.auth.gr/imglnks/usimg/8/8e/IMSLP55380-PM LP114416-BERTON_Airs.pdf; and the piano version is at http://cataloguelabs.bnf.fr/ ark:/12148/cb43868698n (accessed 15 January 2016).

31. Hindman, "Concert Life in Ante-Bellum Charleston," 412–13; Butler, *Votaries of Apollo,* 155. Aimé also sang in New Orleans; see Baron, *Concert Life in Nineteenth-Century New Orleans,* 143, 285–89, 290. George Willig noted on his edition of Boieldieu's "Simple innocente et Joilette" that it was sung by Mr. Aimé.

32. La Société Française first met in Fayolle's Long Room in 1819, and later the German Turn Verein met there; see Charleston County Public Library, "King Street (1–98)," http://www.ccpl.org/content.asp?id=15640&action=detail&catid=6 (accessed 10 February 2016). See also Butler, *Votaries of Apollo,* 247. In a list of immigrants arriving in Charleston, Peter Fayolle's name appears for 1806, according to Hemperley, "Federal Naturalization Oaths, Charleston," 122.

33. Death date given in Ella, *Musical Sketches,* 271.

34. This information is taken from a column celebrating the birthdays of musicians in *Le Foyer,* 28 December 1865, 6.

35. He was still there in 1827 when *A Dictionary of Musicians: From the Earliest Ages to the Present Time,* by Sainsbury and Choron was printed. His name appears on p. 74. A notice of Bégrez singing at Hanover-Square Rooms appeared in *New Monthly Belle Assemblée* 11 (July 1839): 48.

36. *Boston Evening Post,* 18 July 1822.

37. Fétis, *Biographie universelle des musiciens,* 14.

38. First published in *Orphéon: Répertoire de musique vocale 1. sans accompagnement . . . 1,* no. 11 (1840); just "Naderman" in *Bibliographie de la France* [formerly de *l'Empire français*] *ou, Journal* (1820): 265.

39. See Bailey, *Music and the Southern Belle,* 84.

40. *Charleston Courier,* 26 October 1815; Hindman, "Concert Life in Ante-Bellum Charleston," 162, 370, 409, 411–12.

41. Sarah Rutledge to Elizabeth Lowndes, 20 January 1820, Pinckney-Lowndes Papers, in Harriott Horry Rutledge Ravenel Papers (11/332a/5), South Carolina Historical Society, Charleston. I am grateful to the anonymous reader for drawing my attention to this reference.

42. Ravenswaay, *St. Louis,* 242.

43. Virginie Bridon (Paris, 1794–1860, St. Louis, MO). Daughter of Vincent Louis François Bridon (1764–1814) and Catherine Barbe Hoffet (1760–1833). Married Greuhm 23 Nov. 1819 in DC, then Baroness Greuhm married Col. Luke Edward Lawless (1781– after 1846) 23 May 1825. She was later known as Virginia de Greuhm Lawless.

44. The first edition of the work is available for viewing at http://gallica.bnf.fr/ ark:/12148/btv1b525029477. Accessed 18 Sept. 2016.

45. Holcombe, *South Carolina Marriages*, 46.

46. A family of Girauds moved from Charleston to San Antonio sometime between 1830 and 1850. Her death date is unknown, and she is not listed as teaching music in the 1850 United States census, http://tree.nicolehernandez.com/pafg11.htm. Tickets for a concert in 1823 were advertised to be sold at Peter Fayolle's "house" at 80 King Street, so they may have all lived in the same residence (*Southern Patriot and Commercial Advertiser,* 11 February 1823).

47. January 1830, quoted in Hindman, "Concert Life in Ante-Bellum Charleston," 170–71.

48. Hindman, "Concert Life in Ante-Bellum Charleston," 385.

49. *Savannah Daily Gazette,* 20 November 1819.

50. The South Carolinian Emmala Reid wrote in her diary that "Mrs. Pinkind" (Angélica Giraud Pinkind), who was also known as "Madam Giraud," was a Polish countess who was exiled from her homeland and happened to be an opera singer. Louise Vandiver recorded that Mrs. Pinkind was the first woman violinist in the United States, traveling from New York to Charleston and then to Pendleton and Anderson. This story might be seen as a confused case of women named "Giraud," except for the fact that in the Charleston Museum, several sets of pieces for violin and piano belonging to one Aniela Niecieska survive in a binder's volume that belonged to E. B. Grimball (SMB 22). Reed and Oliver, *A Faithful Heart,* 34, quotes Vandiver, *Traditions and History of Anderson County,* 23, on Giraud in the western part of South Carolina. The woman in Anderson had previously married Count Giovanni Giraud (1776–1834), an Italian dramatist born in France. Women did not begin playing the violin in the United States until at least the mid-century. Evidence suggests, however, that the honor of being the first woman to do so goes to Aniela Niecieska (1827–89), the woman known in western South Carolina as Angélica Giraud Pinkind. The present author discovered Niecieska's music in SMB 22 in 2015. Niecieska, who was indeed Polish, performed on the violin at Hibernian Hall in Charleston in 1850 (Hindman, "Concert Life in Ante-Bellum Charleston," 631). Camille Urso (1840–1902) toured as a violin virtuoso and is usually credited with being the first woman to play onstage in the United States. Born in Nantes to musician parents, Urso debuted in New York City in 1852. In 1855 the Urso family took up residence in Nashville, Tennessee. See the Camille Urso Collection at the University of South Carolina, http://library.sc.edu/ digital/collections/ursoabout.html. Accessed 10 Nov. 2017. Aniela Niecieska's performance predated that of Camille Urso. Niecieska's daughter Antoinette taught music, according to the 1880 census.

51. *Charleston Courier,* 26 October 1815; Hindman, "Concert Life in Ante-Bellum Charleston," 162.

52. Hindman, "Concert Life in Ante-Bellum Charleston," 409.

53. Ibid., 411.

54. Advertised on 12, 14, 15, and 17 Feb. 1823, *City Gazette and Commercial.*

55. When Mrs. Giraud, her sisters, and Miss Bridon presented a concert about a month later, Jacob Bond I'On's name was not among the managers (*Southern Patriot and Commercial Advertiser,* 25 March 1823).

56. She may have married and continued to perform under a different name.

57. British Library, H. 2827.f, binder's volume of Louisa Hevael[?]. The name was cut off in the process of binding. This volume contains some of the same composers found in the Aiken-Rhett House collection, including Panseron, Clapisson, and Paër.

Chapter 4: French Connections

1. The contents of SMB 218 are in appendix A.

2. E. E. Ulmo composed several songs that were published in the 1840s and 1850s. He took an organist's post in Richmond in 1842 and taught there in the same year. See Stoutamire, *Music of the Old South,* 167. Little is known about Ulmo prior to this, but he is listed in Charleston in the 1828 directory as a shoemaker, in the 1830 United States Census, and as a property owner in Savannah in 1840. The 1870 New Orleans directory lists him as a professor of music. Such moving about was not uncommon for professional musicians in the nineteenth century.

3. An inventory with hands can be found in appendix A.

4. This date can clearly be seen printed on each song in the publication. A copy of the third volume is available online at http://gallica.bnf.fr/ark:/12148/bpt6k859348n .r=antoine%20romagnesi (accessed June 2016).

5. In the inventory for SMB 48, I have listed nine hands. This is perhaps an overly careful assignment as some of the texts match, and some of the music—particularly that in the single gathering—matches somewhat.

6. See especially O'Brien, *Placing the South,* "Britain and the South," 26–47; McInnis, *The Politics of Taste,* 25–27; Garrett, "Entertainment of the Most Beautiful Kind"; and Kilbride, *Being American in Europe,* "English Association: 1750–1783," 9–44. Even though Kilbride's chapter deals with an earlier period, the use of "Anglo-American" throughout the rest of the book implies that the connection lasted at least until the Civil War.

7. State University of New York, University at Buffalo, Special Materials, FVM 1.

8. Several of her published romances have been bound into a volume entitled *Recueil de musique p[ar] la Comtesse de St. Didier,* now held at the University of Michigan (M 1495 .C72 183-). I am grateful to Kristen Castellana for making a digitized version of this binder's volume available.

9. This volume is now in the Music Library, Special Materials, University of Buffalo, State University of New York, FVM 1.

10. An inventory of these sources can be found online at http://library.buffalo.edu/ music/special-materials/french-vocal-music/ (accessed January 2016).

11. Slightly later Italian and French opera melodies came to dominate the repertory performed by southern women, but opera music was just beginning to infiltrate the American market in the 1820s. The heyday of Donizetti, Bellini, Verdi, Meyerbeer, and others was the 1840s–60s.

12. Harriet was descended from Rev. Frances Le Jau (1665–1717), who was born into a Huguenot family in France, ordained in the Anglican Church in England, and became first rector of St. James Church, Goose Creek, Carolina. He arrived in Carolina in 1706 and has been called "the most influential Anglican clergyman in Carolina" (Prioleau and Manigault, *Register of Carolina Huguenots,* 2:1031).

13. Details on French musicians from Saint Domingue who worked in Charleston after 1804 are given in Butler, *Votaries of Apollo,* 189.

14. See above, p. 22.

15. See chapters 6–8 and 10.

16. "Tessitura" refers to the compass of most of the notes in a given musical work.

17. "Deh calma ciel bel sonno" had renewed popularity during the 1850s in the series *Jenny Lind's Operatic Songs.*

18. Sometimes he incorporated Scottish folk tunes in *La dame blanche,* rendering some of his music less demanding.

19. See Bailey, "Binder's Volumes as Musical Commonplace Books."

20. "La ci darem la mano," the somewhat illicit duet in which Don Giovanni seduces Zerlina, occurs in several graduation programs and binder's volumes from the antebellum period, suggesting that the true meaning of the text, or the action in the opera, remained a mystery to the singers.

Chapter 5: Harriet Lowndes Aiken's Opera Collection

1. Garrett, "Entertainment of the Most Beautiful Kind," 33, noted that the configuration of the Aiken-Rhett House did not allow for the two parlors found in other upper-class American homes and suggested that the family must have had a semipublic space upstairs as well.

2. National Archives Microfilm Publication M575, roll 2, 1820–73 ; Records of the U.S. Customs Service, Record Group 036, National Archives Building, Washington, D.C.; in Lyla Sparks, comp., *Atlantic Ports, Gulf Coasts, and Great Lakes Passenger Lists, Roll 2: 1820–1873* [database online] (Provo, Utah: Ancestry.com Operations, 2001).

3. *Records from Record Group 287, Publications of the U.S. Government; Record Group 85, Records of the Immigration and Naturalization Service [INS] and Record Group 36, Records of the United States Customs Service: The National Archives at Washington, D.C.* lists the date of arrival as 18 November 1820.

4. Garrett, "Entertainment of the Most Beautiful Kind," 9. Garrett stated that the 1828 visit was William's first overseas, but this is incorrect.

5. Russell, *Legacy of a Southern Lady,* 95, said that the Aikens first left for Europe in 1833, but evidence in some of Harriet's music contradicts this statement. William returned to New York from Liverpool on 4 April 1836 aboard the ship *Roscoe,* and Harriet may have accompanied him.

6. The scores are not complete as we think of them today: in some cases recitatives and instrumental parts have been omitted. They contain most of the music, however, and would have been considered "complete" scores by 1830 standards.

7. All of Harriet's opera scores are piano-vocal, not full orchestra versions.

8. Butler, *Votaries of Apollo.*

9. On the general practices of book ownership, see Miller, *Books Will Speak Plain.*

10. Emily Wharton Sinkler to Thomas Wharton, 6 December 1845, quoted in LeClercq and Sinkler, *An Antebellum Plantation Household*, 22.

11. See below, pp. 128–30.

12. Quoted in LeClercq and Sinkler, *An Antebellum Plantation Household*, 23.

13. Emily Wharton Sinkler to Thomas Wharton, 13 December 1845, quoted in ibid., 22. The daughters of Dr. Francis Kinloch Huger (1773–1855), Elizabeth Pinckney Huger (1804–82) and Harriet Horry Huger (1822–57), were close friends of Emily.

14. Emily Wharton Sinkler to Mrs. Thomas I. Wharton, 13 December 1845, quoted in LeClercq and Sinkler, *An Antebellum Plantation Household*, 23; Pringle, *A Woman Rice Planter*, 8.

15. Leclercq and Sinkler, *An Antebellum Plantation Household*, 22.

16. Coxe, *Memories of a South Carolina Plantation*.

17. Kilbride, *Being American in Europe*, 39.

18. Russell, *Legacy of a Southern Lady*, 95–96.

19. The books are *L'histoire de la revolution française,* "signed H. L. Aiken / Paris / 1837," and *Oeuvres completes des Comte Xavier du Maistre,* signed "H. L. Aiken / Paris / 1837"—both now in the Charleston Library Society.

20. Russell, *Legacy of a Southern Lady*, 95–96.

21. McInnis et al., *In Pursuit of Refinement*, 49–51, 228, 317; Garrett, "Entertainment of the Most Beautiful Kind," 52.

22. [Unknown] to Francis Kinloch Middleton, 24 February 1839, Cheves-Middleton Papers, South Carolina Historical Society, Charleston, quoted in McInnis, *The Politics of Taste*, 297.

Chapter 6: The Aiken Family and Henrietta's Music Collection

1. Boyd, "The Parlor Companion," 4–5, claimed that Henrietta Wyatt's sister Violette taught at a ladies' academy in Manchester, England.

2. O'Brien, *Placing the South,* "Britain and the South," 26–47; McInnis, *The Politics of Taste*, 25–27; Garrett, "Entertainment of the Most Beautiful Kind"; Kilbride, *Being American in Europe,* "English Association: 1750–1783," 9–44.

3. Quoted in Zierden and South Carolina Historic Charleston Foundation, "Aiken-Rhett House," 19. The contents of the Aiken-Rhett House have been rigorously examined in studies such as Garrett, "Entertainment of the Most Beautiful Kind"; Zierden and South Carolina Historic Charleston Foundation, "Aiken-Rhett House"; Tew, "A Study of the Aiken-Rhett Stew Stove"; and Bachand, "A Season in Town."

4. Bremer and Howitt, *The Homes of the New World,* 1:389. Fredrika saw fellow Swede Emilie Holmberg Hammarsköld, a much-respected teacher and performer in the South, while in Charleston (ibid., 1:267).

5. Information is too scant to claim they traveled throughout Europe on each journey.

6. William Porcher Miles, South Carolina College, to Harriet Lowndes Aiken, 24 June [no year], Aiken Family Correspondence, Charleston Museum. A professor at the college, Miles became mayor of Charleston in 1855 and later a U.S. representative for South Carolina.

7. Mr. Boudet and his daughter Victoire advertised a music school in Savannah in 1820 (*Savannah Gazette,* 14 October 1820), but I have not been able to establish connections between this family and Pauline Boudet in Charleston. A Mr. Boudet from France advertised as a portrait artist in Charleston in several papers in 1838.

8. Passenger list for the *Columbia* in *Charleston Courier,* 15 November 1848.

9. Mary Chesnut's account of Henrietta's 1862 wedding in Flat Rock can be seen frequently in literature about the Aikens. She described it as an opulent affair, despite the lack of availability of finery for most of the women in attendance, made all the more memorable for a fire that broke out. See Chesnut and Williams, *A Diary from Dixie,* 212.

10. This musical club remains a mystery. Helen to Henrietta Aiken, 13 March, Historic Charleston Foundation, 2009.016.1k. She wrote, "Ma chere cousine." Several references to Harriet by Eliza Middleton appear in Fisher et al., *Best Companions,* 251.

11. Margaret Ann "Meta" Morris Grimball, "Journal of Meta Morris Grimball, SC, December 1860–February 1866," entry for 10 June 1861 (p. 35), Southern Historical Collection, University of North Carolina, Chapel Hill. Her binder's volume, SMB 35 in the Charleston Museum, evinces a competent pianist and singer.

12. It is tempting to speculate that these women, or their heirs, may have given the volumes to Henrietta because of her reputation as a musician and music lover.

13. Books in the Charleston Library Society have dates that suggest a journey in 1837, when Henrietta would have been less than a year old. It is doubtful that she would have made this trip at so young an age.

14. SMB 19 is her copy of *Échos de France;* SMB 189 is *Méthode de vocalisation;* and SMB 228 is a French edition of Rossini's *Semiramide.*

15. There are some gaps in the numbering of the SMS and SMB items in the Charleston Museum.

16. A complete list of the SMS pieces in the Charleston Museum that might be associated with the Aiken-Rhett-Lowndes extended family group constitutes appendix B.

17. It is possible, though not probable, that one of her descendants too was a serious pianist and inherited piano music—the proverbial "box of music in the attic"—that is not included in the Charleston Museum collection. However, the manner in which the house was preserved—shutting down rooms and not giving or selling items belonging to the family—seems to preclude this possibility.

Chapter 7: Henrietta's Earliest Music and First European Journey

1. Calhoun and Wilson, *The Papers of John C. Calhoun,* 318.

2. The hotel is now the Fondation Maison de la Chimie at 28, rue Saint-Domingue. A walk today through the areas of Paris where Charlestonians resided in the antebellum period still reveals a degree of the opulence that attracted families such as the Aikens.

3. Gabriel Manigault diary, 52, Manigault Family Papers, Southern Historical Collection, University of North Carolina, Chapel Hill. The previous tenant had been William R. King (1786–1853) of Alabama, the American minister who was elected vice president in 1852; see http://www2.lib.unc.edu/mss/inv/m/Manigault_Family.html# folder_10#1 Accessed 6 June 2016. He also found that, as with other French apartments of the period, at the Hôtel de la Rochefoucauld one could not enter the drawing room

without first traversing the dining or breakfast room. Such an arrangement differed from American household organization, where the parlor—the nearest equivalent to the drawing room—stood as a semipublic room. See Halttunen, *Confidence Men and Painted Women,* 59. The Aiken-Rhett House differed from most southern residences, and Garrett has suspected a semipublic room upstairs as well ("Entertainment of the Most Beautiful Kind," 33).

4. Gabriel Manigault diary, 52, Manigault Family Papers, Southern Historical Collection, University of North Carolina, Chapel Hill.

5. Gabriel mentioned that the "travelers" (possibly the Aikens) had been to Greece, Egypt, and Spain (Manigault diary, 60).

6. A. and W. Galignani and Co., *Galignani's New Paris Guide.*

7. Too little survives of Henrietta's handwriting before 1860 to be able to determine if the writing in her books and on her music is Harriet's or her own. The implications for the present study do not depend on distinguishing one from the other.

8. Anna Smith of the Charleston Library Society kindly found the Aiken books among the society's collection for my research.

9. These are discussed below.

10. On Essler in Charleston, see Pease and Pease, *Ladies, Women, and Wenches,* 56–57.

11. Keates, *The Siege of Venice,* 90.

12. Filippini, *Donne sulla scena pubblica,* 114.

13. Louisa Rebecca McCord also owned some controversial music; see the McCord family's struggle in this in part 3, p. X. Accessed 6 June 2016.

14. Available online at http://babel.hathitrust.org/cgi/pt?id=uc1.31175035175937;view=1up;seq=5 (accessed February 2016).

15. Tunley, *Salons, Singers, and Songs,* 24–25, has described the Zimmerman salon in Paris as "almost Parnassian in status."

16. Charles Sumner recorded hearing Adelaide Kemble sing and play at a soiree in Paris in 1838, providing proof that at least some Americans were invited to these events (Pierce, *Memoir and Letters of Charles Sumner,* 274).

17. These are discussed below.

18. In contrast, the Bertini method described below teaches the trill on p. 184, near the end of the book. On piano tutorials used in the United States, see Brubaker, "A History and Critical Analysis of Piano Methods."

19. Nineteenth-century pianos were sold by the number of octaves and the type of wood used.

20. Zimmerman, *Encyclopédie du pianiste compositeur,* ii, 60.

21. Quoted in Johnson, *Listening in Paris,* 257.

22. I explored this change in repertory choices in "Reconstructing Women by Reconstructing Repertory," a paper given at Southern American Studies Association in Atlanta, February 2016.

23. This type of nocturne is not the duet for voices found among her mother's music collection but the piano genre made famous by Field and Chopin.

24. A fugue is essentially a musical composition based on a single theme that runs throughout much of the piece. Imitation and counterpoint are its main characteristics,

and these are almost the opposite of the homophonic (melody-based) works preferred by young women in this period.

25. See, for example, the extensive list of offerings at Oliver Ditson's store in Boston given in *American Publishers' Circular and Literary Gazette*, 9 August 1856, 484.

26. An online version of the Dubois edition from the 1820s is available through the Hathi Trust at http://hdl.handle.net/2027/uc1.31175014535044. Accessed 9 November 2016.

27. See Bailey, "Binder's Volumes as Musical Commonplace Books," 453–56.

28. See Bailey, *Music and the Southern Belle*, 84, 93.

29. Saint-Saëns, *Musical Memoirs*, 8–9. In the 1840s Henrietta might have played on one of the older instruments, but she certainly would have been familiar with the heavier action of mid-century pianos.

30. Weitzmann et al., *A History of Pianoforte-Playing*, 150–51.

31. Clark, *Anthology of Early American Keyboard Music*, xii. I have not seen anything to indicate that Thibault used the Chiroplast with his students.

32. Thibault, ed., *Kalkbrenner's Exercises*, 1

33. John Siegling's biography appears in the introduction to this book.

34. On this institution, see Smith, *Music, Women, and Pianos*. Marie Siegling published an account of her life entitled *Memoirs of a Dowager* in 1908.

35. *Boston Evening Transcript*, 20 May 1844, received from the *New York Express.*

36. Havana was a regular stop on the concert circuit and an important city for performing musicians and southerners in general. Carrie Holt, from Canada, a music teacher in antebellum North Carolina, South Carolina (including Charleston), and Florida, traveled there, as did Octavia Walton Le Vert.

37. Born María de Las Mercedes de Jaruco, she spent her childhood in Havana until she married General Merlin in Madrid. See Tunley, *Salons, Singers, and Songs*, 23, 8.

38. This was one of several works Marie Siegling had published in Baltimore while living in Europe; others include "La Capricieuse" and "La Gracieuse" in 1845; and "Souvenir de Charleston," "Encouragement: I Will Not Chide Thy Love," and "The Recall: Come Back Oh Come!" in 1846. On these, see Bailey, *Music and the Southern Belle*, 141–43, 154–55.

39. The Spanish baritone Manuel Garcia II (1805–1906) was a remarkable pedagogue who meshed an older Italian singing style with nineteenth-century ideas about the science behind vocal production. He was the inventor of the first laryngoscope and was the brother of both Pauline Viardot and Maria Malibran, two celebrated opera stars. Countess Merlin also studied with Garcia. See Tunley, *Salons, Singers, and Songs*, 45.

40. Stark, *Bel Canto*, 3.

41. The first part of this treatise appeared in 1841.

42. In 1859 John Sullivan Dwight included an advertisement for Breusing as "Importer of Foreign Music" (and the "Dépôt of Erard's Grand Pianos") in *Dwight's Journal of Music.* Carl, or "Charles" as he was known, owned the store where Gustave Schirmer, of "G. Schirmer" publishing fame, began. Schirmer and Bernard Beer bought Breusing's business in 1862. See Hoxie, *New York Supreme Court*, 20. See also Sanjek, *American Popular Music*, 85.

43. Zierden and South Carolina Historic Charleston Foundation, "Aiken Rhett House," 21. The U.S. Census of that year lists her age as twenty. See also note 7.

Chapter 8: Henrietta's Music, 1850–57

1. Letter from Walters and Walker addressed to Col. Singleton, Flat Rock, N.C., 5 July 1851, Singleton Papers no. 668, Southern Historical Collection, University of North Carolina, Chapel Hill; quoted in Garrett, "Entertainment of the Most Beautiful Kind," 39. The Aikens purchased Powers's *Proserpine* in 1857.

2. Mary Huger Lowndes was the daughter of Sabine Elliott Huger and Charles Tidyman Lowndes. She and Henrietta were first cousins. Researchers on ancestry.com provided two different dates for Mary's birth, 1832 and 1836. The passenger list of 1851 gives her age as eighteen, certifying the earlier birth date. I address Mary's music collection in the Conclusion.

3. These Mallards were possibly daughters of Thomas Mallard of Liberty County, Georgia, who had at least three daughters. The daughters of southern politicians often spent time in Washington when their fathers held positions there. Fellow southerners formed their social circles.

4. The first edition came out in 1853. Later volumes give the publisher as Durand & Fils, who purchased Flaxland's business at the end of December 1869.

5. *Échos de France* was part of a series, and the back page of this volume lists the indexes for *Échos d'Italie* and *Échos d'Allemagne*. All spell the first word the same way. *Échos d'Italie* includes arias by Donizetti, Meyerbeer, Mercadante, Stradella, Rossini, Handel, Bellini, Gluck, and—somewhat surprisingly since he is not at all associated with Italy—Beethoven. The song in question is his famous "Adelaide." There is an appendix for this volume, listed as *Paroles espagnoles* by [Sebastián] Yradier. *Échos d'Allemagne* consists of songs by Mendelssohn, Kücken, Spohr, Reissiger, Weber, and, again, Beethoven. That Beethoven's contribution to the German-emphasis volume is "Le délire du coeur, mon doux penser" belies the French origin of the series.

6. On the performance of Lully and Rameau in nineteenth-century France, see Ellis, *Interpreting the Musical Past,* 135–41.

7. These compositions can be found in Harriet's SMB 47.

8. A letter from Burnet to Henrietta written before their engagement indicates that Harriet was not pleased with the match. Burnet asked Henrietta to consider her own happiness, rather than that of her parents. See A. B. Rhett to H. A. Aiken, Aiken-Rhett Papers, Charleston Museum. Since Burnet's father, Robert Barnwell Rhett, had famously and publicly been at odds with William Aiken over the question of secession, her parents' opposition is understandable.

9. This version of "La Fidanzata" is IT\ICCU\RMR\0290859 at Biblioteca e Archivio musicale dell'Accademia nazionale di S. Cecilia-Roma-RM, no date.

10. In Hofmeister, *Handbuch der musikalischen Literatur,* 569.

11. Louisa Rebecca's copy (in SMB 29) was a manuscript probably prepared by her voice teacher during the Civil War; see below.

12. John Siegling sold the 1851 edition published by Oliver Ditson in Boston. On Lablache, see Cheer, *The Great Lablache.* Henrietta's *Méthode de vocalisation* (SMB 190) does not indicate a place of purchase.

13. Basvecchi was a violinist and composer, and his chief claim to fame seems to have been as teacher of the violinist Barrett Isaac Poznanski (1840–96). Grove and Fuller-Maitland, *Grove's Dictionary of Music and Musicians,* 3:803–4, stated that Poznanski began his violin study with Basvecchi and made his debut when he was eight years old. However, *Grove's Dictionary* said that Charleston was in Virginia, which was clearly incorrect because he mentioned the Ladies Calhoun Monument Association. An article on Poznanski published in 1857 described Basvecchi as an Italian violin teacher (*New York Weekly Review* 8 [1857]: 274).

14. Early February proved to be an impressive week for concerts, because just three days later Madame Rosa De Vries, the reigning queen of opera in New Orleans, and her opera troupe put on a "Grand Concert" at Hibernian Hall (*Charleston Courier,* 13 February 1855, p. 2).

15. *Charleston Courier,* 10 May 1856, p. 3.

16. *Charleston Mercury,* 24 March 1857. Apparently Basvecchi was popular enough to have a horse, owned by John Cantey, named after him (*Charleston Mercury,* 12 May 1857).

17. His passport application, dated 17 March 1858, stated that he was born in Recanati, Italy (Federal Court records, District of South Carolina, Books 1–12, 1789–1861). See Hemperley, "Federal Naturalization Oaths, Charleston," 115.

18. This concert by Basvecchi included Mrs. D. Bailey and Messrs. Reeves and Greatorex. Mrs. Bailey and Mr. Reeves sang "The Parting Kiss" by Basvecchi, and she performed the ever-popular "Di tanti palpiti" by Rossini. See *Charleston Mercury,* 20 May 1857. Musicians associated with an 1855 Charleston Calhoun Monument Association concert included the Sloman sisters, Elizabeth and Ann, local music composers and teachers from England; and Victor Petit, a Frenchman who ran a music school in Charleston. Victor Petit was the father of Herminie Petit Barbot, who became a major part of Charleston's sacred music scene throughout the second half of the nineteenth century. For more information on the Slomans and the Petits, see Bailey, *Music and the Southern Belle,* 58, 169–70. A report of the Calhoun proceedings is available online at https://archive.org/stream/ahistorycalhoun01lamagoog/ahistorycalhoun01la magoog_djvu.txt (accessed May 2016).

19. *Macon Telegraph,* 16 June 1883.

20. I wish to thank Dr. Giulio Ongaro for graciously correcting and translating the Italian lyrics.

21. *Ossia* indicates an alternative version that the performer may use instead of the original.

22. These marks were made with pencil on a score written in ink.

23. Such qualities have been outlined throughout Bailey, *Music and the Southern Belle.* See also the sheet music image on "La Piganino" (1867) in Tatham, *The Lure of the Striped Pig,* 145.

24. Harriett Lowndes Aiken to Mr. Heywood, Aiken-Rhett Papers, Charleston Museum.

25. Act 1 opens with this tale of Count di Luna.

26. English translation by Charles Jeffreys (New York: Firth, Pond & Co., 1856).

Chapter 9: After 1857

1. Aiken-Rhett Papers, Charleston Museum. I am grateful to Karen Emmons for a photocopy and transcript of this document. This journey lasted fifteen months.

2. This event showed over sixteen thousand works of art, the largest ever in the United Kingdom.

3. Lady Paget Walburga wrote in 1858 that "though Fenton's was a fashionable [hotel], our rooms were small and dark, furnished like a common lodginghouse. . . . I had to write my letters on my knees or on the window-sill, or on the top of a box, as there was no table. The dirt and darkness of these rooms was [*sic*] most repulsive" (Walpurga, *Embassies of Other Days*, 1923, 1:84). Samuel Morse stayed there for ten days in 1856–57. Napoleon I's stepdaughter, the Queen Consort of Holland and mother of Napoleon III, stayed at Fenton's in 1831. See Cheetham, *Louis Napoleon and the Genesis of the Second Empire*, 1:75; Turner, *The Liberal Education of Charles Eliot Norton*, 126.

4. Wagner's wife Minna had an illegitimate daughter, Natalie, who worked at the hotel in late 1852/early 1853 (Walton, *Richard Wagner's Zurich*, 215).

5. Russell, *Legacy of a Southern Lady*, 97.

6. Fellow southerner Octavia Walton Le Vert wrote of several performances she attended while in London and Paris at about the same. See Bailey, *Women, Music and the Performance of Gentility*, forthcoming.

7. Coghlan, *A Hand-Book for Italy*, 156.

8. Henrietta owned several other German pieces; however, Breusing imported most of these. They are discussed below.

9. In areas where a large percentage of the population was German, such as Columbus, Georgia, one finds more influence from German musicians.

10. While Henrietta's version lacks a date, the catalog at the Bibliothèque Nationale de France, Paris, gives the earliest publication a date of 1857 (Cotage G. 48 A, catalog number FRBNF42810181).

11. Garrett, "Entertainment of the Most Beautiful Kind," 5. She quoted various sources concerning William's arrest, including an 1863 letter to Lincoln. Jefferson Davis apparently forgave William and dined with him in 1863. See Chesnut and Williams, *A Diary from Dixie*, 321–22.

12. This version of "Oh, Whisper What Thou Feelest" came from the publishers Lee & Walker in Philadelphia and appears to be unique to Henrietta's collection. No other copies have been found, and no date is on this copy.

13. Both are marked "To Etta / from / May," and one has a date that is now too faint to read. That they have consecutive shelf marks is suggestive; see below. SMS 625 is a fifth edition, and both came from the firm of Firth, Pond & Co. in New York.

14. Her name also appears frequently in a binder's volume owned by Anna Smith, SMB 38. Other names in this volume include a family member, Elvira C. Huger, and EML (unknown).

15. Two books of hymns owned by Henrietta date from after the war. The earlier is *The Additional and Selected Hymns from "Hymns, Ancient and Modern" and "Hymns for Church and Home"* (texts only, published in New York), which bears the inscription "Clauda from Etta / 1870." She also owned *The Hymnal, Revised and Enlarged* (Episcopal) of 1892, which she signed "Mrs. A. B. Rhett." Her copy of *Psalms and Hymns,* New

York, 1833, (texts only) is signed "Henrietta Aiken." These items are in the Charleston Library Society.

16. One can imagine that with various cousins, nieces, and others visiting the family, music that was not in a binder's volume could easily be picked up and taken home by the wrong person.

17. Published in New York by Firth, Pond & Co.

18. A lied is a German solo song, almost always with piano accompaniment. Schubert composed over six hundred lieder, although in the United States, those of Abt were more popular. Just after the war, lieder by Robert Schumann appeared in southern parlors and were printed several times in the *Southern Musical Journal* (Savannah, 1870s).

19. Louisa Rebecca McCord also had this.

20. This version occurs on p. 15 in Seule's collection *Complète des mélodies . . . avec acc.t de piano: Paroles françaises de Mr Bélanger,* vol. 1, Bibliothèque Nationale de France, Paris.

21. 2009 .016.1r., Historic Charleston Foundation.

22. Emma Taber to A. B. Rhett, 4 January 1866, 2009.016.1b, Historic Charleston Foundation. Emma also mentioned that Burnet enjoyed hearing Laurie sing. Emma Taber married Augustus Barton Knowlton in September of that year.

23. Possibly Maria Louisa Wagner Legare (1820–73), of Charleston.

24. Elise Rhett to Henrietta Aiken Rhett, 2 March 1866, 2009.016.1c, Historic Charleston Foundation.

25. On uninscribed works in this collection, see chapter 10, (pp. 143–51).

26. There was a piano at the Aiken-Rhett House from before the war, but no known record describes what happened to it (conversation with Valerie Perry, May 2016). From 1 December 1863 until 20 April 1864, William Aiken's house served as Beauregard's headquarters. William was arrested and taken to Washington when Charleston surrendered in 1865, and the house was looted. Jehossee Plantation had been plundered in 1862, but family still went there until the late-nineteenth century. His lands were returned to him in 1866. See Zierden and South Carolina Historic Charleston Foundation, *Aiken-Rhett House,* 20.

27. Marie H. Cottenet to Harriet Lowndes Aiken, 13 October 1867, Harriett Lowndes Aiken Personal Correspondence, Aiken Collection, Charleston Museum.

28. Pringle, *Chronicles of Chicora Wood,* 85. At least one of hers (the last one) was an upright piano.

29. Conversation with Valerie Perry, manager of the Aiken-Rhett House, May 2016.

Chapter 10: Other Music That Might Have Belonged to Henrietta

1. The numbering of SMS volumes in the Charleston Museum is not complete; therefore there are some gaps in the numbers.

2. SMS 372 has "Henrietta Aiken" in full.

3. These include 250, 251, 351, 428, 438, 439, 450, 453, 462, 563, 571, 576, 578, 581, 585, 615, and 630. Two others by Niedermeyer (SMS 462 and 615) might also have been Harriet's choice, based on her earlier connection with Madame Giraud.

4. Of the isolated manuscript copies, SMS 500, "Questo cor ti giura amore" (from Rossini's *Demetrio e Polibio*), stands out because it is tied with a ribbon.

5. A few advertisements mentioned figured bass—also called "thorough bass"—as part of music lessons. For example, per an announcement in the *Charlotte Democrat* on 22 January 1861, Miss H. M. Hammarskold would begin "giving instructions on the Piano, in Singing, and in Thorough Bass" on the 28th of that month. Hammarskold had studied music at the Royal Academy of Music in Stockholm. She may have been the same woman who sang in concerts in various places in South Carolina.

6. Not all voice methods from the nineteenth century explained "portamento" the same way. See Stark, *Bel Canto*, 165–66.

7. See above, 000.

8. *New Orleans Daily Picayune*, 22 June 1845. The *New York Herald*, 13 September 1843, listed him as an officer in the Company of Italian Volunteers. He was still with this group on 1 February 1847.

9. See Altrocchi, *The Golden Wheel*, 139–40. Additionally, there are a few manuscripts in the hand of Antonio Bagioli, but I have not been able to establish a connection with Henrietta.

10. If Altrocchi left New York and settled permanently in Italy in 1845, Henrietta would have been too young to study voice with him in New York.

11. A list of all of the opera arias is in appendix B.

12. Henrietta never had a full-length portrait made, and one of the stories circulating around Charleston is that she was not attractive. In this case her music talent may have been especially encouraged as a means to attract suitors, although being the richest heiress in the state would seem to negate a need for such. Burnet wrote to her after he had proposed, acknowledged her parents' dislike of the potential union, and asked that in this one thing she not obey them, implying that she otherwise did.

13. Bushman, *The Refinement of America*, xix.

Chapter 11: The McCord Family

1. Dawson, *A Confederate Girl's Diary*. Bailey, *Music and the Southern Belle*, 43, has examined Sarah's descriptions of music while she was fleeing the Union army. An excerpt from her diary is available in Tick and Beaudoin, *Music in the USA*, 245–49.

2. Housed now in "Manuscripts, Plb (Smythe, Louisa McCord)," South Caroliniana Library, University of South Carolina, Columbia. The date 1928 is given in the catalog record. See editions of Louisa Susanna Cheves McCord's writings in McCord, edited by Richard Cecil Lounsbury; as well as Clinton, *Half Sisters of History* and *Civil War Stories;* Fought, *Southern Womanhood and Slavery;* and O'Brien, *Conjectures of Order.*

3. On the efforts of southern women to reinvent a history of life before the war, see in particular Cox, *Dixie's Daughters;* and Heyse, "The Rhetoric of Memory-Making."

4. On the Cheves family, see McLeod, "Louisa S. McCord and the 'Feminist Debate.'"

5. This point holds for the wealthiest, as well as those who sought to rise into the highest social circles, such as William Aiken Sr. and Langdon Cheves. Alternative

strategies can be seen in others. For example, while Jennifer Green has agreed that planter status was the "pinnacle of status" in the South ("Education and Professionals in the Old South," 178), she challenged the popular view that it was the goal of most southern men (*Military Education and the Emerging Middle Class in the Old South*, 10).

6. These included Inverary (which he called Upper Delta) and Telfair (Lower Delta) on the Savannah River; both of these are now known as Delta Plantation. Cheves also did not want to oppose Henry Clay for the Speaker's position in 1815.

7. Fought, *Southern Womanhood and Slavery*; McCord, *Political and Social Essays*; McCord, *Poems*; McCord, *Selected Writings*. I will refer to the mother as "Mother Louisa" to distinguish her from "Louisa Rebecca." Neither woman was called by these names during the nineteenth century.

8. Smythe, "Recollections of Louisa McCord Smythe," 30.

9. Fraser, "Louisa C. McCord," 6–7.

10. Ibid., 4.

11. Fought, *Southern Womanhood and Slavery*, 88. Langdon Cheves had acquired Lang Syne, in Calhoun County, through his marriage to Mary Dulles. He purchased Inverary and Smithfield, combining them into a single plantation, Delta, of over eleven hundred acres. His sons divided this property when Cheves died. See Martin et al., *Northern Money, Southern Land*, 140; Rowland et al., *The History of Beaufort County*, 319.

12. Smythe, "Recollections of Louisa McCord Smythe," 9. David McCord brought ten stepchildren from his previous union with Catherine Muldrip to the marriage, but Mother Louisa had little interaction with them. O'Brien has given one of the most detailed accounts of his contributions in *Conjectures of Order*, 783, 816, 900, 914–15, 1099.

13. See, for example, Brophy, "Louisa McCord and Antebellum Southern Legal Thought."

14. McCord, *Poems*, 6.

15. Ibid. Fought, *Southern Womanhood and Slavery*, has dealt with these issues throughout. On women writers in the South in general, see Wells, *Women Writers and Journalists*. On Mother Louisa's place among southern intellectuals, see O'Brien, *Conjectures of Order*, 716, 905, among others.

16. Cogan, *All American Girl*, 5; Welter, "The Cult of True Womanhood." See also Jane Turner Censer's synthesis of these roles in *The Reconstruction of White Southern Womanhood*.

17. Jane Caroline North, "Journal of an Excursion to the Virginia Springs, No. 2," entry of 12 September 1851, quoted in O'Brien and Southern Texts Society, *An Evening When Alone*, 174.

18. Quoted in McCord, *Poems*, 8.

19. Ibid., 10.

20. According to Louisa Rebecca, the whole family had wished to move to the Hawaiian Islands but could not afford to do so. Louisa McCord sold the house at Lang Syne to have enough money to get to Canada. See Smythe, "Recollections of Louisa McCord Smythe," 77.

21. Ibid., 100, 102. This would not be an unreasonable inference given Mother Louisa's relationship with her own father, whom she undoubtedly missed while away

at school. Louisa Susanna McCord studied French with the émigrés Charles Picot and his wife. See McCord, *Poems,* 2.

22. Smythe, "Recollections of Louisa McCord Smythe," 24. According to Louisa Rebecca, Hannah attended the South Carolina Female Institute in Barhamville, which would have been near their home in Columbia ("Recollections of Louisa McCord Smythe," 22; Rembert, "Barhamville").

23. Smythe, "Recollections of Louisa McCord Smythe," 22.

24. Ibid., 18, 24, 10. See also J. William Harris, *Society and Culture in the Slave South.*

25. In this context "books" refer to pieces of music published as a collection, such as Henrietta Aiken's *Échos de France* and Louisa Rebecca's daughter's Kuhlau pieces (below).

26. Smythe, "Recollections of Louisa McCord Smythe," 4.

27. Ibid., 8. Lieber left the South to take a position at Columbia College (now University in New York). He is famous for many reasons, including opposing secession; collecting records from the Confederate States of America after the war; writing the "Lieber Code" (sometimes called the "Lincoln Code"), which lays out rules of war; and serving as a diplomat between the United States and Mexico. See Mack et al., *Francis Lieber and the Culture of the Mind.*

28. She recalled Brendan's fondness for bacon, noting that it contradicted his otherwise observant diet (Smythe, "Recollections of Louisa McCord Smythe," 11–12).

29. Fought, *Southern Womanhood and Slavery,* 25.

30. See below.

31. Smythe, "Recollections of Louisa McCord Smythe," 1. Being that she was two when they left Pendleton, these memories may be those of her older siblings.

32. Ibid., 20. On such productions, see Lewis, "Tableaux Vivants."

Chapter 12: Louisa Rebecca's Antebellum Music Collection

1. Louisa's name, as "Louisa R. McCord," appears on the cover of SMB 30, but her husband's name, Augustine Smythe, is on the plate inside. It presumably formed part of the family's collection after the war.

2. SMB 27 shows many signs of use, such as ornamentation added to both the piano and vocal parts of "Una voce poca fa" and a moustache drawn on the image of Anna Bishop on "Ah Where Flee So Rapidly."

3. Some have suggested that binder's volumes would not be used in music performance after they were bound because large volumes are unwieldy. Louisa Rebecca's, however, are not too large—simple songs were much shorter than long arias and piano variation sets—and could have been used.

4. Dates given in brackets for Louisa Rebecca's binder's volumes belong to catalog entries in the Library of Congress (Washington, D.C.), the British Library (London), and libraries at the University of Cambridge, the University of Glasgow, Duke University, the University of Virginia, and the University of Michigan.

5. Macfarren's series of Scotch songs apparently ran from 1859 to 1867, according to the British Library entry (Music.H.1225c). If they were not published before 1859,

Louisa Rebecca would have had to buy them when the family sailed home that year. The fifth song in SMB 30 may have been purchased in England as well.

6. The fingering incorporates the earlier-styled numbering system in which the thumb is marked by an "X," not "1" as in more modern publications.

7. Henrietta Aiken too owned "Kathleen Mavourneen" (SMS 516), as did many southern women.

8. Isolated examples exist, but usually under special circumstances. For example, Kate and Eliza Berry of Nashville, Tennessee, had luxurious sheet music that was up-to-date and often included images (now in the Center for Popular Music, Middle Tennessee State University). Their father, however, owned a prosperous and prestigious bookstore, and his connections probably made it more likely that they received the latest publications.

9. See http://dc.lib.unc.edu/cdm/compoundobject/collection/sheetmusic/id/7263/rec/1. Accessed 10 June 2016 .

10. Indeed several of Louisa Rebecca's sheet music pieces are inscribed "Paris Oct. 1858," even though she acquired them elsewhere. For example, "Die Schönsten Augen," a German-language setting of a text by Heine, lists publishers in London and Philadelphia in German, but she wrote "Louisa R. McCord / Paris Oct. 1858" at the top.

11. Rheyn is an unusual name and appears irregularly in the U.S. Census of 1840. I have located only one John Rheyn, and he was born in 1832, rendering it unlikely that he published this 1847 composition.

12. Quoted in Clark, *South Carolina*, 288.

13. Southern women, from as far afield as New Orleans to Virginia, frequently numbered their pieces of sheet music.

14. Charlotte "Lizzie" Oakes was the composer's niece. Charlotte Elizabeth Oakes was born in 1832 to J. B. and Margaret G. Oakes of Charleston. He was listed as a "Broker" from Maine in the 1850 census; his wife was from Massachusetts. See Oak et al., *Oak—Oaks—Oakes*, register 92. Sallie's father, James Cureton Doby, was a planter of elite status: he owned 230 slaves in Kershaw County.

15. On such societies, see Greene, *A Singing Ambivalence;* Strickland, "How the Germans Became White Southerners."

16. Von Bulow toured the United States in the 1870s (Lott, *From Paris to Peoria,* 266). Abt was welcoming to the Fisk Jubilee Singers (Hubbard, *The American History and Encyclopedia of Music,* 63).

17. "Gleanings from German Musical Papers," *Dwight's Journal of Music* 3, no. 5 (7 May 1853): 35.

18. For example, one of Nora Gardner's binder's volumes, CPM 144, has the same Abt song (published in 1864–65) but with German words. Margaret Wingfield's version in a binder's volume from Music Library, University of North Carolina at Chapel Hill, came from the 1854 edition of the series *Gems from the German: A Collection of the Most Admired Songs of Schubert, Mendelssohn, Abt & Others* (UNC, old series, 45, 020).

19. Operas by these composers were made popular through sheet-music copies of their works as well as through performances organized by Max Maretzek at the Academy of Music in New York in the 1850s (Crawford, *America's Musical Life,* 181).

Chapter 13: Europe in 1858–1859

1. Scarborough, *Masters of the Big House*, 42.

2. On the need for male chaperones, see Censer, *The Reconstruction of White Southern Womanhood*, 22.

3. Smythe, "Recollections of Louisa McCord Smythe," 23

4. The McCords' journey began in New York City on 7 July 1858. They embarked for Liverpool on the steamship *Persia*. In Paris, Mother Louisa consulted Jules Sichel and other opthamologists, who famously recommended she wear tinted glasses. They arrived in New York on 26 October 1859 (McCord, *Poems*, 347).

5. Smythe, "Recollections of Louisa McCord Smythe," 23.

6. Ibid., 12–15.

7. Death certificate, 4 June 1865, Paris 8e-Paris (Paris, Ile-de-France, France): Archives départementales de Paris, Bretonnière, Victor Joseph Barthélémy.

8. Smythe, "Recollections of Louisa McCord Smythe," 23.

9. Ibid., 25.

10. [Anne] Catherine Boykin Jones diary , 29 June 1851, diary, [A] CBJ diaries, 29 June 1851, SHC.

11. Golombek, *Chess*, 142.

12. Hall-Witt, *Fashionable Acts*, 227–28. See also Crawford, *America's Musical Life*, 182; Johnson, *Listening in Paris*, 221–23.

13. Le Vert, *Souvenirs of Travel*, 1:116–17. She had also seen several operas and plays in London. On Octavia Walton Le Vert, see Bailey, *Women, Music, and the Performance of Gentility*, forthcoming.

14. Caroline married Lucien Murat, a Frenchman living in exile in New Jersey, in 1831. He was the son of the King and Queen of Naples (1808–15), Joachim Murat and Caroline, Napoleon Bonaparte's sister.

15. The Prestons were at the time residents of Rome and were visiting Paris when the McCords saw them. Louisa Rebecca apparently confused the American minister in Paris at this time, John Y. Mason, with the Confederate emissary to Paris beginning in 1861, James Mason, of Mason and Slidell fame in the famous Trent affair.

16. Smythe, "Recollections of Louisa McCord Smythe," 26–27.

17. Ibid., 28.

18. Le Vert traveled to Europe twice in the 1850s, in 1853 and 1857.

19. John R. Thompson to his father, 13 September 1854, John R. Thompson Papers, University of Virginia; quoted in O'Brien, *Conjectures of Order*, 122. The data I have examined suggest that most of the southerners who traveled to Europe during the antebellum period chose to associate with fellow southerners and did not mix with Parisians.

20. He opened his establishment here in 1847. Flaxland was known to be a friend of Wagner.

21. Their hotel, the Hôtel Meurice, was nearby on boulevard des Italiens. Henrietta Aiken too had music from Flaxland. The other music stores included those of Pleyel, Meissonier, Leduc, and Offenbach.

22. In his popular *Life of Wagner*, 35, Louis Nohl called Puget "a favorite amateur balladist" and noted that she was preferred even to Wagner or Berlioz, who complained that they could not get anyone to listen to their music.

23. Marie Siegling, a Charleston singer and composer, also dedicated a piece to Maria, Queen of Saxony. Most likely Siegling's dedication refers to Maria Anna of Bavaria (1805–77), who was Queen Consort of Saxony from 1836 to 1854. Whether Puget's does as well I do not know. Florence Launay's *Les compositrices en France au XIXe siècle* has many references to Puget. The decidedly Roman Catholic "Ave Maria" in Louisa Rebecca's volume does not seem to have been an issue, despite most Americans' deep distrust of the religion.

24. In 1859 Ash Wednesday fell on 9 March. This establishment was recommended in John Murray, *A Handbook for Travellers*, 61.

25. Ibid., 63.

26. Smythe, "Recollections of Louisa McCord Smythe," 32.

27. *Penny Magazine,* 12 April 1845, 144.

28. John Murray, *A Handbook for Travellers,* 97.

29. Smythe, "Recollections of Louisa McCord Smythe," 32.

30. *Penny Magazine,* 12 April 1845, 144.

31. "Music and the Drama," *Athenaeum* no. 1617, 23 Oct. 1858, p. 528.

32. While this may look like a pun on "caffe" and "wretched" by the English writer, the name in fact belonged to Carlo Zanobi Cafferecci, who published popular tunes in Naples between 1840 and 1870.

33. Alessandro Carrera, "Folk Music and Popular Song from the Nineteenth Century to the 1990s," 325–36, in Barański and West, *The Cambridge Companion to Modern Italian Culture,* 326. See also Borgna, *Storia della canzone italiana.* On the implications of such music and the Risorgimento, see Gossett, "Le 'edizioni distrutte' e il significato dei cori operistica nel Risorgimento."

34. Forsyth and Crook, *Remarks on Antiquities, Arts, and Letters,* 148.

35. Smythe, "Recollections of Louisa McCord Smythe," 34, 18. This meeting suggests that Louisa Rebecca took her lessons at the South Carolina College, which was an all-male school.

36. Ibid., 34.

37. Ibid., 34–35.

38. Ibid., 24.

39. J. A. F. Maitland, "Hawes, William (1785–1846)," rev. David J. Golby, in *Oxford Dictionary of National Biography,* http://www.oxforddnb.com/view/article/12649 (accessed 28 December 2015). She was also a frequent performer in music festivals and house concerts. See, for example, notices of her performances in Norwich Festivals in Legge and Hansell, *Annals of the Norfolk & Norwich Triennial Music Festivals,* 91–93.

40. Maria Hawes's "Thou Are Lovelier" was published in the United States as well as Great Britain. The composer was paid £73 10s. in 1842 to sing at the Norwich Music Festival. See Legge and Hansell, *Annals of the Norfolk & Norwich Triennial Music Festivals,* 88. On this occasion Hawes sang her own "Thou Art Lovelier," as well as other works.

41. See Bailey, "The Multifaceted Career of Sarah Davis Smith," 170–72.

42. This itinerary resembles that of other southerners, such as Anne Catherine Boykin Jones of Georgia.

Chapter 14: The Civil War and Beyond

1. Smythe, "Recollections of Louisa McCord Smythe," 36, 42.

2. Ibid., 46–48; on the new lyrics, ibid., 38–39.

3. Two examples serve to illustrate how musicologists and historians have investigated aspects relative to women, music, and the Civil War. James Davis's thoughtful *Music along the Rapidan* takes a refreshing approach to music and soldiers during the war, but it is a book predominantly about men. Drew Gilpin Faust's *Mothers of Invention* (1996) is one example of how historians have interrogated women's lives during the same period, but details on music were not a focus of this study.

4. A previous cataloger made a note of the southern imprints in this binder's volume.

5. "Gems" tells us where southerners could buy music: Blackmar in Augusta; Townsend North's and Duncan's in Columbia (S.C.); J. W. Blandin's in Selma (Ala.); J. J. Richards's in Atlanta; W. N. White's in Athens (Ga.); and at three sellers in Richmond—West & Johnston, J. W. Randolph, and P. H. Taylor. From Stephen Foster's "Parthenia to Ingomar," we can add Schreiner in Macon, Schreiner & Oxen's in Savannah, Bloch and Snow in Mobile, Logemann & Hollenberg in Huntsville (Ala.), T. S. Whitaker in Wilmington (N.C.), and Oates and Catlin in Augusta.

6. J. William Harris has found that Mother Louisa "benefited from the lively intellectual circle that centered on South Carolina College" (Harris, *Society and Culture in the Slave South,* 51). Madame R. Acélie (Aliza) Togno had moved from her fashionable boarding school in Charleston to this area in June 1861 in order to assume leadership of the popular South Carolina Female Institute at Barhamville (just outside of Columbia), which was noted for its music instruction. Mme. Togno had excellent teachers in her faculty, according to Louisa Rebecca, even during this dire period. See an 1855 image of Togno in Lowcountry Digital Library, Charleston, S.C., http://lcdl.library.cofc.edu/lcdl/catalog/lcdl:51333#!prettyPhoto. Langdon Cheves Jr. received a 21 January 1856 letter from Mme. Togno regarding the appropriateness of her school; see Langdon Cheves Jr. Papers, South Carolina Historical Society, Charleston. See also Scarborough, *Masters of the Big House,* 78.

7. Smythe, "Recollections of Louisa McCord Smythe," 50, 53. A neighbor whose daughters also studied lessons with Torriani took him back to the school.

8. His son Ferdinando was one of Jeanette MacDonald's voice teachers. This school had other musicians around at the time, but Torriani clearly had the best track record as voice teacher. See Bailey, *Music and the Southern Belle,* 126–27. Also, in a brief biography of Mme. [Aimee] Torriani, the author noted that her father, Angelo, was "for many years the chef d-orchestre with Maritzek, the old-time impresario" (Ingram A. Pyle, *Book Notes: A Monthly Literary Magazine and Review of New Books* 6 [1901]: 555). This association has been confirmed in Lawrence et al., *Repercussions,* 145n. See also the description in Turk, *Hollywood Diva,* 42. An announcement in the *Southeast Missourian* stated that Torriani was a director of the Metropolitan Opera Company "in the days of Patti and the DeReszkes" (4 December 1928, p. 1, col. 1).

9. "Death of Angelo Torriani," *Chicago Tribune,* 28 August 1893.

10. *Charleston Mercury,* 27 October 1861.

11. On the contents of these binder's volumes, see Bailey, *Women, Music, and the Performance of Gentility*, forthcoming.

12. Smythe, "Recollections of Louisa McCord Smythe," 50.

13. It is possible, however, that she bought it locally, it being leftover stock from the previous decade.

14. Torriani may have copied it directly from his own copy. There is a copy in the Library of Congress: M1.A12Z, vol. 24, Case Class, available online at https://www.loc.gov/item/sm1851.681530/. Accessed 3 June 2016.

15. This song remained popular throughout the nineteenth century and has appeared in collections as far away as Australia. See Preston, *Music for Hire*, 322; National Library of Australia, Bib ID 3413887, http://catalogue.nla.gov.au/Record/3413887. Accessed 10 Dec. 2015. Welzel published it in Brooklyn in 1854, LOC M1.A12Z, vol. 59, Case Class.

16. Ditson published it in Boston, but no date was given on his publication either. Miller & Beacham in Baltimore (1853–64) too published the nocturne.

17. Eva Thornton's book is Music Library, University of North Carolina at Chapel Hill, UNC, old series, 82. Eva (b. 1848) lived in Sussex, Virginia, and married Solomon Williams in 1866. Mary Glenn's volume is in the Historic Sheet Music Collection, Duke University (conf0300). No biographical details of Mary Glenn have come to light. This "nocturne" typifies those of Chopin with an arpeggiated left-hand part accompanying a melody in the right hand that consists of filigree ornamentation.

18. For example, Tom Elmore, *Scandalous Lives* (e-book), chap. 2, has reported that bacon went from one dollar per pound in 1863 to five dollars in 1864. Even more striking, he found that a barrel of flour could sell for as high as twelve hundred dollars in Columbia in 1864.

19. Harris, *Society and Culture*, 60. After this dedication follows a poem for Langdon. See McLeod, "Louisa S. McCord and the 'Feminist Debate,'" for context in her writings.

20. Fought, *Southern Womanhood and Slavery*, 180; Clinton, *Civil War Stories*, 97.

21. Historic Sheet Music Collection, David M. Rubenstein Rare Book and Manuscript Library Center for Popular Music, Middle Tennessee State University, Duke University (DHSM), b038; Center for Popular Music, Middle Tennessee State University (CPM), sheet music vol. 154. Clementi's music appeared on Charleston concert programs earlier in the century; an example is the one Miss Bridon gave in October 1815 (see part 1).

22. The move to older music took place in Europe before it did in the United States. For a discussion of this trend in France, see Ellis, *Interpreting the Musical Past*.

23. No date appears on Louisa Smythe's version. It was the version that G. Schirmer published throughout most of the twentieth century in familiar yellow books. Born in Rome, Clementi won a reputation for his keyboard skills while still young. He traveled to England for the first time in 1766 and in 1775 moved to London, the city with which he is most associated. Like many musicians of the day, he took a variety of positions, such as "conductor" at the King's Theatre in Haymarket. Beginning in 1779 his popularity grew, due in large part to his op. 2 sonatas, which were considered especially difficult.

24. "Rondo" in this period meant an instrumental work in which the first theme (A) returns throughout the composition. The structure is typically ABACA[BA]. Perhaps the most familiar rondo is Mozart's so-called "Turkish Rondo," the final movement of the Sonata in A, K. 331.

25. Douglas Shadle, *Orchestrating the Nation,* has examined the influence of German music in the United States, particularly in orchestral music. Tick, "Passed Away Is the Piano Girl," discussed the shift in what was expected of young women pianists at the end of the nineteenth century.

Conclusion

1. O'Brien, *Placing the South,* 125, found that southern history is often written so that a part is made to represent the whole. I have borrowed "synecdoche" in the context of how southern history has been told from his writing.

2. Levenstein, *Seductive Journey,* 53.

3. Italian composers—e.g., Bellini, Rossini, Verdi—lived and had their operas performed in Paris, and the Louvre held many Italian paintings and sculptures.

4. Tew, "A Study of the Aiken-Rhett Stew Stove," 1.

5. Garrett, "Entertainment of the Most Beautiful Kind," 59.

6. The contents of SMB 32 are included in appendix A.

7. Zogbaum's also brought in music from Fiot in Philadelphia, per SMB 32.

8. Or at least not the music that found its way into SMB 32. Music of this difficulty must have been preceded by simpler fare that has not survived, but it would have predated 1850.

9. See Bailey, "The Multi-Faceted Career of Sarah Davis Smith."

10. For a list of the contents, see appendix A.

11. Mary Rhett's biography is a sad one. Widowed when her first husband, John Vanderhorst, died in 1864, she became addicted to alcohol. She married John Williams Lewis in 1869. See Davis, *Rhett,* 561. See also Taylor et al., *The Leverett Letters.*

12. She owned one particularly curious title: "Valse à cinq temps," a waltz in five beats instead of three. Several waltzes in this meter appeared in New Orleans at about this same time.

13. The contents of SMB 53 are in appendix A.

14. She was the sister of Adèle "Della" Allston, mentioned in the introduction.

15. Their bookplate exists in only a few of these binder's volumes, but their distinctive index page appears in others.

16. The entire episode has been recounted in Bailey, *Music and the Southern Belle,* 126–27.

17. He also taught the opera star Sallie Isabella McCullough, who was another student at the South Carolina Female Institute and a colleague of Bessie. Her story is told in Bailey, *Women, Music, and the Performance of Gentility,* forthcoming.

18. Pringle, *Chronicles of Chicora Wood,* 178.

19. These were Charles Zimmerman, age sixty; Henry Schaller, age thirty; Augustus Keopfer, age thirty-eight; John Thurston, age twenty-eight; and Nathan Peterson, age twenty-six. The other woman was Louisa P. Hotchkiss, age thirty-nine, from Connecticut. Additionally, the 1860 census included two free men of color as musicians:

Joe Randal, whose combined worth was $3500; and Caepha Gunley, whose combined worth was $575.

20. In 1976 Jean Boyd proposed an edition of music from the Aiken-Rhett Collection, but the editor declined publication because this type of project was not popular at that time. Since the 1970s a number of scholars have worked to add American music history to the musicological canon. Should such a venture be proposed today, it would surely meet with approval. See Boyd, "The Parlor Companion."

21. Emily's binder's volume can be seen in the excellent edition by Slobin et al., *Emily's Songbook*.

22. See, as an example, Hanning, *Concise History of Western Music,* 431.

23. The implications of Pierre Bourdieu's social theory aptly applied to southern women and their use of music. See, for example, his *Distinction: A Social Critique of the Judgement of Taste* (1984).

Appendix A

1. Dates were taken from other resources as none is given in SMB 218.

2. See http://www.justanothertune.com/html/lsabdl.html for more information. Accessed 11 June 2016.

3. See http://hz.imslp.info/files/imglnks/usimg/5/53/IMSLP257671-PMLP417909 -romanmechantvil.pdf. Accessed 10 Dec. 2015.

4. See http://gallica.bnf.fr/ark:/12148/bpt6k859348n.r=antoine%20romagnesi. Accessed 3 Dec. 2016.

Bibliography

Newspapers, Magazines, and Nineteenth-Century Journals

Athenaeum [London]
Bibliographie de la France [formerly de *l'Empire français*] *ou, Journal*
Charleston Courier
Charleston Mercury
Charlotte Democrat
Dwight's Journal of Music [New York]
Macon Telegraph
New Monthly Belle Assemblée [London]
New Orleans Daily Picayune
New York Evening Standard [New York]
New York Herald
New York Review
New York Weekly Review
Penny Magazine [London]
Rochester Telegraph
Savannah Daily Gazette
Savannah Republican
Southern Patriot and Commercial Advertiser [Charleston, S.C.]

Libraries and Archives

Aiken Family Book Collection. Charleston Library Society, Charleston, S.C.
Aiken Family Papers. Charleston Museum, Charleston, S.C.
Aiken-Rhett Collection. Charleston Museum, Charleston, S.C.
Aiken-Rhett Correspondence. Historic Charleston Foundation, Charleston, S.C.
Bound Music Collection, circa 1700–1970. Earl Gregg Swem Library, College of William and Mary, Williamsburg, Va.
Cheves-Middleton Papers. South Carolina Historical Society, Charleston.
Grimball, Margaret Ann Meta Morris. Diary, 1860–66. Southern Historical Collection, University of North Carolina, Chapel Hill.

Historic Sheet Music Collection. David M. Rubenstein Rare Book and Manuscript Library, Duke University, Durham, N.C.

Levy, Lester. Sheet Music Collection. Johns Hopkins University, Baltimore, Md.

Lowndes, William and Thomas. Letters, 1795–1846. David M. Rubenstein Rare Book and Manuscript Library, Duke University, Durham, N.C.

Manigault Family Papers, 1824–97. Southern Historical Collection, University of North Carolina, Chapel Hill.

Nineteenth-Century Sheet Music Collection. Music Library, University of North Carolina, Chapel Hill.

Pinckney-Lowndes Papers. In Harriott Horry Rutledge Ravenel Papers, South Carolina Historical Society, Charleston.

Singleton Papers. Southern Historical Collection, University of North Carolina, Chapel Hill.

Smythe, Louisa McCord. Papers. South Carolina Historical Society, Charleston.

Smythe, Louisa McCord. "Recollections of Louisa McCord Smythe." South Caroliniana Library, University of South Carolina, Columbia.

Special Materials. State University of New York, Buffalo.

University Library. Cambridge University.

Urso, Camilla. Collection. Irvin Department of Rare Books and Special Collections, University of South Carolina Library, Columbia.

Books, Articles, and Dissertations

A. and W. Galignani and Co. *Galignani's New Paris Guide.* Paris: A. and W. Galignani, 1842.

Abel, E. Lawrence. *Singing the New Nation.* Mechanicsburg, Pa.: Stackpole Books, 2000.

Ahlquist, Karen. *Democracy at the Opera: Music, Theater, and Culture in New York City, 1815–60.* Music in American Life. Urbana: University of Illinois Press, 1997.

Alderman, Edwin Anderson, Joel Chandler Harris, and Charles William Kent, eds. *The Library of Southern Literature: Biography.* New Orleans and Atlanta: Martin & Hoyt, 1908–13.

Altrocchi, Paul Hemenway. *The Golden Wheel: A Collection of Poetry.* Bloomington, Ind.: Xlibris, 2007.

Alvarez, Eugene. "Southern Hospitality as Seen by Travelers: 1820–1860." *Studies in Popular Culture* 2, no. 1 (1979): 23–35.

Bachand, Marise. "A Season in Town: Plantation Women and the Urban South, 1790–1877." Ph.D. diss., University of Western Ontario, 2011. http://ir.lib.uwo.ca/cgi/viewcontent.cgi?article=1383&context=etd. Accessed 10 June 2015.

Bailey, Candace. "Binder's Volumes and Women of Color in the Antebellum South: The Case of the Johnson Sisters." Paper presented at the Eighth Triennial Porter-Campbell Symposium, American Music Research Center, University of Colorado, Boulder, October 2016.

———. "Binder's Volumes as Musical Commonplace Books: The Transmission of Cultural Codes in the Antebellum South." *Journal of the Society for American Music* 10, no. 4 (November 2016): 446–69. doi:10.1017/S1752196316000353.

———. "The Multifaceted Music Career of Sarah Davis Smith in Mid–Nineteenth Century Middle Tennessee." *Tennessee Historical Quarterly* 76, no. 2 (Summer 2017): 160–81.

———. *Music and the Southern Belle: From Accomplished Lady to Confederate Composer.* Carbondale: Southern Illinois University Press, 2010.

———. "Reconstructing Women by Reconstructing Repertory." Paper presented at the Southern American Studies Association, Atlanta, Ga., February 2016.

Barański, Zygmunt G., and Rebecca J. West, eds. *The Cambridge Companion to Modern Italian Culture.* Cambridge Companions to Culture. Cambridge and New York: Cambridge University Press, 2001.

Barbier, Patrick, and Robert Gust Luoma. *Opera in Paris, 1800–1850: A Lively History.* Portland, Ore.: Amadeus Press, 1995.

Baron, John H. *Concert Life in Nineteenth-Century New Orleans: A Comprehensive Reference.* Baton Rouge: Louisiana State University Press, 2013.

Bashford, Christina. "Historiography and Invisible Musics: Domestic Chamber Music in Nineteenth-Century Britain." *Journal of the American Musicological Society* 63, no. 2 (2010): 291–360. doi:10.1525/jams.2010.63.2.291.

Beckert, Sven, and Julia B. Rosenbaum, eds. *The American Bourgeoisie: Distinction and Identity in the Nineteenth Century.* Palgrave Studies in Cultural and Intellectual History 9. New York: Palgrave Macmillan, 2010.

Bellaigue, Christina de. *Educating Women: Schooling and Identity in England and France, 1800–1867.* Oxford and New York: Oxford University Press, 2007.

Bennett, Susan Smythe. "The Cheves Family of South Carolina (Continued)." *South Carolina Historical and Genealogical Magazine* 35, no. 4 (1934): 130–52.

Bibliographie de la France. Paris: For Cercle de la librairie, 1864.

Biget-Mainfroy, Michelle, ed. "Boieldieu, Les Frères Jadin, Ladurner: Un style de clavier Nouveau pour une institution nouvelle." In *Le Conservatoire de Paris, 1795–1995,* edited by Anne Bongrain, Yves Gérard, and Marie-Hélène Coudroy-Saghai, 57–65. Paris: Editions du Buchet/Chastel, 1996.

Borgna, Gianni. *Storia della canzone italiana.* Roma: Laterza, 1985.

Borsay, Peter, and Jan Hein Furnée, eds. *Leisure Cultures in Urban Europe, c.1700–1870: A Transnational Perspective.* Manchester: Manchester University Press, 2015.

Bowes, Frederick Patten. *The Culture of Early Charleston.* Chapel Hill: University of North Carolina Press, 1942.

Boyd, Jean Ann. "The Parlor Companion: An Anthology of Music from the Aiken-Rhett House." Typescript. Historic Charleston Foundation, Charleston, S.C., 1976.

Bremer, Fredrika, and Mary Howitt. *The Homes of the New World: Impressions of America.* 2 vols. New York: Harper, 1853.

Brenner, Betty, and J. Francis Brenner. *The Old Codgers' Charleston Address Book.* Charleston, S.C.: Old Codger's Press, 2000.

Brophy, Alfred L. "'A Revolution Which Seeks to Abolish Law, Must End Necessarily in Despotism': Louisa McCord and Antebellum Southern Legal Thought." *Cardozo Women's Law Journal* 5, no. 1 (1998): 33–77.

Brown, Edward E. "A History of Theatrical Activities at Mobile Theatre, Mobile, Alabama, from 1860–1875." Ph.D. diss., Michigan State University, 1952.

Brown, Lydia. "Alessandro Parisotti's Arie Antiche: Its Transformation into the Schirmer '24 Italian Songs and Arias' and a Survey of Contemporary Performing Editions." Ph.D. diss., Juilliard School, 2006.

Broyles, Michael. *Beethoven in America*. Bloomington: Indiana University Press, 2011.

Brubaker, Debra. "A History and Critical Analysis of Piano Methods Published in the United States from 1796 to 1995." Ph.D. diss., University of Minnesota, 1996.

Buckingham, James Silk. *The Slave States of America*. 2 vols. London and Paris: Fisher, Son & Co., 1842.

Burgess, George, and Episcopal Church. *Hymns for Church and Home*. Philadelphia: J. B. Lippincott, 1860.

Bushman, Richard Lyman. *The Refinement of America: Persons, Houses, Cities*. New York: Vintage, 1993.

Butler, Nicholas Michael. *Votaries of Apollo: The St. Cecilia Society and the Patronage of Concert Music in Charleston, South Carolina, 1766–1820*. Columbia: University of South Carolina Press, 2007.

C. "Music and the Drama" *Athenaeum* [London] no. 1617, October 23, 1858, p. 528.

Calhoun, John C., and Clyde Norman Wilson. *The Papers of John C. Calhoun*. Vol. 34, 1846–47. Columbia: University of South Carolina Press, 1991.

Calhoun, John C., Robert Lee Meriwether, William Edwin Hemphill, Clyde Norman Wilson, South Caroliniana Society, South Carolina, and Department of Archives and History. *The Papers of John C. Calhoun*. Columbia: Published by the University of South Carolina Press for the South Caroliniana Society, 1959.

Cavicchi, Daniel. *Listening and Longing: Music Lovers in the Age of Barnum*. Middletown, Conn.: Wesleyan University Press, 2011.

Censer, Jane Turner. *The Reconstruction of White Southern Womanhood, 1865–1895*. Baton Rouge: Louisiana State University Press, 2003.

Chase, George B. "The Lowndes Family of South Carolina: A Genealogical Sketch." *New England Historical and Genealogical Register* 30 (1876): 141–64.

———. *Lowndes of South Carolina, an Historical and Genealogical Memoir*. Boston: A. Williams, 1876.

Cheer, Clarissa Lablache. *The Great Lablache, Nineteenth Century Operatic Superstar: His Life and His Times*. Bloomington, Ind.: Xlibris, 2009.

Cheetham, Frank Halliday. *Louis Napoleon and the Genesis of the Second Empire: Being a Life of the Emperor Napoleon III to the Time of His Election to the Presidency of the French Republic, with Numerous Illustrations Reproduced from Contemporary Portraits, Prints and Lithographs*. London and New York: John Lane, 1909.

Cheshire, Rt. Rev. Joseph Blount. *An Historical Address Delivered in Saint Matthew's Church, Hillsboro, N.C., on Sunday, August 24, 1924: Being the One Hundredth Anniversary of the Parish*. N.p., 1925.

Chesnut, Mary Boykin, and Ben Ames Williams. *A Diary from Dixie*. Boston: Houghton Mifflin, 1949.

Clark, J. Bunker. *Anthology of Early American Keyboard Music 1787–1830: Part 1*. Madison, Wis.: A-R Editions, 1977.

Clark, Thomas Dionysius. *South Carolina: The Grand Tour, 1780–1865*. Columbia: University of South Carolina Press, 1973.

Clinton, Catherine. *Civil War Stories.* Athens: University of Georgia Press, 1998.

———. *Half Sisters of History: Southern Women and the American Past.* Durham, N.C.: Duke University Press, 1994.

Cogan, Frances. *All American Girl: The Idea of Real Womanhood in Mid–Nineteenth Century America.* Athens: University of Georgia Press, 2010.

Coghlan, Francis. *A Hand-Book for Italy . . . Including Every Information Explanatory of the Routes . . . for an Entire Tour, from Recent Personal Visits. . . .* London: H. Hughes, 1845.

Cox, Karen L. *Dixie's Daughters: The United Daughters of the Confederacy and the Preservation of Confederate Culture.* Gainesville: University Press of Florida, 2003.

Coxe, Elizabeth Allen. *Elizabeth Allen Coxe: Memories of a South Carolina Plantation during the War.* Privately printed for my family and friends, 1912.

Crawford, Richard. *America's Musical Life: A History.* New York: W. W. Norton, 2001.

Crew, Danny O. *Presidential Sheet Music: An Illustrated Catalogue of Published Music Associated with the American Presidency and Those Who Sought the Office.* Jefferson, N.C.: McFarland, 2001.

Cuthbert, Robert B. *Flat Rock of the Old Time: Letters from the Mountains to the Lowcountry, 1837–1939.* Columbia: University of South Carolina Press, 2016.

Davidson, Chalmers Gaston. *The Last Foray: South Carolina Planters of 1860, a Sociological Study.* Columbia: University of South Carolina Press, 1987.

Davies, James. "Julia's Gift: The Social Life of Scores, c. 1830." *Journal of the Royal Musical Association* 131, no. 2 (2006): 287–309.

Davis, William C. *Rhett: The Turbulent Life and Times of a Fire-Eater.* Columbia: University of South Carolina Press, 2001.

Davis, James A. *Music along the Rapidan: Civil War Soldiers, Music, and Community during Winter Quarters, Virginia.* Lincoln: University of Nebraska Press, 2014.

Dawson, Sarah Morgan. *A Confederate Girl's Diary.* Boston and New York: Houghton Mifflin, 1913.

Dwight. John Sullivan. *Dwight's Journal of Music,* 3/5 (7 May 1853): 35.

Eigeldinger, J.-J. "Chopin and Pleyel." *Early Music* 29, no. 3 (August 1, 2001): 389–98. doi:10.1093/earlyj/XXIX.3.389.

Ella, John. *Musical Sketches, Abroad, and at Home.* Vol. 1. London: Ridgway, 1869.

Ellis, Katharine. *Interpreting the Musical Past: Early Music in Nineteenth-Century France.* Oxford and New York: Oxford University Press, 2005.

Episcopal Church. *The Additional and Selected Hymns: From "Hymns, Ancient and Modern," and "Hymns for Church and Home."* New York: Dutton, 1870.

Fant, Jennie Holton, ed. *The Travelers' Charleston: Accounts of Charleston and Lowcountry, South Carolina, 1666–1861.* Columbia: University of South Carolina Press, 2016.

Fétis, François-Joseph. *Biographie universelle des musiciens et bibliographie générale de la musique. [vol. 2] / par F.-J. Fétis. . . .* Paris: Didot, 1866. http://gallica.bnf.fr/ark:/12148/bpt6k69718c. Accessed 12 August 2016.

———. "Boieldieu, Adrien." *Grove Music Online.* Oxford Music Online. Oxford University Press. Accessed 16 January 2016.

Filippini, Nadia Maria. *Donne sulla scena pubblica: Società e politica in Veneto tra Sette e Ottocento.* Milan: FrancoAngeli, 2006.

Finson, Jon W. *The Voices That Are Gone: Themes in Nineteenth-Century American Popular Song.* Oxford and New York: Oxford University Press, 1997.

Fisher, Eliza Middleton, Mary Hering Middleton, and Eliza Cope Harrison. *Best Companions: Letters of Eliza Middleton Fisher and Her Mother, Mary Hering Middleton, from Charleston, Philadelphia, and Newport, 1839–1846.* Columbia: University of South Carolina Press, 2001.

Forsyth, Joseph, and Keith Crook. *Remarks on Antiquities, Arts, and Letters during an Excursion in Italy, in the Years 1802 and 1803.* Newark: University of Delaware Press, 2001.

Fought, Leigh. *Southern Womanhood and Slavery: A Biography of Louisa S. McCord, 1810–1879.* Columbia: University of Missouri Press, 2003.

Fox-Genovese, Elizabeth, and Eugene D. Genovese. *The Mind of the Master Class: History and Faith in the Southern Slaveholders' Worldview.* Cambridge: Cambridge University Press, 2005.

Fraser, Jessie Melville. *Louisa C. McCord.* M.A. thesis, University of South Carolina, Columbia, S.C., 1919.

Gacs, Ute. *Women Anthropologists: Selected Biographies.* University of Illinois Press, 1988.

Garrett, Elizabeth W. "Entertainment of the Most Beautiful Kind: The House of William and Harriet Aiken, 1833–1860." Master's thesis, University of Delaware, 2005. ProQuest (305350715).

Geoffroy-Schwinden, Rebecca. "'L'école des jeunes filles de Madame Campan: Musique, performance et genre au Lendemain de la révolution française.'" Paper presented at Columbia University in Paris, 2013.

———. "Madame Campan's Music Curriculum for Girls: Post-Terror Discipline of the Female Body." Paper presented at Université Paris, 2015.

Gillespie, John. *Five Centuries of Keyboard Music.* Courier Corporation, 2013.

Golombek, Harry. *Chess: A History.* 1st edition. New York: Putnam, 1976.

Gossett, Philip. "Le 'edizioni distrutte' e il significato dei cori operistica nel Risorgimento." *Il Saggiatore Musicale* 12, no. 2 (2005): 339–87.

Green, Jennifer R "Education and Professionals in the Old South: Schooling's Impact on Career and Social Class." In Delfino, Susanna, Michele Gillespie, and Louis M. Kyriakoudes. *Southern Society and Its Transformations, 1790–1860,* 176–94. Columbia, Mo.: University of Missouri Press, 2011.

———. *Military Education and the Emerging Middle Class in the Old South.* Cambridge: Cambridge University Press, 2008.

Greene, Victor R. *A Singing Ambivalence: American Immigrants between Old World and New, 1830–1930.* Kent, Ohio: Kent State University Press, 2004.

Grier, Katherine C. *Culture and Comfort: Parlor Making and Middle-Class Identity, 1850–1930.* Washington, D.C.: Smithsonian Institution Press, 1997.

Gross, Steve, Susan Daley, and Henry Wiencek. *Old Houses.* New York: Stewart, Tabori & Chang, 1995.

Grove, George, and J. A Fuller-Maitland. *Grove's Dictionary of Music and Musicians.* New York and London: Macmillan, 1904.

Hagy, James William. *Directories for the City of Charleston, South Carolina: For the Years 1849, 1852, and 1855.* Baltimore: Genealogical Publishing Company, 1998.

Hall, Margaret Hunter, and Una Pope-Hennessy. *The Aristocratic Journey: Being the Outspoken Letters of Mrs. Basil Hall Written during a Fourteen Months' Sojourn in America, 1827–1828.* New York and London: Putnam, 1931.

Hall-Witt, Jennifer. *Fashionable Acts: Opera and Elite Culture in London, 1780–1880.* Durham: University of New Hampshire Press; Hanover: University Press of New England, 2007.

Halttunen, Karen. *Confidence Men and Painted Women: A Study of Middle-Class Culture in America, 1830–1870.* New Haven, Conn.: Yale University Press, 1982.

Hancock, Claire. *Paris et Londres au XIXe siècle: Représentations dans le guides et récits de voyage.* Paris: CNRS, 2003.

———. "'Your City Does Not Speak My Language': Cross-Channel Views of Paris and London in the Nineteenth Century." *Planning Perspectives* 12, no. 1 (1997): 1–18. doi: 10.1080/026654397364753.

Hanning, Barbara. *Concise History of Western Music.* 5th ed. New York: W. W. Norton, 2014.

Hemperley, Marion R. "Federal Naturalization Oaths, Charleston, South Carolina, 1790–1860." *South Carolina Historical Magazine* 66, no. 2 (1965): 112–24.

Heyse, Amy Lynn. "The Rhetoric of Memory-Making: Lessons from the UDC's Catechisms for Children." *Rhetoric Society Quarterly* 38, no. 4 (2008): 408–32.

Hibberd, Sarah. "'Dormez donc, mes chers amours': Hérold's *La somnambule* (1827) and Dream Phenomena on the Parisian Lyric Stage." *Cambridge Opera Journal* 16, no. 2 (2004): 107–32.

Hindman, John Joseph. "Concert Life in Ante-Bellum Charleston." Ph.D. diss., University of North Carolina at Chapel Hill, 1972. ProQuest (302623106).

Hofmeister, Friedrich. *Handbuch der musikalischen Literatur: Oder, Allgemeines systematisch-geordnetes Verzeichnis der in Deutschland und in den angrenzenden Ländern gedruckten Musikalien auch musikalischen Schriften und Abbildungen, mit Anzeige der Verleger und Preise.* Liepzig: Hofmeister, 1854.

Holcombe, Brent. *South Carolina Marriages, 1800–1820.* Baltimore: Genealogical Publishing Co., 1995.

Holden, Amanda. *The New Penguin Opera Guide.* London: Penguin, 2001.

Hoxie, N. B., and Henry Day, *New York Supreme Court.* New York: Evening Post Steam Presses, 1876.

Hubbard, William Lines. *The American History and Encyclopedia of Music: History of American Music.* Toledo and New York: Irving Squire, 1908.

Jain, Jules-Gabriel. *The American in Paris during the Summer, Being a Companion to the "Winter in Paris."* London: Longman, Brown, Green, and Longmans, 1844.

John Murray (Firm). *A Handbook for Travellers in Southern Italy: Being a Guide for the Provinces Formerly Constituting the Continental Portion of the Kingdom of the Two Sicilies.* London: J. Murray, 1862.

Johnson, James H. *Listening in Paris: A Cultural History.* Berkeley: University of California Press, 1995.

Jones Wilson, Jennifer. "The Impact of French Opera in Nineteenth-Century New York: The New Orleans French Opera Company, 1827–1845." Ph.D. diss., City University of New York, 2015. ProQuest (1706911584).

Kassler, Michael. *The Music Trade in Georgian England.* Farnham and Burlington, Vt.: Ashgate, 2011.

Kearns, William, and William Reeves, eds. *Report of Proceedings: Ph.D. in Music Symposium, April 5–7, 1985.* Boulder: College of Music, University of Colorado, 1988.

Keates, Jonathan. *The Siege of Venice.* London: Pimlico, 2006.

Keats, John, and John Barnard. *John Keats: The Complete Poems.* Harmondsworth, Middlesex; and New York: Penguin Books, 1988.

Kilbride, Daniel. *Being American in Europe, 1750–1860.* Baltimore, Md.: Johns Hopkins University Press, 2013.

———. "Travel, Ritual, and National Identity: Planters on the European Tour, 1820–1860." *Journal of Southern History* 69, no. 3 (2003): 549–84. doi:10.2307/30040010.

Kimball, Bruce A. *The "True Professional Ideal" in America: A History.* Totowa, N.J.: Rowman and Littlefield, 1996.

Kirk, Elise K. *American Opera.* Urbana: University of Illinois Press, 2001.

Kmen, Henry A. *Music in New Orleans: The Formative Years, 1791–1841.* Baton Rouge: Louisiana State University Press, 1966.

Kobbé, Gustav. *Kobbé's Complete Opera Book.* London: Putnam, 1922.

Krummel, Donald William, and Stanley Sadie. *Music Printing and Publishing.* New York: W. W. Norton, 1990.

Lablache, Luigi. *A Complete Method of Singing: Being an Analysis of the Principles by Which Study Should Be Regulated in Forming & Developing the Voice, in Acquiring Flexibility and in Cultivating the Taste; With Illustrative Examples, Exercises, & Progressive Studies in Vocalisation. . . .* London: Chappell, 1840.

Launay, Florence. *Les compositrices en France au XIXe siècle.* Paris: Fayard, 2006.

Lawrence, Vera Brodsky, and George Templeton Strong. *Repercussions, 1857–1862.* Strong on Music, vol. 3. Chicago: University of Chicago Press, 1999.

Le Vert, Octavia Walton. *Souvenirs of Travel.* 2 vols. New York: Derby & Jackson, 1859.

LeClercq, Anne Sinkler Whaley, and Emily Wharton Sinkler. *An Antebellum Plantation Household: Including the South Carolina Low Country Receipts and Remedies of Emily Wharton Sinkler.* Columbia: University of South Carolina Press, 1996.

Legge, Robin Humphrey, and W. E. Hansell. *Annals of the Norfolk & Norwich Triennial Music Festivals: MDCCCXXIV, MDCCCXCII.* London: Jarrold and Sons, 1896.

Lemmers, Frédéric. "Fétis et l'enseignement du chant en belgique." *Revue Belge de Musicologie/Belgisch Tijdschrift Voor Muziekwetenschap* 62 (2008): 147–61.

Levenstein, Harvey. *Seductive Journey: American Tourists in France from Jefferson to the Jazz Age.* Chicago: University of Chicago Press, 2000.

Levine, Lawrence W. *Highbrow, Lowbrow: The Emergence of Cultural Hierarchy in America.* William E. Massey Sr. Lectures in the History of American Civilization 1986. Cambridge, Mass.: Harvard University Press, 2002.

Lewis, Elizabeth Wittenmyer. *Queen of the Confederacy: The Innocent Deceits of Lucy Holcombe Pickens.* Denton: University of North Texas Press, 2002.

Lewis, Robert M. "Tableaux Vivants: Parlor Theatricals in Victorian America." *Revue Française D'études Américaines,* no. 36 (1988): 280–91.

Loesser, Arthur, Edward Rothstein, and Jacques Barzun. *Men, Women and Pianos: A Social History.* Rev. ed. New York: Dover, 2011.

Loewenberg, Alfred. *Annals of Opera, 1597–1940.* 3d ed. rev. and corrected. Totowa, N.J: Rowman and Littlefield, 1978.

Lott, R. Allen. *From Paris to Peoria: How European Piano Virtuosos Brought Classical Music to the American Heartland.* Oxford and New York: Oxford University Press, 2003.

Macfarlane, Helen Louise. "'Il faut savoir l'italien pour déchiffrer une romance française': Italian Presence in the French Romance 1800–1850." Ph.D. diss., University of Southampton, 2015.

Mack, Charles R., Henry H. Lesesne, and University of South Carolina, eds. *Francis Lieber and the Culture of the Mind: Fifteen Papers Devoted to the Life, Times, and Contributions of the Nineteenth-Century German-American Scholar with an Excursus on Francis Lieber's Grave: Presented at the University of South Carolina's Bicentennial Year Symposium Held in Columbia, South Carolina, November 9–10, 2001.* Columbia: University of South Carolina Press, 2005.

Magaldi, Cristina. "Music for the Elite: Musical Societies in Imperial Rio de Janeiro." *Latin American Music Review / Revista de Música Latinoamericana* 16, no. 1 (1995): 1–41. doi:10.2307/779977.

Martin, Chlotilde R., Robert B. Cuthbert, and Stephen G. Hoffius. *Northern Money, Southern Land: The Lowcountry Plantation Sketches of Chlotilde R. Martin.* Columbia: University of South Carolina Press, 2009.

Matthews, Catherine Taylor, J. Tracy Power, and Frances Wallace Taylor. *The Leverett Letters: Correspondence of a South Carolina Family, 1851–1868.* Columbia: University of South Carolina Press, 2000.

McCord, Louisa Susanna Cheves. *Louisa S. McCord: Poems, Drama, Biography, Letters.* Ed. Richard Cecil Lounsbury. Publications of the Southern Texts Society. Charlottesville: University Press of Virginia, 1996.

————. *Louisa S. McCord: Political and Social Essays.* Ed. Richard Cecil Lounsbury. Publications of the Southern Texts Society. Charlottesville: University Press of Virginia, 1995.

————. *Louisa S. McCord: Selected Writings.* Ed. Richard Cecil Lounsbury. Publications of the Southern Texts Society. Charlottesville: University Press of Virginia, 1997.

McInnis, Maurie D. "'An Idea of Grandeur': Furnishing the Classical Interior in Charleston, 1815–1840." *Historical Archaeology* 33, no. 3 (1999): 32–47.

McInnis, Maurie Dee. *The Politics of Taste in Antebellum Charleston.* Chapel Hill: University of North Carolina Press, 2005.

McInnis, Maurie Dee, Gibbes Museum of Art (Charleston), and Historic Charleston Foundation. *In Pursuit of Refinement: Charlestonians Abroad, 1740–1860.* Columbia: University of South Carolina Press, 1999.

McLeod, Cindy A. "Louisa S. McCord and the 'Feminist Debate.'" Ph.D. diss., Florida State University, 2011. ProQuest (902634500).

Melnick, Ralph. "College of Charleston Special Collections: A Guide to Its Holdings." *South Carolina Historical Magazine* 81, no. 2 (1980): 131–53.

Miller, Julia. *Books Will Speak Plain: A Handbook for Identifying and Describing Historical Bindings.* Ann Arbor, Mich.: Legacy Press, 2014.

Minnegerode, Meade. *The Fabulous Forties 1840–1850: A Presentation of Private Life.* New York: Putnam, 1924.

Minnen, Cornelis A. van, and Manfred Berg. *The U.S. South and Europe: Transatlantic Relations in the Nineteenth and Twentieth Centuries.* Lexington: University Press of Kentucky, 2013.

Moore's Irish Melodies: With Symphonies and Accompaniments. Wilmington, Del.: Michael Glazier, 1981.

Morgan, Elizabeth. "The Accompanied Sonata and the Domestic Novel in Britain at the Turn of the Nineteenth Century." *19th-Century Music* 36, no. 2 (2012): 88–100.

Mullaney-Dignam, Karol. *Music and Dancing at Castletown, County Kildare, 1759–1821.* Dublin and Portland, Ore.: Four Courts Press, 2011.

The New England Historical and Genealogical Register. Boston: Society, 1876.

Nohl, Ludwig. *Life of Wagner.* Trans. by George P. Upton. Fifth edition. Chicago: A. C. McClurg, 1897.

Newman, Nancy. *Good Music for a Free People: The Germania Musical Society in Nineteenth-Century America.* Rochester, N.Y.: University of Rochester Press, 2010.

Oak, Henry Lebbeus, New England Historic Genealogical Society, and Ora Oak. *Oak—Oaks—Oakes: Family Register, Nathaniel Oak of Marlborough, Mass., and Three Generations of His Descendants in Both Male and Female Lines.* Los Angeles: Out West, 1906.

O'Brien, Michael. *Conjectures of Order: Intellectual Life and the American South, 1810–1860.* Chapel Hill: University of North Carolina Press, 2004.

———. *Placing the South.* Jackson: University Press of Mississippi, 2011.

O'Brien, Michael, and Southern Texts Society, eds. *An Evening When Alone: Four Journals of Single Women in the South, 1827–67.* Publications of the Southern Texts Society. Charlottesville: Published for the Southern Texts Society by the University Press of Virginia, 1993.

Orr, N. Lee. *Alfredo Barili and the Rise of Classical Music in Atlanta.* Atlanta: Scholars Press, 1996.

Pearson, Lennart. "When Fredrika Bremer Came to Charleston." *Swedish-American Historical Society Quarterly* 56, no. 4 (2005): 214–30.

Pease, Jane H., and William H. Pease. *A Family of Women: The Carolina Petigrus in Peace and War.* Chapel Hill: University of North Carolina Press, 1999.

Pease, Jane H., and William Henry Pease. *Ladies, Women, and Wenches: Choice and Constraint in Antebellum Charleston and Boston.* Chapel Hill: University of North Carolina Press, 1990.

Pease, William H., and Jane H. Pease. "Traditional Belles or Borderline Bluestockings? The Petigru Women." *South Carolina Historical Magazine* 102, no. 4 (2001): 292–309.

Perkins, Edwin J. "Langdon Cheves and the Panic of 1819: A Reassessment." *Journal of Economic History* 44, no. 2 (1984): 455–61.

Pierce, Edward Lillie. *Memoir and Letters of Charles Sumner.* London: Sampson Low, Marston, Searle & Rivington, 1878.

Pope, Christie Farnham. *Preparation for Pedestals: North Carolina Antebellum Female Seminaries.* Chicago: University of Chicago Press, 1977.

Preston, Katherine K. *Music For Hire: A Study of Professional Musicians in Washington, 1877–1900.* Stuyvesant, N.Y.: Pendragon Press, 1992.

———. *Opera on the Road: Traveling Opera Troupes in the United States, 1825–60.* Music in American Life. Urbana: University of Illinois Press, 1993.

Pringle, Elizabeth Waties Allston. *Chronicles of Chicora Wood.* New York: Scribner, 1922.

———. *A Woman Rice Planter.* New York: Macmillan, 1913.

Prioleau, Horry Frost, and Edward Lining Manigault. *Register of Carolina Huguenots.* Vol. 2, *Dupre-Manigault.* N.p.: Lulu Com, 2010.

Putnam, George Palmer. *The Tourist in Europe: Or, A Concise Summary of the Various Routes, Objects of Interest, &c in Great Britain, France, Switzerland, Italy, Germany, Belgium, and Holland; with Hints on Time, Expenses, Hotels, Conveyances, Passports, Coins, &c; Memoranda during a Tour of Eight Months in Great Britain and on the Continent.* New York: Wiley & Putnam, 1838.

Pyle, Ingram A. *Book Notes: A Monthly Literary Magazine and Review of New Books.* Vol. 6. New York and Chicago: Seigel-Cooper, 1901.

Radford, John. "The Charleston Planters in 1860." *South Carolina Historical Magazine* 77, no. 4 (1976): 227–35.

Ravenel, Harriott Horry. *Charleston: The Place and the People.* New York and London: Macmillan, 1906.

Ravenel, Harriott Horry, and Mrs. St. Julien Ravenel. *Life and Times of William Lowndes of South Carolina, 1782–1822.* Boston and New York: Houghton Mifflin, 1901.

Ravenswaay, Charles Van. *St. Louis: An Informal History of the City and Its People, 1764–1865.* St. Louis: Missouri History Museum, 1991.

Reed, Emmala, and Robert T. Oliver. *A Faithful Heart: The Journals of Emmala Reed, 1865 and 1866.* Women's Diaries and Letters of the South. Columbia: University of South Carolina Press, 2004.

Rembert, Sarah H. "Barhamville: A Columbia Antebellum Girls School." *South Carolina History Illustrated* 1 (1970): 44–48.

Rickards, Maurice, et al. *The Encyclopedia of Ephemera: A Guide to the Fragmentary Documents of Everyday Life for the Collector, Curator, and Historian.* New York: Routledge, 2000.

Riis, Thomas L. "The Music and Musicians in Nineteenth-Century Productions of Uncle Tom's Cabin." *American Music* 4, no. 3 (1986): 268–86. doi:10.2307/3051610.

Robinson, Philip, and Sarah Hibberd. "Gail [Garre], (Edmee) Sophie." *Grove Music Online.* Oxford Music Online. http://www.oxfordmusiconline.com.prox,y.Iib.duke.edu/groyemusic/view/10.1093/gmo/9781561592630.001.0001/omo-9781561592630-e-0000010493. Accessed 16 April 2018.

Rohr, Nancy M., ed. *An Alabama School Girl in Paris, 1842–1844: The Letters of Mary Fenwick Lewis and Her Family.* Huntsville, Ala.: Silver Threads, 2001.

Rosen, Robert N. *The Jewish Confederates.* Columbia: University of South Carolina Press, 2000.

Rowland, Lawrence Sanders, Alexander Moore, and George C. Rogers. *The History of Beaufort County, South Carolina: 1514–1861.* Vol. 1. Columbia: University of South Carolina Press, 1996.

Russell, Ann Ratliff. *Legacy of a Southern Lady: Anna Calhoun Clemson, 1817–1875.* Clemson, S.C.: Clemson University Digital Press, 2007.

Ruth, John A. *Social Culture: A Treatise on Etiquette, Self, Culture, Dress, Physical Beauty and Domestic Relations, Together with Social, Commercial and Legal Forms.* Springfield, Mass.: King-Richardson, 1902.

Sainsbury, John S, and Alexandre Choron. *A Dictionary of Musicians, from the Earliest Ages to the Present Time.* London: Printed for Sainsbury and Co., 1827.

Saint-Saëns, Camille. *Musical Memories.* Boston: Small, Maynard, 1919.

Sanjek, Russell. *American Popular Music and Its Business: The First Four Hundred Years.* Vol. 2, *From 1790 to 1909.* New York: Oxford University Press, 1988.

Scarborough, William Kauffman. *Masters of the Big House: Elite Slaveholders of the Mid-Nineteenth-Century South.* Baton Rouge: Louisiana State University Press, 2003.

Schirmer, Gustave. *Twenty-Four Italian Songs and Arias.* New York: Hal Leonard, 1948.

Schuman-LeClercq, Mary Regina [Siegling]. *Memoirs of a Dowager.* Self-published, 1908.

Shadle, Douglas. *Orchestrating the Nation: The Nineteenth-Century American Symphonic Enterprise.* 1st edition. New York: Oxford University Press, 2015.

Siegling Music House, Inc. *The Test of Time, 1819–1919: A Brief Resume of the Hundred Years of the Impressive History of the South's Foremost and America's Oldest Music House.* Charleston, S.C., 1919.

Slap, Andrew L., and Frank Towers. *Confederate Cities: The Urban South during the Civil War Era.* Chicago: University of Chicago Press, 2015.

Slobin, Mark, James W. Kimball, Katherine K. Preston, Deane L. Root, and Emily McKissick, eds. *Emily's Songbook: Music in 1850s Albany.* Recent Researches in the Oral Traditions of Music 9. Middleton, Wis.: A-R Editions, 2011.

Small, Christopher. *Musicking: The Meanings of Performing and Listening.* Hanover, N.H.: University Press of New England, 1998.

Smart, Mary Ann. "Parlor Games: Italian Music and Italian Politics in the Parisian Salon." *Nineteenth Century Music* 34, no. 1 (Summer 2010): 39–60, 106.

Smith, Jewel A. *Music, Women, and Pianos in Antebellum Bethlehem, Pennsylvania: The Moravian Young Ladies' Seminary.* Bethlehem, Pa.: Lehigh University Press, 2008.

Stark, James. *Bel Canto: A History of Vocal Pedagogy.* 2d ed. Toronto and Buffalo: University of Toronto Press, 2003.

Stephen, Sir Leslie, and Sir Sidney Lee. *Dictionary of National Biography.* London: Smith, Elder, 1908.

Stoutamire, Albert. *Music of the Old South: Colony to Confederacy.* Rutherford, N.J.: Fairleigh Dickinson University Press, 1972.

Strickland, Jeffery. "How the Germans Became White Southerners: German Immigrants and African Americans in Charleston, South Carolina, 1860–1880." *Journal of American Ethnic History* 28, no. 1 (2008): 52–69.

Tatham, David. *The Lure of the Striped Pig: The Illustration of Popular Music in America, 1820–1870.* Barre, Mass.: Imprint Society, 1973.

Tawa, Nicholas E. *Sweet Songs for Gentle Americans: The Parlor Song in America, 1790–1860.* Bowling Green, Ohio: Bowling Green University Popular Press, 1980.

Tew, Julia Anne. "A Study of the Aiken-Rhett Stew Stove." M.S. thesis, Clemson University, 2013.

Thibault, C., ed *Kalkbrenner's Exercises for the Piano Forte: Perfected by C. Thibault.* 3 vols. New York: J. Hewitt, [n.d.].

Thomas, Ella Gertrude Clanton, and Virginia Ingraham Burr. *The Secret Eye: The Journal of Ella Gertrude Clanton Thomas, 1848–1889.* Chapel Hill, N.C.: University of North Carolina Press, 1990.

Thornwell, Emily. *The Lady's Guide to Complete Gentility: In Manners, Dress and Conversation, in the Family, in Company, at the Pianoforte, the Table, in the Street, and in Gentlemen's Society; Also a Useful Instructor in Letter Writing, Toilet Preparations, Fancy Needlework, Millinery, Dressmaking, Care of Wardrobe, the Hair, Teeth, Hands, Lips, Complexion, Etc.* New York: Derby & Jackson, 1858.

Tick, Judith. "Passed Away Is the Piano Girl." In *Women Making Music: The Western Art Tradition, 1150–1950,* edited by Jane M. Bowers and Judith Tick, 325–49. Urbana: University of Illinois Press, 1986.

Tick, Judith, and Paul E. Beaudoin. *Music in the USA: A Documentary Companion.* Oxford: Oxford University Press, 2008.

Todd, William Burton, and Ann Bowden. *Sir Walter Scott: A Bibliographical History, 1796–1832.* New Castle, Del.: Oak Knoll Press, 1998.

Trimpi, Helen P. *Crimson Confederates: Harvard Men Who Fought for the South.* Knoxville: University of Tennessee Press, 2010.

Tsou, Judy and William Cheng. "Duchambge [Du Chambge; nee du Montet], (Charlotte-AntoinettePauline)." *Grove Music Online* http://www.oxfordmusiconline .com,proxx.lib.duke.edu/KTovemusic/view/10.1093/amo/9 781561592630.001.0001/ omo-9781S61592630-e-0000008251. Accessed 7 April 2017.

Tunley, David. *Salons, Singers, and Songs: A Background to Romantic French Song 1830–1870.* Aldershot and Burlington, Vt.: Ashgate, 2002.

Turk, Edward Baron. *Hollywood Diva: A Biography of Jeanette MacDonald.* Berkeley: University of California Press, 1998.

Turner, James. *The Liberal Education of Charles Eliot Norton.* Baltimore, Md.: Johns Hopkins University Press, 2002.

United States Bureau of Customs and National Archives and Records Service. *Copies of Lists of Passengers Arriving at Miscellaneous Ports on the Atlantic and Gulf Coasts and Ports on the Great Lakes, 1820–1873.* Washington, D.C.: National Archives and Records Service, General Services Administration, 1972.

Vandiver, Louise Ayer. *Traditions and History of Anderson County.* Atlanta: Ruralist Press, 1928.

Walpurga Ehrengarde Helena (von Hohenthal) Paget, Lady. *Embassies of Other Days: And Further Recollections.* London: Hutchinson & Co., 1923.

Walton, Chris. *Richard Wagner's Zurich: The Muse of Place.* Rochester, N.Y.: Camden House, 2007.

Watson, Bradley C. S. "Who Was Francis Lieber?" *Modern Age* 43, no. 4 (Fall 2001): 304–10.

Watson, Charles S. *The History of Southern Drama.* Lexington: University Press of Kentucky, 2009.

Watson, Harry Legare II. "'Bitter Combinations of the Neighborhood': The Second American Party System in Cumberland County, North Carolina." Ph.D. diss., Northwestern University, 1976. ProQuest (302829819).

Weitzmann, Karl Friedrich, Otto Lessmann, and Theodore Baker. *A History of Pianoforte-Playing and Pianoforte-Literature*. New York: G. Schirmer, 1893.

Wells, Jonathan Daniel. *The Origins of the Southern Middle Class, 1800–1861*. Chapel Hill: University of North Carolina Press, 2004.

———. *Women Writers and Journalists in the Nineteenth-Century South*. Cambridge: Cambridge University Press, 2011.

Welter, Barbara. "The Cult of True Womanhood: 1820–1860." *American Quarterly* 18, no. 2 (1966): 151–74. doi:10.2307/2711179.

Zierden, Martha A., and South Carolina Historic Charleston Foundation. *Aiken-Rhett House: Archaeological Research*. Charleston, S.C.: Charleston Museum, 2003.

Zimmerman, J. *Encyclopédie du pianiste compositeur*. Paris: L'Auteur, 1840